The Literary Life of Yājñavalkya

SUNY series in Hindu Studies

Wendy Doniger, editor

The Literary Life of Yājñavalkya

STEVEN E. LINDQUIST

SUNY
PRESS

Cover: The Goddess Sarasvati appears before Yājñavalkya.

Published by State University of New York Press, Albany

Printed in the United States of America

For information, contact State University of New York Press, Albany, NY
www.sunypress.edu

Library of Congress Cataloging-in-Publication Data

Name: Lindquist, Steven E., author.
Title: The literary life of Yājñavalkya / Steven E. Lindquist.
Description: Albany : State University of New York Press, [2023] | Series: SUNY series in Hindu Studies | Includes bibliographical references and index.
Identifiers: ISBN 9781438495620 (hardcover : alk. paper) | ISBN 9781438495644 (ebook)
Further information is available at the Library of Congress.

10 9 8 7 6 5 4 3 2 1

Contents

Acknowledgments

There is some truth to the platitude that no person is an island, but if I may modify this slightly (with tongue planted firmly in cheek), he or she *is* a subcontinent.

I view the history of the Indian subcontinent—and in the book before you, the literary life of Yājñavalkya—as a complex and varied interaction of peoples and the objects they produce; of intersecting ideologies, aspirations, material interests, alliances, conflicts, and frustratingly, but inevitably, a degree of historical chance that remains elusive to analysis. I am keenly aware that any attempt to make a cohesive narrative out of a small aspect of this complexity—in my case, one literary figure in the religious history of what is known as Hinduism today—must be, by definition, incomplete. This incompleteness is often a cause of frustration to scholars, and indeed it is that frustration that propels many of us forward. But, at the end of the day, I think, there is a certain poetic beauty to realizing that humans, their literary products, and their history are ultimately irreducible to any single narrative or final interpretation.

This is as true of the texts and people we study as of ourselves. As I think of the path that led to this book, I cannot help but get lost in the matrix of mentors, colleagues, friends, and family who have played a role in my academic trajectory, though a role that can be opaque, sometimes to both of us. Like with the stories of Yājñavalkya, I find myself connecting various dots in my own autobiographical thinking and realize that any such story can be told in different ways and each version can be satisfying in its own right. Though I am convinced I have left out significant influences, I hope my preamble makes clear that this is not intentional in the least and is probably inevitable.

This book grew out of a dissertation from The University of Texas at Austin and members of that committee were always insightful, critical, helpful, and kind. Most directly, Patrick Olivelle was my mentor in this project and remains so in various ways. He was the one who first pointed me towards Yājñavalkya and the *Bṛhadāraṇyaka*, but he was also eager to let me take the work in my own direction. Patrick was always willing to discuss the particularities of the Sanskrit language and its literature, but also my many ideas and drafts. He was and is a thorough, yet generous, critic. Joel Brereton was a constant source of detailed knowledge of the late Vedic period and its literature. Martha Selby shared her knowledge of all things literary and much more. Janice Leoshko taught me to "read" images and "see" text, while Cynthia Talbot asked hard historical questions in gentle ways.

In regard to debts more recent, I would like to express my thanks to: Philip Lutgendorf, Timothy Lubin, and Caley Smith for reading the whole manuscript and offering detailed comments; Herman Tull for a close reading of chapter 2; Stephanie Jamison for reading or hearing different parts at different times and always providing insightful feedback; Laurie Patton for her several collaborations and consistently generous comments on several aspects of my work over the years; Michael Witzel for past correspondence on our mutual interest in Yājñavalkya; and Christian Novetzke for his critical insights on my work and his good humor.

Several colleagues and friends in North America and Europe have been a source of inspiration and critical feedback: Brian Black, David Brick, Simon Brodbeck, Laura Brueck, the late Steve Collins, Neil Dalal, Donald Davis Jr., Madhav Deshpande, William Ellison, Jim Fitzgerald, Andrew Fort, Oliver Freiberger, John Robert Gardner, Robert Goodding, Peter Gottschalk, A. Gardner Harris, Edeltraud Harzer, James Hagerty, Alf Hiltebeitel, Hans Hock, Ronald Inden, the late Stanley Insler, Richard Larivierre, Andrea Marion, Karline McClain, Mark McClish, John Nemec, Jason Neelis, Leslie Orr, Deven Patel, Parimal Patil, Ajay Rao, Andy Rotman, Richard Salomon, Adheesh Sathaye, Federico Squaricini, George Thompson, Jarrod Whitaker, and Robert Yelle. An earlier version of one section of chapter 2 was originally published in the *Journal of Indian Philosophy* (Lindquist 2008) while another was published in a volume in honor of Dr. G. U. Thite (Lindquist 2004). I am grateful to those editors and their teams. My thanks to the anonymous reviewers of the book manuscript, the kind and diligent editorial staff at SUNY Press, and especially Wendy Doniger of the University of Chicago.

Several people and institutes made my research and my time in India both productive and pleasurable. The Bhandharkar Oriental Research Institute (Pune) was my central place of work in India. Special thanks to Dr. Saroja Bhate and the late Dr. M. G. Dadphale for their kind assistance in many matters. I also spent a fruitful year at Adyar Library and Kuppuswami Research Institute in Chennai.

Many Sanskritists shared their time and immense knowledge during my research trips to India. Dr. Ganesh Thite was my Sanskrit guide throughout the length of this project and was a wonderful resource on *brāhmaṇa* literature and Indian sacrifice more broadly. Dr. Srikant Bahulkar also shared his Sanskrit expertise with me on many occasions. While in Chennai, K. Srinivasan was another of my Sanskrit guides, and I fondly remember our many animated discussions about various Upaniṣadic passages. Dr. Pushpa Kale in Pune read Śaṅkara's commentaries with me, and while they are not directly part of this book, appreciation of later traditional systems of interpretation is found within. Other colleagues in India that deserve my dear thanks are: Dr. Pradeep Mahendiratta, Purnima Mehta, Madhav Bhandare, Gayatri Chatterjee, and Ramu Pandit.

My colleagues at Southern Methodist University deserve my thanks for providing me a place that I am happy to call my academic home. Special thanks Richard Cogley and Mark Chancey for guiding me through the crucial early years. My home department consists of colleagues who are not only supportive, but who have also been a source of friendly competitiveness, good humor, and honesty—an all-too-rare combination.

In reverse temporal order, this project was made financially possible by two University Research Council faculty grants at Southern Methodist University, The University of Texas at Austin Continuing Fellowship, the Fulbright-Hays Doctoral Dissertation Research Abroad Fellowship, and the American Institute of Indian Studies Junior Fellowship.

Finally, a special and dear thanks to my family. My parents, Rey and Lois Lindquist, were always supportive, even when they prodded me to "get that paper done." My wife, Lisa Owen, read "that paper" more times than either of us dare to count. She has been a pillar of kindness, love, and patience. In one sense, producing a book is like raising a child—with the care, love, defensiveness, and frustration that comes along with it—and Lisa has been an ideal intellectual co-parent. This metaphorical child, though, has since been supplanted by an actual one, and both our co-parenting and her steadfastness continues. My son, Evan, has taught me more about life in a few short years than I could have imagined. Though he has repeatedly distracted my attention from actually getting "that paper" done, my debt is to him.

To return to the metaphor from the start: a subcontinent—though possessing the intricacies of connections between lands, peoples, and cultures—like a person, ultimately stands on its own. Everything in this book, while deeply influenced by so many, is fundamentally my own doing. Any weakness or flaw is mine alone.

I dedicate this book to the memory of my loving father,
Reynold Lindquist (1939–2023).

Abbreviations

AGS	*Aśvalāyana Gṛhyasūtra*
AP	*Agni Purāṇa*
ĀpDhS	*Āpastamba Dharmasūtra*
AV	*Atharvaveda*
BĀU	*Bṛhadāraṇyaka Upaniṣad*
BĀUK	*Bṛhadāraṇyaka Upaniṣad* (Kāṇva)
BĀUM	*Bṛhadāraṇyaka Upaniṣad* (Mādhyandina)
BĀUBhā	*Bṛhadāraṇyaka Upaniṣad Bhāṣya*
BaudhDhS	*Baudhāyana Dharmasūtra*
BhG	*Bhagavadgītā*
BhP	*Bhāgavata Purāṇa*
CU	*Chāndogya Upaniṣad*
BP	*Brahmāṇḍa Purāṇa*
GauDhS	*Gautama Dharmasūtra*
JB	*Jaiminīya Brāhmaṇa*
KP	*Kūrma Purāṇa*
KS	*Kāṭhaka Saṃhitā*
KṣB	*Kauṣītaki Brāhmaṇa*
KṣU	*Kauṣītaki Upaniṣad*
LP	*Liṅga Purāṇa*
MārkP	*Mārkaṇḍeya Purāṇa*
MBh	*Mahābhārata*
PP	*Padma Purāṇa*
PrU	*Praśna Upaniṣad*
ṚV	*Ṛgveda*
ŚB	*Śatapatha Brāhmaṇa*
ŚBK	*Śatapatha Brāhmaṇa* (Kāṇva)

ŚBM	*Śatapatha Brāhmaṇa* (Mādhyandina)
SP	*Skanda Purāṇa*
SV	*Sāmaveda*
TB	*Taittirīya Brāhmaṇa*
TS	*Taittirīya Saṃhitā*
VaDhS	*Vasiṣṭha Dharmasūtra*
VāP	*Vāyu Purāṇa*
VP	*Viṣṇu Purāṇa*
VS	*Vājasaneya Saṃhitā*
VVRI	Vishveshvaranand Vedic Research Institute (Vedic Word Concordance)
YS	*Yājñavalkyasmṛti*
YV	*Yajurveda*

Introduction

Narrative and Method

Yājñavalkya is perhaps the most important literary-historical figure in ancient India prior to the Buddha.[1] He is attested to throughout the late Vedic ritual, philosophical, Epic, and Purāṇic literature (8th century BCE and well into the common era)—specifically, in the *Śatapatha Brāhmaṇa* (ŚB), the *Bṛhadāraṇyaka Upaniṣad* (BĀU), the *Mahābhārata* (MBh), and various Purāṇas. The Hindu tradition views him as the founder of the White Yajurveda (YV) school of ritual practice, which he is said to have received from the Sun (*āditya*).[2] Further, he is credited with writing a legal treatise, the *Yājñavalkyasmṛti* (YS), and is considered one of India's earliest and best known thinkers. In secondary scholarship he is also associated with a number of firsts in Indian religious literary history: the first person to discuss *brahman* and *ātman* thoroughly; the first to put forth an (albeit limited) theory of *karma* and reincarnation; the first to renounce his household life; the first to dispute with women in religious debate (*brahmodya*); and the first to discuss religious and philosophical matters with his wife. Throughout early Indian history, then, Yājñavalkya was seen as a priestly bearer of ritual authority, a sage of mystical knowledge, and an innovative propagator of philosophical ideas and religious law. In modern times, for many in the tradition he personifies the hoary past of the Veda, Vedic orthodoxy, and the beginnings of Vedāntic philosophical discourse.

In spite of Yājñavalkya's significance in ancient Indian literary history, he has only been approached in limited studies through philosophical and positivist-historical lenses—that is, the early narratives of Yājñavalkya have been viewed as the beginnings of formal philosophy and/or the emphasis has been placed on isolating the "real" Yājñavalkya and his teachings.[3] The later narratives concerning Yājñavalkya have been treated perfunctorily, if at all, and are generally taken as "mythic" fabrications. Yājñavalkya has never been taken seriously as a literary figure through the variety of texts in which he appears and has not been given the treatment he deserves. This is all the more ironic given that Yājñavalkya, because of his importance, is mentioned in nearly every introductory text on Hinduism or work on ancient Indian philosophy.[4]

The principal goal of this book is to analyze the early literary and historical construction of Yājñavalkya as a cultural icon in late Vedic, Epic, and Purāṇic literature[5] and to discuss how Yājñavalkya is composed and recomposed in religious texts in different historical contexts with different (literary, doctrinal, and sociological) intentions. Thus, I will critically analyze the early Yājñavalkya texts in regard to both their literary *and* social components—that is, how literary and lived worlds intersect in the construction of a social identity and literary memory across time.

Literary Background

Who is Yājñavalkya and what is his literary portrayal? These questions are central to this book and are dealt with at length in the following chapters. It is, however, prudent to give a brief summary to frame the narrative that is to follow.

Yājñavalkya first appears in the Brāhmaṇa literature (especially the ŚB, ca. 8th century BCE), an ancient genre of hieratic commentary devoted to ritual minutiae, stories, and myths—all of which have the overall purpose of explaining the various sacrificial acts and their relation to the gods, the phenomenal world, and humankind. He is portrayed as a ritual specialist giving his opinion on a variety of ritual actions and interpretations. Most of the passages are succinct and do not provide any detailed information about this individual (such as lineage, associations, etc.) nor do they provide much of a context. They do, however, give a sense of Yājñavalkya's character—a ritual specialist with a tendency towards sarcasm or wit. The majority of the passages are short, consisting of little more than a paragraph when translated into English. The form these passages often take is a series of opinions on a particular sacrificial point, although Yājñavalkya does appear in a few passages where his statement or opinion is the only one given.

In the later books of ŚB we encounter longer narratives in which Yājñavalkya is one of the principal characters, though shorter passages do occur as well. It has been argued by some that these longer narratives are more philosophical, indicating a shift from the earlier portrayal of Yājñavalkya and are themselves perhaps "mythical." It should be pointed out, however, that while one may see a shift in the character of Yājñavalkya, I show how the topics discussed are still intimately tied to his previous portrayal (albeit perhaps more abstractly in some cases) showing a clear attempt at consistency. Such longer narratives also give us a context to Yājñavalkya's appearance, something quite obscure in the single passages which simply list various ritualists' opinions on some particular point.

In the *Bṛhadāraṇyaka Upaniṣad* chapters 3 and 4 (ca. 6th century BCE), Yājñavalkya is the central character in a rather lively public debate and then in a private discussion, both set in the court of Janaka, the famed king and sponsor.[6] In the public debate of BĀU 3, other well-known ritual specialists have also gathered as well to participate. This debate spans such topics as sacrifice, life, death, and immortality, and climaxes with the rather dramatic defeat of the famous ritualist Śākalya, thus establishing Yājñavalkya as the most learned in the Vedas. Chapter 4 of BĀU shifts to a private religious discussion between Yājñavalkya and Janaka and continues by elaborating several of the themes presented in chapter 3. Chapter 4 then concludes with an even more private discussion, presumably in the domestic context, between Yājñavalkya and his wife, Maitreyī. In the sixth and final chapter of BĀU, we are told that Yājñavalkya is viewed as the founder of the White Yajurvedic school of ritual interpretation and that he received the sacrificial formulae of the White Yajurveda Saṃhitā from the Sun (*āditya*).

Yājñavalkya again appears in the *Mahābhārata* (MBh), the Epic poem dated roughly between the 4th century BCE and 2nd century CE.[7] While he is mentioned only briefly in a few passages, we do have one longer passage in the Śāntiparvan where Yājñavalkya is the central figure. Here he is seen teaching Janaka the doctrine of Yoga-Sāṅkhya, quite appropriate for this didactic book. Interestingly, after Yājñavalkya teaches his version of this doctrine, we step out of this dialogue proper and are told a story about how Yājñavalkya received the White Yajurveda *and* composed or compiled the ŚB, a new detail in his biography.

Finally, Yājñavalkya appears in a number of Purāṇic texts, often in the context of explaining the origin of the Vedas. In these various texts we encounter what I show to be recompositions of earlier material. We also have different stories about how and why Yājñavalkya split with his teacher to form his own ritual school, how he had to purify himself to receive the White Yajurveda from the Sun, and how he is seen as the founder of the White Yajurvedic tradition. Details of these tellings are premised on the earlier stories, stories which must have come to constitute a more widely held literary world surrounding the figure of Yājñavalkya. The composers of these texts interpret the figure more freely than those before them, and the literary life of this figure greatly expands.

Throughout the expanse of the literature under question here, there are a number of topics and themes that will be revisited throughout the chapters of this book. First, Yājñavalkya's wit or sarcasm is quite particular to this literary figure and makes him unique in ancient Indian literature, particularly amongst philosophers. Even in the earliest material, such as the ŚB, we find Yājñavalkya associated with many instances of clever wordplays, short and witty retorts, and derisive statements towards other Brahmins or opinions. While such comments may not be solely limited to the figure of Yājñavalkya, their overwhelming prevalence here and in the later literature that exploits such a characterization, I argue, clearly defines him as a distinct literary figure. In this sense, by looking at the use of sarcasm attributed to this figure, we see the foundation of his personality developing in the earliest literature.

In tracing the use (and nonuse) of this character trait diachronically, an intriguing pattern starts to emerge. For example, in the early material the sarcasm associated with Yājñavalkya *only* appears in situations where he is taken as authoritative by the tradition and not in situations where his opinion is an option or even disputed. I argue that this character trait of the figure of Yājñavalkya was viewed positively by the White Yajurvedic tradition and that his sarcasm was seen as justified by his correct (to their minds) interpretation of the matter at hand. This use of sarcasm develops and expands in the later books of ŚB and throughout the BĀU, culminating in Yājñavalkya's authority becoming absolute, when he begins to be portrayed as *always* correct in his opinion whether on ritual procedure, in public debate, or in private discussion. As sarcasm can be variously understood—such as humorous or rude—in this early context it might be best understood as "pride in correct knowledge," as it was apparently a positive trait (he was, after all, correct in those interpretations) and the sarcasm adds rhetorical force to his authority. In fact, the sarcasm associated with Yājñavalkya positions him as an ideal spokesperson for a newly emerging tradition—authoritative in his own right, but particularly in deriding the establishment with which he was competing.

When we approach Yājñavalkya's appearance in the MBh, his characterization changes; his character is still based on the same model of Yājñavalkya that was established in the early literature, but it is understood and deployed differently. Yājñavalkya's characteristic wit appears relatively absent in the MBh tellings, but his authority has risen greatly. This may be because the White Yajurvedic tradition is no longer a new contender in the Vedic sacrificial world and derisive competition was less necessary, though its position may not yet be as secure as others as it is often portrayed as a historically "younger" Veda. Here, Yājñavalkya is portrayed as a *r̥ṣi* (sage) of the ancient past and is said to have been present in Indra's heaven to perform the *rājasūya* (royal consecration ceremony). This mythical association authorizes him to perform the same rite for Yudhiṣṭhira on earth. It is clear that Yājñavalkya's status has grown in the Brahminical world and this figure plays an integral role in various parts of the text. In a longer passage associated with Yājñavalkya, I suggest that a lack of his characteristic sarcasm from earlier material may have prompted hagiographical elaboration about how Yājñavalkya came to have knowledge of the White Yajurveda and what his relationship to the Sun god was. In this sense, even though the characteristic sarcasm is absent, the composers, in elaborating a story of Yājñavalkya's past, are reminding us that we are still dealing with the same figure from the older literature.

In the Purāṇic material, this sarcastic trait is variously understood, sometimes negatively and sometimes positively. Given the depth of time between the Purānic compositions and those of the Vedic period, the composers had more liberty to explore his personality for their own ends. Here we encounter different stories that attempt to explain how Yājñavalkya could receive a "new" Veda (and what "new" means in the context of simultaneously being "ancient") and how his personality played a role in that reception. In one text, it is suggested that Yājñavalkya's teacher misunderstood a statement by Yājñavalkya and was insulted. Yājñavalkya then appealed to the Sun god for a new Veda since he had been compelled to return the Black Yajurveda to his teacher. In another text, we are told that Yājñavalkya did, apparently intentionally, insult his teacher and had to undergo penance. His penance pleased the Sun to such a degree that the Sun god chose to grant him a new Veda. In another story, which is a retelling of the *Bṛhadāraṇyaka* story, Yājñavalkya is not sarcastic or arrogant at all, but all of the other Brahmins present in a public debate are said to have this trait. In this case, what could be understood as a negative trait associated with a particular *ṛṣi* is placed onto the other Brahmins in the debate and thus the character of Yājñavalkya is "sanitized" while inverting the moral message of the story.

The rather unique trait of sarcasm attributed to Yājñavalkya, as I argue throughout this book, is a defining trait that positioned him as particularly appropriate to be taken as the founder of the White Yajurvedic tradition. A close reading of the texts suggests that it is this characteristic that ideally situates him as the spokesperson for the tradition: he is a leader who can justify his own tradition's practices in contrast to an already established orthodoxy, even—or especially—if that means denigrating others in the process. It is, however, also a trait that the tradition had to reconcile itself with once the tradition and its founder became established. In the later literary traditions (the Purāṇas), the composers are concerned with this unique trait, in part because they lacked the same agonistic need of the earlier tradition. In these cases, we find that their interest lies in explaining his sarcasm or arrogance, especially how such an ambivalent trait can be associated with such a renowned sage.[8] Some of these texts try to explain this characteristic away ("it was based on a misunderstanding") or elaborate how, if viewed as a character flaw, it can be overcome (such as through penance).

A second related theme that we find throughout the literature on Yājñavalkya is his association with other, newer religious traditions or practices. For example, from the MBh onward Yājñavalkya is associated with apparently different traditions of *yoga*. While the earliest material does not discuss Yājñavalkya in relation to *yoga*—it is likely that a distinct mainstream tradition as such did not exist at the time—it appears that Yājñavalkya's authority is being put to a different use in later material. Here we find that his philosophical discussions on the nature of the self (*ātman*) and the universal principle (*brahman*) from the earlier material are reinterpreted in the context of mental and physical conditioning that are supposed to aid in the realization of certain larger truths.

As Yājñavalkya is associated with a new Yajurveda, he paradoxically becomes viewed as an ancient *ṛṣi*. Here I argue that Yājñavalkya becomes emblematic of "the new within the ancient" and his association with *yoga* and other traditions is a means of claiming ancient authority for newly developing traditions. This becomes particularly clear in the Purāṇas where there is the dual concern of explaining the origin of Yājñavalkya (as a "new" sage among ancient ones) with newly emerging (or newly "Sanskritizing") traditions devoted to Śiva or Rāma or valorizing apparently new rites or pilgrimages. As such, the character of Yājñavalkya becomes a means to put the present into the past to make a claim to authority for a tradition. To put this another way: a "new" sage is made "old," but then his new "oldness" is utilized to claim "oldness" for other newly developing traditions, thus creating a mutually reinforcing temporal circle. In this way, the ancient may newly appear in the world, but its newness becomes an ironic feature in the creation of authority, rather than a bug.

Another central theme in the literature is how Yājñavalkya becomes seen as an idealized priest in relation to kings. In the ŚB we see the beginning of this association with King Janaka, himself an idealized king who sponsors Brahmins and, at least on one occasion, is said to know more than Brahmins about a particular rite and its significance. In the BĀU, Yājñavalkya is closely associated with Janaka, and he proves himself to be the wisest Brahmin at a debate held at Janaka's court. Later in the same text it is said that Yājñavalkya teaches Janaka about the nature of life, death, and the cosmos in a private discussion. In later literature, Yājñavalkya appears often with Janaka, but he also is associated with other kings as well. His kingly associations parallel his ritual associations with the *aśvamedha* (royal horse sacrifice) and the *rājasūya* (royal consecration), emphasizing the dependent relationship of kings and Brahmins.

From these precedents, there are suggestive reasons why Yājñavalkya becomes associated with the legal tradition (*dharmaśāstra*) where his name is attributed to a particular legal text (the *Yājñavalkyasmṛti*). Based on a comparison with the figure of Manu and the famous legal text attributed to him, I argue that Yājñavalkya fulfills a similar ideological function as Manu, albeit from the other side of the dominant *varṇa* coin. While Manu is an idealized king, Yājñavalkya has become an idealized Brahmin, specifically through his relationships with kings, and both represent class-based claims to a tradition of *dharma*.

Finally, the major concern of this book is how we can trace the life of a literary figure across time and texts and how we can query these recompositions for what they tell us, not only about how a larger tradition developed out of a smaller one, but also about how various people understood this figure in recomposing him. By viewing the recomposition of Yājñavalkya as a literary figure in different literature, we are granted a window into the concerns and motivations of those later compositions. If we view these recompositions as a form of commentary on earlier literary productions, we can analyze these later traditions in a new manner. We can look at what aspects of an earlier narrative were known and/or were important to different composers by looking at hagiographical expansion (such as later narratives focused on Yājñavalkya's wives or on the origins of the Vedas), hagiographical inversion (such as the narrative of Yājñavalkya's sarcasm being transposed onto others), and hagiographical contraction (such as removing certain details altogether or collapsing a story to focus on one particular part).

It is in the historically later narratives that the figure of Yājñavalkya becomes an increasingly well-known figure—both because the audience progressively widens in the transition between genres in the oral literature and also due to a broadening creative license on the part of the authors to explore or expand on those literary precedents. This does not mean that later composers were not bound to collectively held notions of who this figure was, but that certain genres and contexts allowed for a certain freedom in how those authors might compose or recompose. I suggest that we think of this process as the "literary memory" that these composers had of Yājñavalkya—a ritualist, a debater with a strong wit, and a philosopher with two wives—where the authors were not necessarily rigidly bound to a specific textual tradition, but were apparently well aware of it and found different means to work within its larger contours for their own ends.

By talking about the "life" of a literary figure, we are also talking about the lives of various individuals who found this literary figure interesting, useful, or religiously compelling for any number of different reasons. This diachronic and narratological approach to the figure of Yājñavalkya is, as far as I am aware, the first of its kind. Generally speaking, portrayals of Yājñavalkya beyond the early material have been simply dismissed by scholars or rather perfunctorily treated. In fact, I would argue that exploring how a figure attains such a status, and more so, what such a status means, grants a unique view into how particular ancient Indians understood their tradition. Further, to dismiss the narratives as myth or the like ignores the fact that there are many different stories about Yājñavalkya coming from many different traditions which grants a view into how *different* people used the figure in their compositions for *different* ends.

"Literary Lives"

I have argued elsewhere as a devil's advocate against scholarship that attempts to find a "real" Yājñavalkya within the literary presentation of this figure in an effort to illuminate the problems with such approaches.[9] This book begins with the assumption that, given the current state of scholarship, the search for a historical individual in this case will only produce very limited results. While I do not think that such studies should be abandoned altogether, more sophisticated theoretical models need to be developed if one wishes to pursue this route. What is necessary in such attempts is an analysis of how narrative and history are interrelated as well as an explicit discussion about the criteria used to determine if something can be considered "legend," "myth," or "fact." As I have shown (Lindquist 2011b), no attempt so far has been adequately able to demarcate a "real" Yājñavalkya—more often than not, the logic employed to do so can simply be turned on itself or equally compelling alternatives can be given. Further, a more sophisticated view of literature must be adopted by those concerned with the early material as regards the notion of narrative or narrativeness, that is formal characteristics that make certain speech into narratives. As is well accepted, if not always analyzed, all speech is motivated to some end, whether that end is rather banal or more insidious (from pleasantries, to sharing of information, to an attempt to convince or deceive). Any narrative, whether told for the first time or repeated for generations, takes on formal literary structures and employs narrative devices which do not necessarily say anything about its historicity, but do speak to the motivations of composers. These devices do not mean that what is being told is historically true or not, but it does mean that the speech is motivated towards various ends and narrative structures and devices are employed to support those ends. As Roland Barthes (1972), among others, has shown, we are always surrounded by narrativity whether it be in our speech acts, our advertising, our view of our own individual lives, or in our other cultural productions. Unlike others concerned with Yājñavalkya, I take the nature of these narratives as the starting point of analysis, rather than as the conclusion.

The early textual evidence as we have it does not appear to lend itself, as far as I can determine, to the drawing of a firm line between who is the "real" historical Yājñavalkya and who is not. While there most likely was a real historical individual at some point in early Indian history, where to determine the beginning and the end of a "person" in the early literature remains analytically unclear.

For my purposes, I take the portrayal of Yājñavalkya in the literature as a *literary* figure. Within the confines of literature, we can compare and evaluate the various portrayals to analyze who this figure was as part of the literary imagination of ancient Indians and how that literary imagination creates a literary memory over time. Rather than proposing any grander theory to explain legend, myth, or mythic development, the following chapters look at the various ways that a series of narratives (i.e., those surrounding Yājñavalkya) and history (the contexts, whether material or ideological) intersect. Dominick LaCapra (1994) has made the useful heuristic distinction between the "documentary" and the "work-like" aspects of a text, where the former is the object of sociological and historical scrutiny and the latter the object of literary criticism. Following this bifurcation, I will analyze certain historical developments in early Indian history and their relationship to textual production. Thus, by avoiding entirely the question of a "real Yājñavalkya," the focus of this monograph is *what Yājñavalkya represents, to whom,* and *why*. Such a focus allows us to view the development of Yājñavalkya as a literary figure across time and contexts. We can, by approaching Yājñavalkya as a literary figure, analyze the pronouncements and stories attributed to him as well as the motivations of the communities who preserved these texts as indicative of various (historical) concerns, ideas, and beliefs. Thus, by not searching for the "authentic" person or teaching, this book looks at what people believed and why across time.

In this fashion, a literary view of Yājñavalkya focuses on aspects of the texts which have been largely overlooked.[10] For example: we can analyze plot, character, literary structures and devices, themes and thematic change, and note the use of hyperbole, sarcasm, and narrative tension. More importantly, we can analyze what all this tells us not only about the rise to authority of a particular figure, but also about those communities that created and maintained these stories in a variety of genres.

Chapter 1 is concerned with Yājñavalkya in the earliest literature, the ŚB. In this chapter, I deal with Yājñavalkya in two sections: his portrayal in ŚBM (Mādhyandina) books 1–5 and then in books 11–13 (both along with the correlate passages in the other recension of the same text, ŚBK [Kāṇva]). After briefly discussing the name "Yājñavalkya" itself and the literary history of the ŚB, I analyze the form and meaning of the different passages in which Yājñavalkya appears, focusing on the form and function of what many have called his "sarcastic" nature. It is here that I elaborate the contours of what constitutes "sarcasm" in the context of this figure. Moreover, I will propose a topography of the statements attributed to Yājñavalkya, which shows that not only was Yājñavalkya *not always* authoritative in his pronouncements, but that the authoritativeness and sarcasm attributed to him increases in parallel fashion across the texts. I also discuss the historical reasons for this development: as the tradition of the White Yajurveda was establishing itself in the frontier northeastern region, it needed a spokesman for what must have been seen as a fringe tradition. In this fashion, Yājñavalkya's sarcastic portrayal serves as an ideal soapbox for this tradition—one which not only establishes the White Yajurveda as a legitimate sacrificial school, but also one which criticizes, even mocks, the then current western (Kuru-Pañcāla) establishment. In the later books of ŚB, I will also suggest that a template of Yājñavalkya has begun to be established—that is, the character and narrative basis that will influence most, though not necessarily all, of his other literary portrayals. Chapter 1 is furnished with more philological rigor than the following chapters, but as I explain below, this is unavoidable.

Chapter 2 analyzes the most important text associated with Yājñavalkya, the *Bṛhadāraṇyaka Upaniṣad*. It is in this text that Yājñavalkya is found in an elaborate narrative about the nature of the sacrifice (*yajña*), life, death, the self, and rebirth. This text, similar to narratives found in later ŚB books, comprises a lively debate, but with rather deadly consequences. Not only will I discuss the various passages and their meaning, but I will also focus on how the text coheres as a whole. I will investigate the thematic links between the sections and how the various sections develop a single coherent plot and climax (BĀU 3), followed by a distinct but interrelated continuation of these themes (BĀU 4). I propose that the entire Yājñavalkyakāṇḍa, while not a single narrative, is a series of narratives that thematically coheres as a larger "teaching narrative." This teaching narrative progresses through BĀU 3 and 4 coinciding with an increasing privacy in the contexts of these teachings (from the public to the private court, concluding with a private dialogue between a husband and wife).

In this chapter, I will also discuss the various literary devices which serve to hold this narrative together. Particular attention will be paid to how the BĀU account is consistent with the portrayal of Yājñavalkya in the ŚB, not necessarily suggesting a real individual, but certainly suggesting an attempt at consistency on the part of the literary tradition. It is here too that the topography of sarcasm and authority from chapter 1 will be discussed anew: I show that the authority attributed to Yājñavalkya, coupled with his characteristic sarcasm, is a firmly established pairing. While this trait begins in the ŚB, the notion of "pride in correct knowledge" is entrenched by BĀU—that is, all sarcastic expressions are justified in context based on the fact that Yājñavalkya is *always* correct in his interpretations of the sacrifice, life, death, and rebirth. Further, I show that this "philosophical" text is ultimately polemical—it is inherently an *argument against* western forms of ritual understanding and an *argument for* the newly establishing/established eastern hegemony.

A subsection in chapter 2 is devoted to women in the BĀU, as this is the first literary occurrence of women involved in abstract, philosophical debate. This section focuses on how gender is constructed in this text and how the role of women is related to the portrayal of Yājñavalkya and the larger narrative. Another section in this chapter concerns the interpretation of BĀU 3.9.28, a riddle-poem which has caused problems for scholars and the indigenous tradition alike. As this riddle-poem is the conclusion of the debate of BĀU 3, it is necessary to take a fresh look at what it may mean, particularly regarding the nature of rebirth. This is particularly important, because contrary to common opinion (e.g., Horsch 1966), a close reading shows that Yājñavalkya is clearly associated with a newly emerging idea of rebirth.

The first two chapters, particularly chapter 1, are the most philologically detailed chapters in the book. Though I am sympathetic to the nonspecialist reader, I hope he or she will understand that this was unavoidable for two main reasons. First, at the heart of this book is the methodological principle that stories need to be taken seriously in their appropriate linguistic and historical context. As such, close linguistic and textual scrutiny is the hallmark of all that follows. Because of this, primary text and translation is employed throughout the body of the text (and separately as an appendix for the whole of chapters 3 and 4 of the BĀU), not only to justify my own interpretations, but also to give the reader an appreciation for the interpretive complexity that is involved. This linguistic and textual scrutiny, though, is most intense where the language or larger context is obscure. This is particularly true of the *brāhmaṇa* material in chapter 1. Since *brāhmaṇas* are ritual technical manuals for the early Vedic practitioner, they assume a knowing audience—an audience intimately familiar with a vast array of religious texts and practices which are obscure not only to the nonspecialist, but often also to the specialist separated by thousands of years and miles. I spend a significant part of chapter 1 teasing out the plausible context and meaning of these passages, which often requires teasing out the meaning of individual phrases or words.

A second reason that this level of detail is unavoidable in these chapters, in this case especially in the textual analysis of chapter 2, is that the literary background of Yājñavalkya becomes established here, and later composers explicitly and implicitly refer to it in their compositions. Chapter 2 discusses the literarily and historically most important narratives about Yājñavalkya found in the BĀU. My close literary analysis of this text not only *lays out* the groundwork of my own chapters that follow, but also *is* the groundwork for the composers of the later portrayals of this figure. I argue that this text codifies a template of this figure, and it is this template that later authors draw upon, even when challenging or circumventing it. This template, then, must be understood in detail in order to understand those later literary developments. Since my interpretations are tied intimately to my understanding of the primary text, the text and translation (including notes) of BĀU 3–4 are included in a separate appendix. This is done not only to give access to the larger narrative to the nonspecialist reader, but to lay bare my interpretative moves to specialists.

The reader who is not familiar with Sanskrit or early India is advised to not become bogged down in the philological details of these chapters. In order to assist in this, each chapter has several thematic sections which are intended to both focus on some of the most interesting details in these sections (such as the use of sarcasm attributed to Yājñavalkya or the historical anomaly of females participating in what were normally all-male arenas) and also provide brief summaries to create a broader picture of this literary figure. If a larger picture is the goal, the details create and justify that picture. The reader should be rewarded in the chapters that follow, not because that material is uncomplicated or less interesting, but because those passages are predicated on the earlier material and are also less complicated philologically, at least for my purposes.

In chapter 3, I consider the role of Yājñavalkya in the MBh. I analyze and discuss the brief references throughout certain books of this text. Particularly, I focus on the one long narrative concerning Yājñavalkya and how, at least on an initial reading, his appearance seems anomalous—he is teaching the metaphysics of Yoga and Sāṃkhya, doctrines he has never been associated with before. However, I show how Yājñavalkya's appearance is not so anomalous after all. Yājñavalkya's main appearance is principally in the Śāntiparvan, a later didactic text which focuses especially on Yoga and Sāṃkhya, but it is also a text concerned with justifying new teachings under older, more established garb. Thus, by the time of the MBh, Yājñavalkya was established as a sage of the past and new doctrines are being attributed to his authority, making a claim to ancient precedence.

It is also in the MBh where the first discernible hagiographical tendencies concerning Yājñavalkya begin. The MBh contains a story about how Yājñavalkya broke away from his teacher of the Black Yajurveda, how he purified himself for his transgression against his *guru*, how he received the White Yajurveda from the Sun for his penance, and how and why he compiled or composed the ŚB. This story itself also seems, at first glance, anomalous with respect to Yājñavalkya's larger teaching on Yoga-Sāṃkhya as it is not thematically related and appears simply attached to the end. While it may be that this passage is a later addition, I suggest that it is an intentional, necessary part of the longer passage. The reason for this, I argue, is that this passage in the MBh has fundamentally altered the template of Yājñavalkya established in the ŚB and the BĀU. As I show in chapters 1 and 2, a foundational characteristic of Yājñavalkya that is developed is his sarcasm. In the MBh, Yājñavalkya's sarcastic wit is nowhere to be found—in fact, Yājñavalkya appears almost without a personality, a perhaps reverential portrayal of a venerated sage. This longer passage is a dry listing of the fundamental tenets of a particular view of Yoga-Sāṃkhya, which is purely didactic and Yājñavalkya might appear to be little more than a mouth to put that teaching into. It is here that I suggest that there was a perceived need for the inclusion of a brief hagiography, as well as the ascription of the White Yajurveda and the ŚB to Yājñavalkya, *because of* the lack of sarcasm or apparent connection to his earlier portrayal and association with ritual. This is to say that there is a lack of connection to the template that had previously defined Yājñavalkya as a literary character so a connection had to be forged through hagiography. Not only does this passage serve as an entertaining conclusion to the discussion of Yoga-Sāṃkhya (perhaps one of its intents, given its dry nature), but it also makes clear that we are dealing with *the same literary figure* found in the ŚB and the BĀU, something otherwise not necessarily obvious.

While chapter 3 discusses what appears to be the first clear hagiographical trend in any Yājñavalkya narrative, the narrative shows that by this period Yājñavalkya was an established figure, even an ancient *ṛṣi*. In chapter 4, I will discuss how this hagiographical trend is greatly expanded in the Purāṇic ("legendary/historical") accounts. As I will demonstrate, the Purāṇic narratives about Yājñavalkya center on five major themes: (1) retellings of the BĀU/ŚB; (2) a concern with names and origins (specifically, the division of the Vedas and the perceived split between the White and Black Yajurveda); (3) Yājñavalkya in relation to *yoga*; (4) the relationship of kings and Brahmins; and (5) Yājñavalkya in relation to the *dharmaśāstra* tradition.

Analyzing these five themes, I argue, allows us not only an insight into what stories, narrative structures, and character portrayals these authors were familiar with from the earlier sources, but they also grant us a view into how later composers understood the previous narratives in the composing of their own. Reading these later stories as explicitly or implicitly based on earlier ones allows us to view these later compositions as a form of commentary, granting us insight into how this figure was interpreted and reinterpreted across time.

Chapter 4 concludes with the all-too-brief ascription of the *Yājñavalkyasmṛti* to Yājñavalkya. As the evidence is extremely meager, I only tentatively suggest possible reasons why this text was ascribed to him based on a comparison with the figure of Manu and a composite view of Yājñavalkya across time.

This book then concludes with "Yājñavalkya and Ancient Indian Literary Memory." Recently, it has been shown that it can be fruitful to view Indian images as having "lives."[11] This is to say that images are reinvented and reinscribed with meaning over time—depending on their context, both physical (such as how and where they are installed) and more abstract (such as how they are offered to, and venerated by, particular communities). Like images, religious-literary figures also have "lives," here the lives within a particular story or cluster of stories, but also lives across time and space which are reinvented and reinscribed with meaning depending on the needs and motivations of the particular communities that maintain, venerate, and elaborate the narratives surrounding such figures.[12] This book is, at its base, about how these two "lives" intersect.

1

The Origins of a Sage

Although Yājñavalkya is one of the most prominent figures in the literary history of what can be called early Hinduism, especially in the emergence of late Vedic religion and society, he does not appear at all in the earliest Vedic literature. Yājñavalkya's first appearance in the literary record is in the *Śatapatha Brāhmaṇa* (ŚB).[1] Yājñavalkya's absence in the earlier material has been noted by Macdonell and Keith ([1912] 1967) with some degree of surprise—both apparently expected such a consequential figure to have a longer literary genealogy or at least appearances in contemporaneous texts.[2] This expectation of a longer literary genealogy implies that, to Macdonell and Keith, the figure of Yājñavalkya had, by the time of the later Vedic texts, such as the *Bṛhadāraṇyaka Upaniṣad* (BĀU), gone beyond any "realistic" portrayal and had entered the realm of "legend."[3] The expectation that Yājñavalkya should appear in texts of other schools further implies that Yājñavalkya's school, the White Yajurveda, was mainstream enough, either geographically or ritualistically, to warrant mention in the texts of other traditions. As I will point out below, the lack of earlier textual references probably has more to do with the rise to authority of an anomalous figure at a particular point in time, rather than with a long period of hagiographical elaboration (which, in this case, only clearly occurs in the MBh and Purāṇas, and only in specific instances). Further, as recent historical research into the geographical placement of Vedic texts indicates (Witzel 1987a, 1989, 1997; Mylius 1965, 1972), the White Yajurvedic tradition, especially the composition of the ŚB, was an eastern "fringe" development whose mention in the mainstream traditions of the day would have been unlikely.

The Name Yājñavalkya

As the name Yājñavalkya does not appear in the earlier literature, it would seem a prudent starting place to consider what this name may mean when it is first used. As with many Sanskrit names, there are often secondary meanings that may help determine family lineage or even indicate something about the character himself.[4] However, along with the absence of this name in the earlier record, we are also at a loss to interpret its meaning when it first appears in the ŚB.[5]

The first part of the compound is rather straightforward—the masculine noun *yajña* is the Vedic "sacrifice," comprising any number of possible offerings to the gods accompanied by *mantras*. The most elaborate form of *yajña*, the *śrauta* ritual, includes the pressing and offering of *soma*, a plant with possible mind-altering properties.[6] The term *yājña* is the appropriate strengthening (*vr̥ddhi*) of the vowel to indicate relation to the principal term.[7] Thus, as a name, it would mean "the son of Yajñavalka." This would be useful if a Yajñavalka appeared in the textual record. He does not.

The most significant difficulty in understanding this name, however, is the lack of a satisfactory explanation for *-valkya-*. The *-ya-* suffix is a standard nominal derivation and poses little problem—it denotes a relation to the principal term in an adjectival sense and is commonly used in patronymics. Mayrhofer (1986, 410) has proposed that *°*valka-* is related to *varcas* ("luster, brilliance"). The linguistic variation of r/l in Vedic and classical Sanskrit is well attested (Witzel 1989, 107–108).[8] Mayrhofer points to *R̥gveda* (R̥V) 3.8.3 = 3.24.2 *várco dhā yajñávāhase*, where the words are associated with each other, yet not in compound. The compound "Yajñavalka" could then mean "illustrious at/in/through the sacrifice." Yājñavalkya would then be the "son of someone who is illustrious at/in/through the sacrifice."

The indigenous interpretation is, linguistically, of little help, but it is perhaps culturally more meaningful. Śaṅkara explains *-valkya-* based on a comparison with √*vac*, meaning "to speak," and sees Yājñavalkya as a "speaker at/of the sacrifice" (*Br̥hadāraṇyaka Upaniṣad Bhāṣya* [BĀUBhā] 1.4.3).[9] This is consonant with what we know of

Yājñavalkya, constantly engaged in debate both in and about sacrifice, but the trouble lies in the fact that this is linguistically unlikely, if not impossible. The root √*vac* cannot be linguistically related to the later attested verb √*valk* (where would the inserted *l* have come from?), and both more likely have separate linguistic histories. While it is common in scholarship to point to the root √*valk* (i.e., "to speak") independently of an association with √*vac*,[10] it must be noted that according to Vishveshvaranand Vedic Research Institute (VVRI) the verbal root √*valk* only appears in the literature *historically later* than the name itself (i.e., later than the ŚB).

However, if an attempt at an etymology of Yājñavalkya's name does not bear much fruit, we are still in the position to examine the development of the character of Yājñavalkya in the early literature. In fact, the portrayal of Yājñavalkya's personality is quite lively and intriguing, particularly given the rather stiff portrayals of other figures in the Brāhmaṇa literature, and this will constitute a major portion of this chapter. However, before moving directly into an analysis of the portrayal of this figure it is necessary to briefly place the ŚB, and in our case Yājñavalkya, within a broader historical context.

Literary and Historical Background

White and Black Yajurveda

As is well known,[11] the Vedic corpus is generally viewed as encompassing four genres: the Saṃhitās (or *mantra*-type texts, each associated with a particular priestly group), consisting of the *R̥gveda*, *Sāmaveda*, *Yajurveda*, and *Atharvaveda*; the Brāhmaṇa texts, consisting largely of prose commentary; the Āraṇyakas, or "wilderness" texts, thought to be more esoteric than the Brāhmaṇas though quite similar in style; and the Upaniṣads, usually viewed as philosophical-mystical texts that progressively move away from the ritual worldview of the preceding texts. These distinctions, needless to say, are rather artificial: Brāhmaṇa, Āraṇyaka, and Upaniṣad are variously attached to different texts of the various liturgical schools (lit. "branches," *śākhā*) and these text-types are often part and parcel of other text-types.[12] Further, one must bear in mind that such stratification of text-types is not necessarily chronological—text production and compilation of various genres continued simultaneously and delineation can only be carried out on a case-by-case basis.

The text and the school that Yājñavalkya is associated with is the Yajurveda Saṃhitā of the *śuklayajurveda* ("White Yajurveda"),[13] as opposed to the *kṛṣṇayajurveda* ("Black Yajurveda"). Broadly, the Yajurveda is a compendium of the *yajus* or sacrificial formula of the *adhvaryu* priest, the priest responsible for the majority of ritual actions (and their accompanying *mantras*) in a *yajña*. As has been noted quite early by scholars (for example, Caland 1932, the fundamental difference between the White Yajurveda and the Black is that the White has separate *mantra* and Brāhmaṇa texts, whereas in the Black they are mixed. Witzel (2003, 134ff.) has pointed out that though there is variation in content between schools, the White Yajurveda (YV) Saṃhitā is not recited with the standard accent of the ŚB (*bhāṣika* accent). Instead, it follows the western (Kuru-Pañcāla) accenting system. This may suggest that the *Vājasaneya Saṃhitā* (VS) was recomposed in a more western location or perhaps that it was intentionally recomposed in the western accent system to claim higher authority for their text. While the separation of Brāhmaṇa and *mantra* portions of a text is largely a formal one, there are traces even in the early literature that the differentiation of the White YV from the Black YV fostered competition, even derision.[14]

The Black Yajurveda, of which we have three main versions, largely consists of the Brāhmaṇa and *mantra* portion mixed together in a single text,[15] while the White Yajurveda has a separate Brāhmaṇa, called the *Śatapatha Brāhmaṇa* (ŚB), an extensive text concerned with the ritual actions of the *adhvaryu* priest and the larger religious import of those rituals and ritual actions. The ŚB is known to us in two different, but closely similar, recensions: the Mādhyandina (M) and the Kāṇva (K) (see trans. Eggeling [1882–1900] 1993, intro., vol. 12; Witzel 1987a, 1989, 1997; and Brereton 2006).[16]

Place and Time of the White YV/ŚB

While my concern here is not the larger and more detailed linguistic arguments that have been made about the placing and dating of ŚB (see Mylius 1965; Witzel 1987a, 1989, 1997), it is necessary for us to briefly summarize the historical situation that the latest scholarship has been able to deduce. As Witzel (1989; see also 1997) has convincingly shown, in elaborating Oldenberg's (1971) earlier summary, the ŚB grew out of and was part of a newly evolving cultural center of people who had immigrated to northeastern India.[17]

Based on river names and broader geographical knowledge evidenced in the texts, as well as research in possible dialectical variations, Witzel has placed the composition of the ŚB (in both the Mādhyandina [ŚBM] and Kāṇva [ŚBK] recensions) in northeastern India (specifically, in northern Bihar). However, as with most of our early Indian texts, the ŚB is a compiled text, probably at the hand of various editors, and it contains any number of interpolations in the course of its history. As many have pointed out, there is a general tripartite split in the text: ŚBM books 1–5 and 11–13, which consist of the "Yājñavalkya sections," and books 6–10 where the principal authority is Śāṇḍilya (and Yājñavalkya does not appear at all). Weber pointed out long ago (1961) that books 6–10 appear to be from a more western region than the other books. This theory has been greatly elaborated by Witzel's work (1989) on dialectical variation within Vedic texts, particularly the ŚB. Through the tracing of a multitude of grammatical forms, certain particular terms (i.e., *punarmr̥tyu, pāpa,* etc.), particles (*svid,* etc.), and other peculiarities of the language, there is little doubt that the ŚBK and ŚBM mutually influenced the production of the other and that their place of production was geographically close—with ŚBK having a slightly more western location in northeastern India (perhaps in northwestern Bihar) and overlapping with the Kosala region (in eastern Uttar Pradesh) and ŚBM in Videha (in northeastern Bihar).[18] Witzel (1997, 314) summarizes this dialectical relationship: "the main Kosala YV text, the Kāṇvīya Brāhmaṇa (ŚBK), often participates in *western* linguistic developments, while on the basis of geographical location, one would expect eastern forms such as found in the closely related ŚBM . . . However, while the ŚBM and ŚBK are ultimately based on the western, Kuru-Pañcāla model of *śrauta* ritual, they are opposed to the strictly western form of the ritual and its texts."

Dating the ŚB

The dating of the ŚB is, as with all dating of ancient Indian texts, necessarily relative. Our dating of one text requires the dating of other texts (for example, in the case of the *Ṛgveda*, its relationship to Avestan texts as well as later texts such as *Sāmaveda* [SV], *Atharvaveda* [AV]). The situation with the ŚB is no different: we must have relative dates of the texts that precede and postdate the text to propose a date somewhere in the middle.[19] While the internal chronology of sections or passages of ŚB and BĀU is greatly complicated as well as contested, that of the ŚB and BĀU *as a whole* is fairly well accepted.[20]

The ŚB is generally placed at about the 8th century before the common era, with the necessary caveat of "give or take a century." A principal reason for this dating is that the ŚB, as well as the BĀU (the final book of ŚB), appears to be pre-Buddhist. The BĀU is clearly younger than the ŚB as a whole. Since the life of the historical Buddha has been dated roughly within the 5th to 4th centuries, the BĀU may have been composed roughly in the 7th–6th centuries and the thirteen other books of the ŚB in the 8th century. While there has been some scholarly disagreement about the pre-Buddhist nature of the BĀU, no firm evidence has been brought forward to seriously challenge the established relative dating.[21] The internal evidence of BĀU suggests an *urbanizing* environment and not the *urbanized* environment of the Pāli texts (see Olivelle 1998). In BĀU there is no direct mention of cities, but rather of debates occurring in Videha, a region without an expressed capital. Of course, there is the court of Janaka in BĀU 3–4, but there is no evidence from which to suggest administrative capacities, division of labor, or any other standard sociological and material indicators from which to determine what type of town or city may have been present at that time. Rather, the BĀU suggests people were settling in the eastern region most likely in the early phases of the second urbanization in Indian history (Allchin 1995; Erdosy 1988; Olivelle 1993, 56–62).

The ŚB, however, does not suggest an urbanized or even urbanizing world, but rather a village-based system with gradual immigration into more eastern regions. The text retains more archaic forms of language,[22] and thus, as a whole, appears to predate the BĀU. As mentioned before, however, while the text *as a whole* may predate the BĀU, this does not mean *the whole* text does—in fact, books 11–13 of ŚBM ≈ 13–15 ŚBK have compositional similarities with the BĀU and are likely closer in compositional date than the early books.

Tracing the Early Yājñavalkya

Yājñavalkya's appearance in the earliest literature has been the focus of a number of works (Tsuji 1943/1981 as cited by Witzel 2003; Renou 1948; Ruben 1947, 1954; Horsch 1966; Fišer 1984; Witzel 1987b, 2003; Brereton 1997; and Hock 2002). Some of these works have attempted to show that Yājñavalkya throughout the ŚB and BĀU is one and the same individual (Tsuji, Witzel), and other works argue that there are multiple Yājñavalkyas—a historical one and a mythologized one—particularly when discussing the historically later portions of ŚB and BĀU (Ruben, Renou, Bronkhorst, Horsch, Fišer). Hock (2002) and Brereton (1997), in their studies of the Yājñavalkya section of the BĀU, however, have avoided this question and focused rather on the constructed nature of the discourse and what that discourse tells us, not necessarily about a "real" individual, but about how a tradition viewed itself and constructed its discourse for different ends.[23] Here I intend to follow this latter model with the ŚB, something that has not been done to date. This is to say, that while recognizing the larger historical development from the Black Yajurveda to the White Yajurveda, particularly in regard to the ŚB, my concern is with the nature of those passages attributed to or containing Yājñavalkya, what they may tell us about how a tradition viewed this figure, and how these portrayals are directly connected to his later appearances. Thus, while I will argue that there is a progression from the early to the later books in ŚB regarding how Yājñavalkya is portrayed, I do not think that this progression necessarily supports the larger arguments made by others about who the "actual" Yājñavalkya might have been.

While Fišer (1984) and Witzel (2003) both claim to be assessing the personality of Yājñavalkya, their works consist largely of an accumulation of the various Yājñavalkya passages, with little content or character analysis. Witzel has gone much further than Fišer in attempting to show a "personal" language of Yājñavalkya that is "witty" and "innovative." In contrast, Fišer takes the individual pronouncements of Yājñavalkya as relating to a historical individual and sees the later stories (ŚBM books 11–13 and the BĀU) as a progressively elaborated hagiography. Neither has paid special attention to the Kāṇva recension (except as an occasional counterpoint to the Mādhyandina text) nor has either scholar paid close attention to exactly how and why Yājñavalkya's language appears witty or sarcastic and how such rhetoric may have evolved in the tradition. Both have, however, suggested topographies for understanding the Yājñavalkya passages: Fišer proposes a formal typography (based on the nature of discourse, whether individual pronouncement or larger narrative); Witzel has proposed looking at the Yājñavalkya passages thematically—based on whether they pertain to ritual, myth, Yājñavalkya's innovativeness, etc. I will attempt a topography that combines the two, systematically analyzing each passage in both recensions to show where the points of comparison and divergences lie. My particular interest is in how and why Yājñavalkya's pronouncements may be seen as witty or sarcastic and where and when his pronouncements appear to be taken as authoritative or not. Through this combined approach, I show that there is a parallel historical development of Yājñavalkya's authority and sarcasm across the books, but not one that should lead us to discount certain stories as "legend." Such stories or passages could certainly be "real" incidents regarding an established, even venerated authority, or they could be the beginnings of a budding hagiography. There is no way, I contend, to tell the difference (Lindquist 2011b).

Before discussing the passages directly, a discussion of certain literary terms is in order. Any number of scholars have described (as I have above) Yājñavalkya as "witty" and "innovative" (Witzel 2003, throughout), "somewhat raffish" (Brereton, 1997, 2), or "humorous, sarcastic, and often irreverent" (Olivelle, 1998, 486). These are all apt descriptions of Yājñavalkya in many of the passages and, in what follows, I further discuss the nature of wordplays, critiques, and even derision found in these passages. In so doing, I refer to particular passages as "satiric," "ironic," or "sarcastic." However, the use of these terms (particularly the first two) should not be confused with Euro-American literary theorizing on particular genres of literature. As is well known, irony and satire have elaborate and long histories as formal genres of literature in the West. Needless to say, this is not the case in the Indian context. All of our early texts are religious in nature, and formal literary theory (*alaṃkāraśāstra*) is a later development. Further, this later Indian theorizing does not address the Vedic canon. The commentarial tradition on the Veda, which precedes formal literary criticism, does not discuss the literary aspects directly, such as the personality traits of Yājñavalkya, as its concern is the teachings, rather than the person or story. This is, of course, absolutely logical if one views the texts as *apauruṣeya* ("not of human origin").[24] Thus, I use such literary terms in their adjectival form (i.e., ironic, satiric) to indicate types of discourse possible in any genre, rather than as indicating a genre in itself. *Sarcasm* has less of an interpretation-laden formal history, and I use it in noun-form. Here, I use *sarcasm* in its common usage: as discourse which is intended to deride or ridicule another (whether person, group, institution, or oneself). Sarcasm may be ironic or satiric, but it is not necessarily so. It is often humorous, though humor is usually a means to an end, rather than the primary goal. The rhetorical force of sarcasm is generally not apparent in individual phrases, but only emerges from context through juxtaposition, understatement, contradiction, and the like.

Table 1.1

Mādhyandina	**Kāṇva**
1.1.1.9	2.1.1.7
1.3.1.21	2.2.4.17
1.3.1.26	2.2.4.19
1.9.2.12	2.8.3.11 (Yājñavalkya not mentioned)
2.3.1.21	1.3.1.13
2.4.3.1–12 (no final *íti*)	1.3.2.1–12 (no final *íti*)
2.5.1.2	1.4.3.2
3.1.1.4–5	4.1.1.3–4 (no final *íti*)
3.1.2.21	4.1.2.12
3.1.3.10	4.1.3.9
3.8.2.24–25	4.8.2.18
4.2.1.7	5.2.1.5
4.6.1.10	5.8.1.11
4.6.8.7	absent
5.5.5.14	7.5.3.11
11.3.1.2–4 (≈ JB 1.19–20)	3.1.4.3–4
11.4.2.17 (no final *íti*)	13.4.2.12 (no final *íti*)
11.4.3.20	13.4.2.19
11.6.2.1–10 (≈ JB1.22–25?)	13.6.2.1–11
11.6.3.1–11 (≈ JB 2.76–77)	13.6.3.1–10
12.4.1.9–10 (≈ JB 1.58–59)	14.7.1.7
13.5.3.6	absent

As has been stated, Yājñavalkya is mentioned a number of times in the ŚB, though these passages are not exactly parallel in both recensions. The major differences between the two recensions, as they concern Yājñavalkya, are more a matter of arrangement than of direct content. As we shall see, however, often a slight rewording in one recension may cause us to doubt our interpretation of the other. Further, there is one case in ŚBK where the passage is not attributed to Yājñavalkya (as it is in ŚBM) and a few other passages in both recensions where it is not entirely clear where the discourse of Yājñavalkya ends (as there is the omission of a final *íti*, a discourse marker similar to a quotation mark). These have been noted in the chart below and will be dealt with in detail shortly.

The number of passages where Yājñavalkya appears (excluding BĀU) are twenty-three in M and twenty in K. The following concordance (table 1.1) shows the Yājñavalkya passages within the *Śatapatha Brāhmaṇa* in both recensions (and their correlates in the *Jaiminīya Brāhmaṇa*).

This chart shows a rather remarkable consistency in the retention of passages concerning Yājñavalkya, where the main difference overall is within the ordering of the text. For example, books 1 and 2 are inverted between recensions, though similar passages are retained. So also, ŚBM book 3 ≈ ŚBK book 4; ŚBM book 4 ≈ ŚBK book 5; ŚBM book 5 ≈ ŚBK 7. Viewed in this fashion, the ŚBM Yājñavalkya books are 1–5 and 11–13. In ŚBK, they are books 1–5, 7, and 13–14. Thus, while there is variation among and between books, the overall structure of the Yājñavalkya sections framing a middle portion has been maintained (with the exception of ŚBK 7).

Yājñavalkya in ŚBM 1–5 ≈ ŚBK 1–7

ŚBM Book 1 ≈ ŚBK Book 2

(1) Yājñavalkya's first appearance in the ŚBM is at 1.1.1.9 ≈ ŚBK 2.1.1.7. This passage is part of a discussion about whether the patron of the sacrifice takes food after performing the *agnihotra* at the end of the first day of fasting (*upavasatha*) during the new and full moon sacrifice (*darśapūrṇamāsa*; cf. KatyāŚS 2.1.13 and also 4.15.36 on *upava-*

satha). Yājñavalkya is listed here as giving an opinion that is contrary to that of Āṣāḍha Sāvayasa, who asserts that the fasting vow must entail complete abstention from food until the sacrifice is performed on the second day. Āṣāḍha's opinion is based on the fact that a patron cannot eat anything before the gods eat, because it would be against the proper etiquette of being a host (as the gods are said to be abiding with the patron during the sacrifice, *devā́n vásataḥ*, ŚBK). Yājñavalkya, however, sees a problem in not eating at all because a similar fast is required in a different type of sacrifice, a sacrifice to the ancestors. Yājñavalkya agrees that the patron cannot eat before the gods, but full fasting would confuse the type of sacrifice and the object of the offering (whether deities or ancestors). Yājñavalkya's answer is a wordplay as well as a logical play on "how to eat without eating," followed by Brāhmaṇa-style commentary.

> *tád u hovāca yā́jñavalkyaḥ | yádi nā̀śnā́ti pitr̥devátyo bhavati yády u 'śnā́ti devā̄n átyaśnātī́ti sa yád evā̀śitam ánaśitaṃ tád aśnīyā̄d íti yásya vaí havir ná gr̥hṇánti tád aśitam ánaśitaṃ sa yád aśnā́ti tenā́pitr̥devatyo bhavati yády u tád aśnā́ti yásya havir ná gr̥hṇánti téno devā̄n nā́tyaśnāti* || (9)
>
> Regarding this, however, Yājñavalkya said: "If he does not eat, he has the fathers as his deity; [and] if he does eat, he eats before the gods [have eaten]: Food which when eaten is 'not eaten'—that he should eat." [The food] that they do not take as an offering, even though eaten, [is considered] as 'not eaten.' Therefore when he [the patron] eats [the 'not eaten' food], he does not have the fathers as his deity; and if he eats what they do not take as an offering, he does not eat before the gods. (9)

The lines that follow make it clear that this opinion is taken as authoritative. The text goes on to say that a sacrificial patron should eat forest plants or fruit from trees (*sa vā́ āraṇyám evā̀śnīyāt | yā́ vāraṇyā óṣadhayo yád vā vr̥kṣyàm*), i.e., those foods not offered in the sacrifice which are therefore categorized as "not eaten." Following this, the text reinforces Yājñavalkya's opinion, by pointing out that Barku Vārṣṇa once asked for beans to eat because they are not offered in the sacrifice. This option is then rejected based on the similarity of beans to rice and barley (which are offered). It is then reiterated that only forest foods or fruits should be eaten.

The Kāṇva version of this passage is almost identical. The principal substantive difference is that a qualification is included: one who becomes "one who has the fathers as his deity" is one who is *ávīrya*, "without virility." Consequently, one retains "virility" by not having "the fathers as his deity" (i.e., by not abstaining from all food). In this fashion, a consequence is listed for one who confuses the two rituals by the type of fast he carries out. The Kāṇva further adds *devān vásataḥ* ("the abiding gods") which clarifies that the gods are guests currently in attendance and one should not eat before them.[25]

The play on logic that Yājñavalkya is using defines only ritually offered food as "eaten food" and other food as "not-eaten food." The wordplay is obvious in the Sanskrit: *yádi nā̀śnā́ti pitr̥devátyo bhavati yády u 'śnā́ti devān átyaśnātī́ti sa yád evā̀śitam ánaśitaṃ tád aśnīyād íti*, playing on various forms of the verbal root √*aś*, to eat.

(2) During the same sacrifice, ŚBM 1.3.1.21 ≈ ŚBK 2.2.4.17 discusses the "eyeing of the ghee" which takes place after the girdling of the patron's wife. After the patron's wife looks down upon the ghee, reciting certain mantras, the *āgnīdhra* priest carries this ghee to the east. The question here is whether the ghee is then to be placed inside the sacrificial altar or not. If it is put inside the altar, the text says that the wives of the gods would be separated from their husbands (who are sitting around the outside of the altar) and the patron's wife would become separated from her husband (via metonymic equivalence). Yājñavalkya, in an apparently conservative move, argues that "rules are rules" and whether someone is excluded or not is irrelevant.

> *tád āhuḥ | nā̀ntarvédy ā́sādayed áto vaí devā́nām pátnīḥ sáṃyājayanty ávasabhā áha devā́nām pátnīḥ karóti paraḥpúṁso hāsya pátnī bhavatī́ti tád u hovāca yā́jñavalkyo yathādiṣṭam pátnyā astu kas tad ā́driyeta yát paraḥpuṁsā́ vā pátnī syād yáthā vā yajño védir yajña ā́jyaṃ yajñā́d yajñaṃ nírmimā íti tásmād antarvédy evā́sādayet* || (21)

Regarding this, they say, "He should not place it within the altar [because] from that very [ghee] they make the oblation to the wives of the gods. He thus makes the wives

> of the gods excluded, and his [the patron's] wife is [then] outside the circle of men [i.e., separate from her husband]." Regarding this, however, Yājñavalkya said, "Let it be for the wife as it is ordained (*yathādiṣṭam*). Who should care if the wife be outside the circle of men or the like?[26] The altar is the sacrifice, and the ghee is the sacrifice, I will make the sacrifice from the sacrifice!" Therefore, let him place it within the altar. (21)

As with our previous passage, the last line tells us that Yājñavalkya's opinion is taken as authoritative. Eggeling had mistranslated this passage, based on a misunderstanding of the compound *paraḥpuṁsā́*, taking it to mean "consort with other men."[27] Outside of misconstruing the compound-type, such sexual indiscretion, not to mention the dismissal of it on Yājñavalkya's part, appears out of place in this ritual context. Eggeling ([1882–1900] 1993, 12: 76n2) further remarks that he is unsure whether this remark is to be attributed to Yājñavalkya because of a difference in the Kāṇva version. However, his translation does not coincide with the critical edition of the Kāṇva which does suggest the passage should be attributed to him. It is possible, however, that Eggeling's version of ŚBK had significant variants. ŚBK 2.2.4.17 reads (underlined passage omitted in Eggeling's translation of ŚBK):

> . . . *tád u hovāca yā́jñavalkyo 'ntarvédy evā́sādayet íti hovāca yathādiṣṭaṃ pátnyā astv íti yat sā́ paraḥpuṁsā́ vā syā́d yád vā kas tayā́rtha íti hovāca yajño védir yajña ā́jyaṃ yajñā́d yajñaṃ nírmimā íti tásmād antarvédy evā́sādayet* |[28]

If we recognize that both the ŚBM and ŚBK versions are largely the same and that no sexual innuendo is intended, the passage is quite clear: the "rules are the rules" (*yathādiṣṭa*) and any perceived problem of separating the wives of the gods from their husbands is irrelevant according to Yājñavalkya. Yājñavalkya justifies this by equating the altar and the ghee to the sacrifice and then to each other (again, in standard brāhmaṇic wordplay: *yajño védir yajña ā́jyaṃ yajñā́d yajñaṃ nírmimā*). While there may be an underlying sexism in Yājñavalkya's pronouncement, it is not one that suggests sexual indiscretion.

(3) ŚBM 1.3.1.26 ≈ ŚBK 2.2.4.19 is related to the above, in that it is also concerned with the ghee. Normally, the *adhvaryu* is to look down at the ghee after having purified the water with strainers (*kuśa* grass) covered with ghee. Some *adhvaryu* priests, it appears, have the patron of the sacrifice look down at the ghee. Yājñavalkya is here refuting this practice with what appears to be a sarcastic retort.

> *athā́jyam ávekṣate | tad dhaíke yájamānam ávakhyāpayanti tád u hovāca yā́jñavalkyaḥ kathaṃ nu ná svayám adhvaryávo bhávanti katháṁ svayaṃ nā́nvāhur yátra bhū́yasya ivāśíṣaḥ kriyánte kathaṃ nv eṣām átraivá śraddhā́ bhavatī́ti yāṃ vai kā́ṃ ca yajñá 'ṛtvíja āśíṣam āśā́sate yájamānasyaiva sā tásmād adhvaryúr evā́vekṣeta ||* (26)
>
> Now he [Adhvaryu] looks down on the ghee. Here some make the patron of the sacrifice look down. Regarding this, however, Yājñavalkya said, "How is it that [the patrons of sacrifice] themselves do not become Adhvaryu priests? How is it that they do not themselves recite the formula when even greater requests are made [in other ritual acts]? How can these [patrons] have trust in this?" That request which the priests ask for during the sacrifice, that is the patron's alone.[29] Therefore only the Adhvaryu should look down on [the ghee]. (26)

This passage is somewhat confusing, unless one consults the Kāṇva for the larger context under discussion. In the Kāṇva it is clear that when a patron is made to look down at the ghee, he is to request a reward for himself from the gods: *tā́ṁ svayam ā́śāsātā íti tád u hovāca yā́jñavalkyaḥ,* "'What request here [that he may have], he should request that.' Regarding this, however, Yājñavalkya said . . ." The logical point that Yājñavalkya is making is about an inconsistency in the ritual practice of others: it is the *adhvaryu*'s role to make requests for the patron and not the patron himself, as others apparently have him do. The "trust" mentioned is the trust in the *adhvaryu* to make requests to the gods on the patron's behalf (and not, for example, on behalf of himself) as well as trust in the efficacy of the rite.

Yājñavalkya's argument can be summarized as follows: (1) patrons should not function as *adhvaryus* (i.e., by making a request from the gods), even in the single act; (2) if the *yajamāna* is the one to look down at the ghee and make a request (i.e., function as the *adhvaryu*), the *yajamāna* would not have trust in the priest in the other ritual acts where greater rewards are asked for (i.e., why would the *yajamāna* similarly not be the one to request those and how does he know the priest will properly request the reward for him?); (3) to solve this problem the priest must do it, otherwise it would undermine the priests' status in other ritual acts. Yājñavalkya's rather conservative answer "that the priest should do all such acts" is an attempt at consistency in ritual acts so as not to undermine the foundation of sacrifice—trust (*śraddhā*). The sarcasm in this passage lies in the fact that Yājñavalkya is saying that the *adhvaryu* priest (that is, himself as well as his own priestly class) would be superfluous if the patron does the ritual act as others suggest. It suggests that those not properly trained (i.e., the *yajamāna*) would be acting as priests. The sarcasm here lies in the rhetorical questions that cannot be answered, and thereby the realization that the foundation of other people's practice is flawed.

Of importance is the fact that the Kāṇva omits the statement regarding trust in the institution of priests. Thus, while Yājñavalkya asking how the patron is not equivalent to the priest is sarcastic, it is not extended into a criticism of priests as a whole as in Mādhyandina.

(4) This passage occurs in the context of the "after offerings" of the Patnisaṃyāja (ŚBM 1.9.2.12 ≈ ŚBK 2.8.3.11).

> *sa yátra devā́nāṃ pátnīr yájati | tát purástāt tiráḥ karoty úpa ha vai tā́vad devátā āsate yā́van ná samiṣṭayajur júhvatīdáṃ nú no juhvatv íti tā́bhya evaìtát tiráḥ karoti tásmād imā́ mānuṣyà stríyas tirá ivaivá puṃsó jighatmanti yā́ iva tu tā́ ivéti ha smāha yā́jñavalkyaḥ* || (12)

> When he offers to the wives of the gods, he conceals it [the offering][30] from the eastern side.[31] Before they offer the *samiṣṭayajus*, the male deities sit [thinking], "Let them offer to us!" Therefore he hides [the offering] from them; and Yājñavalkya once said, "Human women desire to eat[32] apart/hidden from men. Of the sort that they [human woman] are, of that sort they [wives of gods] are." (12)[33]

Witzel (2003, 118) has argued that the desiderative of "to eat" on the part of women suggests a derisiveness in this passage—that is, Indian women traditionally eat after men/husbands, and the desiderative indicates that the women are waiting hungrily for the men to finish.

It is unclear whether this interpretation of the verb should apply here, as the text simply says *tirás* ("apart/hidden") and not *paścāt* ("after"). Fišer (1984, 68–69) has also suggested that the verb √*ghas* is generally used for women eating (while √*aś* is used for men), and the use of √*ghas* elsewhere implies a "devouring." While this may be the case in other passages, I find it difficult to read a particularly derisive meaning in this passage, principally because we are told that the male gods are the ones initially hoping that the offering is given to them. That is, the male gods are also *desiring to eat* by asking for the offering, and the use of the desiderative with the wives parallels this. Witzel is correct that women generally eat separately from men and Fišer in that the history of the term itself may suggest sexism, but in this passage it is the male gods who initially desire to eat. As I read it, the gods and their wives are the same in their desire to eat, and further, like the wives of the gods, human women want to eat separately from men (perhaps as an issue of decorum or propriety). The parallelism in the passage is firstly between the gods and their wives and, secondly, between the female gods and human females. Parallelism seems the principal point of this passage, rather than any derision.[34]

Interestingly, the Kāṇva does not include *ha smāha yā́jñavalkyaḥ*.[35] While in the previous passages we have seen that the Kāṇva version of the text contains many clarifications (perhaps added secondarily), here the text omits Yājñavalkya altogether. In the Kāṇva tradition, then, the desiderative use of the verb is not attributed to a particular person, further suggesting that any intentional derision may be out of place.

(5) The final Yājñavalkya passage in this book concerns the concluding rites of the New/Full Moon sacrifice (ŚBM 1.9.3.16 ≈ ŚBK 2.8.4.10). After the main sacrifice and after the three "Viṣṇu strides," the *adhvaryu* pours water which is to be caught in the hands of the patron of the sacrifice. This ritual action is to correct or "heal" any ritual error committed during the course of the sacrifice.

> *sa údīkṣate | svayambhū́r asi śréṣṭho raśmir íty eṣa vai śréṣṭho raśmir yát sū́ryas tásmād āha svayambhū́r asi śréṣṭho raśmir íti varcodā asi várco me dehī́ti tv èvā̀hám̐ bravīmī́ti ha smāha yā́jñavalkyas tad dhy èvá brāhmaṇénaiṣṭávyaṃ yád brahmavarcasī syā̄d íty úto ha smāhaupoditeyá eṣa vāva máhyaṃ gā́ dāsyati godā gā́ me dehī́ty evaṃ yaṃ kā́maṃ kāmáyate sò 'smai kā́maḥ sámr̥̥dhyate* || (16)

> He looks up [at the sun, chanting] "You are self-existent, the best ray of light!" [VS 2.26a]. Indeed, the sun is the best ray of light, and therefore he says, "You are self-existent, the best ray of light." Yājñavalkya once said, "But I for one say, 'You are the giver of luster, give me luster.' For this is to be desired by a Brahmin, that he should have the luster of *brahman* (*brahmavarcasin*)." Aupoditeya once said, "He indeed will give me cows!" [upon my saying] 'You are the cow-giver, give me cows!'" In this way, whatever he wishes for [and modifies the mantra accordingly] that wish is granted to him. (16)

In this passage,[36] we are told that Yājñavalkya strives to "have the luster of *brahman*," that is, true knowledge of the sacrifice and the universe, prefiguring his claim to be the *brahmiṣṭha* ("most learned in *brahman*") in the BĀU. Interestingly, Yājñavalkya here is changing or adding onto the original VS mantra and supplying his own Brāhmaṇa-like commentary to justify that change. Witzel takes Yājñavalkya's modification of the *mantra* as an "innovative and authoritarian tendency" (2003, 114), and Fišer takes his change as authoritative, though offers no explanation (1984, 61–62). However, I think that Yājñavalkya, unlike in the other passages, is probably not taken as authoritative in this passage in quite the same sense as these two scholars have suggested, but rather he stands as but one example of how the *mantra* can be modified depending on one's desire: *yaṃ kā́maṃ kāmáyate* . . . As such, Yājñavalkya's modification of the *mantra* is simply a variation, but an authoritative tendency can be seen in *the form* his modification takes. The fact that his modification of a *mantra* is followed by a structurally similar modification (ŚBM, by Aupoditeya; ŚBK, by Tumiñja Aupoditeya Vaiyāghrapadya), and the fact that the text ends by stating that the *mantra* is to be composed based on one's desire, suggests that his modification itself was not necessarily authoritative but rather the way he modified the *mantra* itself was.

What has gone unnoticed is that this is the first (and only) ŚB passage where Yājñavalkya is formally being associated with the Sun (*sūrya*, though *āditya* in BĀU), an association that later becomes central to Yājñavalkya's biography. Fišer, in discussing the BĀU as "legend," notes that in BĀU 6.5.3 Yājñavalkya received the white sacrificial formulas (*yajus*) from the Sun (*āditya*) but states "to make more out of these data than merely to state them would mean to plunge into pleasant, but totally unwarranted speculations" (1984, 86). This BĀU passage, however, has a direct precedent in the above ŚB passage. In an early part of the ŚB, Yājñavalkya is asking the sun for "luster/brilliance" (*varcas*) whereas in BĀU the Sun is said *to have given it to him* in the form of the white (*śukla*) sacrificial formula (*yajus*). Fišer obviously views BĀU 6.5.3 as simply a fiction, but given the lack of context there, what does it mean to be "coming from the sun"? Must we take the BĀU passage as an unanchored elaboration, as Fišer does (perhaps anachronistically influenced by Epic or Purāṇic accounts)? Much more likely, it seems to me, is that the later text is acknowledging and/or extending upon Yājñavalkya's individual praise or reverence for the Sun already found here in ŚB. In this way, the White Yajurveda "origin" in the Sun found in the BĀU has its own literary origin in ŚB.

In the whole of ŚBM book 1 ≈ ŚBK book 2, three of the five passages discussed contain *tád u hovāca,* and in each case Yājñavalkya is taken as authoritative with his opinion placed in the ultimate position. In the final case, Yājñavalkya's opinion appears only as a valid option, not an authoritative statement (note that in these other two passages, the phrase used is *ha smāha yā́jñavalkyaḥ*). While Witzel is right that a *mantra* generally is not modified other than in gender and number, such greater modifications must have been at least occasionally acceptable as Aupoditeya does the same, and this last passage ends leaving the *mantra* formulation open to choice. We have seen that Yājñavalkya is taken as authoritative in this book, yet not universally so (though, he is not said to be wrong) and that his connection to the Sun found in BĀU has an older precedent.

ŚBM Book 2 ≈ ŚBK Book 1

In ŚBM 2 ≈ ŚBK 1, there are only three references to Yājñavalkya, which consist of two proclamations (one where he is said to be wrong!) and a long mythical justification for the performance of the First Fruits rite (*āgrayaṇeṣṭi*), which is taken as authoritative.

(1) ŚBM 2.3.1.21 ≈ ŚBK 1.3.1.13 concerns the Agnihotra (explicitly stated in K) and is a justification for one particular act—the act of sipping water and licking the milk out from the bowl/spoon after the main ritual. Immediately previous to this passage it is suggested that an offering can be made so that the animals that are excluded

(M; or "all beings," K) can partake in the sacrifice. Yājñavalkya does not differ from the opinion that the rite is related to other creatures (including cattle), but rather points out that the sipping of water and the licking of milk is sufficient for all creatures to partake of the benefit of the sacrifice. To understand the passage, one must know that normally in a *havis* sacrifice all offering matter taken out of the bowl with the spoon is offered to the deities. In this sacrifice, however, the remnants of the milk are drunk.

> *tád u hovāca yā́jñavalkyaḥ | na vaí yajñá iva mántavaí pākayajñá iva vā ítīdaṁ hí yád anyásmin yajñé srucy àvadyáti sárvaṃ tád agnaú juhoty áthaitád agnaú hutvòtsr̥pyā́cāmati nírleḍhi tád asya pākayajñásyevéti tád asya tát paśavyàṃ rūpáṃ paśavyò hí pākayajñā́ḥ* || (21)

> Regarding this, however, Yājñavalkya said, "It [the *agnihotra*] should not be thought of like a [*havis*] sacrifice, but [rather] like a domestic sacrifice (*pākayajña*); because in the other [*havis*] sacrifice he offers in the fire all that he cuts off [of the offering and puts] into the offering spoon. But here, having offered in the fire and stepping aside,[37] he sips [water] and licks out [the milk]; and this is like [the offering] of that domestic offering." This is the animal form of that [Agnihotra], because the domestic sacrifice relates to cattle. (21)

Again, this passage begins with *tád u hovāca* and is the concluding statement on the topic, suggesting Yājñavalkya's opinion is different than the preceding opinion and that his opinion is most likely the authoritative one.

(2) ŚBM 2.4.3.1–12 ≈ ŚBK 1.3.2.1–12: This long passage begins a larger discussion about the *āgrayaṇeṣṭi*—the Offering of the First Fruits made at the beginning of harvest season. There is substantial variation between K and M in minor details, but not in a fashion that is useful for our understanding of Yājñavalkya. Yājñavalkya tells a classical myth about the battle between the gods and the *asura*s to explain why the First Fruits Offering is performed. It appears that Yājñavalkya is disagreeing with the prior reasoning of Kahoḍa Kauṣītaki's regarding the performance of the rite. Another possibility is that Yājñavalkya is simply expanding on Kauṣītaki's interpretation. The larger problem in interpreting this passage as a disagreement or simply as Yājñavalkya expanding on Kauṣītaki's interpretation is that Kauṣītaki's interpretation is limited in scope. Kauṣītaki says that because the essence of plants (presumably, particularly at the new harvest) belongs to heaven and earth, it should thus be offered before human beings can eat it.

> *tád u hovāca kahóḍaḥ kaúṣītakiḥ | anáyor vā́ ayaṃ dyā́vāpr̥thivyo ráso 'sya rásasya hutvā́ devebhyó 'themam áśnāméti tásmād vā́ āgrayaṇeṣṭyā́ yajata íti || (1)*
>
> Regarding this, however, Kohaḍa Kauṣītaki said, "This juice/essence [of the plant] is of these two, heaven and earth. Having offered of this juice/essence to the gods, now we will eat it. Therefore, he performs the First Fruits Offering." (1)

Yājñavalkya's opinion is largely in agreement, particularly when he repeats the same rationale for the offering (8, 10). However, what the myth told by Yājñavalkya does is give a greater context for the reasons for offering the first fruits and who the first fruits are offered to. The myth can be summarized as follows: the gods interceded on behalf of humankind to rid the poison that the *asuras* put into edible plants and then they held a race to determine who among them receives the offerings from humankind; Agni and Indra won that race, so they are the principal deities of the offering. Further justification is then given for offering to the All-Gods (*viśvadeva*s), heaven and earth, etc. The myth ends by stating that the First Fruits Offering makes all plants wholesome (i.e., edible and safe). If Yājñavalkya is challenging Kauṣītaki's opinion at all, it is simply because Kauṣītaki's answer was an incomplete one. Note here that we have our first instance of Yājñavalkya disagreeing with or elaborating upon someone's opinion from an established, more western school (Kauṣītaki is the main protagonist of *Kauṣītaki Brāhmaṇa* [KṣB]).

It has been pointed out by Fišer (1984, 58–59) that we do not have an *iti* to mark the end of Yājñavalkya's speech. However, neither Fišer nor Witzel notes that there is an indication that Yājñavalkya's speech continues after the myth is completed: his manner of dismissing another's opinion is exactly parallel to his dismissal found in ŚBM

1.3.1.21 ≈ ŚBK 2.2.4.17 (regarding women being separated from their husbands). Immediately following the myth, our passage shifts to a standard Brāhmaṇa-style listing of others' opinions on ritual actions in the First Fruits Offering and then proceeds to argue against it. According to the text, some ancient Indian priests speculated that offering on a single potsherd (in the manner the myth suggests) would cause the offering to be "turned around/upside down" (*paryābhut*), that is, make it ineffectual and dangerous.[38] The authoritative response is that "turning around/upside down" of the offering is not a ritual error because the ritual already has its "firm basis" (*pratiṣṭha*) in the *āhavanīya* fire. So, as the text continues, if the offering should turn around even ten times or more,[39] "what of it?" (K *kas tenā́rthaḥ;* M *na tad ā́driyeta,* "one should not heed/care about this"). The answers in both recensions are direct parallels to the answers that Yājñavalkya gave regarding women at ŚBM 1.3.1.21 ≈ ŚBK 2.2.4.17: M *kas tad ā́driyeta,* "who should care" about women being separated from their husbands? Or, K: *kas tayā́rtha,* "what of her" who is separated? Both recensions, consistent in themselves in both passages (though varying from each other),[40] suggest indirectly that the tradition viewed Yājñavalkya as speaking in lines 10 and probably through 12, in what appears to be the same dismissive tone.

(3) The final passage in this book is ŚBM 2.5.1.2 ≈ ŚBK 1.4.3.2 and it is perhaps the most interesting, not so much in its content as in the larger implication. In this passage, Yājñavalkya is said to be directly contradicting the R̥V. As with our one instance in book 1, Yājñavalkya is not taken as authoritative here. His interpretation, however, does not appear optional, but rather simply in contradiction to established tradition. Here, a creation myth is being told and Yājñavalkya's opinion is inserted in the middle of the myth.

> *sá aikṣata prajā́patiḥ | yáthā nv èvá puraikó 'bhūvam evám u nv èvā́py etarhy éka evā̀smī́ti sá dvitī́yāḥ sasr̥je tā́ asya páraivá babhūvus tád idám̐ kṣudrám̐ sarīsr̥pam̐ yád anyát sarpébhyas tr̥tī́yāḥ sasr̥ja íty āhus tā́ asya páraivá babhūvus tá imé sarpā́ etā́ ha nv èvá dvayī́r yā́jñavalkya uvāca trayī́r u tu púnar r̥cā ||* (2)

> Prajāpati reflected, "As I was previously alone/singular, so also am I now alone/singular." He created a second [class of beings]; [but] they just perished—they are those

> small reptiles other than snakes. He created a third [class of beings], they say; [but] his [creation] also perished—they are snakes. Yājñavalkya, said they [the creations] are of two kinds only, but they are of three kinds according to the R̥gveda. (2)

It appears, but it is not entirely clear, that Yājñavalkya viewed the first two creations as non-distinct; that is, that "snakes" and "small reptiles" were produced in a single creation. According to the ŚB: birds were the original creation, reptiles the second, and snakes the third. ŚBM 2.5.4.1 ≈ ŚBK 1.4.3.3 adds a further creation of mammals that did not perish because they survived on mother's milk. Witzel (2003, 112) has suggested two possible ways to interpret Yājñavalkya's statement: (1) Yājñavalkya's opinion was an attempt to collapse the creations of "perished beings" together, and the second category intended was mammals or (2) reptiles and snakes were viewed as a single category, and birds were the second. Opinion one, however, seems unlikely as the creation of mammals had not yet occurred in the text, and the cited R̥V passage only refers to three "perished creations." As with the single passage in book 1, we have here an example where Yājñavalkya's opinion was not accepted (M *trayī́r u tu púnar r̥cā́*, in K, *trayyás tu púnar r̥cā́ bhavanti*). This passage appears to follow a general pattern of Yājñavalkya's non-authoritative statements not closing a discussion. In this case, given that the passage is closed with citing the authoritative R̥V, Yājñavalkya's interpretation must be wrong.

Throughout ŚBM 2 ≈ ŚBK 1, we find the pattern that we found previously. Yājñavalkya, while generally taken as authoritative, is not universally so—in fact, he is here found to be in contradiction to the established and universally accepted (among Vedic Brahmins, that is) authority of the R̥V. The other two pronouncements, which take his opinion as authoritative, are concerned with sacrificial explanations (of the drinking of the milk and of the offering of First Fruits). This pattern continues in the other books.

ŚBM Book 3 ≈ ŚBK Book 4

(1) ŚBM 3.1.1.4–5 ≈ ŚBK 4.1.1.3–4: This passage is concerned with the selection of a place for sacrifice in the *agniṣṭoma*.

tád u hovāca yā́jñavalkyaḥ | vārṣṇyā́ya devayájanaṃ jóṣayitum aima tát sātyayajñò 'bravīt sárvā vā́ iyáṃ pr̥thivī́ devī́ devayájanaṃ yátra vā́ asyai kvà ca yájuṣaivá parigŕ̥hya yājáyed íti | (4) *r̥tvíjo haivá devayájanam | yé brāhmaṇā́ḥ śuśruvā́ṁsó 'nūcānā́ vidvā́ṃso yājáyanti saìvā́hvalaitán nediṣṭhamā́m iva manyāmaha íti* | (5)

Regarding this, however, Yājñavalkya said, "We went to choose a place to sacrifice on behalf of Vārṣṇya. Sātyayajña then said, 'Indeed, this whole earth is a deity[41]—after encompassing [it] with *yajus* [sacrificial formula], wherever on this [earth] that he would offer sacrifices, that is the place of sacrifice.' (4)

It is, however, the officiating priests that are the place for the sacrifice. When Brahmins, who are wise, learned, and versed in sacred lore perform the sacrifice, then they are without crookedness. We think [that sacrificial place is] nearest [the gods?]." (5)

This passage in M seems rather straightforward. In relating a previous event (i.e., looking for a place to sacrifice for Vārṣṇya), Yājñavalkya gives Sātyayajña's opinion on the "place of the sacrifice" (*devayájana*). Sātyayajña contends that any place on earth, duly consecrated with sacred formula, is a proper place for sacrifice. Yājñavalkya takes a more abstract and apparently innovative view, one that places sole authority in the priests—wherever there are learned priests to perform the sacrifice is a proper sacrificial ground.

However, a difficulty arises with this passage in determining the extent of Yājñavalkya's speech given the variations in K.[42] M's placement of the two *íti*s makes it rather clear that Yājñavalkya is said to have spoken both passages, where the first *íti* is to mark the indirect speech of Sātyayajña, and the second to mark off Yājñavalkya's differing opinion in 5. This follows the format of the previous passages where the authoritative opinion is listed last.

However, ŚBK has four *ítis* placed differently: the first to mark off Vārṣṇa's (M Vārṣṇya) intent to sacrifice and the second to close Yājñavalkya's speech. Sātyayajñi's (M Sātyayajña) name is marked off with the third *íti*, and the fourth *íti* concludes Sātyayajñi's speech. Making it clear that Sātyayajñi is no longer speaking, the text concludes: "This he did indeed think."

> *tád u hovāca yā́jñavalkyo vā́rṣno 'yakṣyateti tásmai devayájanam ī́kṣitum ayaméti sò 'bravīt sā́tyayajñir íti . . . íti etád u ha sá mene . . .*

The K text continues in a similar fashion as above, but does not conclude with a final *íti* (which would suggest that all of this is a narration of Yājñavalkya). Thus, the Kāṇva seems *not* to attribute any of Sātyayajña's statement or the rest of the passage to Yājñavalkya. Swaminathan translates (2000, 3:3):

> About this, Yājñavalkya said, "We went to look for a place for him for sacrifice as this Vārṣna intended to sacrifice." Sātyayajñi said, "This whole earth is divine. Wherever, having enclosed a place with *Yajus* (chant), one sacrifices, that is a sacrificial place." This is indeed what he thought.

I suspect, however, that M retains the older, more correct reading. I further suspect that K intends one to assume a final *íti* (marking Yājñavalkya's speech), as we have seen earlier with the longer myth in book 1 where there is a shift in topic marking the close of speech. In support of this interpretation it should also be noted that if Yājñavalkya's speech only consisted of "We went to look for a place for him for sacrifice as this Vārṣna intended to sacrifice" it would seem superfluous, even nonsensical, in the larger context of the passage.

(2) ŚBM 3.1.2.21 ≈ ŚBK 4.1.2.12 is one of the most interesting and controversial passages because Yājñavalkya says that he eats cow-meat (specifically of a milk-cow, *dhenu*, not cows in general, *go*) during the Agniṣṭoma.

> *áthainaṃ śā́lāṃ prápādayati | sá dhenvaí cānaḍúhaś ca nàśnīyād dhenvanaḍuhau vā́ idaṃ sárvaṃ bibhṛ̥tas té devā́ abruvan dhenvanaḍuhau vā́ idaṃ sárvaṃ bibhṛ̥to hánta yád anyéṣāṃ váyasāṃ vīryàṃ tád dhenvanaḍuháyor dádhāméti sa yád anyéṣāṃ váyasāṃ vīryàm ā́sīt tád dhenvanaḍuháyor adadhus tásmād dhenúś caivā̀naḍvā́ṃś ca bhū́yiṣṭhaṃ bhuṅktas tád dhaitát sarvā́śyam iva yó dhenvanaḍuháyor aśnīyad ántagatir iva taṃ hā́dbhutam abhíjanitor jāyā́yai garbhaṃ nírabadhīd*[43] *íti pāpám akad íti pāpī́ kīrtis tásmād dhenvanaḍuháyor nāśnī̀yāt tád u hovāca yā́jñavalkyo 'śnā́my evā̀hám aṁsalaṃ ced bhávatī́ti* | (21)

> Now [the Adhvaryu] causes him to enter into the hall. He should not eat either the milk-cow or the ox, for the milk-cow and the ox indeed support everything here [on earth]. The gods said, "Indeed, the milk-cow and the ox support everything here: [thus] we will bestow on the ox and the milk-cow whatever vigor belongs to other species!" They gave the milk-cow and the ox whatever vigor belonged to other species; and therefore the milk-cow and the ox consume the most. Should one eat an ox or a milk-cow, it would be as if an eating of everything, [that is] a going to destruction. [It may be that] to him a strange thing is born [where people would say?] "he expelled a fetus from a woman," "he committed a sin"—he is renowned as a sinner.[44] Therefore he should not eat the milk-cow and the ox. Regarding this, however, Yājñavalkya said, "I, for one, eat it, provided that it is fatty/tasty."

Others have tried to interpret this passage as discussing the enjoyment of the products of the milk-cow (i.e., milk) or ox (i.e., labor) and not the flesh itself (most recently, by Swaminathan 2000, 3:9).[45] While it is true that a grammatical object in the sentences may remain unexpressed, this interpretation is unlikely. First, the root √*aś*, usually meaning "to eat" but also "consume," is unlikely to mean "to enjoy," particularly of something not literally consumed (such as "labor"). Second, the point is that the milk-cow and the ox themselves are said to support everything and eat the most (i.e., everything), naturally leading to rather disastrous results (according to some) if they themselves are eaten. The reason for this is clear—along with an equivalence between eating and destruction, the milk-cow gives milk for drinking and the ox hauls loads for farming, hence they are vitally important to society. Finally, and most importantly, *aṁsalá* (fleshy/fatty), though rare, is *only* used in the context of flesh in the early literature (Fišer 1984, 69–70), and there is no occurrence in which it is clearly associated with milk and certainly makes no sense in the context of "labor."

Recently, Mehendale (1977) has tried to argue that this "fleshiness" is a sacrificial criterion, pointing to ŚBM 3.8.4.6 where *aṁsala* is equated with the "sacrificial essence" (*medha*). Mehendale then suggests that Yājñavalkya's statement at the end of this passage is not sarcastic or irreverent, but rather it is an attempt at applying a ritual criterion in determining whether the meat should be eaten or not. However, while interesting, I don't find this argument necessarily convincing. It would require us to take one passage (ŚBM 3.8.4.6) as solely authoritative for the other occurrence of the same term. While Mehendale's interpretation is an important starting point and it is certainly suggestive, there are compelling reasons to disagree with it. One problem with his interpretation is that the meaning of the term appears rather generic in our passage and to assume a larger ritual-technical gloss, without more of a justifying context, appears unnecessary. This is particularly true because if *aṁsala* were meant as an important sacrificial criterion, we would expect to find other uses where that meaning is clear (in fact, *aṁsala* here is more likely a wordplay; see below).

Moreover, there is a parallel (R̥V 1.162.12ab) in the context of cooking the sacrificial meat during the course of a horse sacrifice that also clearly points to the sumptuousness of the offering and the desirousness of Brahmins wanting to eat it. Here the animal is being cooked, and the appetites of those in attendance are being aroused. In this regard, it is important to remember that very down-to-earth human needs and desires also appear within sacrificial texts. "Those who inspect the prizewinner when cooked and who say about him 'It smells good! Take it off (the fire)!' and those who draw near in hopes of a share of the meat of the stead—let the applause of those urge us on" (Jamison and Brereton 2014, 1: 345).

Moreover, an interpretation like Mehendale's overlooks what I contend is the larger import of the passage. Whether Yājñavalkya *actually* ate the meat of the milk-cow or ox, as the sacrificial essence or otherwise, is in one sense irrelevant in this passage (though I see no reason not to take his claim at face value). Yājñavalkya's criticism is ultimately of the logic employed by the other Brahmins and, more so, the overly dramatic consequences of eating the meat. If Yājñavalkya was meant to be saying that he eats the meat of the milk-cow or the ox if it were "the essence of the sacrifice," his answer would not directly address the larger arguments which precede his statement. His statement would be disconnected from the argument about why one should not eat such meat. Rather it appears to me that Yājñavalkya is answering in the affirmative, while critiquing the overly dramatic consequences claimed by the other Brahmins should one eat the meat. Yājñavalkya is not directly addressing the arguments of others about the "milk-cow and ox supporting the world," not to mention the dire consequences of having a deformed child. His statement is a sarcastic dismissal (akin to ŚBM 1.3.1.21 ≈ ŚBK 2.2.4.17), suggesting their logic and concerns are absurd and what lies before them is a well prepared offering that should be consumed.

This passage further suggests that certain Brahmins (and probably Yājñavalkya) ate the meat of a milk-cow or ox as there would not be a rule against eating such meat if some people did not do so. It is likely that this longer passage is an example of an internal debate among Vedic Brahmins about the eating or not eating of certain animals (even milk-cows). In our passage here, we have one example of what must have been a much larger debate about the nature of eating meat. The important point here is that Yājñavalkya clearly dismisses the other Brahmin's elaborate argument against it. Again, this passage concludes with *tád u hovāca* and closes the section, but the sarcasm might mitigate to what degree Yājñavalkya's opinion is an authoritative affirmation as opposed to a dismissal of others.

Further, similar to his appearances elsewhere, Yājñavalkya here is using a wordplay: *aśnā́my evā̀hám aṁsalam* ("I eat the meat [provided it] is tasty / fatty"). The repetition of *am/ām* clusters is a play on sound, which is probably why such a rare word, counter to Mehendale's argument, is used. This is consistent with other wordplays we find in the text (such as ŚBM 1.3.1.21 ≈ ŚBK 2.2.4.17), but those wordplays are more often clever justifications of particular acts and are not derisive or dismissive in themselves. Further, note how the last part of this phrase may have been heard: *ahámamṃsalaṃ*, where **-(m)aṁsa-* would suggest *māṃsa* ("meat!"), an oral pun and probably the main reason for the use of a rare word.[46] This passage is similar to the dismissive passages mentioned earlier as well as the passage where Yājñavalkya is cursed to die by a *caraka-adhvaryu* (ŚBM 3.8.2.24–25 ≈ ŚBK 4.8.2.18; see #4 below). Thus, Yājñavalkya is authoritative in this passage, but with regard to the proper formulation of Brāhmaṇa logic—clever, short, and specific.

(3) Another prideful and perhaps sarcastic passage is attributed to Yājñavalkya in this same book. ŚBM 3.1.3.10 ≈ ŚBK 4.1.3.9 discusses the anointing of one's eyes in the consecration of the Agniṣṭoma.

> *athā́kṣyā̄v ā́nakti | árur vai púruṣasyā́kṣi praśā́n maméti ha smāha yā́jñavalkyo durakṣá iva hāsa pū́yo haivā̀sya dūṣī́kā té evà̀tad ánaruṣkaroti yad ákṣyāv ānákti* (10)

> Now he anoints the eyes. Yājñavalkya once said "Wounded (sore?), indeed, is the eye of man, [but] mine is soothed." His eyes were very bad; their secretion was pus. So then he makes his eyes healed by anointing them. (10)

Whether this passage is sarcastic or not is not clear. Certainly, it is prideful as Yājñavalkya is saying that, in contrast to the rest of humankind, his eyes are healthy since he has anointed them (Witzel 2003, 115–16). However, whether to ascribe this pridefulness *solely* to the figure of Yājñavalkya (as Witzel does) is unclear—what the passage attributed to Yājñavalkya appears to be doing is praising the act of anointing the eyes with ghee and butter. Thus, the passage is about the efficacy of the act itself, transforming the regular ("wounded") eye of man into the "healed" eye for purposes of the sacrifice. In support of the argument that this passage is meant more as praise for the act itself, rather than personal pride, Yājñavalkya's statement is just that, a statement—there is no one he is disagreeing with here, and the text confirms the authority of his statement immediately afterward. One possibility that has not been considered before is that Yājñavalkya may be here creating his own *mantra* to be used when the act of anointing is carried out. Immediately prior to this passage (9), the *adhvaryu* is anointing his body with VS *mantras* (VS 4.3) followed by a Brāhmaṇa explanation of the *mantra* in relation to the act itself. This passage follows that exact same form. If so, it would support a prideful and innovative interpretation of Yājñavalkya's character.

(4) In ŚBM 3.8.2.24–25 ≈ ŚBK 4.8.2.18, Yājñavalkya is recalled as having an encounter with another *adhvaryu* Brahmin, perhaps of the Black Yajurveda or perhaps simply a wandering priest (*caraka*, though simply *brāhmaṇa* in K). This longer passage is quoted in full, to make Yājñavalkya's sarcasm clear.

> *hutvā́ vapā́m evā́gre 'bhighārayati | átha pr̥̥ṣadājyaṃ tád u ha cárakādhvaryavaḥ pr̥̥ṣadājyám evā́gre 'bhíghārayanti prāṇā́ḥ pr̥̥ṣadājyam íti vádantas tád u ha yā́jñavalkyaṃ cárakādhvaryur anuvyā́jahāraivám̐ kurvántaṃ prāṇaṃ vā́ ayám antáragād adhvaryúḥ prāṇá enaṃ hāsyatī́ti | (24) sá ha sma bāhū́ anvavékṣy āha | imaú palitaú bāhū kvà svid brāhmaṇásya váco babhūvéti na tad ā́driyetottamo vā́ eṣá prayājó bhavatīdaṃ vaí haviryajñá uttamé prayājé dhruvā́m evā́gre 'bhíghārayati tásyai hí prathamāvā́jy-*

abhāgau hoṣyan bhávati vapām vā átra prathamā́ṃ hoṣyán bhavati tásmād vapā́m evā́gre 'bhíghārayed átha pr̥ṣadājyam átha yát paśuṃ nā̀bhighāráyati ned áśr̥tam abhighāráyāṇī́ty etád evā̀sya sárvaḥ paśúr abhíghārito bhavati yád vapā́m abhighāráyati tásmād vapā́m evā́gre 'bhíghārayed átha pr̥ṣadājyam | (25)

Having offered, he bastes first the omentum, then the clotted ghee. Now the Caraka-Adhvaryus baste first the clotted ghee, saying that the clotted ghee is breath. Indeed, a Caraka-Adhvaryu cursed Yājñavalkya for doing so (i.e., basting the omentum first) [saying], "This *adhvaryu* has shut out the breath; the breath will spring from him!" (24)

But he [Yājñavalkya], looking at his arms, said, "These gray-haired arms—what has become of a Brahmin's word?" He should not heed that [objection of the Carakas]. This is the last fore-offering (*prayāja*)—and being a *havis*—offering [he,] at the last fore-offering, first pours ghee into the *dhruva*-spoon, getting ready to offer the first two butter-portions with it. Here, he will offer the omentum first—therefore he should baste first the omentum, then the clotted ghee. [Though he does not baste the whole victim with ghee,][47] "lest he baste the uncooked," the one who bastes the omentum, his whole animal becomes basted with ghee. Therefore he should baste first the omentum, then the clotted ghee. (25)

The meaning is rather clear—Yājñavalkya's arm hair has turned grey (i.e., he is old), and certainly he has never had the "breath spring from him" (i.e., died) for basting the omentum in the fashion he does and, according to the rest of the passage, as all White YV *adhvaryus* should do. He thus chastises the other Brahmin, and even Brahmins as a whole, saying "What has become of a Brahmin's word?"—that is, this Brahmin is wrong, or worse, lying.

Translating *anu-vi-ā-√hr̥* as "to curse" is problematic in this passage, but for the lack of a better alternative it has been used. The problem lies in the fact that Yājñavalkya's response shows that not only did his "breaths springing from him" not happen then and there, it also had not occurred previously (i.e., he has grown old doing the very same ritual practice). Thus, the "curse" is not so much of a "curse" as it is a truth-act: if Yājñavalkya's basting of the omentum first means that one shuts out one's breath (i.e., he dies), then it should have occurred previously as Yājñavalkya apparently carried out the rite in this fashion his whole life.

ŚBK is more diplomatic in its treatment of this passage in not mentioning any specific group of Brahmins. The passage begins simply, "Some say . . ." (*tad vā́ āhuḥ*) and later states that an unspecified priest (*brāhmaṇa*) cursed Yājñavalkya. Interestingly, Yājñavalkya's retort is not spoken directly to the Brahmin who cursed him, but rather is an apparent death-bed retort: "[When] old, worn-out, and lying down, Yājñavalkya said, 'These gray-haired arms—what has become of a Brahmin's word?'" (*sthávriro jī́rṇiḥ śáyāna imaú palitaú bāhū abhūtā́ṃ kva svid evá brāhmaṇásya váco babhūvéti*).

In ŚBM 3 ≈ ŚBM 4 we have two general ritual pronouncements of Yājñavalkya which are taken as authoritative, one remembrance (in K, on the death-bed) of Yājñavalkya sarcastically mocking another Brahmin's threat, suggesting that not all Brahmins are to be trusted, and one sarcastic retort at the overelaborate ritual logic of other Brahmins.

ŚBM Book 4 ≈ ŚBK Book 5

(1) ŚBM Book 4 ≈ ŚBK Book 5 contains three passages related to Yājñavalkya, though there is no parallel in K for the last of these. ŚBM 4.2.1.7 ≈ ŚBK 5.2.1.5 is concerned with the drawing of two cups of *soma* to drive away two demons, Śaṇḍa and Marka, during the day of the *soma*-feast of the Agniṣṭoma. The question being considered is whether the cups of *soma* are to be drawn for the demons (to coax the demons to the sacrifice so that they can be driven away) or for the gods.

> *ápi hovāca yā́jñavalkyaḥ* | *no svid*[48] *devátābhya evá gṛhṇīyāmā3 víjitarūpam iva hìdam íti tad vai sa tán mīmāṃsā́m evá cakre net tú cakāra* | (7)
>
> Also Yājñavalkya said, "We should we not draw (portions) for the deities, should we? For this rite has something of the form of conquest." This, however, he just considered, but did not practice. (7)

This passage is unique among all Yājñavalkya passages, because rather than listing an opinion as authoritative or not, or even as an option, it instead lists a speculation. This speculation of Yājñavalkya, though, follows the standard Brāhmaṇa logic of similarity. One may infer that the passage is not taken as authoritative, as Yājñavalkya just (*eva*) considered this alternative and there is no explicit recommendation to follow this practice.[49] Also, in contrast to authoritative passages which begin *tád u hovāca,* this text begins *ápi hovāca* (M) or *utá ha smāha* (K).

K here is quite similar to M. However, rather than *víjitarūpam iva,* this text contains *víditaṃ hī́dam,* "this is well known." It is difficult to reconcile this reading with the passage, however, because if the practice of drawing the *soma* cups for the gods is well known, why then is Yājñavalkya said to only speculate on this rather than practice it? Here it appears that M contains the better reading.

(2) ŚBM 4.6.1.10 ≈ ŚBK 5.8.1.11 lists Yājñavalkya's opinion in contrast to Buḍila Āśvatarāśvi (K Buḷila) concerning the pressing of the *soma* during the *dvādaśāha vyūḍhachandas* (the Sacrifice of 12 Days of Transposed Meters). However, the question dealt with here concerns whether the *soma* should be pressed symbolically (Buḍila's opinion) or actually pressed (Yājñavalkya's opinion). Since this is an offering for the deity Soma, Yājñavalkya's point is that the offering should be done differently than it is for other gods as a way of emphasizing Soma's uniqueness.

> *tád u hovāca yā́jñavalkyaḥ | abhy èvá ṣuṇuyān na sóma índram ásuto mamāda nā́brāhmāṇo maghávānaṃ sutā́sa ity ṛ́ṣiṇābhyánūktaṃ na vā́ anyásyai kásyai caná devátāyai sakṛ́d abhíṣuṇoti tád anyáthā tátaḥ karoti yátho cānyā́bhyo devátābhyas tásmād abhy èvá ṣuṇuyād íti* | (10)
>
> Regarding this, however, Yājñavalkya said, "He should press [because] 'The unpressed *soma* did not delight the mighty Indra, nor the pressed [given] without sacred formula,' was declared by a *ṛṣi* (ṚV 7.26.1). For no other deity does he press only once—thus he is doing differently than what he does for other deities. Therefore he should press [once]." (10)

Here, in contrast to the example in book 2, Yājñavalkya is not in contradiction to the ṚV, but is rather using the ṚV as a proof text for his opinion that a single pressing is proper. Again, his opinion stands in the final position of this discussion, suggesting that his opinion is authoritative. K has no significant variants for our purposes.[50]

(3) ŚBM 4.6.8.7 is unique to the M recension. This passage occurs in the consecration (*dīkṣā*) section of the Gavām Ayanam ("Leading of the Cows Sacrifice").

> *rā́jānaṃ prá́ṇayati | údyata evaìṣá ā́gnīdhrī́yo 'gnir bhávaty áthaita ékaikam evólmukam ādā́ya yathādhiṣṇyáṃ vipárāyanti taír eva téṣām úlmukaiḥ prághnantī́ti ha smāha yā́jñavalkyo ye táthā kurvantī́ty etan nv ékam áyanam* | (7)
>
> He leads forward the king (Soma). That *āgnīdhrīya* fire has been elevated. Then they take one fire-brand each [from the fire at the hall-door] and return to their respective *dhiṣṇya* hearths: "They who do so," said Yājñavalkya, "hit/slay with those fire-brands of theirs." This is now one way. (7)

It is clear in this passage that, once again, Yājñavalkya is not taken as authoritative, but his opinion is simply listed as an option. Further, the passage that immediately follows this (ŚBM 4.6.8.8) offers another alternative to Yājñavalkya—that the priests go to where they will perform the animal offering. The topic turns back to the larger issue of lighting the *āhavanīya* in 4.6.8.9, suggesting that Yājñavalkya's opinion is an option, but probably not even the preferred option.

The three passages found in book ŚBM Book 4 ≈ ŚBK Book 5 cover the spectrum of possibilities regarding authoritativeness. In one case Yājñavalkya simply contemplated a practice, but did not perform it. In another, his opinion is taken as authoritative, but in the final passage his opinion is simply an option. In no passage does the sarcasm that we saw earlier attributed to Yājñavalkya occur.

ŚBM Book 5 ≈ ŚBK Book 7

(1) Yājñavalkya appears only one time, in Book 5.5.5.14 ≈ ŚBK 7.5.3.11, in a sacrifice devoted to Indra, the *sautrāmaṇī*.

> *átho hainayā́py abhícaret | etáyā vaí bhadrasenám ājātaśatravam ā́ruṇir abhícacāra kṣipraṃ kílāstr̥ṇutéti ha smāha yā́jñavalkyó 'pi ha vā́ enayéndro vr̥trásyāsthā́nam achinad ápi ha vā́ enayāsthā́naṃ chinatti yá enayābhicárati tásmād u hainayā́py abhícaret.* (14)

> Now, indeed, one may also practice magic with this [offering]. For it was with this that Āruṇi bewitched Bhadrasena Ājātaśatrava. "He knocked him down quickly," Yājñavalkya used to say. And with this [offering], indeed, Indra also cut off Vr̥tra's retreat and, indeed, he who practices magic with this cuts off the retreat [of his enemy]. Therefore one may also practice magic with this offering. (14)

Previous translations of this passage are enigmatic at best. However, counter to Eggeling, Witzel (following Eggeling), and Swaminathan, Fišer has pointed out (1984, 60n11) that the verbal root must be √*str̥*, "to knock down" and not √*str̥̄*, "to spread / strew." Thus, it appears that Yājñavalkya's statement is a simple declaration that Āruṇi (perhaps Uddālaka?) did practice magic with this offering and it was quite effective—it "knocked him [the enemy] down quickly." This is not an opinion, but rather an endorsement of the efficacy of the practice.

Authority and Sarcasm, Part I

Throughout the early books of the ŚB, the picture of Yājñavalkya is a diverse one. In eleven passages, Yājñavalkya is shown to be authoritative on ritual interpretation in a variety of contexts: the new and full moon sacrifice (book 1); the *agnihotra,* the First Fruits Sacrifice, and the Four-Monthly Sacrifice (book 2); the *agniṣṭoma* (books 3 and 4); the consecration and the Sacrifice of Twelve Days (book 4); and the *sautrāmaṇī* (book 5). All of these passages place Yājñavalkya's opinion in the ultimate position to indicate his authoritativeness, though occasionally the text will continue with a brief Brāhmaṇa-style commentary to reinforce that opinion. Seven of these authoritative passages begin with the phrase *tad u hovāca,* indicating that Yājñavalkya's opinion is in contrast to someone else's, but since it occupies the ultimate position it is the preferred opinion. In one case (the eating of meat, ŚBM 3.1.2.21 ≈ ŚBK 4.1.2.12), the passage appears authoritative, but that may be mitigated by the sarcastic intent of the passage. In two cases where *tad u hovāca* is not used, Yājñavalkya is praising a ritual action and his view is not contrasted with another's (ŚBM 3.1.3.10 ≈ ŚBK 4.1.3.9; ŚBM 5.5.5.14 ≈ ŚBK 7.5.3.11), while in another example his answer is the rather blunt "what of it/who should care?" which closes the topic (ŚBM 1.3.1.21 ≈ ŚBK 2.2.4.17).

Yājñavalkya's authority in the early books, however, is not absolute. In ŚBM 1.9.3.16 ≈ ŚBK 2.8.4.10, his opinion is listed as an optional means to construct a *mantra*. In ŚBM 4.6.8.7 (not in K), his view of the meaning of the fire-brand and the action of the priests is listed as an option. In another case, we are told that Yājñavalkya just considered one ritual possibility (*tan mīmāṃsām eva*) but did not practice it (*net tu cakāra*). Yājñavalkya's opinion in one passage is in contrast to the R̥V, and the ŚB indicates that his opinion is incorrect. Counter, however, to Bronkhorst's seeing this conflict with the R̥V as the historical predecessor to Yājñavalkya's "legendary" debate with Śākalya (a representative of the R̥V), in ŚBM 4.6.1.10 ≈ ŚBK 5.8.1.11 Yājñavalkya uses the R̥V as a "proof text" that the *soma* needs to be pressed at least once.

Interestingly, Yājñavalkya, who has often been described as innovative, is shown in a number of passages to be quite conservative. In one passage (ŚBM 1.3.1.21 ≈ ŚBK 2.2.4.17), Yājñavalkya dismisses the concern of separating the wife from the husband with "what of it?" in a "rules are the rules" fashion. This same phrasing is also used in ŚBM 2.4.3.12 ≈ ŚBK 1.3.2.12, suggesting that this passage might also be attributed to Yājñavalkya. In ŚBM 2.4.3.1–12, Yājñavalkya uses a classical myth of creation to explain the reasons for the carrying out of the First Fruits Sacrifice. In ŚBM 4.6.1.10 ≈ ŚBK 5.8.1.11, Yājñavalkya refers to the R̥V to support his opinion. In ŚBM 3.1.1.4–5 ≈ ŚBK 4.1.1.3–4, Yājñavalkya places *all authority* for carrying out the sacrifice exclusively within the priestly class, because according to him the learned priests make up sacrificial ground itself. In ŚBM 1.3.1.26 ≈ ŚBK 2.2.4.19, Yājñavalkya attempts to preserve the traditional trust (*śraddhā*) in the priests by arguing for a consistency of ritual practice.

This conservatism, however, does not vitiate Yājñavalkya's innovativeness. Rather, the presentation of him as conservative serves to reinforce the authority of his innovation, particularly appropriate in the conservative context of the Vedic tradition. In many of these cases, the innovativeness is couched in the standard Brāhmaṇa-style logic we see elsewhere. ŚBM 1.1.1.9 ≈ ŚBK 2.1.1.7 plays on the word "to eat" (√*aś*), where Yājñavalkya is said to rather cleverly show that eating certain foods is not really eating. In ŚBM 1.9.3.16 ≈ ŚBK 2.8.4.10, Yājñavalkya modifies a *mantra* and states that his goal is to be "brilliant in *brahman*" (*brahmavarcasin*). Though his modification is only optional, it appears to follow the appropriate formulation. In another instance, Yājñavalkya is said to create a new way to carry out ritual acts (ŚBM 4.6.8.7; not in K), but again in an acceptable fashion. Yājñavalkya even restrains his own innovativeness, such as when he is said to consider certain innovations, but then reject them himself (ŚBM 4.2.1.7 ≈ ŚBK 5.2.1.5).

In comparing the sarcasm or derision that is often associated with Yājñavalkya with his established, though not universal, authority in his own tradition, an interesting pattern can be seen in these five books. The graph below (table 1.2) shows this pattern in ŚBM (for convenience, K has been omitted from this chart; cf. the previous chart for comparison).[51]

Table 1.2

(1) Sarcastic/prideful passages		
	(a) Authoritative	1.3.1.21; 1.3.1.26; 3.1.3.10; 3.8.2.24–25
	(b) Probably authoritative	3.1.2.21
(2) Non-sarcastic/prideful passages		
	(a) Authoritative	1.1.1.9; 2.3.1.21; 2.4.3.2–12; 3.1.1.4–5; 4.6.1.10
	(b) Not authoritative	2.5.1.2; 4.2.1.7
	(c) Optional	1.9.3.16; 4.6.8.7
	(d) Praising established practice	5.5.5.14
(3) Not clear whether Yājñavalkya is being sarcastic		
	(a) Authoritative	1.9.2.12

As can be seen, sarcasm only occurs when Yājñavalkya's opinion is taken as authoritative, that is, when the practice or interpretation associated with him is the preferred one. This indicates that Yājñavalkya is not being portrayed in the textual tradition as "irreverent" in a negative fashion, but rather that the combination of sarcasm with authoritativeness serves as a rhetorical reinforcement of the position stated or as an emphatic dismissal of others. In all cases of sarcasm, the derision is towards others that are either directly or indirectly expressed (in the case of ŚBM 3.1.3.10 ≈ 4.1.3.9, the "others" would be all other humans). Thus, while Yājñavalkya's opinion is taken as authoritative in the text, others' positions are intentionally derided.

In ŚBM 3.1.2.21 ≈ ŚBK 4.1.2.12, I contend that Yājñavalkya is taken as authoritative in a different light—that is, in his dismissal of the other Brahmins' overly elaborate and overly dramatic argument regarding what would happen should one eat the meat of a milk-cow or ox. As the various examples have shown, the passages attributed to Yājñavalkya in ŚBM books 1–5 ≈ ŚBK 1–5 and 7 are most often straightforward and succinct, even single sentences. In regard to the meat-eating, it is the other Brahmin's elaborate rationale that Yājñavalkya is dismissing in a single aural pun—"I, for one, eat it, provided that it is fatty/tasty" (*aśnā́my evā̀ham aṃsalaṃ ced bhávatī́ti*).

In the context of this attribution of sarcasm to Yājñavalkya, another interesting pattern emerges. Though, on the whole, the Mādhyandina recension appears to contain better, probably earlier readings, I have pointed out that the Kāṇva recension sometimes appears to include a larger context for certain passages—even if that only means including a single extra word which adds clarity.[52] There is also another type of variation in K, which is important in this discussion of sarcasm. The K recension contains slightly different readings of certain passages *where the sarcastic intent is minimal or less pointed*. For example, ŚBK 2.2.4.19 (ŚBM 1.3.1.26) does not contain the criticism of priests as a whole ("How can these [patrons] have trust in this?").[53] ŚBK 4.8.2.18 (ŚBM 3.8.2.24–25) mentions only that a Brahmin cursed Yājñavalkya, whereas M states that it is a Brahmin who is a *carakādhvaryu* priest, probably a representative of the Black Yajurveda. Further, in K the sarcastic response is a death-bed retort by Yājñavalkya and not a face-to-face confrontation as it appears in M.

While it is true that the statistical relevance of these few passages can be questioned, one must still ask why this portrayal is one-sided—that is, why is it that the Kāṇva contains the more ambivalent passages with regard to sarcasm while the M is more direct? It is possible that these variations are simply an issue of the differing textual transmission of K. There is, however, another possibility which is suggestive, if not definitive. If, as Witzel (1989) has pointed out, the K recension was geographically slightly more western than the M recension, this means that K would likely have been more directly influenced by the already established Kuru-Pañcāla Black Yajurvedic tradition. As such, this textual tradition would have been in more direct contact with the establishment that it was in direct religious competition with. The less sarcastic portrayals of Yājñavalkya could have been strategic—this is to say, that while the Kāṇva White YV tradition viewed Yājñavalkya as authoritative and in contradistinction to the Black YV, it would have created difficulties were the contrast more directly stated (i.e., a Brahmin is critiqued, but he is not explicitly said to be a *carakādhvaryu*). The Mādhyandina, however, being geographically further east probably had less contact or was less under the authority of an already established tradition. As such, there may have been a certain freedom in textual production and religious understanding, one which allowed for more explicit, sarcastic criticism of others.

Yājñavalkya in ŚBM Books 11–13

Yājñavalkya appears in the later books of ŚBM seven times (five times in book 11; once each in 12 and 13). As I pointed out, others (such as Bronkhorst) have focused on the perceived change in narrative form in these later books—from general pronouncements to more elaborate narratives. This often has been taken as indicative of a shift from historical statement to legend. However, in looking at the passages both individually and as a whole, I do not see such a sharp distinction in form. It is true that these books are where we find longer narratives about Yājñavalkya, but there are a variety of narrative forms in these books, suggesting the shift in form doesn't necessarily mean a shift into the "clearly legendary." Four of the passages (ŚBM 11.4.2.17≈ ŚBK 13.4.2; ŚBM 11.4.3.20 ≈ ŚBK 13.4.3; ŚBM 12.4.1.9–10 ≈ ŚBK 14.7.1; ŚBM 13.5.3.6) are single statements, one of which consists of a short statement about Yājñavalkya and is not speech attributed to him. As for the three longer narratives, 11.3.1.1–4 (≈ ŚBK 4.1.4.3–4) is a short discussion between Yājñavalkya and king Janaka; 11.6.2.1–10 (≈ ŚBK 13.6.2) is an amusing passage where Yājñavalkya outwits other

Brahmins to learn the secret of the *agnihotra* from king Janaka; and 11.6.3.1–11 (≈ ŚBK 13.6.3.1–10) is a longer debate between Śākalya and Yājñavalkya, the predecessor of the famous debate found in BĀU 3.9 (Lindquist 2011a). Thus, the types of narrative found in these books are split, albeit with a slight emphasis on the single statements that we have seen earlier. For convenience the longer passages are summarized, rather than translated in full.

(1) ŚBM 11.3.1.2–4 ≈ ŚBK 3.1.4.3–4 (*Jaiminīya Brāhmaṇa* [JB] 1.19–20) is a small dialogue between Yājñavalkya and Janaka concerning the nature of the *agnihotra*.

> *tád dhaitáj janako vaídehaḥ* | *yā́jñavalkyam papracha vétthāgnihotrám yājñavalkyā3 íti véda samrāḍ íti kím íti páya evéti* | (2)

> Regarding this, Janaka of Videha asked Yājñavalkya, "Do you know the *agnihotra*, Yājñavalkya?"
> "I know it, O King," [he said].
> "What is it?"
> "It is just the milk."

Following this, Janaka asks a series of reductive questions:[54] if milk is not present, what would one sacrifice with? Yājñavalkya answers, "with rice and barley" (*vrīhiyavā́bhyām*); if there is no rice and barley? and so on. The final question is if there was no water, then what would one sacrifice with?

> *sá hovāca* | *ná vā́ iha tárhi kíṃ canā̀sīd áthaitád á́hūyataivá́*[55] *satyám śraddhā́yām íti véthāgnihotrá́ṃ yājñavalkya dhenuśatám dadāmīti hovāca*[56] | (4)

> He [Yājñavalkya] said, "If there were nothing at all here, it is just offered—[that is,] truth in trust."
> "You know the *agnihotra*, Yājñavalkya. I give you a hundred cows."[57] (4)

The point of this passage is rather clear: if there are neither sacrificial offerings nor the sacrificial fire present, one can still carry out the *agnihotra* through their abstract equivalents, truth (*satyám*) and trust (*śraddhā́*). As Bodewitz has pointed out, this passage does not give rules for emergency situations (i.e., how to worship should one be lacking materials), but rather is a dialogical lead-up to the conclusion: "the point beyond which one cannot proceed, the final truth" (trans., 1973, 236). This truth, which according to Bodewitz implies speaking the truth, meditation upon the truth, etc., suggests a way of living that is superior to the ritual proper.

This passage, however, does not appear to contain a new teaching, but is rather a proof text of sorts for what is stated immediately before it. Prior to this passage, ŚB 11.3.1.1 (ŚBK 3.1.4.2) states that "fire, indeed, is trust, and ghee is truth" (*téja evá śraddhā́ satyám ā́jyam*), foreshadowing the conclusion of the story. Thus, this narration of a discussion between Yājñavalkya and Janaka is not presenting a new teaching but is elaborating and verifying the conclusion already accepted as true. This is to say that this passage functions as a proof story. The conclusion is authoritative, but no innovation is apparently attributable to Yājñavalkya.

It is in this passage that we first encounter the "giving of cows." Hock (2002) has discussed what he calls the "cow theme" in BĀU 4—that is, how the "giving of cows" serves to formally mark parts of discourse in the text, often followed by a shift in topic that is more abstract than what was before.[58] In BĀU 4, the "giving of cows" is followed by another teaching and more cow-giving until the discourse is formally closed. In this passage in ŚB, however, it serves to end the discussion with Yājñavalkya. Interestingly, it is Janaka's giving of cows that verifies and reinforces that the teaching is correct. Thus, this is a scene not only of royal patronage of religious teaching, but also of royal endorsement of that teaching.[59] Whether we are supposed to consider Janaka as knowing the answers to his own questions is not clear, but it is clear that he at least knows the proper answer when he hears it.

The variation of this story found in JB (1.19–20) has been the subject of some discussion. Oertel (1902, 328) is the first person that I am aware of to note the correspondences between these passages. Caland (1998, 102) also compares this passage of JB with ŚB and finds that it agrees more directly with the K version in the beginning and the M recension further on.[60] Bodewitz (trans., 1973, 62), however, has pointed out that the main differences in the latter part of the passage do not concern content so much as the use of particular words (i.e., K *abhaviṣyat*; M *syāt*). If Witzel's geographical placement of the JB is correct, than it is more likely to have been influenced by K (or a K-inspired version).

Following Bodewitz and Caland, it seems that this JB passage is a direct borrowing from the ŚB (perhaps from a variant version that we no longer possess and/or undergoing further changes under the Jaiminīyas). As Bodewitz points out, JB 1, which is concerned with the *agnihotra,* is a later addition to this Brāhmaṇa and "most likely [this] section is later than ŚB in both recensions."

One significant change, from a narrative point of view, is that the JB omits the final equation in the introduction (fire being faith and ghee being truth)[61] which foreshadows the final answer of Yājñavalkya. Why this is the case is unclear, as it disconnects the introduction from the following narrative. It may be, however, that the JB is attributing a newness to the teaching of Yājñavvalkya, suggesting the innovation was his own and that the story is not functioning as a proof text. This would be in line with a general heightened authority of Yājñavalkya found in JB.

Another significant variation is what follows the ŚB narrative. In the ŚB version, the story involving Yājñavalkya and Janaka ends (11.3.1.4). This is clear, not only in comparison with other narratives where the cow-giving marks a conclusion (something akin to "you answered the questions, here is your reward"), but also because what follows in the text is disconnected from the dialogue ("concerning this, there are these verses," M *tád apy éte ślókāḥ*; K *éṣo 'sti ślókaḥ*). The following ŚB passages (11.3.1.5–8) then discuss the issue of performing the *agnihotra* while away from home and what it is that connects the sacrificer to the ritual performance carried out at home in his absence. This appears as standard Brāhmaṇa-style commentary not placed in the mouth of any particular individual.

The JB, however, reinterprets or recomposes this passage. In the JB, rather than the dialogue of Yājñavalkya and Janaka ending, the story continues and what appears as Brāhmaṇa-style commentary in ŚB is made into a dialogue between Yājñavalkya and Janaka. This is quite clear in that JB, rather than introducing apparently anonymous versus, concludes 1.19 with *atha hainam upajagau*: "Then he recited to him (the verse)" (trans., Bodewitz 1973, 63). The subject "he" must refer to Janaka asking a question of Yājñavalkya in the form of a verse. Yājñavalkya then responds but is referred to repeatedly as *vājasaneya* (derived from *vājasani,* "winning the prize" or "victorious") in the JB.

Bodewitz notes that the use of the term *vājasaneya* suggests a borrowing from the ŚB (1973, 63), though his reasons are not explicit.

I believe, however, that Bodewitz must be correct. The VVRI indicates no use of the term *vājasaneya* prior to the final book of the ŚB and then only in the final chapter of the BĀU (6).[62] In BĀU, and in JB, it is quite clear that this is being used as an epithet for Yājñavalkya and is clearly meant to indicate his association with the "sun." This term may also designate that Yājñavalkya was by that point considered the founder or leader of the school of the White Yājurveda (BĀU 6.5.6), indicating a point at which his authority was considered foundational, even absolute (see chapter 2). It is also understood by most scholars that chapters 5–6 of the BĀU are the last additions to the ŚB. This suggests that the JB borrowed from the ŚB at some point after this addition.

Another major reason to take the JB version as a late adaptation of an already formed (or forming) ŚB version is that the ŚB appears to be a more logical composition in the sense that when the topic shifts (from the means to perform the *agnihotra* without the proper implements to a different discussion on the *agnihotra*), it is no longer a dialogue. As was mentioned earlier, the giving of cows marks the end of this particular discussion and the following line introduces authorless and subjectless verses (M *tád apy éte ślókāḥ*; K *éṣo 'sti ślókaḥ*). The JB appears to be a recomposition of the ŚB version.[63]

It should be pointed out that the recomposing of JB is not without its own logic, even if this logic appears as a later adaptation from a text-critical perspective. The logic of the JB composition appears to be as follows. First, since the *brāhmaṇa* in the ŚB version does not actually end until after these additional passages (11.3.1.8), one may suspect that the JB redactors felt they must have been directly connected to what preceded them. Clearly, both sets of passages are about the *agnihotra* (albeit different aspects of it). Most interestingly, though, the ŚB passage contains, after the Yājñavalkya dialogue (11.3.1.5–8), a series of *iti*s (quotation marks, of a sort) without attributing the passages to any particular individual. It would be rather natural then for the JB redactors to assume the dialogue is supposed to continue and thus recompose the passage to fit that interpretation by adding the later name. Following Bodewitz, however, it is clear that the innovation lies with the JB and that the earlier version is the ŚB.

(2) ŚBM 11.4.2.17 ≈ ŚBK 13.4.2.12, also concerned with the *agnihotra*, is a single pronouncement in the same format as found in the first five books. Here Yājñavalkya is said to be giving an alternative interpretation for when the gods "fill the gold cups." The issue is how one is to prepare the offering.

> *tád u hovāca yā́jñavalkyaḥ | yád vā́ upastī̀ryā́vadā́yābhighārā́yato tád evàināḥ sámtarpayati tā́sām sámtr̥ptānāṃ devā́ hiraṇmáyāṃś camasā́n pūrayante . . .*

> Regarding this, however, Yājñavalkya said, "When, after making an underlayer [of ghee and] after cutting [sacrificial portions], he bastes [them] with ghee. Indeed, he satisfies[64] them [the offerings] and [after the offerings are] satisfied the gods fill the gold cups."

This passage does not conclude with an *íti* as one would expect, but in fact appears to switch to another topic in the same section.[65] The lines that follow are concerned with another priest (Śaulvāyana) who criticizes a householder and his sacrificial session. We must assume that Yājñavalkya's discourse ends here, though it is curious that K also lacks an *íti* (i.e., if this was perceived as an oddity or error, it would have been easy enough to correct). Again, this is the ultimate statement on "how to satisfy the offering" and appears authoritative.

(3) ŚBM 11.4.3.20 ≈ ŚBK 13.4.3.19 is not a pronouncement by Yājñavalkya, but rather is an explanation of one particular rite, the Mitravindā́ ("Find an Ally"). This passage is unique in that it is a (remembered?) association of Yājñavalkya and Janaka used as an explanation of a sacrifice.

> *tā́ṃ haitāṃ gótamo rāhūgaṇáḥ | vidā́ṃ cakāra sá ha janakam vaídeham pratyútsasāda tā́ṃ hāṅgajídbrāhmaṇéṣv ánviyeṣa tā́m u ha yā́jñavalkye viveda sá hovāca sahásram bho yājñavalkya dadmo yásmin vayaṃ tváyi mitravindā́m anvávidāméti vindáte mitráṃ rāṣṭrám asya bhavaty ápa puna[r]mr̥tyúṃ jayati sárvam ā́yureti yá eváṃ vidvā́n etayéṣṭyā́ yájate yó vaitád evaṃ véda* | 20

> Now Gotama Rāhūgaṇa[66] had discovered this [sacrifice]. It went away to Janaka of Videha. He sought it out in the Brahmins versed in the *aṅgas*[67] and found [√*vind*] it in Yājñavalkya. He [Janaka] said, "We give you, Yājñavalkya, a thousand [cows] in whom we found [√*vind*] the Mitravindā́."

> He finds Mitra [or an "ally"] and possesses the kingdom, conquers repeated death and gains all life whoever knows in this way and performs this, he knows thus.

This passage comes at the end of the myth of the creation of the Mitravindā́, presumably as a justification or perhaps elaboration of the rite and is the same in ŚBK. In this case the authority does not lie in what Yājñavalkya may have said or not, but it is clear that the tradition holds him in high authority by associating him with this sacrifice. Further, not only does Yājñavalkya know the sacrifice when others do not, but the gift of "one hundred" cows seen elsewhere is now "one thousand."

Most interesting here, though, is the double-meaning of the name of the sacrifice and that it was "found" in Yājñavalkya. Mitravindā́ or "Find Mitra" is also a play on words, one that is common in the older sources (Witzel 2003, 123 n73). The word *mitra* can be the proper name of a god, an "ally," an "agreement/contract," or, later, a "friend." Here the wordplay—less a pun and more the magical equivalence we have seen earlier—is between "ally" and the god Mitra. The text is telling us that not only did Janaka find (√*vind*) the apparently lost sacrifice to Mitra (Mitravindā́), but he also finds (√*vind*) an ally/friend (*mitra*), Yājñavalkya. This magical equivalence is then between the relationship of Janaka with Yājñavalkya—which may have already been a stereotyped relationship of the ideal king and Brahmin—and the double meaning of *mitra*. As Janaka had to find the knowledge of this sacrifice in Yājñavalkya, Yājñavalkya's authority is placed above other Brahmins with a rite originally associated with a R̥V *r̥ṣi*, Gotama Rāhūgaṇa.

(4) ŚBM 11.6.2.1–10 ≈ ŚBK 13.6.2.1–11[68] is a long passage and can be summarized as follows:

King Janaka came across three Brahmins (Śvetaketu Āruṇeya,[69] Somaśuṣma Sātyayajñi[70] and Yājñavalkya). He proceeded to ask each of them how they performed the *agnihotra*. The final and most subtle answer is given by Yājñavalkya, upon which Janaka gives one hundred milk cows (*dhenuśata*) to him. However, while Janaka tells Yājñavalkya that he has inquired most closely (*amīmāṁsiṣṭha*) into the rite, he also tells Yājñavalkya that he does not know the rising/departure (*ut* √*kram*), the goal (*gati*), the support (*pratiṣṭḥa*), the contentment (*tr̥pti*), the return again (*punarāvr̥tti*), or the renascent world (*loka pratyutthāyina*) of the two oblations under discussion. The king leaves while the Brahmins decide whether to challenge the king again because he bested them.[71] Yājñavalkya convinces them not to, pointing out that there is a public loss of face if they lose to a *rājanya* and no honor in beating him. However, Yājñavalkya then sneaks away to find the king and learn about the *agnihotra*. Upon receiving the knowledge of the rising, the goal, etc. from him, Yājñavalkya grants Janaka a boon. Janaka asks for the right to question Yājñavalkya whenever he likes (*kāmapraśna*). The passage concludes by saying "Thereafter Janaka was a Brahmin" (*táto brahmā́ janaká āsa*).

What is particularly interesting in this passage is that Yājñavalkya is said to convince the other Brahmins not to engage the king in further debate, yet he chases after the king (presumably, in secret) to learn about the *agnihotra*. While on a surface reading it may appear that Yājñavalkya is contradicting his own warning to the other Brahmins, on a closer reading it is clear that he is not. What Yājñavalkya is doing here is exploiting a loophole in his warning to the other Brahmins to his own advantage.[72] Yājñavalkya's criticism of debating with a *rājanya* is that it would lead to no gain if they won, but the loss of prestige were they to lose. What Yājñavalkya does then is not debate *publicly* with Janaka, but rather he approaches him *privately* by sneaking off in secret to be taught. In this manner, he is not doing what he told the other Brahmins they should not do and avoids the consequence of a public loss of face through a clever play on logic.

At the end of the story, Yājñavalkya is said to grant Janaka the boon of questioning him at will (*kāmapraśna*) and we are told "Thereafter Janaka was a Brahmin" (*táto brahmā́ janaká āsa*). There are a number of reasons to suspect that the statement that "Janaka was a Brahmin" is not meant in a literal sense.[73] As Fišer (1984, 73) points out, one would have expected a form of √*bhū* ("to become"), indicating a transformation from one state of being to another, rather than √*as*, which usually denotes a *being* in that state. However, I only partially agree with Fišer's explanation that this passage indicates that Janaka was "equal to Brahmins in knowledge and had the right to dispute with them at his own discretion" (73). While Janaka's knowledge may have been greater than Yājñavalkya's in this one passage, the other portrayals of Janaka are solely as a questioner (BĀU 4) or facilitator (as in the ŚBM 11.6.3.1ff ≈ ŚBK 13.6.3.1–10 below, or the BĀU 3 debate). There is no passage in ŚB or BĀU where Janaka "disputes" with Brahmins. Even in the above passage, Janaka is not "disputing" with other Brahmins: he asked how each performs the *agnihotra,* tells them that they all are only partially correct, and then he simply leaves. In BĀU 4 (dealt with in chapter 2), where Janaka actually uses the boon, he only asks Yājñavalkya questions for the sake of his release (*vimokṣa*), not to dispute with him.

I agree with Fišer that this passage is probably about Janaka being equal in knowledge to the others, but I think the import of the statement that "Thereafter Janaka was a Brahmin" is more about the boon he chose. Janaka was a Brahmin because he has been granted the boon to ask Yājñavalkya questions as he wishes. The boon grants him the right to question at will, which must have been normally reserved for Brahmins—that is, those schooled in the ritual knowledge who would properly understand the teachings. As Janaka has shown himself schooled in such knowledge—here, he even knows more than Yājñavalkya about the *agnihotra*—he transcends normal *varṇa* boundaries, and he is granted such a right for future encounters with Yājñavalkya.

Another reason not to accept the statement literally is because such an interpretation is mitigated by a larger theme in this narrative. One of the main points of this narrative is to place "proper knowledge" over "birthright" with regard to *both* Yājñavalkya and Janaka, a theme that is also fairly common in late Vedic literature (Lindquist 2011c). Yājñavalkya comes to Janaka to learn about a ritual that *should be* best understood by Brahmins, not a *rājanya.* Janaka claims a boon that *would normally* be reserved for Brahmins. In emphasizing that proper knowledge is more important than birthright,[74] the text is also criticizing the other Brahmins present—they are concerned solely with their own pride and public persona and not the proper knowledge that Janaka possesses. They want to beat him in debate, not learn the *agnihotra.* While Yājñavalkya is also concerned with his public persona (as he goes to Janaka in private), he is more concerned with acquiring the knowledge of the *agnihotra.*

JB 1.22–25 will be dealt with briefly because, while it is comparable to the above dialogue in certain ways, it is also a rather different narrative. In this version, five Brahmins (Āruṇi, Vājasaneya, Barku Vārṣṇa, Priya Jānaśruteya, and Vaiyāghrapadya) go to Janaka to discuss the *agnihotra* saying that Janaka "considers himself superior to us in the dispute" (trans., Bodewitz 1973, 72).[75] After Janaka questions them about the *agnihotra* and they answer, Janaka points out to them that they do not know the goal or the means of the *agnihotra*. Each of them grant him a boon if he can explain the goal and the means to them. He does and chooses as his five boons to grant each of the five Brahmins one thousand cows and five hundred horses.

There is an apparent overlap in the JB version and the ŚB version, particularly in regard to their answers of offering the sun into the fire and then the fire into the sun as the proper way to perform the *agnihotra*. However, this theme is common and does not indicate that these two versions came from a similar source (trans., Bodewitz 1973, 38–39, 235, 240ff.). Further, outside of a similar narrative structure (one, it may be added, that is rather common to *brahmodyas*), there is little to suggest any direct link between the JB and the ŚB: the introductory matter is rather different in the JB; Vājasaneya plays a relatively minor role (he is neither the first nor the last to give his opinion); Janaka is here teaching all the Brahmins (not just Yājñavalkya); and the ending is completely unique in that even though Janaka was granted five boons, he uses those boons *to give the Brahmins cows*, thus reasserting his idealized role as patron of priests.

(5) ŚBM 11.6.3.1–11 ≈ ŚBK 13.6.3.1–10 ≈ JB 2.76–77 (elaborated version found at BĀU 3.9; see chapter 2) is the second long narrative in ŚB where Yājñavalkya's pride and sarcasm are quite clear.

Janaka of Videha had performed an elaborate sacrifice and set aside a thousand cows for whomever of the assembled Brahmins was the most learned in *brahman* (*brahmiṣṭha*). Yājñavalkya laid claim to the cows, and the other Brahmins challenge his claim.

> *té hocus tvám̥ svin nó yājñavalkya bráhmiṣṭho 'sī3 sá hovāca námo 'stu bráhmiṣṭhāya gókāmā evá vayám sma íti*[76] ||2||

> They said, "Are you really the most learned in *brahman* among us?"
>
> He [Yājñavalkya] said, "Homage to him who is most learned in *brahman*. We are just desirous of cows."

The sarcastic intent of this passage is quite clear—Yājñavalkya, apparently tongue-in-cheek, claims that the sole intent of the assembled crowd is to acquire cows, rather than any higher religious purpose. This passage is both ironic and sardonic: Yājñavalkya is still claiming that he is the *brahmiṣṭha* among them by laying claim to the cows, while at the same time mocking the assembled Brahmins as a group (including himself).

When Vidagdha Śākalya volunteers to be the representative of the Brahmins and challenge him, Yājñavalkya chides him, saying "Have these Brahmins made you the fire-quencher?" (*tvā́ṃ svichākalya brāhmaṇā́ ulmukāvakṣáyaṇam akratā3 íti*). The point of this metaphor is: if Śākalya is the fire-quencher (presumably a device for calming a coal-fire), then Yājñavalkya is calling himself the "fire," that is, the one bold enough to take the cows and to claim to be the *brahmiṣṭha*. The insult lies in the fact that Yājñavalkya is insinuating that Śākalya is simply a tool of the other Brahmins who are perhaps too timid to challenge him directly. The name Vidagdha, which is often translated as "clever," also has the meaning of "burnt up." Thus, the outcome of this debate is foreshadowed in this character's name: he is the fire-quencher who actually gets engulfed by the fire himself.

Śākalya proceeds to challenge Yājñavalkya by asking about the "actual" number of gods, and Yājñavalkya's answers progressively reduce the "actual" number from 3,306 gods down to one. He then asks Yājñavalkya who the thousands of gods are, and Yājñavalkya says that there are really only thirty gods and the larger number is actually their powers (*mahiman*). Śākalya proceeds interrogating Yājñavalkya.[77] The culminating question is: "Who is the one god?" Yājñavalkya answers that the one god is "breath" (*prāṇa*). At this point, Yājñavalkya curses Śākalya to die on a particular day in a particular way. The reason for the curse was not because Śākalya had insulted Yājñavalkya, but because Śākalya made a (fatal) mistake in his questioning: Yājñavalkya said, "You have asked me beyond the deity which is not to be asked beyond" (*anatipraśnyā́ṃ mā devátām átyaprākṣīḥ*) and proceeds to describe the fatal consequences that await Śākalya. In the end, we are told that Śākalya actually did meet such a fate.

A difficulty arises in this passage in determining who the deity (*devatā*) is that is being asked beyond. Eggeling ([1882–1900] 1994, 44: 117n2) suggests that it is Prajāpati (11.6.3.9) based on similar phrasing found at BĀU 3.6.[78] In this ŚB passage, however, there are four other questions that intercede between the mention of Prajāpati and Yājñavalkya's threat. In this context, one would have naturally expected the threat earlier as there is no clear reason why Śākalya would have been permitted to ask those four questions. Instead, I suspect that

Eggeling is taking "deity" too literally. Up until ŚB 11.6.3.9, recognizable deities are mentioned: Vasus, Rudras, Ādityas, etc. culminating with Indra and Prajāpati. In 11.6.3.10, Śākalya asks about other deities: the three deities, the two, the one and a half,[79] and the one. The answers on Yājñavalkya's part are more abstract: the three deities are the three worlds, the two are food and breath (*prāṇa*), the one and a half is the wind, and the one is breath (*prāṇa*). However, all of these are also referred to as *devátās*, so there is no reason to assume that Prajāpati is the deity meant in Yājñavalkya's threat.

It appears that Śākalya's error was in pushing the discussion beyond "breath" (*prāṇa*). Though breath was mentioned in conjunction with food earlier, breath in that context probably refers to the individual breath that sustains the body as does food. As a singular deity in Yājñavalkya's final answer of breath, it is probably understood not only as the fundamental principle of life (as with food), but also the fundamental principle of the cosmos. Śākalya's error, then, is in inquiring about the basis of everything, presumably a topic that is off-limits. As "the one" it is irreducible.

The JB version is quite similar to the ŚB, but shows clear signs of being later and probably being influenced by a hypothetical BĀU version of the text. First, Yājñavalkya is called Vājasaneya when he claims the cows to be his own, clearly showing that the text is later than much of the BĀU, where the term *vājasaneya* does not appear until the late chapter 6. Second, JB includes the word *somya*, "dear one," suggesting his student Sāmaśravas who is mentioned by name in BĀU and called *somya* but is entirely absent in ŚB. Also, the JB (as does the BĀU) mentions that Yājñavalkya's initial answer regarding the number of gods is in accordance with the *nivid* (lit. "saying"), which is also absent in the ŚB.

(6) ŚBM 12.4.1.10 ≈ ŚBK 14.7.1.7 (JB 1.59)[80] is a single pronouncement about the expiatory rites in the *agnihotra*, in this case, what one should do if the milk-cow lies down during the ceremony. It is possible that the statement attributed to Yājñavalkya is sarcastic, but it is unclear as what immediately follows his statement appears to take it quite seriously. 12.4.1.9 mentions the opinion of others—that the expiation consists of a number of *mantras* and the giving away of the milk-cow to a Brahmin that one will not visit. The rationale appears to be that there was a ritual error, so giving the ritual error away (i.e., the cow who sat down) solves this problem.

> *tád u hovāca yā́jñavalkya*[81] | *áśraddadhānebhyo haibhyo gaúr ápakrāmaty ā́rtyo vā́ ā́hutiṁ*[82] *vidhyantī́tthám evá kuryād daṇḍén-aivaìnāṁ*[83] *vipiṣyótthāpayed íti . . .*
>
> Regarding this, however, Yājñavalkya said, "Indeed the cow leaves from those who have no trust. They pierce the offering with affliction. He should do it just like this—prodding her with a stick he should make her get up." (12.4.1.10)

Yājñavalkya's criticism here is blunt, if not sarcastic. He calls those others who give away the cow "unbelieving" or "untrusting" (*áśraddadhāna*); that is, by giving the cow away they do not trust that their expiation with *mantras* was ritually efficacious. This is a serious charge as trust is paramount in the performance and efficacious outcome of Vedic sacrifice.

Whether or not Yājñavalkya's statement about prodding the cow is a sarcastic or ironic dismissal of the others' opinion is unclear. It may be interpreted as sarcastic in that Yājñavalkya is saying that if it is a ritual error if the cow sits down, then just make it stand up—a dismissal of the elaborate logic that the other Brahmins employ (similar to ŚBM 3.1.2.21 ≈ ŚBK 4.1.2.12 regarding meat-eating). A difficulty, however, in reading this passage as sarcastic is that the text continues in a rather formal way, justifying Yājñavalkya's practice. Immediately following his statement, the text explains that this is what anyone would do if an animal (such as a horse) were to get tired (consonant with a sarcastic intent), but then adds that by pushing the cow forward with a stick "the world which one wants to obtain, that [world] he attains" (*yám svargám lokáṃ samī́psati taṃ sáṃaśnute*).

This passage, through proper Brāhmaṇa-style logic, then is verifying Yājñavalkya's interpretation as correct which would seem to downplay any sarcastic intent. Āruṇi's opinion follows after, probably supporting Yājñavalkya's interpretation, but suggesting that the sitting down of the cow is not in itself a ritual error. As we have seen in books 1–5, however, the sarcasm attributed to Yājñavalkya *only* appears when he is taken as authoritative in his interpretation. Thus, I suspect the statement attributed to Yājñavalkya is, in itself, sarcastic or mildly humorous, but the composers of the Brāhmaṇa take it seriously along with Āruṇi's opinion, and the tone is muted.

(7) The final passage attributed to Yājñavalkya is ŚBM 13.5.3.6 (not present in K), a single pronouncement against the previously listed views of Satyakāma Jābāla, the two Saumāpa Mānutantavyas, Śailāli, Bhāllaveya, and Indrota Śaunaka regarding the ritual act of offering the *vapā* (omentum) during the *aśvamedha* ("horse sacrifice").

> *átha hovāca yā́jñavalkyaḥ* | *sakṛ́d evá prājāpatyā́bhiḥ pracáreyuḥ sakṛ́d devadevátyābhis tád evaìnān yathādevatáṃ prīṇātī́ áñjasā yajñásya sámsthām úpaiti ná hvalatī́ti* | (6)
>
> Now Yājñavalkya said, "They should go forth simultaneously with [the omentum] of those connected with Prajāpati [i.e., his victims] [and] simultaneously with those consecrated to [other] gods. In this way, he satisfies them deity after deity—he goes directly to the completion of the sacrifice [and] does not falter." (6)

As we have seen in many other cases, Yājñavalkya's single pronouncement comes at the end of a list of others' opinions. Interestingly, this is the only passage in pronouncement form that begins *átha hovāca*, rather than *tád u hovāca*. The reason for this change seems rather clear—immediately prior to Yājñavalkya's statement, the text tells us that the others' opinions are not accepted and implies that Yājñavalkya's is authoritative as his opinion immediately follows (*etád áha téṣāṃ váco 'nyā́ tv èvā́ta sthítiḥ*, "this, indeed, is their advice, but the established [practice] is different from this"). Here, then, it is not necessary to again frame Yājñavalkya's speech with *tád u* as it is already clear that his opinion is in contradistinction to others and is the correct one.

Authority and Sarcasm, Part II

We saw that in books 1–5 Yājñavalkya appeared in a variety of ritual settings with a variety of interpretations on particular ritual acts. We have also seen that his opinion was not always accepted (he considered certain interpretations but did not practice them, he was in contradiction to the R̥V, etc.). Further, Yājñavalkya's sarcasm only occurred in situations where his interpretation was correct, indicating the continuation of the theme of "pride in correct knowledge," where the sarcasm is justified by context.

In books 11–13, the variety in ritual settings has decreased: five of the seven passages are about the Agnihotra rite, the other two are about the Mitravindā and Aśvamedha, respectively. In these books, however, there is a variety of narrative styles, rather than a variety of ritual contexts. While in books 1–5 all statements are pronouncements, whether authoritative or not, in book 11 we find one example of a third-person narrative about Yājñavalkya and the Mitravindā (11.4.3.20), one passage where Yājñavalkya and Janaka are used to reinforce an accepted practice (11.3.1.1–4), and two longer narratives, one where Yājñavalkya is taught by Janaka (11.6.2.1–10) and another where Śākalya is "schooled" by Yājñavalkya (11.6.3.1–10). Four of the passages in books 11–13 include Janaka, though only in one (11.6.2.1–10) does he play any narrative role beyond simply framing a debate or eliciting answers from Yājñavalkya.

Three of the passages are pronouncements which are similar to those found in books 1–5. In one passage (11.4.2.17), Yājñavalkya is said to baste the omentum from the underside first, which is so that the gods "fill the gold cups" (*hiraṇmáyāṃś camasā́n pūrayante*). In another passage (12.4.1.10), he criticizes the other Brahmins as unbelievers and solves the ritual error of the cow lying down by making it get back up. In the third passage (13.5.3.6), he states that the omenta are to be offered simultaneously for Prajāpati and other gods. All of these passages utilize arguments similar to those that we have seen in the earlier books to justify his interpretations.

The sarcasm and wit associated with Yājñavalkya in the early books also occurs here: Yājñavalkya deceives the other Brahmins so as to find out the secret of the Agnihotra himself (11.6.2.1–10); he insults other Brahmins along with Śākalya in a narrative about "proper knowledge" which also includes a moral about when to stop questioning (11.6.3.1–11); and Yājñavalkya, perhaps in a sarcastic fashion, solves the ritual error of the cow lying down by simply making it get back up again (12.4.1.10).

In these three books there is another interesting trend related to Yājñavalkya's sarcasm and authority: he is *always* portrayed as authoritative. Unlike in the earlier books, where Yājñavalkya's opinion is optional or contradicted, in every case in the later books his opinion is authoritative. Even in the case where Yājñavalkya tricks other Brahmins to learn the secret of the Agnihotra, the subtext is that what he did was proper so as to learn the real meaning it.

It has been argued by others (Bronkhorst, Fišer, etc.) that the shift in narrative forms found in the later books of the ŚB indicates a "classical" (Fišer) and "legendary" (Bronkhorst) portrayal of

Yājñavalkya. The focus of this argument particularly has been on the longer narratives found in the text as well as Yājñavalkya's association with Janaka. The problem, however, is that even these passages seem consistent with the portrayal of Yājñavalkya in the other passages: Yājñavalkya's characteristic sarcasm and wit are employed against Śākalya (11.6.3.1–11); his wit is used to trick the other Brahmins in 11.6.2.1–10; and in 11.3.1.1–4 Yājñavalkya explains to Janaka in proper Brāhmaṇa fashion how to sacrifice without offerings or a fire.

Whether or not these stories of Yājñavalkya are "true," there is another interesting point that needs to be made. As we have seen, the two longer narratives regarding Yājñavalkya occur in SB 11.6 ≈ ŚBK 13.6, but what has not been pointed out is that *all* of ŚB 11.6/13.6 are narratives that are *thematically linked to each other*: they are all stories about "proper knowledge." ŚB 11.6.1.1 ≈ ŚBK 13.6.1 is a story about Bhṛgu, son of Varuṇa, who thinks himself superior in knowledge to his father. His father sends him traveling in various directions where he sees horrible acts of men killing other men and men eating other men. Finally, having seen two women flanking a man who was black with yellow eyes he returns home in terror. His father realizes that Bhṛgu has seen what he is supposed to and teaches him the symbolic meaning of these people in relation to the Agnihotra.

This episode is followed by the episode of Yājñavalkya being taught by Janaka about the Agnihotra and then the story of Yājñavalkya and Śākalya. Read sequentially,[84] the Bhṛgu story is about one's father being the proper teacher—and that a son should not think himself wiser than the father—while the second story is about a different type of "father/son" relationship between Yājñavalkya and Janaka (lit. "father"!). While the first story is about familial relations and the possession of knowledge, the second is about class relations and the possession of knowledge. Both focus on the means necessary for acquiring proper knowledge: by realizing that one does not know everything, one may acquire more/proper knowledge.

The third story about Yājñavalkya and Śākalya is less obviously connected to the first two, but it is connected nonetheless. This story is also about the hierarchy of knowledge, albeit not directly in a familial setting. Śākalya is the (unjustifiably) arrogant priest challenging the obviously superior, if (justifiably) arrogant, Yājñavalkya. If the first story is about a father teaching his arrogant son that he does not know more than the father, the second is a king teaching

Yājñavalkya the same. The third story is also about arrogance, but this time on Śākalya's part. In this case, both Yājñavalkya and Śākalya are arrogant, but Yājñavalkya's arrogance (calling other Brahmins *gokāma*, etc.) is justified throughout the story as he answers all the questions correctly (a character trait I have called "pride in correct knowledge"). Śākalya's arrogance in challenging Yājñavalkya is *not* justified, and his head shatters apart because of it. If the first two stories can be said to be about *acquiring* correct knowledge, the third is about propriety in claiming to possess that knowledge.[85]

The consequence of Śākalya dying is as much a matter of trying to *publicly* best Yājñavalkya as it is because of Śākalya's asking too far into the nature of the deities. As we saw with the Yājñavalkya and Janaka passage, someone loses face (or in this case, "head") in a public challenge, and since Śākalya attempts to "quench" the "fire" publicly, he himself is "quenched."

In conclusion and in segue to the portrayal of Yājñavalkya in the BĀU, a structural connection of the above three stories with the BĀU needs to be pointed out. One aspect of the narrative structure of the above three stories taken as a whole directly relates to the structure of BĀU 3–4. In fact, as we will see, the interrelationship of the three stories is the *exact structural inverse* of what we find in BĀU 3–4. The three passages in the ŚB progressively move from the privacy of (Bhr̥gu's) family, to a private teaching at court, to a public debate at a sacrifice where Śākalya is said to die. BĀU 3–4 is inversely structured on a progressive *privatization* of the discourses: from the open court (where Śākalya dies), to Yājñavalkya teaching Janaka (another inversion) privately at court, to Janaka stepping down from his seat to become Yājñavalkya's student, to the privacy of the home where Yājñavalkya discusses immortality with his wife, Maitreyī (also analyzed in chapter 2). The only real structural difference in this inversion is that a single story in the ŚB (Bhr̥gu being taught by his father at home) is split in the BĀU—Janaka becomes Yājñavalkya's student at court and Yājñavalkya discusses immortality with his wife at home.

While this could suggest to some that such an organizational (inverted) parallel of the ŚB stories with the BĀU supports a "legendary" reading of either or both, there is, I contend, no way to determine which accounts or any are historically "true" or not. What this *does* show us, though, is that the narrative structural template of BĀU 3–4 is prefigured in the ŚB. This is to say that the compilers of the BĀU may have modeled their text on the arrangement of the ŚB 11.6/13.6 *as a whole* and not just on the Yājñavalkya passages in it, suggesting that both (ŚB and BĀU 3–4) are more closely linked than has been assumed.

2

The Mature Yājñavalkya and the *Bṛhadāraṇyaka*

Yājñavalkya's most elaborate portrayal is in the *Bṛhadāraṇyaka Upaniṣad,* the concluding section of the *Śatapatha Brāhmaṇa* (ŚBM book 10.6.4–5 and 14 ≈ ŚBK 16). Yājñavalkya appears for the most part in chapters 3–4 of the *Bṛhadāraṇyaka Upaniṣad* (BĀU), those chapters which the tradition names after him: the Yājñavalkyakāṇḍa or "Yājñavalkya Section."[1] As was pointed out at the conclusion of the previous chapter, there seems to be a structural parallel (albeit in inverse fashion) between ŚBM 11.6/ŚBK 13.6 and BĀU 3–4. ŚBM 11 ≈ ŚBK 13 is the only Brāhmaṇa chapter containing significantly long narratives about Yājñavalkya.[2] In BĀU 3–4 we have four stories in which Yājñavalkya appears, and I will suggest how and why, based on the parallel with ŚBM 11 ≈ ŚBK 13, these stories, although functioning independently, could have been conceived of as interconnected when the text was compiled. I will first discuss the nature of the text and the context in which it was produced, however, before turning to the BĀU proper and Yājñavalkya's portrayal in it.

The BĀU consists of three sections, each with a traditionally ascribed name: chapters 1–2 are called the Madhukāṇḍa (the "Honey Section"); chapters 3–4, the Yājñavalkyakāṇḍa (the "Yājñavalkya Section"); and chapters 5–6, the Khilakāṇḍa ("Supplementary Section"). As Olivelle (1998, 29) has pointed out, this text must have had at least three major editorial stages: the first consists of the individual passages, narratives, etc. which were preserved within the oral tradition; the second phase in which different editors at different times compiled the three sections independently; and the final phase when the three sections were brought together as a cohesive text known as the *Bṛhadāraṇyaka Upaniṣad*. The first section (chapters 1–2), concerned largely with praising the *udgīta* chant of the *udgātṛ* priest, gets its name from BĀU 2.5, a passage where *madhu* ("honey") is the principal subject. The Yājñavalkyakāṇḍa (chapters 3–4) gets its name from Yājñavalkya, the principal protagonist. Chapters 5 and 6 are recognized by the tradition as an amalgamation of various topics and appear, even by their title ("The Supplementary Section") not to be a narratively or thematically structured whole.[3]

While the Upaniṣads are most often viewed as a discrete genre by the later indigenous tradition, they (particularly the oldest Upaniṣads, the BĀU and *Chāndogya Upaniṣad* [CU]) overlap thematically and structurally with the Brāhmaṇas, to the point where separating them becomes somewhat artificial. Indeed, the fundamental starting point in the early Upaniṣads is to discuss various aspects of ritual, whether it is to praise a particular chant, or to explain the cosmological significance of a ritual act or the sacrifice as a whole. It is fair to say, however, that much (if not all) of the BĀU postdates the preceding ŚB chapters, though it is clearly possible that certain passages of BĀU may predate certain parts of the ŚB. For this reason, combined with an apparent lack of Buddhist influence in the text, the general scholarly consensus dates this text roughly to the 6th–5th centuries BCE.[4]

Yājñavalkya outside the Yājñavalkyakāṇḍa

Yājñavalkya appears twice in the Madhukāṇḍa and twice in the Khilakāṇḍa. What is most notable about these passages is that they are consistent with the portrayal of Yājñavalkya in the ŚB proper. In two cases, Yājñavalkya's opinion on ritual matters is cited and taken as authoritative (1.4.3, 6.3.7–8).[5] One case (2.4) is a longer narrative of a discussion that Yājñavalkya purportedly had with his wife Maitreyī about immortality (again, authoritative),[6] while another (6.5.3) lists Yājñavalkya in a lineage of teachers and proclaims that he received the White Yajurveda from the Sun. Thus, as with the late ŚB books, we have a variety of narrative styles and settings. We do not, however, have any apparent sarcastic intent in any of these passages. This is easily explained by the fact that Yājñavalkya is not portrayed in contrast to different priests' opinions and confirms what we have seen earlier: sarcasm is only used to reinforce an interpretation in contrast to others.

(1) The first passage in which Yājñavalkya appears outside of the Yājñavalkyakāṇḍa is BĀUK 1.4.3 ≈ BĀUM 1.4.4–5,[7] a passage that is embedded within a larger myth about the creation of the first man. This first man was the sole being (*ekākin*) in the world, but found no pleasure in his existence as he was alone. Since his size was equal to that of a man and woman combined,

> *sá imám evā̀tmā́nam dvedhā̀pātayat | tátaḥ pátiś ca pátnī cābhavatām | tásmād idám ardhabṛgalám*[8] *iva sva íti ha smāha yā́jñavalkyaḥ | tásmād ayám ākāśá striyā́ puryáta evá | tāṁ sámabhavat táto manuṣyā̀ ajāyanta* || (3)
>
> He split this body into two and became a husband and wife. Therefore, Yājñavalkya said "We two are, in some way, two halves of a block." The space here [heart?], therefore, is just filled by the woman. He copulated with her and from this human beings were born.

The passage continues by explaining the creation of cattle, one-hoofed animals, goats, etc. and concludes that the "self" (*ātman*) is "dearer than a son, it is dearer than wealth, it is dearer than everything else" (*putrā́t préyo vittā́t préyo 'nyásmāt sárvasmāt*).

As with the passages we have seen in the ŚB, this passage simply lists Yājñavalkya's opinion followed by a Brāhmaṇa-style endorsement of his interpretation. This passage also follows the pattern where non-dialogic passages containing Yājñavalkya use *íti ha smāha* (in contrast to *tád u hovāca*), but are taken as authoritative.

Though there is nothing remarkable about Yājñavalkya in this passage in comparison to the ŚB—indeed, it is almost structurally identical to those passages—the teaching of this passage culminates with the *ātman* and the notion of "dear" (*priyaḥ*). This is a thematic difference from the contexts surrounding Yājñavalkya in the ŚB, where the common topic was ritual explanation. While this teaching is not directly attributed to Yājñavalkya (he is only quoted once to explain/justify this interpretation), it is interesting that Yājñavalkya appears in a passage that culminates in "dearness." This doctrine of "dearness," though rephrased, is attributed to Yājñavalkya in BĀU 2.4 and 4.5, where it is the starting point of a discussion with his wife, Maitreyī, on the nature of immortality. It seems it is not possible to determine which passage preceded the other—that is, whether Yājñavalkya here is associated with the doctrine because of his teachings to his wife or vice versa, but it is interesting that there is this thematic overlap as it shows an attempt at consistency in Yājñavalkya's literary portrayal across chapters.

(2) Yājñavalkya also appears in BĀUK 6.3.7 ≈ BĀUM 6.3.15, a passage that explains how to carry out ritual offerings to attain "greatness" (*mahat*). The text, in its authoritative, authorless voice explains how to offer ladles of ghee along with the appropriate *mantras*. The remaining ghee that is not poured in the offertory fire after each offering is placed in a separate receptacle. At the end of the rite, the person drinks the remaining ghee (in this way, sharing the offering with the gods), and then he is supposed to recite the lineage (*vaṁśa*). Yājñavalkya's name occurs within this *vaṁśa*, as a student of Uddālaka, a relationship that does not have a precedent in the ŚB. In fact, even in the BĀU (3.8) Yājñavalkya bests Uddālaka in debate, a passage where one would expect a mention of their relationship were this passage to view Yājñavalkya as Uddālaka's student. Most likely, chapters 5–6 have retained a different tradition(s),[9] where they viewed Yājñavalkya as Uddālaka's student (as also in 6.5.3). Given the long genealogy here (six generations of students), this is clearly a remembered association.

> *taṁ haitam uddālaka āruṇir vājasaneyāya yājñavalkyāyāntevāsina uktvovācāpi ya enaṁ śuṣke sthānau niṣiñcej jāyerañ chākhāḥ praroheyuḥ palāśānīti* |
>
> After telling this to his pupil Vājasaneya Yājñavalkya, Uddālaka Āruṇi said: "Even if one were to sprinkle this [mixture] upon a dried-up stump, branches would sprout and leaves would grow."

The text continues with each pupil then conveying the same message to his own pupil: Yājñavalkya to Madhuka Paiṅgya; Madhuka Paiṅgya to Cūla[10] Bhāgavitti; Cūla Bhāgavitti to Jānaki Āyasthūṇa; Jānaki Āyasthūṇa to Satyakāma Jābāla; and Satyakāma to his pupils. This passage concludes that one should only disclose this teaching to a son or pupil.

Most interesting in this passage is that it is the first time that Yājñavalkya is called Vājasaneya.[11] The ŚB does not contain a family name (nor any family) connected with Yājñavalkya. I suspect that the inclusion of the family name here is for consistency: all other teachers/ students mentioned have names which consist of two parts. Further, the larger point of the lineage in the passage is to emphasize that the teaching is not to be given to people other than *sons* or *students* (*tam etaṃ nāputrāya vānantevāsine vā brūyāt*, BĀU 6.3.12 ≈ BĀUM 6.3.20). Thus, the use of two names for the individuals connects each of them directly to a family lineage (i.e., "sons") and the relationship of these individuals to each other is a teaching lineage (i.e., "students"). In this fashion, the form of the lineage presented here is itself a proof-text in support of the secrecy of this rite. This is confirmed by the fact that the text, in order to conclude the lineage, simply states that Satyakāma Jābāla told this teaching to his pupils, whose names are not expressed (6.3.12 ≈ BĀUM 6.3.20). This is to say that by not expressing the names in the final lines, the lineage is able to conclude without needing to explain another relationship of a named person.[12]

This passage is also consistent with the ŚB passages where a statement attributed to Yājñavalkya is used as a validation of a ritual act. Yājñavalkya, however, is not the first nor the last in this lineage, suggesting that while he is an established authority, he is not necessarily thought of as the sole spokesman for the tradition.

(3) Yājñavalkya's final appearance outside of the Yājñavalkyakāṇḍa occurs in the concluding lineage (BĀU 6.5.1–4 ≈ BĀUM 16.4.29–33). At the end of each section of BĀU (1–2; 3–4; 5–6) a different genealogy is given.[13] The first two genealogies (2.6 and 4.6) consist of patronymics, and while they begin and end the same, they differ in the middle. All three genealogies trace their origin back to *brahman*. The final genealogy begins with matronymics, but switches to patronymics two generations prior to the inclusion of Yājñavalkya.[14] Outside of the first person mentioned (Pautimāṣya, the "son of Pautimāṣi") and its conclusion with *brahman*, this genealogy is radically different than the previous two. Yājñavalkya is said to be taught by Uddālaka, and Uddālaka by Aruṇa (presumably his father, hence the full name of Uddālaka Āruṇi in 6.3.7).

Most interestingly, this genealogy also includes the "Sun" (Āditya), which is not present in the other two genealogies.[15] When the text reaches this point, it breaks away from the genealogy proper to comment on the Sun.

> *ādityānīmānī śuklāni yajūṁṣi vājasaneyena yājñavalkyenākhyā-yante* |
>
> These White Yajus ("formulas") from the Sun have been declared[16] by Vājasaneya Yājñavalkya.

These lines were probably a conclusion to an earlier formulation of *ādhyāya* ("chapter") 6, or they were perhaps added on secondarily to conclude the genealogy. The following (BĀU 6.5.4) must have been added on after that, which is suggested by *samānamā sāṃjīvīputrāt*; "[the lineage] is the same up to the son of Sāñjīvī" before it continues the genealogy, again with a matronymic.

As I pointed out in chapter 1, this connection of Yājñavalkya to the Sun is not new to the BĀU. In ŚBM 1.9.3.16 ≈ ŚBK 2.8.4.10, Yājñavalkya is already associated with the Sun (ŚB, *sūrya*; BĀU, *āditya*), suggesting an early, perhaps intimate, relationship with the Sun as Yājñavalkya takes the liberty to modify a *mantra* composed for *sūrya*. While others take this BĀU passage as simply "hagiography,"[17] such an interpretation is not entirely clear in the text itself. What the text does tell us is that Yājñavalkya is taken as the sole authority for White Yajurvedins—he is credited with possessing the *mantras* due to divine influence. Whether that divine influence is hagiographical[18] remains unclear, but it is clear that the mention of it here becomes the basis of later hagiography (such as in the *Mahābhārata* and later).

While the mention of Yājñavalkya in 6.5.3 suggests that his authority is absolute, this absolute authority was probably limited to how he was viewed within his own tradition. Indeed, in the Yājñavalkyakāṇḍa, one of the main points of the narrative is to establish Yājñavalkya's authority *over other* traditions. What should be noted is that the narrative variety we found in the ŚB (proclamations, short narratives, longer narratives) is quite similar to the variety we find in the BĀU. Whether or not such debates took place as recorded is not possible to determine, but the narratives do make it quite clear that Yājñavalkya was the leading authority, at least for one tradition.

Yājñavalkya inside the Yājnavalkyakāṇḍa

Along with the short proclamations discussed above, we also have longer narratives in the BĀU. The main difference, and not one upon which claims for historicity can be made, is that the narratives in the Yājñavalkyakāṇḍa are longer and are grouped together, resulting in a larger narrative structure. This, however, is not completely novel. As I have argued earlier, the basic structure of BĀU is the same as ŚB 11.6, albeit in reverse. As ŚB 11.6 is the only place where longer narratives of Yājñavalkya are placed together ŚB (along with the story of Bhṛgu), the parallelism suggests it was the basis of the Yājñavalkyakāṇḍa.

The Yājñavalkyakāṇḍa consists of one long narrative (BĀU 3) and three shorter narratives (4.1–2; 4.3–4; and 4.5). The long narrative of BĀU 3 is composed of units, which can be read separately as each closes with a particular teaching about the self, *brahman*, the sacrifice, etc. Each question posed by Yājñavalkya's interlocutors is set off by the same formulaic phrases (beginning *atha hainam* X *papracha*, "Then X asked him"; and concluding *tato ha* X *upararāma*; "Therefore X ceased questioning"). At least in compilation, however, it is clear that these "mini-narratives" are to be also seen as a larger unit—the chapter as a whole—but also under the superstructure of BĀU 3–4 combined. The same is true of BĀU 4—parts can be read independently (that is, as narratively complete in themselves) or as a narrative whole, either as an independent chapter or inclusive of BĀU 3 as a larger unit. As Hock (2002) has pointed out, these narratives in chapter 4 are bracketed by the repetition of the "giving of cows." If the principal binding link of the narratives in BĀU 3 is the debate at the court of Janaka, the principal binding link of BĀU 4 is Janaka in discussion with Yājñavalkya, and in 4.5, with Maitreyī. Before discussing what I have called the "teaching narrative" which progresses in contexts of increasing privacy and which binds these two chapters together, a brief discussion of the structure of the text is in order. Brereton (1997) and Hock (2002) have both proposed schemas for understanding the structure of chapters 3 and 4, respectively, and I am indebted to their work, though I occasionally disagree with their conclusions or propose to read the structure of the text somewhat differently.

Bṛhadāraṇyaka 3

As has been mentioned, BĀU 3 consists of a series of narratives, all bound together in a larger narrative of a religious debate at Janaka's court. It is clear that the original frame to this story was ŚBM 11.6.3 ≈ ŚBK 13.6.3 (Renou 1948), where a similar debate occurred, but it was only Śākalya who questioned Yājñavalkya. In that story, Yājñavalkya foretold of Śākalya's death for "asking beyond" *prāṇa* ("breath").

BĀU 3 utilizes this story as a frame, but also greatly modifies and elaborates on it. BĀU 3 begins similarly to the ŚB account—Janaka is holding a sacrifice and declares a contest to determine the most learned in *brahman* (*brahmiṣṭha*). However, rather than one Brahmin challenging Yājñavalkya as in the ŚB, he is questioned by a series of eight Brahmins (with Gārgī questioning on two occasions). Witzel (1987b, 402–403) has pointed out that a number of figures attending the debate represent different western schools, particularly the *Ṛgveda* (ṚV) (summarized below). All, including Yājñavalkya, are stated to be Kuru-Pañcāla Brahmins at the beginning of the text.

dramatis personae[19]

Aśvala represents the Āśvalāyana Ṛgvedic school.
Kahola Kauṣītakeya is a descendent of the reputed author of the Ṛgvedic *Kauṣītaki Brāhmaṇa* and *Āraṇyaka*.
Uddālaka Āruṇi is famous in the *Chāndogya Upaniṣad* and comes from a territory west of Videha.
Gārgī's name indicates she is from the Gārga clan which "seems to represent the (originally) more Western schools." (Witzel 1987b, 403). Gārgī is treated separately below.
Śākalya (or his tradition) composed the *padapāṭha* of the Ṛgveda.

Aśvala, Kahola, and Śākalya are all associated with the ṚV, while Uddālaka and Gārgī are probably western. The remaining three (Jāratkārava Ārtabhāga, Bhujyu Lāhyāyani, and Uṣasta Cākrāyaṇa) are less known. Sāmaśravas, Yājñavalkya's student, is mentioned tangentially as the one who drives away the cows for Yājñavalkya. Fišer has argued that since certain characters are not known in the previous record, this text has "no historical value." He continues: "Neither a *hotar* of Janaka by [the] name Aśvala nor a disciple of Yājñavalkya called Sāmaśravas appears anywhere else in the Veda" (1984, 76).

To claim that this suggests "no historical value" is questionable reasoning on Fišer's part, if not counter to the logic used in his larger argument. Fišer has argued that the debate appears contrived—that is, it is a clear fiction determined to exalt Yājñavalkya. One would then, following his logic, expect *more known* characters to indicate the fictitious nature of the text, particularly to exalt the position of Yājñavalkya. The fact that there are three lesser known figures could then argue for the possibility of a historical precedent for this story. Further, we know that Yājñavalkya has been associated with Uddālaka (Āruṇi in ŚBM 5.5.5.14 ≈ ŚBK 7.5.3.11) and Kahoḍa Kauṣītaki (ŚBM 2.4.3.1–12 ≈ ŚBK 1.3.2.1–12). Are we to take their portrayal here as historical or not based on that prior textual mention? In any event, simply whether a character did not appear previously in the prior textual record has no historical weight. Whether they are the historically real members of the schools in question is irrelevant for my purposes—what matters is that they *do represent* those schools in the narrative.

Turning to the narrative proper, Brereton (1997) has done a close study on the structure of BĀU 3. It is not necessary to repeat his argument in full, but rather to summarize a few key conclusions that are important here. Brereton has pointed out that (1) different passages (particularly three paired dialogues: the Gandharva passages, Gārgī's two questions, and the repetition of the two "self within all" passages) are thematically linked to each other; (2) that a formal literary ring is formed by answers concerning sets of eight properties or things; (3) that BĀU 3.1 and 3.2 are formally connected by a play on the preverb *ati*;[20] and (4) that the poem at the end of our story (3.9.28) returns to the theme of immortality and death introduced in the beginning. The binding themes in all the dialogues are a concern with the movement in this world and the next and the fundamental principle that lies behind it. His schema of the structure of the narrative also suggests that "perhaps the best way to approach this passage is to read it by the levels indicated in the initial schema rather than sequentially" (Brereton 1997, 14).

I do not disagree with Brereton's analysis or conclusions. In fact, it is the first article of which I am aware to take the literary nature and structure of the text seriously, rather than to follow the standard Indological tendency to parse out the repeated structures as textual accumulations and view them as distinct and unrelated to a larger whole. I would like, however, to propose a different narrative schema for understanding the text, one that follows the linearity of the narrative and shows contributory themes to those pointed out by Brereton. While BĀU chapter 3 contains a number of passages, perhaps from different sources, there are other literary means by which this chapter holds together: plot progression, thematic rings, formal markers of discourse, and narrative tension.

Structure of BĀU 3[21]

(Underlined words in table 2.1 refer either to the overriding theme or to the individual themes of each section)

Table 2.1

Frame: 3.1.1–2 Janaka sets the contest (cf. ŚB 11.6.3.1–2).
Overriding theme of death and immortality
(1) Theme of death and sacrifice

- **(A.1)** 3.1.3–6 Aśvala asks about the four *atimokṣas.*
  - **(A.1.1)** 3.1.7–10 Aśvala asks about their four equivalents.
    - A.1–2 discusses role of individual priests in aiding the *yajamāna* in overcoming death.
- **(A.2)** 3.2.1–9 Ārtabhāga asks about the eight *grahas* and eight *atigrahas.*
  - **(A.2.1)** 3.2.10–14 Ārtabhāga asks what happens when a person dies.
    - B.1–2 Double-meaning of *grahas* and *atigrahas* as sense organ and sense object and two types of sacrificial cups for offering soma. Concludes with death.
- **(A.3)** 3.3.1 Gandharva dialogue: Bhujyu asks where the Pārikṣitas have gone after death.
  - **(A.3.1)** 3.3.2 Bhujyu rephrases question.
    - C.1–2 Concerned with sacrifice (*aśvamedha*) and death.

(2) Theme of *ātman* ("self")

- **(B.1)** 3.4 Uṣasta asks what is the obvious *brahman,* the "self within all."
  - **(B.1.1)** Rephrases question.
    - Retort to Yājñavalkya.
  - **(B.1.2)** Repeats question.
    - Repeats rephrasing of question.
- **(B.2)** 3.5 Kahola asks what is the obvious *brahman,* the "self within all."
- **(B.3)** Rephrases question.

(3) Theme of *brahman* and *ātman* ("self")

(C.1) 3.6 Gārgī asks what this world, water, wind, etc. are woven upon. Concludes with a question about *brahman*.

(C.2) 3.7 Gandharva dialogue: Uddālaka asks about the thread.

(C.2.1) 3.7.2 Asks about the inner-controller.

C.3) 3.8 Gārgī asks what the worlds, time, and space are woven upon.

C.1–3: C.1 pushes the topic to *brahman*. C.2: the thread (the "wind") is probably a metaphor for *brahman*, whereas the inner-controller is *ātman*. C.2 asks about the imperishable (*akṣara*), which is again probably *brahman*.

(4) Culmination: Yājñavalkya and Śākalya (encompassing all the themes)

(D.1) 3.9.1–9 Śākalya asks Yājñvalkya about the numbers of gods (cf. ŚB 11.6.3.4–10).

(D.2) 3.9.10–17 Śākalya asks about the eight persons, foundations, and gods.

3.9.18 Yājñavalkya mocks Śākalya (cf. ŚB 11.6.3.3).

(D.3) 3.9.19–25 Śākalya asks about the regions and their bases.

(D.4) 3.9.26 Questions about the bases of the vital breaths.

The self is *neti neti*, "not this, not that."

(4.1) 3.9.27 Yājñavalkya challenges Śākalya about the person connecting the eight persons and Śākalya dies (cf. ŚB 11.6.3.11).

(4.2) 3.9.28 Yājñavalkya asks from what a human grows after death. Concludes with *brahman*.

Complementary to Brereton's analysis of paired dialogues (Gārgī twice, the topic of *brahman* twice together, and the two Gandharva questions), much of this text is based on a series of doubles: Aśvala asks two thematically related groups of questions (A.1), as does Ārtabhāga (A.2); Bhujyu (A.3) has two questions for Yājñavalkya as does Uddālaka (C.2; both A.3 and B.2 based on knowledge given to them by a Gandharva); Gārgī occurs in two passages (C.1 and C.3), and in the second she repeats her question to Yājñavalkya; in B both questions about *brahman* are also similarly doubled, but B.1 doubles this even one more time.[22]

These paired questions and paired dialogues suggest that a compositional schema was followed. Though it may be that these episodes have come from separate sources, they are remarkably similar in form, suggesting that an editor would have had to manipulate the text for conformity. All this furthermore points to the idea that the text was conceived to be read as a unit.

These various pairs, however, serve different functions: for Aśvala (A.1), Ārtabhāga (A.2), and Uddālaka (C.2), pairing marks a related shift in theme (consonant with Brereton's analysis), covering the topics of movement in this world and the next and also the ultimate foundation;[23] for Bhujyu (A.3), Uṣasta (B.1), Kahola (B.2), and Gārgī (C.1 and 3) pairing serves a slightly different function—it imbues a tension in the narrative. For example, Bhujyu asks Yājñavalkya a question, but his answer is vague. "Where did the Pārikṣitas[24] come to be?" (*kva pārikṣitā abhavan*). Yājñavalkya answers, "They went to where the offerers of the horse sacrifice go" (*agacchan vai te tad yatrāśvamedhayājino*[25] *gacchantīti*). Here Yājñavalkya does not answer the question directly, leaving the actual place where the Pārikṣitas went after death unstated. This compels Bhujyu to rephrase the question, asking where the horse sacrificers go, to which Yājñavalkya answers directly. The same strategy is used with Uṣasta and Kahola asking Yājñavalkya to explain the "self within all" (*ātmā sarvāntaraḥ*) where Yājñavalkya answers elliptically with "that which is within all is your self" (*eṣa ta ātmā sarvāntaraḥ*) which seems little more than a rephrasing of the question. Uṣasta and Kahola are both forced to then ask "which one" (*katamaḥ*) is the self to receive a detailed answer. With Gārgī, she asks the same question about the foundation of the directions and time twice and Yājñavalkya answers both times that the foundation is "space" (*ākāśaḥ*). Only when Gārgī asks about the foundation of space, does Yājñavalkya answer in full, describing the "imperishable" (*akṣara*), by its non-properties.[26]

In these five cases, Yājñavalkya appears to be either dodging the question, trying to get away with an elliptical answer, or suggesting that a proper answer is only elicited by a proper question.[27] I suspect that this is meant to portray Yājñavalkya as sly and as not wanting to share all his knowledge. The effect of this doubling of the questions creates a narrative tension: one is left waiting for the proper answer, knowing that Yājñavalkya's initial answer is incomplete. Such a device not only connects each formally, but also serves to propel the combined content forward, building towards an answer.

There are other such devices which not only show that Yājñavalkya is reticent with his knowledge but also serve to enliven the debate. Uṣasta at 3.4 gets angry with Yājñavalkya, saying that his answer is like saying "this a cow and this a horse" (*gaurasāśva iti*). This is to say, that Yājñavalkya's initial answer is obvious and not sophisticated, a theme that also occurs in chapter 4. Or in 3.7, after Yājñavalkya claims to know the string (*sūtra*) and inner controller (*antaryāmin*), Uddālaka says that anyone can claim "I know, I know" (*veda vedeti*), but one has to explain it to prove that he really knows. Again, it appears that Yājñavalkya is portrayed as holding back his knowledge and only further probing will compel him to answer.

There is one other formal device, the threat of a shattered head, that pushes the story to its climax: an actual head shattering. The first threat of a shattered head occurs at 3.6, where Gārgī makes the mistake of asking about the foundation of *brahman*, itself the foundation of everything. Here Gārgī is allowed to stop questioning Yājñavalkya and thus avoids the consequences. This is followed by Uddālaka threatening Yājñavalkya with the same in 3.7.1, but here the threat is based on whether Yājñavalkya can properly answer the question, which he does and avoids the consequences. Gārgī then (3.8) questions Yājñavalkya a second time, but intensifies the threat as her questions are "two enemy piercing arrows" (*dvau bāṇavantau sapatnātivyādhinau*). Yājñavalkya is able to give the proper answers, avoiding any dire consequences. It is here that Gārgī tries to close the debate, claiming that no one will beat Yājñavalkya. In this fashion, we can view this device as:

> threat (3.6): counter-threat (3.7): intensification of the threat (3.8)

This debate progresses from "the sacrifice and death theme," to a discussion of *ātman*, to *brahman* and *ātman*; it then culminates in Śākalya's long and elaborate questioning (3.9) on the number of gods, the eight persons, the foundations and gods, the regions and their bases, and the bases of the vital breaths. It is here that Yājñavalkya threatens Śākalaya with a shattered head if he is not able to answer his question about the "person who is the hidden connection" (*aupaniṣad*) that connects the worlds, the gods, etc. and takes them away, brings them back, and transcends them. Śākalya is not able to answer:

> *taṁ ha na mene śākalyaḥ | tasya ha mūrdhā vipapāta | api hāsya parimoṣiṇo 'sthīny apajahrur anyan manyamānāḥ* ||(26)

> Alas, Śākalya did not know him. His head did, indeed, shatter apart. Robbers, moreover, stole his bones, thinking they were something else.

It is here that the head-shattering foretold by Yājñavalkya in ŚB 11.6.3 is said to have occurred.[28] Thus, the concluding structure of this text is a progressively intensifying climax to the story—

> threat (3.6): counter-threat (3.7): intensification (3.8): actual head-shattering (3.9)[29]

As I have shown (2011a), death in various forms—both abstract and concrete—are a binding theme in this chapter. Given Yājñavalkya's association with innovativeness, his view of what occurs after death is particularly important, both in his own biography but also in the history of the early religious tradition. This chapter culminates with a riddle on the nature and potential for rebirth and has been the a topic of some discussion, albeit not previously in the larger context that I have laid out.

Yājñavalkya's Riddle (BĀUK 3.9.28)[30]

Following Śākalya's rather graphic defeat at the conclusion of the *brahmodya* of BĀU chapter 3, Yājñavalkya challenges the assembled Brahmins with a riddle regarding the nature of birth and death (3.9.28). Preceding this riddle, Yājñavalkya not only dares any priest to challenge him but also states that they can do so collectively if they so wish. "Now Yājñavalkya said, 'Distinguished Brahmins, let whomever of you who desires question me or let all of you question me. Let whomever desires me to question him or let me question all of you.'"[31]

The all-inclusiveness of this statement implies that not only has Yājñavalkya's superiority been established (both as the questioner and the questioned), but it is also a means by which the other priests are forced to accept his superiority over them, individually and collectively. Having seen Śākalya's head shatter by challenging Yājñavalkya's knowledge of the sacrifice, immortality, and the universe, the Brahmins do not rise to his challenge. Though none accept, Yājñavalkya questions them with a riddle that stands at the conclusion of this chapter as something of an enigma, where the Brahmins stand mute.

It is likely that this riddle may be derived from a separate source as the immediately preceding *te ha brāhmaṇā na dadhṛṣuḥ* ("Those very Brahmins did not dare")[32] is an exact verbal echo of the Brahmins' response when the challenge was put forth by Janaka at the start of our text (3.1.2). This phrase may have, at some historical point, served to close the narrative after the final and most graphic defeat of the most reputed Brahmin. Thus, prior to this addendum, the literary ring may have been that the Brahmins did not dare rise to Janaka's challenge at the beginning and lay claim to be the *brahmiṣṭha* ("most learned in *brahman*") nor did they dare to challenge Yājñavalkya's claim of the same at the end.

At least according to the received texts, however, the debate is not quite over. Yājñavalkya challenges the assembled Brahmins, even though they had declined his offer, with a final riddle on the nature of death and rebirth. This riddle, in itself and in the context of the larger narrative, has been the subject of some debate both because the riddle does not appear to make sense in itself and if it does (such as in Horsch 1966) it does not make sense in the larger narrative (see Brereton 1997). Thus, this section is concerned with not only understanding the riddle and (what I argue is) its possible answer, but also with how this riddle fits into the larger Yājñavalkya narrative. I suggest that not only have modern scholars been confused about the meaning of this riddle, but that the early commentators equally had difficulty reconciling its meaning. This is, I argue, because the riddle itself became confused during the period of its composition and subsequent elaboration. In support of this, I posit what the original riddle was, how it was added to and manipulated, and where and how the original meaning of the riddle became obscured.[33] In the larger context of this chapter, this section also functions as an example of the complex textual interpenetration of both recensions as well as an early affirmation of reincarnation.

The metaphor of a human being and a tree is quite straightforward in the beginning of the riddle of BĀUK 3.9.28 (see table 2.2).[34] Verses 1–3 are particularly detailed in their comparison of a man to a tree in an attempt to show the physical similarities between the two.[35] In verse 4, though, an apparent contradiction in the metaphor is put

Table 2.2

<table>
<tr><td>So Yājñavalkya questioned them
with these verses.</td><td>tān haitaiḥ ślokaiḥ papraccha |</td></tr>
<tr><td>(1) As is a mighty tree,
so truly is man.
His body hairs are leaves,
his skin the outer bark.</td><td>yathā vr̥kṣo vanaspatis
tathaiva puruṣo 'mr̥ṣā |
tasya lomāni parṇāni
tvag asyotpāṭikā bahiḥ ||</td></tr>
<tr><td>(2) Blood flows from his skin,
[as] sap flows from [the tree's] skin.
From the pricked skin [blood] comes,
as sap from a cut tree.</td><td>tvaca evāsya rudhiraṃ
prasyandi tvaca utpaṭaḥ |
tasmāt tad ātr̥ṇṇāt praiti
raso vr̥kṣād ivāhatāt ||</td></tr>
<tr><td>(3) His flesh is the sapwood,
the tendons are the fibers—that's certain.
His bones are the heartwood,
his marrow made equal to [its] marrow (i.e., pith).</td><td>māṁsāny asya śakarāṇi
kināṭaṁ snāva tat sthiram ||
asthīny antarato dārūṇi
majjā majjopamā kr̥tā ||</td></tr>
<tr><td>(4a) A tree, when cut down grows
(4b) again from the root in newer form.
(4c) A mortal man who is cut down by death,
(4d) from what root will he grow?</td><td>yad vr̥kṣo vr̥kṇo rohati
mūlān navataraḥ punaḥ |
martyaḥ svin mr̥tyunā vr̥kṇaḥ
kasmān mūlāt prarohati ||</td></tr>
<tr><td>(5a) Do not say "from semen,"
(5b) that is produced from him while he is alive.
(5c) Just as a tree sprouts from a seed,
(5d) having died, [a person?] is born immediately.</td><td>retasa iti mā vocata
jīvatas tat prajāyate |
dhānāruha iva vai vr̥kṣo
'ñjasā pretya sambhavaḥ ||</td></tr>
<tr><td>(6a) When torn up with its root,
(6b) a tree will not be born again.
(6c) A mortal man who is cut down by death,
(6d) from what root will he grow?</td><td>yat samūlam āvr̥heyur
vr̥kṣaṃ na punar ābhavet |
martyaḥ svin mr̥tyunā vr̥kṇaḥ
kasmān mūlāt prarohati ||</td></tr>
<tr><td>(7a) He is born, [but] not born.
(7b) who would give birth to him again?
(8a) Perception, bliss, brahman,
(8b) That is the gift of the giver, the highest goal.
(8c) for the one who knows this stands firm.</td><td>jāta eva na jāyate
ko nv enaṃ janayet punaḥ |
vijñānam ānandaṃ brahma
rātir dātuḥ parāyaṇam
tiṣṭhamānasya tadvida iti || (28)</td></tr>
</table>

forth as a question: A tree regrows from its root, but from what root (*mūla*) does a man grow if he is cut down by death (*mṛtyunā*)? 4a parallels 4c, and 4b parallels 4d. This can be simplified as:

> (4a) tree cut down (presumably by an axe) = (4c) man cut down by death
>
> (4b) grows again from the root = (4d) grows again from what root?

Thus, at this point, the riddle is asking whether there is a resolution to the possible contradiction: A tree has an obvious, tangible root that facilitates regrowth, but what about a man cut down by death?

Verse 5 qualifies the riddle, excluding the answer of "semen" (*retas*) as the "root" which facilitates rebirth, because the bearer of the semen produces it "while he is alive" (*jīvataḥ*). Verse 5 is, in essence, arguing against another prevalent, older notion that a man is born again through his progeny and therefore attains immortality through procreation (as the children are supposed to carry out certain death rites that will allow the father to pass through the heavenly worlds).[36] Further, the use of the word *jīvataḥ* suggests an implicit argument against the idea that the *ātman* could somehow exist in two places simultaneously—the man is "living" when the seed is produced, so his "self" could not also be the one being reborn. 5cd, which has caused some confusion, is dealt with below.

Verse 6 is a rephrasing of 4, focusing not on the root (as 4b and the interrogative correlate 4d), but the lack thereof.[37] That 6 is intended as a rephrasing of 4 is clear not only from the structural parallel, but also from the exact phrase being repeated twice: *martyaḥ svin mṛtyunā vṛkṇaḥ kasmān mūlāt prarohati* (4cd and 6cd). Lines 6a and 6b take the comparison of the death of a man and that of a tree one step further than 4: a tree torn up with its root (*samūlam āvṛheyuḥ*) is a death without an apparent basis to facilitate rebirth. Implicit in the following question (6d: from what root will he grow?) is whether man's fate is like that of "being uprooted" rather than just "being cut down." Note that 6a/6c and 6b/6d are not exact correlates as are 4b and 4d—man in 6c is still "cut down by death" (*mṛtyunā vṛkṇaḥ*) and is not said to be "torn up with its root" (*samūlam āvṛheyuḥ*) as the tree in 6a.

(6a) tree is torn up with its root ≈ (6c) man cut down by death

(6b) not born again ≈ (6d) from what root will he grow?

The metaphoric symmetry of 4 is ruptured in 6, as the exact parallel would have been the man being "uprooted" by death in 6c. Line 6d is also not a simple interrogative modification of 6b (as 4d is of 4b). Up until this point there is a progressive qualifying of the initial riddle: (a) 4d asks the question; (b) 5 qualifies the question; (c) 6ab again qualifies the question; and (d) 6d repeats the question in the exact form. The riddle, so far, can be simplified as:

Question, 4d: what is man's root?
Qualification, 5ab: answer is not semen
5cd: unclear, though I suggest a comparison of semen and seed, qualifying 5ab.

Qualification, 6ab: A tree can be uprooted,

Question repeated, 6d: but what is man's root?

jāta eva na jāyate

7ab has created the most interpretive difficulties for scholars and traditional commentators alike who attempted to make sense of this riddle. The fundamental problem appears to be that 7a, on a surface reading, denies the premise of the riddle. Literally, *jāta eva na jāyate ko nv enaṃ janayet punaḥ* means: "He is born, [but] not born. Who would give birth to him again?"

Most scholars have felt inclined to read *punaḥ* into the first phrase and translate as: "Once he's born, he can't be born again" (trans. Olivelle 1998, 103) or "Though born, he is not born again" (trans., Roebuck 2000, 70). Translating in such a manner makes it appear more strongly that rebirth (the question from 4) has been denied outright within the riddle itself. Horsch (1966, 159), perhaps the most ardent supporter of this reading, has argued that the text purports an *Anihilationstheorie* (*ucchedavāda*)—that is, there is no "root" to facilitate man's rebirth.

The problem of interpreting 7a is also apparent within the tradition itself. How do believers of karma and reincarnation, which was prevalent by the time of the earliest commentaries, reconcile the apparent denial of such a theory in an authoritative (*śruti*) text? Śaṅkara, for example, utilizes a creative, if obviously fallacious, interpretive strategy. He takes the initial *jāta eva* as an opponent's possible view and the remaining part of the phrase (*na jāyate*) as a response. Madhavananda (trans., 1997, 393) translates this passage in light of the commentary as: "If you think he is ever born, I say, no, he is again born." In this fashion, an apparently negative statement has been made to say exactly its opposite.

That this is a questionable historical (versus religious) argument is quite clear. If the compilers expected the text to be read as Śaṅkara intends, it certainly would have been composed differently to avoid such confusion. An interpretive move such as Śaṅkara's is a strained attempt to make a negative statement which seems contradictory to later tradition into an orthodox one. Śaṅkara is right, however, in noticing that there is a problem with this passage, but not only because it is against tradition as he understands it. This passage would also be counter to the rather obvious intent of the rest of the Yājñavalkyakāṇḍa—whose stated purpose from the beginning is to discuss death, birth into other worlds, and immortality. Further, as I will argue, Śaṅkara was correct in contending that this passage was not intended to deny rebirth—but for reasons different than he himself put forth.

If one were to follow Horsch's view (1966, 159), this whole poem represents an *Anihilationstheorie*—an annihilation of man at death, comparable to the uprootedness of a tree. Horsch sees a direct parallel with 6a and 6c, while 6d is simply a rhetorical question: From what will a man grow again? The answer is apparently "from nothing," because there exists no principle/root from which a man uprooted by death could be born again.

The problems with this interpretation have been most recently pointed out by Brereton (1997, 14n48), and an attempt to find karma/reincarnation theory in this passage has been carried out by Hock (2002, 284ff). Most importantly, as Brereton succinctly pointed out, such an *Anihilationstheorie* would contradict much of what Yājñavalkya has said, both in this section and throughout the text thus far: 3.1.10 discusses worlds won by proper sacrifice; 3.2.13 discusses action and its correlate reward ("good by good action, bad by bad");[38] 3.3.2 states that a "knower" averts repeated death (*punarmṛtyu*); and the discussion of 3.7 focuses on the immortal (*amṛtaḥ*).[39]

A further problem in Horsch's interpretation also arises: Why would an elaborate riddle, culminating a discussion principally concerned with other worlds and immortality, deny its own premise? The riddle, then, would not be much of a riddle if the answer is explicitly stated within it.[40] Adding more complication to Horsch's theory is the fact that BĀUM places this line much earlier: 7ab is in the position of 5cd, 5cd becomes 6ab, and the rest shifts forward accordingly. If this line really was meant to be the answer to the riddle (i.e., there is no root of any kind) then why would it appear so early in BĀUM, making the rest of the riddle unnecessary?

It is in BĀUM, I contend, that what appears interpretively difficult in BĀUK is not so difficult after all. If BĀUM is read in itself (rather than simply as a counterpoint to BĀUK), the apparent problems of K can be seen in a new light.

Hock (2002) is the first scholar, as far as I am aware, to deal directly with this passage in the M recension.[41] His attempt at reconciling the meaning of this passage with the rest of the text is based on Vasudeva's commentary. Hock contrasts what he sees as two fundamentally different understandings of this passage. The first, the supposed "Western (or western-influenced)" (2002, 284–285) interpretation, reads the passage similar to Horsch: "(But once) born is not born (again)."[42] The second, indigenous interpretation (i.e., Vasudeva on BĀUM 3.9.30–34 = BĀUK 3.9.28) is: "He is (already) born; he is not being born (and in the present case we are asking how somebody dead may be born again)."

Hock (2002) gives a grammatical rationale for the difference between the two interpretations. He states, "Although putting a sentence boundary into the middle of the first half-line may be less natural than the [Western] interpretation, this is not a strong enough argument for rejecting the Indian interpretation." (285). I would phrase this somewhat differently, not viewing the issue as a "sentence boundary," but rather as a question of an implied conjunct and which clause is the subordinate clause (*jāta eva* or *na jāyate*). For our purposes the difference in translation, put literally, is between "(But) just born [sub. clause], he is not born/being born"[43] or "He is just born, (but/and) not born/being born [sub. clause]." Of course, both translations require a conjunct term ("but," "and," etc.) and that implied conjunct is debatable. Viewed in this light, for our purposes if not for a larger grammatical argument, there is little difference between the two translations. But the question still remains: What does this phrase mean in the context of the riddle?

As was stated earlier, BĀUM positions 7ab much earlier in the riddle, making Horsch's interpretation more difficult to reconcile with the rest of the text. In fact, on a close reading, the BĀUM version allows for a different contextual reading of the poem, one that presents a more coherent picture of this passage and its relation to the rest of the riddle and BĀU chapter 3 as a whole.[44]

It is here necessary to translate the relevant part of M's version of the poem (verses 1–3 have been left out as they are irrelevant to this argument and the variants are minimal).[45]

(* marks a shift of line order in relation to K)

(4a) When the tree is cut down,

(4b) it grows again from the root in newer form.

(4c) A mortal man who is cut down by death,

(4d) from what root will he grow?

(5a) Do not say "from semen,"

(5b) that is produced from him while he is alive.

(5c)* He is just born, [but/and] not born/being born.

(5d) who would give birth to him again?

(6a)* A[46] tree sprouts from a seed,

(6b) Having died, [a person] is born from another.[47]

(6c)* When a tree is torn up[48] with its root,

(6d) it will not be born again.

(7a)* A mortal man who is cut down by death,

(7b) from what root will he grow?

(7c) Knowledge, bliss, *brahman*,

(7d) That is the gift of the giver,[49] the highest goal.

(8)—for the one who knows this stands firm.

I will first turn to *jāta eva na jāyate* from K and show how it is not so perplexing in M. In this version, as in 5(K), 5ab qualifies the question by excluding one possible answer, semen (*retas*), but 7ab(K) is now in position 5cd, which allows us to read its intent quite differently. Rather than *jāta eva na jāyate* denying the premise of the riddle (as Horsch argues), 5c here is a further qualification of the initial qualification ("Do not say 'from semen'"), as is 6. The text is telling us that a person is not being born (presumably from his own semen), *because he has already been born*, that is, he is alive. 5cd then is a further explanation of why the exclusion in 5a (semen) is correct.[50]

The contrasting verbal forms in this part of the riddle support this interpretation: *jātaḥ* is a past passive participle indicating a completed action while *jāyate* is a present third person singular indicating an action happening or going to happen.[51] Thus, the verb forms themselves indicate the exclusionary nature of the two clauses. The contrasting nature of these two verbs is further reinforced by the placement of *eva*. As *eva*'s primary function is to emphasize the word that precedes it, here that emphasis is exclusionary—it is on the completed nature of the past participle.[52] Viewed in this way, the most proper translation here should be: "he is already (*eva*) born [and] not being born."

Supporting this interpretation is a word play in the M recension. As it cannot be reproduced well in English, I shall point it out in the Sanskrit.

5ab *retasa iti mā vocata* <u>*jīvatas*</u> *tat* <u>*prajāyate*</u>
5cd <u>*jāta*</u> *eva na* <u>*jāyate*</u> *ko nv enaṃ* <u>*janayet*</u> *punaḥ*

What we have here are multiple forms of the verb-root √*jan* (with the often correlated root √*jīv*) used in a rather clever play on grammatical forms—present participle, present indicative (with prefix), a past participle, another present indicative (without prefix), and an optative. In light of what has been argued about the meaning of the passage, these forms seem to support my interpretation: *jīvataḥ* indicates the person's state of being (i.e., alive); *prajāyate* indicates his producing of semen; *jātaḥ* as a past passive participle indicates that it is a completed action (he is *already* born—emphasized by *eva*) and apparently had little to nothing to do with bringing that event about;[53] *na jāyate* indicates he is not *being* born; *janayet* is the proper form for a question, perhaps expressing doubt. This verbal play is lost in BĀUK, as the position of 5cd is shifted to 7ab, where other forms of √*jan* or √*jīv* do not contextually surround it.

Reinterpreting 5cd(K) = 6ab(M)

As I mentioned earlier, another part of this BĀU riddle has caused some difficulty. This difficulty is based on the fact that K includes the particle *iva*, apparently indicating a continuation of the tree/man metaphor. K reads:

> (5c) Just as (*iva*) a tree sprouts from a seed,
> (5d) Having died, [a person?] is born immediately

That these two lines do not elicit an obvious comparison has caused interpretive difficulty: How are a man and a tree being compared here? 5d does not appear to obviously continue the metaphoric comparison in 5c. Particularly important is the final two words of this verse (*añjasā* and *pretya* or *apretya*). As mentioned earlier, Olivelle and Roebuck have adopted the reading of *añjasā apretya* in an attempt to make sense of K.

I have, in my translation, not adopted this reading, and this is because I think M retains the better reading and presents a solution to this interpretive difficulty. First and foremost, my reason for not adopting this reading is that the M recension does not allow for such a *sandhi*—*anyataḥ pretya* does not contain a potential coalesced final *a*/*ā* with a following *a*/*ā* as does *añjasāpretya* of K. Further, the M recension probably retains the more correct reading as it continues the series of repeated ablatives.

(6a) A tree sprouts from a seed
(6b) Having died [a person] is born from another.[54]

What is also striking in the M version of these two lines is that the particle *iva* in K, which would indicate a comparison between the tree and man, is here simply a conjunctive *u*. Hence unlike K, we do not have an explicit comparison between the tree and man.[55] Rather than continuing the man/tree metaphor as in K, M continues with a secondary comparison of the seed of a tree with the seed of a person. M has moved away from the larger metaphor and is focusing on the origin of a person/tree. "From another" (*anyataḥ*) in this context means "from another [seed]." "Having died" (*pretya*) reinforces my interpretation of *jāta eva na jāyate*—it is not a living person being reborn, but a person who has already died.

As I pointed out previously, 6ab(K) and 6cd(K) are not exact parallels—we are not told that the man is uprooted as a tree can be, but instead it is repeated that he is "cut down by death." It is also asked again from what "root" he will be born again.

(6a) tree is torn up with its root ≈ (6c) man cut down by death

(6b) not born again ≈ (6d) from what root will he grow?

In M, however, the placement of the phrase is different (see table 2.3), yielding a radically different reading.

What we appear to have in 6cd(M) is a qualification of what precedes it—a further explanation of a tree and its possibility of rebirth and *not* a metaphorical comparison. 6(M) is no longer a direct metaphor and 6cd has moved even further away from the metaphor and is simply discussing the nature of a tree. This is to say that a tree is

Table 2.3

(6a) A tree sprouts from a seed,
(6b) Having died, [a person] is born from another [seed].
(6c) When a tree is torn up with its root,
(6d) it will not be born again.

similar to a man in that both are born from "seed," but the nature of rebirth is not fundamentally the same—a tree can be uprooted. A "tree torn up with its root" does not have a metaphorical parallel with man in M. Thus all of 6M is a further qualification of "Do not say from seed" and 7M is a repetition of the initial question: a mortal man who is cut down by death, from what root will he grow?

The Development of the Riddle

Up until this point in this section, I have been concerned with trying to understand what this riddle may mean, particularly regarding certain problematic passages that either seem to deny the meaning of the riddle (*jāta eva na jāyate*) or which are confusing (5cd [K]). I have suggested that if we look at the line ordering of M in the first case and the word variations of M in the second, it seems clear that M has retained the proper reading whereas K has a confused version. Thus, Śaṅkara, who was working with the K version of the riddle, was compelled to interpretive extremes to reconcile these passages with the tradition as he understood it, but in so doing he preserved what appears to be the earliest intent of the riddle—that is, that rebirth does occur.

Concomitant, however, with the supposition that one tradition has somehow confused its own text is the need to explain how such a misunderstanding could have come about. What must be emphasized here is that I am not implying some intellectual failing on the part of the K tradition, but rather that the K tradition viewed the riddle slightly differently which led to a different version. In fact, the K tradition, in an attempt to keep the riddle consistent as it saw it, found it necessary to restructure the poem. At some point, the rationale for this restructuring became obscured, yet the fundamental meaning of the riddle was retained by the commentators.

Here it is necessary to posit a "core" to the riddle, one which was modified and expanded upon by both K and M traditions, but in different ways. I have shown so far that the M recension retains what appear to be better readings of the riddle. It is in M, also, that a coherent core riddle is found, where we can trace the accumulations and reinterpretations, culminating in the two versions of the riddle as we have them today.

The original core of the riddle is most likely M 1–4.

(1) As is a mighty tree,
so truly is man.
His body hairs are leaves,
his skin the outer bark.

(2) Blood flows from his skin,
[as] sap flows from [the tree's] skin.
From the pricked skin [blood] comes,
as sap from a cut tree.

(3) His flesh is the sapwood,
the tendons are the fibers—that's certain.
His bones are the heartwood,
his marrow made equal to [its] marrow (i.e., pith).

(4a) When the tree is cut down,
(4b) it grows again from the root in newer form.
(4c) A mortal man who is cut down by death,
(4d) from what root will he grow?

That this is the original core of the riddle is clear principally because of coherency: the metaphor of the man and the tree is maintained throughout; there is no secondary qualification of parts of the riddle; there is no metaphoric rupture (as in the case of "uprootedness"); and the riddle culminates in the question. Further, if this is the core of the riddle, it would be in accord with the rest of the Yājñavalkyakāṇḍa as no answer is given, particularly not one which contradicts the apparent intent of the chapter as a whole.

Verse 5 was probably the first addition to the riddle, excluding the rather popular belief (and rather easy answer) that one is reborn through one's children. Again, note that M here asks the riddle-question again, suggesting that M is attempting to retain the proper form of the riddle by concluding it with a question.

(5a) Do not say "from semen,"
(5b) that is produced from him when living.
(5c)* He is already born, [but] not born/being born.
(5d) who would give birth to him again?

Verses 6–7 were probably the second addition to the riddle, where 6ab is an elaboration of the exclusion of semen. 6cd, however, is a statement about how a tree and man are actually different: a tree can be torn up by its root, but the implication is that, contrary to Horsch, a man cannot. 6cd is apparently acknowledging that the metaphor is not absolute—what else would be the point of mentioning uprootedness when no "root" of man has been established in the first place to allow such a comparison? It is for this reason that man being "cut down by death" (i.e., *not* uprooted) is repeated and then the question is asked again.

> (6a) A tree sprouts from a seed,
> (6b) Having died, [a person] is born from another.
> (6c) When a tree is torn up with its root,
> (6d) it will not be born again.
> (7a) A mortal man who is cut down by death,
> (7b) from what root will he grow?
>
> 7cd and 8 were the final additions, perhaps together or perhaps in stages.[56]

If my hypothetical construction of the editorial stages of this riddle is correct, the question necessarily becomes: How did K "confuse" the riddle? The answer is rather straightforward and also completely understandable: *the K version wanted to retain the consistency of the metaphor.*

In M, after verse 4, the direct metaphor between a man and a tree is dropped almost altogether (the comparison shifts to the seed of a tree and semen). The K version, however, attempts to correct this, specifically by changing an *u* to the comparative *iva*[57] to continue the metaphor. However, a problem occurs in doing so: the question of the riddle is in the way—*jāta eva na jāyate ko nv enaṃ janayet punaḥ* (He is already born [and] not being born. Who would give birth to him again?). K moves this phrase so that 5 reads:

> (5a) Do not say "from semen,"
> (5b) that is produced from him when living.
> (5c) Just as a tree sprouts from a seed,
> (5d) having died, [a person] is born immediately.

By moving what was originally 5cd, the K version is able to continue the original metaphor of a man and a tree. That this was a somewhat unhappy fit and that its sense became confused can be seen by the time of Śaṅkara who himself could not reconcile 5cd, stating the *iva* was *anarthakaḥ* ("without meaning").[58]

If *jāta eva . . .* is moved to allow for a continuation of the metaphor of the man and tree, where would be the most natural place to move it to? Certainly, to the conclusion of the riddle to stand as the final question asked to the assembled Brahmins. This is precisely what the K version does: 5cd is moved to 7ab. However, in moving this line, the original context is lost. As I pointed out earlier, in M there is a play on grammatical forms of √*jan* and √*jīv* which supports the argument that this line originally continued the exclusion of a living person's direct role in his own rebirth. I have also pointed out that *anyataḥ* ("from another") is also probably a better reading and that it is also directly related to the semen/seed qualification under discussion.

The shifting of this line and the loss of its original context was a problem for traditional commentators as well, but while the original phrasing of the poem may have been lost in K, the original meaning—that rebirth does occur—was maintained. Śaṅkara, though taking interpretive stretches, was correct in his interpretation that this riddle does not deny rebirth. As he was committed to his received text, Śaṅkara certainly would not have tried to pull the riddle apart to see a historical development in its form, but instead he made the received text conform with religious truth as he understood it. Unlike Horsch's attempt to take the text at face value and avoid what he must have seen as textual intervention, the intervention on Śaṅkara's part, at least in this case, appears to be correct—the tradition accepted rebirth, so Saṅkara read the text as accepting rebirth.

An Answer to the Riddle?

The riddle poem ends with 8abc(K) and 7cd and 8(M).[59] Both recensions are fundamentally the same: there is a list of the highest principles/attainments ("Knowledge, bliss, *brahman*"), a statement which includes the reward for proper conduct ("That is the gift of the giver, the highest goal"), and a rather common Upaniṣadic statement about proper knowledge and its reward ("for the one who knows this stands firm"). The principal difference is an issue of line order. K ends:

> He is already born, [but] not being born.
> who is he that gives birth to him again?
> Knowledge, bliss, *brahman*,
> That is the gift of the giver, the highest goal.
> —for the one who knows this stands firm.

Whereas M ends:

> A mortal man who is cut down by death,
> from what root will he grow?
> Knowledge, bliss, *brahman*,
> That is the gift of the giver, the highest goal.
> —for the one who knows this stands firm.

Both versions end with the same structural logic: both ask the question of what facilitates rebirth, though the conclusion of M does not contain the problematic *jāta eva na jāyate* that led Horsch to his *Anihilationstheorie*. If the intention of this riddle posed by Yājñavalkya was not to deny rebirth, but rather to find out the principle that facilitates it, is there an answer suggested in this riddle and, further, in the larger context of the chapter?

If the riddle was not intended to deny rebirth, then an answer *is* possible. Though suggestive, rather than definitive, the final lines of the poem appear to be an answer, that is, the principle which facilitates rebirth is *knowledge, bliss, brahman*—likely synonyms. As has been pointed out by Brereton (1997), it is quite common in the Indian tradition to attempt to solve riddles retained in the textual tradition, where the original did not contain an answer. An answer is then attached in an attempt to remove the textual ambiguity.

Whether this was the original answer intended is not entirely clear. Śaṅkara takes it as such, but he takes the answer as not directly positioned in the story proper. It seems possible that once again Śaṅkara may have retained the proper meaning of the riddle. He comments, "The story is finished. The Śruti in its own form now tells us of the root of the universe, about which Yājñavalkya asked the Brāhmaṇas, and gives the words that directly describe Brahman: *knowledge* . . . which is also *bliss* . . . What is that? *Brahman*" (trans., Madhavananda 1997, 393).

I would like further to posit a corroborating possibility to the meaning of the poem as a whole, which is again suggestive and not definitive. Immediately prior to Yājñavalkya's challenge to the assembled Brahmins, Yājñavalkya had given Śākalya a final challenge—one which led to his graphic demise. Yājñavalkya says (3.9.26): "Those are the eight abodes, the eight worlds, the eight deities, the eight persons. I ask you about that person who is the hidden connection (*aupaniṣad*),[60] who carries away, returns, and goes beyond those persons? If you will not tell me, your head will shatter apart!"[61]

As is well known, Śākalya, due to his ignorance, does die.[62] As I suggested at the beginning of this section, Yājñavalkya's final challenge to the assembled Brahmins and their refusal to rise to that challenge probably was an ending to a story from a different source than the poem. There is, however, a logical reason why the poem may be an appropriate fit with the story.

To this I would like to suggest that the final riddle-poem may very well be a "rewriting" (through the metaphor of a tree) of Yājñavalkya's final challenge to Śākalya about the nature of the "person who is the hidden connection (*aupaniṣad*), who carries away, returns, and goes beyond those persons." This "person" and its function is remarkably similar to the "root" of the tree/man in the riddle-poem. It "carries away, returns, and goes beyond," which could refer to/be similar to death, (re)birth and transcendence found in the riddle-poem.[63] Thus, each question is dealing with reality in a different, but interrelated fashion. The sets of eight that Yājñavalkya is apparently referring to is the eight abodes, worlds, deities, and persons which were directly listed earlier in BĀU 3.9.14 (see table 2.4).[64]

It is not pertinent to this discussion to delve into the logic of why particular items are listed in the groups that they are and their interrelation. Needless to say, many are obvious, while others are not. However, what is of importance for this discussion is that cosmic entities or principles are being personified (as *puruṣas*). In a fashion, the above listing encompasses much of the Vedic cosmos whether concrete (e.g., earth, visible appearance, darkness, fire, etc.), abstract (e.g., life, death, truth), this-worldly (semen, women), or celestial or divine (e.g., the waters, Varuṇa, Prajāpati). In this fashion, Yājñavalkya's question to Śākalya at 3.9.27 is asking what the connecting link to all the above is, the foundation to the whole phenomenal world—what destroys ("carries away"), rebuilds anew ("returns"), and transcends ("goes beyond").

I am inclined to think that the riddle-poem is a rephrasing of Yājñavalkya's final question to Śākalya. In 3.9.26, Yājñavalkya's question is about the "person who is the hidden connection" of those entities listed in 3.9.14. Thus, it is a question about the underlying macrocosmic foundation of the universe. In the riddle-poem of 3.9.28, however, it appears to be the same question on the microcosmic level, that is, what is the foundation/root that facilitates man's rebirth. Through the earthly metaphor of a tree, the poem discusses the microcosmic principle behind death ("carries away"), rebirth ("returns"), and transcendence ("goes beyond") of a human being.

Consonant with this interpretation is that just prior to Yājñavalkya's question to Śākalya, Yājñavalkya had just described the *ātman* as *neti, neti* ("not this, not that"). This would suggest that the answer to Yājñavalkya's question to Śākalya was not *ātman* as, again, the answer would have been too apparent and his challenge would have been a nonchallenge (certainly not a "head-shattering" one). I suspect the answer to Yājñavalkya's final question to Śākalya is also *brahman*. In this way, *brahman* is seen as the foundational principle,

Table 2.4

Abodes	Worlds	Deities	Persons (p.)
Earth	fire	the immortal	bodily p.
Passion	heart	women	p. immersed in passion
visible appearances	sight	truth	p. in sun
Space	hearing	the quarters	p. connected with hearing and echo
Darkness	heart	death	shadow
visible appearances	sight	life	p. in mirror
Waters	heart	Varuṇa	p. in waters
Semen	heart	Prajāpati	p. connected w / son

the prime mover behind existence whether of the macrocosmic or the microcosmic. If such is the case, Gārgī's "asking beyond *brahman*" (3.6) is an asking beyond what is the absolute, fundamental principle, similar to Śākalya's "asking beyond *prāṇa*" (in ŚBM 11.6.3).[65] That is, there is nothing beyond what is, by definition, the foundation of everything (i.e., the cosmos, life, death, and also rebirth). Here, *ātman* and *brahman* are not equated, as in the later tradition, but are rather two mutually interrelated principles in the existence of man and his world.[66]

Bṛhadāraṇyaka 4

Following this dramatic ending to chapter 3, chapter 4 opens at Janaka's court. Hock (2002) has most recently analyzed BĀU 4. Like Brereton, he has attempted to find thematic links and literary rings in BĀU 3 and 4 as well as outside of the Yājñavalkyakāṇḍa proper.[67] Hock notes that these narratives are connected to chapter 3 of the BĀU not only through the presence of Yājñavalkya and Janaka, but also through the "giving of cows" repeated throughout. In support of this, one may add also that chapter 4 begins with a discussion of *brahman*, which, as I have shown, was already discussed in BĀU 3.6–3.9. I chart BĀU 4 below in table 2.5:[68]

It is clear that 4.1–2 are to be read together. In 4.1, after explaining the remaining three aspects of *brahman*, Yājñavalkya repeatedly turns down the offer of cows and elephants by telling Janaka that he has not really taught him anything:

> *pitā me 'manyata nānanuśiṣya hareteti* |
>
> My father believed that one should not take a gift without having taught [the giver something].

This phrase is repeated six times throughout 4.1 and concludes this section. BĀU 4.2 begins with Janaka getting down from his seat, apparently an act of servitude or humility towards Yājñavalkya. Thus, it is clear that these two sections are to be read together. 4.2 concludes with Janaka giving himself and Videha to Yājñavalkya.[69]

Table 2.5

Outer frame: Yājñavalkya at Janaka's Court.

Theme of *brahman*

Inner frame: Janaka is formally seated.

4.1 Janaka relates to Yājñavalkya various opinions of others regarding the nature of *brahman* (as speech, lifebreath, sight, hearing, mind, heart). Yājñavalkya says such explanations are incomplete (*ekapād*, "one-footed") and tells Janaka the complete explanation of each view of *brahman* (that is, adding the other three "feet:" the abode, the foundation, and how it should be venerated). In each case Janaka offers cows, bulls, and elephants, but Yājñavalkya refuses because he does not view his explanation as "real" or complete instruction.

Theme of death and *ātman*

Inner frame: Janaka comes down from his seat (presumably, a sign of studenthood towards Yājñavalkya).

4.2 Yājñavalkya teaches what happens to the ātman at death. He concludes by describing the self by its non-principles (ungraspable, undecaying, unbound, etc.). Yājñavalkya says that by knowing this Janaka is *abhaya* ("free from fear"). Janaka offers himself and his kingdom to Yājñavalkya.

Theme of *ātman*, sleep, and death

Inner frame: Yājñavalkya goes to Janaka (presumably, at court).

4.3–4 Yājñavalkya, thinking to himself that he won't tell Janaka the true nature of the self, goes to him and is compelled to teach him due to the boon that was given to him (ŚBM 11.6.2.1–10).

4.3.1–8 Source of the light of the self.

4.3.9–34 Dream and dreamless sleep.

4.3.35–4.2 Description of process of death.

4.3–6 Fate of those who desire at death.

4.6–25 Fate of the desireless at death.

Outer frame: Yājñavalkya and Maitreyī

Theme of immortality, "dearness," and the self

5 Dialogues on immortality and on the nature of the self (5.6–15).

BĀU 4.3–4 and BĀU 4.5 can be read as separate narratives or they can be read together with 4.1–2. Thematically, they are definitely interrelated—they continue the theme of death and immortality, and the principal novelty that is added is the comparison of death with dream and dreamless sleep.

The Teaching Narrative: BĀU 3–4

What has not been discussed in the scholarship on the Yājñavalkyakāṇḍa is that it is also narratively bound together by a larger theme, suggesting one way that various episodes were seen as interconnected. I call this a "teaching narrative"; this is to say that all of chapters 3 and 4 were seen—at least by the editors—as a cohesive whole bound together in theme and structure. This does not mean that, in practice, these episodes were necessarily heard one after the other, but rather that the editors had an editorial plan in how they were put together. Rather than the common scholarly view that these chapters are only nominally connected, I am suggesting that they are more intimately connected than previously recognized.

Hock (2002) has recently shown a number of links between chapters 3 and 4 of the BĀU (specifically regarding death) and I have pointed to the thematic link of *brahman* from BĀU 3.9.28 to 4.1 suggesting a continuation of the narrative. To this I would like to add that there is also a metastructure to these chapters taken together. As I pointed out earlier, ŚB 11.6 ≈ 13.6 is a series of narratives that progressively become more public—from Bhr̥gu's home, to Yājñavalkya then sneaking off to learn about the *agnihotra* at Janaka's court, to a public debate with Śākalya about the number of the gods. In the BĀU we have the same structure but inverted—the Śākalya debate (11.6.3) serves as the beginning, rather than the end, of the larger narrative that goes from the public to the progressively private. The BĀU begins with the public debate that ends in Śākalya's demise and is followed by: Yājñavalkya teaching Janaka at his court; Janaka stepping down from his seat to become Yājñavalkya's student; Janaka needing a boon to compel Yājñavalkya to talk; to Yājñavalkya talking privately with his wife, Maitreyī. All of these episodes flow together in a series of progressively "privatized" discourses—from the public court to the private court and from the private court to the home. In each case, the knowledge imparted by Yājñavalkya is more esoteric and more directly related to the fundamental principles behind birth, death, rebirth, and immortality.

While a binding theme in the narrative is the teachings imparted by Yājñavalkya, there is also a binding theme on the nature of knowledge and how it is acquired. This is evident in the framing of each narrative—a public debate with cows and prestige for the possessor of proper knowledge and a shattered head for one without;[70] a private discussion whereupon Janaka steps down from his seat in an act of humility to receive the proper teaching; the need to compel Yājñavalkya to teach Janaka through a boon; and, finally, the "dearness" towards his wife leading Yājñavalkya to teach her about immortality. All of this suggests that, at least according to the text, not only was Yājñavalkya viewed as the most eminent personage by his tradition, but that knowledge was closely guarded and required proper etiquette to obtain it.[71] This is seen in particular when Yājñavalkya continually compels his interlocutors into reasking or rephrasing their questions by not giving a full answer.

In BĀU 3, the topics covered were concerned with birth, death, rebirth, and immortality, but the concern there was more concrete—the relationship of the priests at the sacrifice to death, where a sacrificer goes after death, the nature of space and time, etc. In chapter 4, however, the topic matter is solely focused on "first principles" (*brahman*) and death in what appears to be an increasingly elaborate and abstracted discussion. Like chapter 3, chapter 4 culminates with verses, probably standing as a final proof-text validating the teachings that precede it. The text concludes with Janaka once again giving himself and Videha to Yājñavalkya and is followed by a *brahmāṇa*-style commentary justifying that *brahman* is the immortal (*amṛtaḥ*) and is free from fear (*abhaya*).

Such an inverted structure of privatized discourse in BĀU 3–4 suggests that it was modeled after ŚB 11.6 ≈ 13.6. This would appear the logical choice for the structure of BĀU as it is only in ŚB 11 ≈ 13 where longer narratives of Yājñavalkya and Janaka appear. This modeling of the structure of the text, however, should not lead one to discount it as "legendary." It simply means that the editor, putting together different accounts into a narrative whole, saw thematic and structural continuity across the passages and perhaps manipulated the text to maintain that continuity. As the chapters concern themselves with the *knowledge* of birth, rebirth, death and immortality, it is quite clever how the structure of the text parallels increasingly abstract knowledge in its various contexts: from public, to private, to one's student, to one's family.

Authority and Sarcasm, Part III

Turning once again to a topic introduced in the previous chapter, when disputing the opinion of others, Yājñavalkya is characteristically sarcastic. As in ŚBK 11.6.3 ≈ ŚBM 13.6.3, Yājñavalkya again claims that the assembled Brahmins are really *gokāma* ("desirous of cows") and are not necessarily assembled for some higher purpose (such as the sacrifice or its explicit goals). Interestingly, in the BĀU Yājñavalkya is not directly sarcastic with his various interlocutors, with the exception of Śākalya. The reason for this is the form of the dialogues themselves. From BĀU 3.1–8, Yājñavalkya is simply answering questions and were it not for an interlocutor, these passages would be remarkably similar in form, if not in content, to Yājñavalkya's proclamations that we encountered in the ŚB.[72]

Yājñavalkya's sarcasm, consistent with the framing from ŚB 11.6.3, reappears in his discussion with Śākalya in 3.9.[73] BĀU 3.9 is, however, a different form of dialogue than those found in the rest of BĀU 3 as well as ŚB 11.6.3. While BĀU 3.9 begins similarly to its predecessor (asking about the true number of gods), it quickly changes to an actual debate—where Yājñavalkya also challenges Śākalya. While the preceding passages of the BĀU are more like questioning sessions *with* Yājñavalkya proving he knows the right answer, the final debate in 3.9 is a challenge *between* Yājñavalkya and Śākalya. BĀU 3 then climaxes in a debate with an obvious winner and loser, though Śākalya loses more than just the debate.

The interlocking series of questions between Śākalya and Yājñavalkya are punctuated by a series of sarcastic statements which mark particular shifts in the dialogue. For example, when Yājñavalkya asks Śākalya about the deity associated with "that person composed of a son" (*ayaṃ putramayaḥ puruṣaḥ*), Yājñavalkya retorts (3.9.18):

> *śākalyeti hovāca yājñavalkyaḥ | tvāṁ svid ime brāhmaṇā aṅgārā-vakṣayaṇam akratā3 iti* (18)
>
> "O Śākalya," Yājñavalkya said, "have these Brahmins made you their fire-quencher?"

This phrase is nearly identical to the one found in ŚB 11.6.3 (*tvā́ṃ svichā́kalya brāhmaṇā́ ulmukāvakṣáyaṇam akratā3 íti*). While Olivelle has pointed out that this charge is more appropriate in the ŚB version of the story (1998, 512), where Śākalya is more obviously the representative of the Brahmins, in the BĀU it functions to mark a thematic shift in the discourse, from the various gods to *brahman* ("formulation of truth"). It may be the case that Yājñavalkya is stating that Śākalya's answer is incorrect, but that is not particularly clear as Śākalya's answer of *prajāpati* ("lord of offspring") would appear to be an appropriate answer to the question. Most likely, this line from ŚB was moved here to mark the shift of discourse, not only thematically, but also to remind the reader of Śākalya's impending doom.

Such an allusion also occurs at BĀU 3.9.25, when Śākalya asks what the "heart" (*hṛdaya*) is founded upon:

> *ahalliketi hovāca yājñavalkyaḥ | yatraitad anyatrāsman manyāsai | yad dhy etad*[74] *anyatrāsmat syāt chvāno vainad adyur vayāṁsi vainad vimathnīrann iti* (25)
>
> "You are an idiot!"[75] Yājñavalkya said, "should you think it is founded on something other than ourselves! Were it founded on something other than ourselves, dogs would eat it or birds would tear it up/steal it away!"

This insult also marks a thematic shift in the discourse: the previous questions by Śākalya were concerned with what certain things (water, semen, the moon, etc.) were founded upon. Here Yājñavalkya says that the heart can only be founded on "ourselves," and Sākalya continues to ask what "you and your self" (*tvaṃ cātmā ca*) are founded on. In this fashion, Yājñavalkya's insulting interjection leads Śākalya to change the topic to the nature of the self (*ātman*).

The sarcasm in BĀU 4 is much more muted, but this is easily explained by the fact that Yājñavalkya is engaged in one-on-one dialogues with either Janaka or Maitreyī. However, when others do appear in the text secondarily, Yājñavalkya's sarcasm emerges. For example, in 4.1.1, Janaka relays Jitvan Śailini's view of *brahman* as speech (*vāc*). Yājñavalkya responds:

> *yathā mātr̥mān pitr̥mān ācaryavān brūyāt tathā tac chailinir abravīd vāg vai brahmeti | avadato hi kiṁ syād iti | abravīt tu te tasyāyatanaṃ pratiṣṭhām |*
>
> "Śailini saying *brahman* is speech is like saying a person has a mother, father, and a teacher—because what could a person have without speech? But did he tell you its abode and foundation?"

Yājñavalkya goes on to teach Janaka the abode and foundation as well as the proper means to venerate these aspects of *brahman*. This structure repeats throughout 4.1 with different Brahmins being associated with different answers, all of which are incomplete and Yājñavalkya has to elaborate upon them. Others have translated this passage following Śaṅkara's interpretation: "Śailini says what anyone would say who had a mother, a father, and a teacher to teach him" (trans., Roebuck 2000, 71). The Sanskrit certainly allows such a translation, and this would be in accord with the fact that Yājñavalkya actually does admit that *brahman* is speech, etc.—only that the answer is not a complete one.[76]

I, among others, view the passage as a sarcastic statement.[77] While Śaṅkara and others view it as Yājñavalkya declaring that the other individuals are "educated" (i.e., taught first by the mother, then the father, and then the teacher), this interpretation is difficult to reconcile with the rest of the text as well as the picture we have of Yājñavalkya. First, in no other passage in all of the early literature is Yājñavalkya *ever* associated with making a positive statement about other Brahmins and their teachings. While he is sometimes associated with a particular rite (to praise it, etc.), he never is recorded in a noncontentious passage with other priests. In fact, all of the sarcastic passages related to Yājñavalkya are against others, and we have no passage or story where Yājñavalkya endorses other priests.

Second, translating following Saṅkara here seems to miss the point of the passage: Yājñavalkya calls their teachings *ekapād*, "one-footed"—that is, incomplete. Why would Yājñavalkya say that the other Brahmins are "educated" if their answers are incomplete? The rationale behind these claims of *brahman* is that a person cannot exist without them (because what could a person have without X?). This seems to be rather simple, straightforward logic which, I think, fits better with translating the remaining passage: "Śailini saying *brahman* is speech is like saying a person has a mother, father, and a teacher." Here, then, both statements are saying that the other teachers' viewpoints are obvious,[78] simple, and incomplete. This interpretation then would be in accord with Yājñavalkya constantly refusing the cows from Janaka, saying that he has not really taught Janaka anything. Even though Yājñavalkya taught him the various abodes and foundations, he himself did not even see this as a real teaching even though his teaching was more elaborate than any of the other priests.

All these cases of sarcasm in the BĀU, I contend, are justified by the narrative as Yājñavalkya is always correct in his interpretation of ritual, the cosmos, and the self. In the same fashion as the ŚB, sarcasm and authority go hand-in-hand. Though there are many cases where Yājñavalkya is not authoritative or simply speculated on a practice in the ŚB, he is not portrayed as sarcastic in those contexts. In both the BĀU and the ŚB, his sarcasm and authority are in tandem.

The use of sarcasm and wit, both in the ŚB and the BĀU, suggests a pattern—sarcasm is always used in a fashion that reinforces Yājñavalkya's opinion and denigrates another's position. Given its consistency, sarcasm clearly is a developed rhetorical strategy within the White Yarjurvedic tradition. The use of sarcasm, however, also suggests that the authority of the White YV tradition was not universally accepted. Such a strategy of sarcastically reinforcing one's opinion through denigrating another (clearly already established) tradition must have developed as the White YV tradition was establishing itself in contradistinction to the Black YV. It should be noted that such sarcasm is not a developed strategy in the Black YV tradition, which is logically consistent with the fact that the authority of that tradition came into place quite early and it may not have had to position itself against another, dominant tradition.

Gender as Argument[79]

If Yājñavalkya's sarcasm has been a point of interest for Indologists, so has also the position of women in the BĀU. The female characters found in the BĀU, especially Gārgī and Maitreyī, have been subject to various (often passionate) mutually exclusive interpretations—characterized often as unwise and intemperate or willful and strong. Most scholars, though, have focused on the question of whether or not the women in this text are actual historical females participating in philosophical debate as equals to men.[80] If taken as real, then this text is used as a proof-text to suggest a more gender-equal past. If taken as unreal, they are dismissed as myth or legend. As such, scholarship has used the characters in this text, to greater and lesser degrees, to extrapolate the roles of women in ancient India as a whole.[81] Thus, the question has always been *what* is represented in this text and not *how* is it presented.

In this section, I will examine the discourses of women in the BĀU in a different manner from most others. My hope is to move the discussion away from its origins as an orientalist argument about the fact or fiction of a text used in a grander discourse of colonial rule. I will here approach the women of the BĀU as characters in a larger philosophical narrative and *not* as agents in history. My concern is how these characters are narratively constructed and how they function in the BĀU within the greater political and philosophical agenda of the text. In this fashion we can then ask questions about the role(s) that these women play within the larger narrative structures, what motives may underlie their portrayal, and how these episodes relate to the larger arguments in the text. Then I will suggest what, if anything, can be said historically about the position of these literary women and how this may or may not relate to Vedic women in the ancient period. It should be pointed out that my arguments are not based on an "actuality" of the events described in the text, but rather on the literary form that those events have assumed. Any whole or partial actuality of events is not necessarily negated by the literary aspects those events may have taken on when transposed to a relatively fixed narrative. Any claims to historical actuality, however, must first deal with literary features of the text, because in the end what we have as evidence are narratives and not people.[82]

Before turning to the passages in question, it is necessary to put the women of our text into a somewhat larger context. This is necessary because, at least as far as the earlier textual record is concerned, the women portrayed in the BĀU do something rather revolutionary—they speak about ritual matters as relative equals to men.[83] Nowhere in the earlier textual record are human women portrayed as taking part in ritual debate, challenging a priest, and even, as we will see below, getting the better of many famed thinkers and ritualists. Such speech on the part of women in the BĀU is not simply a narrative device to get the story going or to introduce a particular theme,[84] though it does this too. One woman in BĀU "speaks boldly"[85] and debates vigorously with men in a philosophical arena, *brahmodya,* apparently previously closed to women.[86] What I hope to show here is that these characters are as much about positioning Yājñavalkya and the newly emerging White Yajurvedic tradition over and above other Vedic traditions as they are about philosophical arguments. Unlike many exclusively philosophical interpretations of this text, I argue that it is a fundamental mistake to disassociate the philosophical argumentation from the grander narrative it is a part of—that is, they function interdependently.

The BĀU, like all ancient Indian texts, was composed by and for men, and any discourse of women is at least one step removed. Our text is produced by Brahmin males to suit their own ends or ideas, and we cannot expect to recover any authentic female voice. As Jamison has noted,[87] looking for any authentic female voice runs counter to the nature of our evidence; the available literature from the early period was mediated through men of the highest castes and must have been modified throughout its history to conform, more or less, to orthodox understandings.

Though a recovery of any authentic voice may not be possible, we are not without means to analyze the roles of women in the BĀU. Since gender is a cultural construction, we may analyze that construction (and the latent motives and ideologies) to view the layers of discourse present. Taking a lead from literary and gender-oriented studies,[88] it is more fruitful in our case to view gender as a constructed entity (i.e., socially) within a constructed entity (i.e., the narrative).

In the BĀU, the female characters are within a larger cohesive narrative[89] that gives us a vantage point for comparison—not only with the same characters in the two different recensions (BĀUK/BĀUM; in Maitreyī's case, the story is told twice in each recension), but also with the other male characters' speech on related topics. While such a comparison does not allow us to extract any authentic female voice, it does allow us to pose several important questions regarding how gender is used in this text: How does the speech of women compare with the speech of men?[90] Why would a literary tradition dominated by men include women in a prominent place in this discussion? What does female speech do in the narrative? Thus, while we may not be able to define "gendered speech" in any definitive way, we can read this text as saying something about *how* women speak *in the text* and under what circumstances they do so in relation to philosophy.

The cast of characters in BĀU 3–4 that are defeated in debate by Yājñavalkya consists of many well-known figures from other textual traditions (the R̥V, in particular, perhaps because of its long-established authority).[91] I have argued in this book that this was a means to establish Yājñavalkya, his tradition, and his region over and above other well-known ritualists. But while many of these characters are famous in other traditions, there are a few characters about whom we know almost nothing. Gārgī, the only female in this debate, falls into this latter category.

Gārgī's Right to Speak

Most of the male characters in the BĀU come from established traditions which suggests the reasoning for their inclusion in the debate. There is no mention, however, of Gārgī in the early sources or those contemporaneous with the BĀU.[92] In BĀU 2.1K/M[93] and in the later genealogical lists of the BĀU, however, there appears to be an established family lineage of Gārgya.[94] In the first BĀU genealogy (2.6K/2.5M) there is no patronymic that could connect Gārgī to a Brahminical lineage establishing her authority to participate in this debate. In the second genealogy (the one concluding the Yājñavalkyakāṇḍa), however, we have: ". . . Gautama from Āgniveśya; Āgniveśya from Gārgya, Gārgya from Gārgya, Gārgya from Gautama . . ." (4.6.1K) and ". . . Pārāśaryāyaṇa from Gārgyāyaṇa, Gārgyāyaṇa from Uddālakāyana . . ." (4.6.2K).[95] In the concluding genealogy list of BĀUM,[96] sons of various Gārgīs are listed: ". . . the son of Pārāśarī from the son of Gārgī; the son of Gārgī from Pārāśarīkauṇḍinī; the son of Pārāśarīkauṇḍinī from the son of

Gārgī; the son of Gārgī from the son of Gārgī; the son of Gārgī from son of Bāḍeyī . . ."

Attempting to historicize such genealogies is problematic at best—many names overlap between the various lists, the relationships between the overlapping individuals do not necessarily correspond, names are repeated which suggest multiple people by the same name, and the lists hearken back to the ancient seers as well as *brahman* as the original progenitor of the lineage. The conclusion to both final M and K genealogies have Yājñavalkya as the original receiver of the White Yajurveda from the Sun, though his name is also within the final list as having received the same from Uddālaka.[97] Though it appears difficult, if not impossible, to reconstruct an actual verifiable historical lineage from these lists, they are nonetheless important in their own right. First and foremost, these lists serve to establish the authority of the texts and certain speakers within the text based on membership within and between priestly families. The names of the combatants of Yājñavalkya, while not necessarily the "real" or same individuals of the distant past, become emblematic of their familial priestly tradition. They are literary synecdoches or familial *bandhus*, if you will, by which the status of the character is confirmed. Though speaking of Purāṇic kingly lineages, what Thapar writes (2000, 709) equally applies here: "Genealogies are a commemoration of those who have passed away and, in some senses they are almost a cult of the dead. They record supposed ancestors, for, the connections do not necessarily have to be biological and are required in order that status be bestowed on those making the claims. . . . Therefore the nature of the connections sought by those constructing the genealogy are significant." In this vein we can then read Gārgī, though without a literary past, as having the necessary authority of genealogy to permit her entrance into such a debate.[98] Though the lists emphasize male students/teachers, Gārgī still has association through family lineage, but it is an association one step removed.[99]

Further, Thapar notes that most Purāṇic genealogies are often manipulated and changed over time to account for current circumstances. There is a grafting on (or removal) of names to genealogical lists. "They [genealogies] are rarely, if ever, faithful records of the past reality, but they can be memories of social relations. As such they are not records of individuals but of groups and generally those ranked high . . . They change over time and are rearranged if need be, the rearrangement being in accordance with the requirements of later times" (Thapar 2000, 709).

While tentative, it appears that each successive genealogy in the BĀU similarly added and modified the preceding one(s) to account for the rise to prominence of particular individuals in the text (and traditions). For example, Gārgya from 2.1 does not appear in a genealogy until 4.6 and Gārgī of 3.6 and 3.8 appears only in the genealogy of 6.5. Yājñavalkya of chapters 3–4 also does not appear in a genealogy until chapter 6.[100] As is well known, BĀU chapters 1–2, 3–4, and 5–6 were likely composed as sets in that same chronological order. The composers or compilers of the successive sections of the text are apparently accommodating the characters found in previous parts of the text, "grafting" them on to later lineages and justifying their roles after the fact.

Gārgī at Court

Gārgī appears in two sections (3.6 and 3.8), and she has the singular distinction of challenging Yājñavalkya twice.[101] Her first questioning session (3.6.1) shifts the topic of discussion from what I have termed the *ātman* theme of Uṣasta Cākrāyaṇa (3.4) and Kahola Kauṣītakeya (3.5) to questions about the nature of the cosmos.[102]

> *atha hainaṃ gārgī vācaknavī papraccha | yājñavalkyeti hovāca | yad idaṃ sarvam apsv otaṃ ca protaṃ ca kasmin nu khalv āpa otāś ca protāś ceti | vāyau gārgīti | kasmin nu khalu*[103] *vāyur otaś ca protaś ceti | antarikṣa-lokeṣu*[104] *gārgīti |*

> Next Gārgī Vācaknavī questioned him. "Yājñavalkya," she said, "This whole world is woven to and fro on the waters, but on what are the waters woven to and fro?"[105]
>
> "On air, Gārgī."
>
> "But on what is the air woven to and fro?"
>
> "On the middle worlds, Gārgī."

This questioning pattern continues in the same fashion, and the answers are summarized as follows: the middle worlds are woven on the worlds of the *gandharvas*; the worlds of the *gandharvas* on the worlds of the sun; the worlds of the sun on the worlds of the moon; the worlds of the moon on the worlds of stars; the worlds of stars on the worlds of gods; the worlds of gods on the worlds of Indra; the worlds of Indra on the worlds of Prajāpati.[106] The questions climax with:

> *kasmin nu khalu*[107] *prajāpatilokā otāś ca protāś ceti | brahmalokeṣu gārgīti | kasmin nu khalu*[108] *brahmalokā otāś ca protāś ceti | sa hovāca gārgi mātiprākṣīḥ | mā te mūrdhā vyapaptat*[109] *| anatipraśnyāṃ vai devatām atipṛcchasi*[110] *| gārgi mātiprākṣīr iti | tato ha gārgī vācaknavy upararāma* ||(1)

> "But on what are the worlds of Prajāpati woven to and fro?"
> "On the worlds of brahman, Gārgī."
> "But on what are the worlds of brahman woven to and fro?"
> Yājñavalkya said, "Gārgī, don't ask about what is beyond this, lest your head shatter apart! You are asking beyond the deity that should not be asked beyond. Gārgī, don't ask beyond [this!]"
> Thereupon, Gārgī Vācaknavī ceased questioning him.

ATI √PRAŚ

As the interpretation of a text is intimately, indeed inextricably, connected with our understanding of the language used, it is necessary here to make a philological aside. This aside, however, is necessary in giving the broader context of Gārgī's role in this text—particularly, how Yājñavalkya is reacting to her inquiry and what her inquiry actually appears to be about—before we turn to Gārgī directly. If, as Patton (1996) and others have argued, gender is "enacted" in discourse, at a more fundamental level, gender is enacted in the particular use of words in that discourse.

Most scholars have taken *ati √praś* to indicate that Gārgī is asking "too many questions," a plausible translation given that the questions she is asking are reductive and repetitive in nature. Read in this way, Yājñavalkya's warning of the "head-shattering" consequences is a means to stop Gārgī's apparent ad infinitum questioning. For example, D. Venkataramiah (1952, 221) writes: "Her array of questions on the origins of things in an infinite regressive series was so exasperating to Yājñavalkya that he had to curb her curiosity by portending death if she persisted."

Such an interpretation has allowed for rather unsubstantiated elaborations on the part of scholars—Gārgī had an "unquenchable thirst for philosophical knowledge" (Kane 1968, 366) or the reverse, she was "exceptionally presumptuous" (Edgerton 1965, 135). Variations on these views are too common to bear repeating.[111] As mentioned earlier, however, these scholarly interpretations make the a priori mistake of viewing these characters as historical agents. While there is nothing methodologically erroneous in determining personality traits of literary figures in particular contexts, it is not an end in itself nor does it necessarily tell us about a *historical* person. One must ask *why* the author portrayed a figure in a particular way and what that portrayal does for the larger narrative.

Translating *ati √praś* as asking "too many questions," I contend, does not fit the context of the dialogue, particularly in regard to Yājñavalkya's elaboration of the "head-shattering" consequences. To translate Yājñavalkya's statement, *anatipraśnyāṃ vai devatām atipr̥cchasi,* as "You are asking too many questions about a deity about whom one should not ask too many questions" does not make sense in the context of the dialogue for the simple reason that Gārgī has only asked one question about *brahman*.[112] One would be hard-pressed to argue that the whole series of questions is really only about one particular world and its associated deity (thus making the series of questions "too many questions"). The passage is, on its most obvious reading, about a series of worlds and how they are interconnected.

Another alternative interpretation could be that "one question" about *brahman* is "one too many" on Gārgī's part. Such an interpretation, though, is problematic because it would go against one of the larger goals of the narrative—to discuss *brahman* and *ātman*, even if circuitously and in the negative.

The parallel *ati √vad* in the oldest Upanishads invariably means "one who out-talks"—that is one who has shown that his knowledge is "beyond" (*ati*) others through debate.[113] This is also the sense that must be understood in 3.9.19, where *ati √vad* must be taken positively.[114] The principal meaning there is not that Yājñavalkya "talked more" than the other priests, but that he "out-talked" them; that is, he had the proper answer to every question. In this context, *ati* only secondarily has anything to do with quantity, where Yājñavalkya "talks more" in the sense that he has the final word.

For these reasons I take *ati √praś* to mean to "ask beyond."[115] In this fashion *ati* is more value neutral ("beyond"), and the context must be used to decide whether "beyond" is to be taken in a positive (e.g., "asked / talked beyond others") or a negative sense (e.g., "asked / talked beyond decorum / appropriateness"). In the context of our passage, where only one question has been asked about *brahman, ati √praś* must mean that to ask "beyond" *brahman* is to ask a question that is either fundamentally misconceived (i.e., there is nothing that *brahman* can be woven on) and / or that the question asked is inappropriate in some other fashion.[116]

Yājñavalkya's Threat

Since Gārgī's questions elicit a hierarchical ordering of the worlds, the fact that it culminates with *brahman* should not come as a surprise. What is a bit surprising here, though, is that Gārgī is the first character in the story to push the discussion to the topic of *brahman*.[117] Previous to Gārgī's questioning, as I argue, there are two principal themes: the first, encompassing 3.1–3, is directly concerned with the sacrifice and death; passages 3.4–5 then shift the discussion to the nature of the self (*ātman*). What Gārgī does in 3.6 is try to move the topic to the nature of *brahman*.[118] The implication of Yājñavalkya's threat is that one cannot ask about the foundation of something that is, by definition, the foundation of everything. In this manner, Yājñavalkya's warning of a "shattered head" is not an attempt to end ad infinitum questioning as others have suggested, but rather it is because the discussion itself *has become finite* and Gārgī simply does not realize it.[119]

Gārgī Fights Back

After Uddālaka's question, which focuses on the inner controller (the *antaryāmin*), and Yājñavalkya's answer, Gārgī once again challenges Yājñavalkya. This time, however, her rhetoric shifts along with the nature of her question. While the other priests that were present sometimes engaged in "spirited" comments while questioning Yājñavalkya (such as 3.4.2 and 3.7.1), perhaps spurred on by their anger (3.1.2), Gārgī's initial questioning in 3.6 appears to be quite passive. This is certainly not the case in 3.8:[120]

> **1.** Next (Gārgī) Vācaknavī said, "Distinguished Brahmins! I will ask him two questions. If he gives me the answers, none of you will ever beat him in this debate about *brahman*."
> "Ask, Gārgī."
>
> **2.** She said, "As a warrior-son of Kāśī or Videha strings his unstrung bow, takes two enemy-piercing arrows in hand, and rises up [in battle], Yājñavalkya, so I rise up against you with two questions. Answer me these two!"
> "Ask, Gārgī."
>
> **3.** She said, "That which is above the sky, that which is below the earth, that which is between the sky and the earth, and that which people call the past, present, and future—on what are these woven to and fro?"
>
> **4.** He said, "That which is above the sky, that which is below the earth, that which is between the sky and the earth, and that which people call the past, present, and future—on space, Gārgī, these are woven to and fro."
>
> **5.** She said, "Honor to you, Yājñavalkya, you sure solved that one for me. Brace yourself for the second!"
> "Ask, Gārgī."
>
> **6.** She said, "That which is above the sky, that which is below the earth, that which is between the sky and the earth, and that which people call the past, present, and future—on what are these woven to and fro?"
>
> **7.** He said, "That which is above the sky, that which is below the earth, that which is between the sky and the earth, and that which people call the past, present, and future—just on space, Gārgī, these are woven to and fro."
> "But *on what* is space woven to and fro?"

8. He said, "That, Gārgī, is the imperishable, and Brahmins speak [of it] as neither gross nor fine, neither short nor long, without blood or fat, without shadow or darkness, without air or space, without contact, without taste or smell, without sight or hearing, without speech or mind, without energy or life-breath, without mouth or measure,[121] without inside or out; it does not eat anything and nothing eats it.

9. "At the command of this imperishable, Gārgī, the sun and the moon remain separate. At the command of this imperishable, Gārgī, the sky and the earth remain separate. At the command of this imperishable, Gārgī, the seconds and hours, the days and nights, the fortnights and months, and the seasons and years remain separate. At the command of this imperishable, Gārgī, some rivers flow east from the snowy mountains and others west, each in their appropriate directions. At the command of this imperishable, Gārgī, men praise donors, gods are dependent on *yajamānas* and the forefathers on the ancestral offering-ladle.

10. "Without knowing this imperishable, if one makes offerings, carries out sacrifices, and performs austerities in this world for many thousand years, Gārgī, his deeds would amount to nothing. One who departs from this world without knowing this imperishable, Gārgī, is wretched. Now, one who departs from this world knowing this imperishable, Gārgī, he is a Brahmin.

11. "This imperishable, Gārgī, is the seer but isn't seen; is the hearer, but isn't heard; is the thinker, but isn't thought of; is the perceiver, but isn't perceived. Other than this, there is no seer. Other than this, there is no hearer. Other than this, there is no thinker. Other than this, there is no perceiver. On this imperishable, Gārgī, space is woven to and fro."

12. She said, "Distinguished Brahmins, you should think yourself big men to have escaped from him by [only] pay-

> ing homage. None of you will ever beat him in this debate about *brahman*!"[122]
>
> Thereupon (Gārgī) Vācaknavī ceased questioning him.

As is readily apparent, the portrayal of Gārgī's tone and manner has changed dramatically. Rather than passively asking a series of reductive questions as she was previously portrayed, Gārgī is shown as forceful, perhaps even hyperbolic, in the way she approaches Yājñavalkya.[123] Rather than attempting to reduce this to her "impetuous" or "over-eager" behavior, we should look first to how this portrayal may function in the larger narrative and consider why Gārgī is portrayed in this manner.

First and foremost, Gārgī's impassioned rhetoric clues the audience to the fact that this is the end (or should be the end) of the debate. Through Gārgī, a "warrior-son" whose questions are "arrows," we are told that the debate has reached its pinnacle and that this is (or should be) the final test of Yājñavalkya's knowledge. The danger of questioning at this abstract level is also made clear through this martial imagery which also serves to foreshadow Śākalya's death (3.9.26). That Gārgī has to repeat her question to get a complete answer not only indicates a general avoidance of sharing one's knowledge (as in 4.3), but also shows that the nature of Gārgī's question has changed when she asks what "space" (not *brahman*!) is woven on. She is not asking *beyond something* here, but she is asking *about it*, and this question is answered in reference to the "imperishable." Yājñavalkya recognizes that the nature of the question has changed when Gārgī repeats the question and asks further "on what is space woven to and fro?"

Appropriately, Yājñavalkya's answer is also the most abstract answer so far in this debate. He describes the imperishable in relation to its "non-properties" (3.8.8), the universe, time, the phenomenal world, and the sacrifice (3.8.9–10). Forming a literary ring, the discussion is brought back to "departing from this world" (introduced in the beginning of the text). In this way, Yājñavalkya's answer in 3.8 encompasses most of the concerns mentioned by his other interlocutors suggesting, as does Gārgī's rhetoric, an end to the discussion.

Now that we have discussed the role of Gārgī's discourse within the larger debate, the question then becomes: But why is the interlocutor a woman? Is there anything particular about these passages that allows us to speculate on the role of women in this debate in the text?

First, I think Gārgī needs to be viewed within a larger cast of anomalous characters found in the Upaniṣads.[124] As I have argued regarding the nature of philosophical and religious knowledge in the hands of kings (even kings teaching Brahmins), the larger theme begun by the Brāhmaṇas[125] and developed by this Upaniṣad and others is the displacement of the ideology of *Brahmins-by-birth* versus *Brahmins-by-practice/knowledge*. Thus, I think it is more fruitful to view women first as among the cast of others who would have presumably be excluded from such knowledge (at least as far as the earlier textual record indicates)—the crazed Raikva,[126] Satyakāma who is without proper lineage,[127] and the various kings who are directly involved in, if not always in control of, discussions on *brahman*.[128] This is to say that we have a significant number of characters in Upaniṣadic stories who, based on earlier textual material, would normally be excluded from such knowledge. Taken together, their inclusion in the Upaniṣads (and the fact that they are shown to have such knowledge) appears to be more of an internal critique and development of the Brahmin worldview and less of a reflection of a historical reality. If women in this Upaniṣad are viewed in this light, the issue appears to be a larger one of a changing ideology behind the possession of knowledge and what that knowledge is. This does not necessarily mean that crazed individuals were sought after for their knowledge or that someone without a lineage could receive religious teaching on *brahman*, but it does mean that there was an ideological shift concerning how such knowledge was viewed.[129] The rise of urbanization, the displacement of the village priest and his realm of control, and the necessity to compete with other priests for royal and other sponsorship must have all played a role in how the sacrifice and knowledge about it was conceived and thus marketed.

"As a Warrior-Son . . ."

Though the women in this Upaniṣad fall into the general class of anomalous characters in the Upaniṣads as a whole, they should also be viewed as distinct in how they are individually constructed. One means of analyzing the specific role of women in this Upaniṣad is to look closely at the language used and what claims that language makes about the right to speak as well as what is spoken about.

The tenor and language of Gārgī's second questioning session radically change from the first, and it is here where we can begin to speculate about the role of this woman in philosophical discussion. The first two passages of 3.8 are unique and important enough to bear repeating:

> **1.** Next (Gārgī) Vācaknavī said, "Distinguished Brahmins! I will ask him two questions. If he gives me the answers, none of you will ever beat him in this debate about *brahman*."
> "Ask, Gārgī."
>
> **2.** She said, "As a warrior-son of Kāśī or Videha strings his unstrung bow, takes two enemy-piercing arrows in hand, and rises up [in battle], Yājñavalkya, so I rise up against you with two questions. Answer me these two!"
> "Ask, Gārgī."

The question to be addressed first is: What is the function of these narrative details? First and foremost, Gārgī asserts her superiority over the other Brahmins present by declaring herself the final interrogator. In so doing, she has also made it possible for Yājñavalkya to prove his claim of being the most distinguished in knowledge of *brahman* (which is one main point of this debate). While it is unique to have a woman in such a debate in the first place (at least, given their absence in other textual sources), it is more curious that Gārgī claims this status, given that some of the assembled priests are well-known ritualists of considerable stature (up to this point, Uddālaka being the most famous). It appears that Gārgī's status as a woman and her claim to be able to close the debate is an indirect insult towards the other Brahmins: it is Gārgī, apparently a female anomaly in the debate, who elicits the most important answer on the nature of the self and claims the debate closed. The importance of Yājñavalkya's answer is corroborated by the language used by Gārgī. His answer is, to extend the metaphor, a "shield" against her "arrows."

Some scholars have noticed the unusual metaphor of Gārgī being a "warrior-son" (*ugraputra*) and have attempted to assign psychological motives to a historical figure (anger, etc.). As I pointed out earlier, however, such assertions are fundamentally flawed, because not only do they go beyond the textual information that is given, but also because they focus on the "actual" (e.g., an "actual" Gārgī and her "actual" temperament, etc.) and not on the constructed nature of the discourse (e.g., *why* Gārgī is portrayed as angry, etc.).

Gārgī's hyperbolic, unprecedented language first and foremost indicates the importance of the questions that she is asking. Her questions invert Yājñavalkya's threat of a shattered head, suggesting that if he cannot answer these he will be struck down (either metaphorically or otherwise). This is actually explicitly stated in M: *tau cen me na vivakṣyati mūrdhāsya vipatiṣyatīti* ("If you do not answer me these two, your head will shatter apart").[130] Further, such language indicates that her questions are the pinnacle of the debate and that this is an appropriate place to end the discussion.

Gārgī's language, however, also does much more than other scholars have suggested: it *masculinizes* Gārgī.[131] Gārgī is metaphorically transformed from a woman into a *male* ("son," m. *putra*). The composer of the text could have employed a gender-appropriate form, such as *ugraputrī* ("daughter of a warrior"), but chose not to. It is most likely that the author is attempting to make a point by choosing the masculine form: Gārgī's gender is being manipulated by the metaphor.

Further, in the context of this all-male debate, Gārgī is made *more male* than her counterparts—she is not a passive male Brahmin asking questions. Up until this point in the debate, the rhetoric has been rather mild, even if a bit prickly. Here, however, it is Gārgī who is a "warrior-son" (*ugraputra*) of the famed Videha[132] or Kāśī wielding "two enemy-piercing arrows" (*dvau bāṇavantau sapatnātivyādhinau*[133]). Though apparently a Brahmin by birth, Gārgī employs the martial imagery of a male Kṣatriya, positioning her above the others present, at least in boldness. Gārgī being masculinized, particularly in this hyperbolic sense, is an emasculating of the other Brahmins present.[134] Gārgī's character is fashioned such that not only is she positioned above the other male priests, but also once again serves to position Yājñavalkya above them if he can answer her questions. Now, not only can Yājñavalkya out-talk the other Brahmins, he can metaphorically do battle with a male warrior. All of this leads to the dramatic conclusion where Śākalya's head shatters apart because he cannot answer the question of Yājñavalkya, bringing the narrative to its climax.

In the context of this single passage, it is clear that there is a literary manipulation of Gārgī's role within an all-male debate. If there is a tendency, however, to circumscribe the gender of discourse of women in this Upaniṣad as a whole, then there should be corresponding evidence from other episodes to support such an interpretation.

Maitreyī the *brahmavādinī*[135]

As with Gārgī, it seems most prudent to discuss what the Maitreyī episodes do in the grander scheme of the narrative first, and then in themselves. We have two narrations of the same story (2.4 and 4.5) that are repeated in each of the two recensions. The second story (4.5) is an elaborated variant of the first and is directly connected to the two chapters about Yājñavalkya that precede it. The second episode may be a more direct statement that Yājñavalkya is leaving for a life of renunciation[136] which closes not only the Maitreyī episode, but the entire Yājñavalkya narrative with his leaving.[137] This fits in appropriately with the discussion of "immortality" (*amṛtatva*) as Yājñavalkya may be nearing the end of his life, and the topic appropriately matches this as well as the import of two chapters taken together.[138]

Like the Gārgī episode, Yājñavalkya's discussion with Maitreyī has been subject to much debate and psychological speculation. Since I have already discussed the flaws of such a view previously, we can set such interpretations aside. As with Gārgī, I wish to focus on what is happening narratively in the episode. Again, I think the language used gives us an indication of how, once again, women's discourse is circumscribed in this text, though in a different fashion than in Gārgī's dialogue. As with the Gārgī episodes, it is also a comparison of the latter Maitreyī narrative with the former that throws light on the discourse of these women.

The two versions of this story are, by and large, the same, though there are a few striking differences which are particularly significant here. The most important differences for my purposes are what is added in the framing of 4.5. In 2.4 the narrative framing is minimal. Yājñavalkya states that he is leaving and wants to make a settlement with two women (presumably his wives as in 4.5). Maitreyī wants to know what would make her immortal. This leads us directly into such a discussion and then the narrative ends. 4.5, in contrast, adds a number of narrative elements: Yājñavalkya is said to leave at the end, the two women are formally introduced as his wives, and most interestingly, the character of each wife is delineated. Maitreyī is said to be a "talker about *brahman*" (*brahmavādinī*)[139] while Kātyāyanī knows "just womanly knowledge" (*strīprajñaiva*).[140]

Such narrative framing is not present in 2.4, so the question is: Why might it be needed here? One strong possibility is the context in which this second episode occurs—it comes at the end of all the Yājñavalkya dialogues, and the episode is formally connected to those previous dialogues by stating that Maitreyī is a *brahmavādinī*. This positions her in the tradition as a valid receiver of Yājñavalkya's knowledge, something that the composer of 2.4 does not need to do as it is not in the context of what I call "the teaching narrative." The formal structure of the Yājñavalkya episodes of BĀU 3–4 is, I argue, a series of progressive and systematic "privatization" of teaching discourses—from public debate (chapter 3), to private discussion (chapter 4.1), to Janaka as Yājñavalkya's student (4.2), to Janaka's compelling Yājñavalkya's knowledge due to a boon (4.3–4.4), and finally to the privacy of the home and spouse (4.5). Maitreyī's dialogue with Yājñavalkya is the culmination of a discourse of privatization—the most intimate of interlocutors, a husband and wife.[141]

The use of the term *brahmavādinī* in the second episode (4.5) also positions the subject matter (*brahman*) with the object of knowledge (*-vādinī*) once again following an apparent shift in the way this knowledge was viewed as discussed earlier—Maitreyī is worthy of such knowledge because of her natural predisposition or intellectual interests.

But why is Kātyāyanī said to be *strīprajñā*? What does this add to our understanding of the text and the women in it? To this, I think there are two answers that are not mutually exclusive. First, it creates a bifurcation of what are apparently two valid forms of "gendered" knowledge: knowledge necessary for a woman to do her assigned tasks in the household and society[142] and knowledge of religious and philosophical matters. Whether or not these two types of knowledge were necessarily mutually exclusive in society (as opposed to in the text) cannot be determined, but within the text the bifurcation suggests that they are exclusive. Kātyāyanī is portrayed as not being interested in such matters which is exemplified by her not taking part in the discussion that follows. By implication, this also means that Maitreyī is not interested in *strīprajñā*—that is, like Gārgī being a "warrior-son," Maitreyī is constructed to be *not* an ordinary female (*strī*). While Gārgī is masculinized in her speech in 3.8, Maitreyī's role within her gender is manipulated before she speaks. The difference lies again in the context—Maitreyī's character does not have to be positioned among other males, but the author apparently feels the need to position her in relation to the subject matter and vis-à-vis a second wife.

The second reason for such a distinction between these two wives is key to understanding the narrative frame of this episode—this frame is concerned with a "settlement" between the wives. By demarcating Kātyāyanī as *strīprajñā*, the text apparently equates a purported "average" female (*strī*) with more worldly matters. The implication is that she will take a settlement of material goods, perhaps in the form of a living stipend given by Yājñavalkya.[143] Maitreyī, being termed a *brahmavādinī*, is portrayed as interested in philosophy, not in physical property or wealth, and this permits the discourse on immortality to take place. In the light of this settlement theme which frames the dialogue, Maitreyī's asking for knowledge about immortality can also be seen as her asking for another type of settlement—knowledge instead of wealth.[144] Thus, in a manner similar to Doniger's recent discussion of women (2000), Yājñvalkya's wives are split—one to fulfill the role as an average wife and one, apparently not average, to permit a discussion on immortality to take place.[145]

Other Women?

Up to this point, I have argued that Gārgī and Maitreyī are narratively constructed *to not be* representative females and that their right to speak on philosophical matters is circumscribed by different processes of modifying discourse. Gārgī, via the metaphor of the warrior-son (*ugraputra*), is masculinized in her own speech, while Maitreyī is made extraordinary in the frame of her discussion with Yājñavalkya. In conclusion to this discussion, I would like to draw attention to two other women in the BĀU who are generally overlooked in any discussion of gender in this text—when scholars speak of women in BĀU they speak of Gārgī and Maitreyī. I suspect that most scholars would be hard-pressed at this point in the discussion to recognize who these two other women may be. The reason for this is rather simple: in the dialogues I am concerned with here, gender circumscription is taken to the extreme—*it has been made absolute.*[146] We do not read the "possessors" of these discourses as female, but as *exclusively male.*

Patañcala Kāpya, we are told, had a daughter (3.3) and a wife (3.7) who were possessed by male *gandharvas*. Through these male *gandharvas*, women's speech is being supernaturally controlled. BĀU 3.3.1 begins:

> *atha hainaṃ bhujyur lāhyāyaniḥ papraccha | yājñavalkyeti hovāca | madreṣu carakāḥ paryavrajāma | te patañcalasya kāpyasya gṛhān aima | tasyāsīd duhitā gandharvagṛhītā | tam apṛcchāma ko 'sīti | so 'bravīt sudhanvāṅgirasa iti |*

> Next Bhujyu Lāhyāyani questioned him. "Yājñavalkya," he said, "[once] we wandered as itinerants [*carakāḥ*; Black Yajurvedins?] among the Madras. We went to the home of Patañcala Kāpya. He had a daughter seized by a *gandharva*.[147]
> We asked him, 'Who are you?'
> He said, 'Sudhanvan Āṅgirasa.'"

and BĀU 3.7.1:

> *atha hainam uddālaka āruṇiḥ papraccha | yājñavalkyeti hovāca | madreṣv avasāma patañcalasya kāpyasya gṛheṣu yajñam adhīyānāḥ | tasyāsīd bhāryā gandharvagṛhītā | tam apṛcchāma ko 'sīti | so 'bravīt kabandha ātharvaṇa iti |*

> Next Uddālaka Āruṇi questioned him. "Yājñavalkya," he said, "[once] we lived among the Madras studying sacrifice in the house of Patañcala Kāpya. He had a wife possessed by a Gandharva.
> We asked him, 'Who are you?'
> He said, 'Kabandha Ārthavaṇa.'"

These two passages frame a larger questioning session of Yājñavalkya challenging whether his knowledge is equal to the celestial *gandharvas*.

The role of these two episodes in the larger structure of the narrative is rather straightforward. BĀU 3.3 functions to thematically mark off what I have called the sacrificial theme (3.1–3). It does so by asking where the Pārikṣitas, ancient performers of the horse sacrifice, went after death. This is an appropriate question to be asked via a *gandharva* because no living person would have direct experience of this. That it is the horse sacrifice (*aśvamedha*) in question is also appropriate because it culminates the sacrificial theme with a question about the most elaborate *śrauta* ritual performed.

BĀU 3.7 also ups the stakes on the theme of the *ātman* (3.6–8). Following from Gārgī's rather simple and direct questions about what the worlds are woven on, Uddālaka uses the *gandharva*'s knowledge as a means to increase the abstraction of the question and answer. He asks what the "thread" (*sūtra*) and the "inner controller" (*antaryāmin*) are on the worldly and divine levels.

In both cases, the literary recourse to a *gandharva* makes sense—the type of knowledge being asked about would be known either to celestial spirits who occasionally possess women or to the people taught by *gandharvas* via such women. Thus Yājñavalkya shows himself to be in possession of supernatural knowledge, as he was not present when these women were possessed. This also reinforces my argument regarding the general shift in the ideology of knowledge that I had mentioned earlier—the *gandharvas* possess this knowledge because of their status whereas Yājñavalkya possesses it because of his true knowledge.

Now the fact that scholars do not refer to Kāpya's daughter and wife as female is significant in light of what I have argued about Gārgī and Maitreyī—they are not seen as female because this text has manipulated their gender. They are textually made male, and the female is, at most, a vehicle for male philosophical speech. This transplantation of gender is brought about by a twofold means—in both cases the story of possession by a male *gandharva* is framed by the male who is doing the questioning (Bhujyu Lāhyāyani and Uddālaka Āruṇi). To support this interpretation even further, it should be pointed out that Patañcala Kāpya's wife and daughter are introduced only in relation to him—no names, which would personalize them and reiterate a gender, are stated.[148] Only the masculine names of the possessors are mentioned. Though these two women are obviously female, the text has degendered them as much as possible. Their gender has been so radically altered that readers are hard-pressed to even notice them as female in the text.

I pointed out in the beginning that any attempt to draw conclusions about women in the BĀU, or about women in general in ancient India, must first take recourse to the literary world that, for us, they inhabit. This is to say that first and foremost we must take a story *as a story* before attempting any larger claims about its historical "actuality" and certainly before we make any claims about particular characters being representative of actual people or of society.

Were Gārgī and Maitreyī actual people and did these events actually take place as recorded? Analytically, I find this to be the wrong question for the simple fact that any definitive answer is impossible given the nature of the evidence. I have argued, however, that in the same manner as kings participating in debate, women must have participated in some fashion in religious debate as there is no positive indication that they did not and certainly indication that they did.

As I have also argued, however, the literary world that the women of the BĀU inhabit is one that is circumscribed for a number of very real ends: to teach about the *ātman* and *brahman*; to mark formal structures in the narrative; to position Yājñavalkya and Videha over and above other traditions and regions, and so forth. In this fashion, women's speech is also circumscribed: Gārgī is masculinized to exalt her position; Maitreyī is marked in contrast to a second wife to show her uniqueness as well as to mark her as a proper recipient of such knowledge; and the daughter and wife of Kāpya are degendered as much as possible since they are simply vehicles of male (supernatural) speech. In each of these cases, the literary construction or manipulation of gender was done by different means: Gārgī through her own speech, Maitreyī through the framing narrative, and the wife/daughter through the gender transplantation of possession.

The BĀU, while giving us the first detailed account about the participation of women in religious debate, tells us also that this participation was textually mediated. Did women have a right to speak in such rarefied philosophical circles and did they then speak? Apparently so, as one would be hard-pressed to imagine the emergence, retention, and popularity of these episodes without some precedent. The text also tells us, however, that the speech of women as recorded here was mediated, and one site for that mediation was gender. In this fashion, the text itself is telling us that these women, whether historical figures or not, were anything but representative of women in any general sense in ancient India.

Conclusion

Chapters 3 and 4 of the BĀU are the foundational narratives in the larger story of Yājñavalkya's literary life. It is in these stories that he is fully established as an authoritative interpreter of the Vedic sacrifice and as the favored priest of King Janaka. Clearly, this portrayal had its precedents in the *brāhmaṇa* passages discussed in the previous chapter, but here that portrayal is fleshed out, in both the sense that these characteristics and contexts are expanded upon, but also in the sense that Yājñavalkya begins to represent a more coherent figure, a literary life that appears, if not historically true-in-life, at least true-to-life.

Taking chapters 3 and 4 together, Yājñavalkya is portrayed as an idealized debater and teacher in a series of different contexts that become progressively more private and domestic. In the public setting, Yājñavalkya establishes himself and the White Yajurvedic tradition over and above the prevailing Vedic orthodoxy, even leading to the death of his most famous interlocutor. In a one-on-one discussion with the king at court, Yājñavalkya shows himself to be the ideal religious counselor to the king—clearly superior to his rivals, but willing to share his most private knowledge for the benefit of the king (rather than simply for a prize). Finally, Yājñavalkya is shown in an apparently private discussion with his wife, Maitreyī, sharing with her his "wealth" of immortality as he prepares to leave. All of these narratives together create the picture of a figure who is the idealized Vedic religious savant in the variety of social contexts in which he is expected to function—the public realm, the semiprivate role as court priest and counselor, and the privacy of the home. And if it is not stretching the interpretation too far, one can also say that the text concludes with the ultimate privacy: Yājñavalkya exits the narrative stage for an apparently solo form of existence, leaving his wife, but also the listener to the story as the text abruptly concludes.[149]

Yājñavalkya is, of course, not just an ordinary human, but is portrayed as a religious virtuoso, a characterization that makes him particularly fitting as the founder of the White Yajurvedic school. Indeed, his sarcasm, which under other circumstances could be interpreted as a negative personality trait, is always justified by the properness of his knowledge over those at whom he is directing that sarcasm. It is this portrayal that serves as the background to the final chapter of the BĀU where he is understood as the receiver of the sacred texts directly from the Sun.

It is with these stories that the later narratives concerned with Yājñavalkya contend, exploring the contours of his sarcasm, the complications of his discussing religious doctrine with women who might normally be excluded, and especially how a "new" form of the Veda can develop when it is, by definition, "ancient." The BĀU, though, is not a "straight-jacket" that severely limits how later composers explore this figure, such as in an exceedingly reverential fashion. While the BĀU itself comes to a close, a "literary life" is more fully opened, where later composers then take it as template from which to work. That is, they were quite familiar with the figure of Yājñavalkya as portrayed in these texts, especially the BĀU, but did not feel the need to slavishly follow them as they explored and expanded upon the contours of his "life."

3

An Ancient Sage and the Paradox of the New

As we have seen in the previous chapters, Yājñavalkya has been portrayed in a variety of fashions: as a priest who contemplated ritual procedures, but did not necessarily pursue them; as an authority, but not one that was universally accepted; and as a spokesman for the eastern fringe of the Vedic heartland, Videha, besting in debate some of the most well-known Kuru-Pañcāla Brahmins. Through all of the portrayals we have also seen a progressive elaboration of Yājñavalkya's sarcastic, even irreverent, personality. By the time of the final redaction of the BĀU,[1] Yājñavalkya's authority appears to have reached its climax within this particular textual tradition when the text tells us that the White *yajus* formulas were received by Yājñavalkya from the Sun, historically establishing him after the fact as the founder of the tradition albeit with a Brāhmaṇa precedent. While this is the final episode regarding Yājñavalkya within the early White Yajurvedic tradition proper, this is certainly not the last we read of Yājñavalkya in the larger Hindu tradition. Though mention of Yājñavalkya in other textual traditions which postdate the BĀU are not statistically numerous in comparison to certain other figures (such as Vyāsa[2] or Vaiśaṁpāyana), they are significant in regard to how purveyors of the Indian tradition viewed Yājñavalkya, what they knew about him, and most importantly, what they thought about him in recasting his role in different literary productions for different ends.

If the BĀU was produced on the cusp of the second urbanization along the Gangetic plain, then the *Mahābhārata* (MBh),[3] the massive poem of some 75,000 stanzas, was produced several centuries thereafter in what must have been a highly urbanized setting.[4] As Pande (1990, 125) observed, "it may be assumed that it [the time of the MBh] was an age in which towns had clearly emerged . . . including merchants and craftsmen, kings and officials." Indeed, the MBh speaks directly about cities and kings, both imagined and semihistorical. Equally important for us, though, is that a variety of renunciate traditions are present in the text which,[5] along with archaeological evidence regarding urbanization, clearly points to a period after the Buddha (roughly 5th century BCE) and concomitant with other *śramaṇa* traditions.[6] It is, in fact, both the Vedic world and the newly emerging traditions of renunciation that the composers of this text contend directly with, albeit in a newly reconstituted orthodoxy (Sutton 2000, 1ff.).

Sutton (2000, 3ff.) argues that urbanization and an emphasis on the notion of the individual were part of the context in which new religious doctrines in the MBh (particularly in regards to renunciation and asceticism) gained prominence. One should also remember, though, that this is also the case with the earliest Upaniṣads that must have preceded Buddhism and the MBh.[7] This does not suggest that Sutton's supposition is incorrect, but rather that urbanization (and its effects) should be viewed as a process where early evidence can be seen in the Upaniṣads, evidence that becomes more and more elaborated by the time of the MBh. The new doctrines—*yoga, ahiṃsā* ("non-violence"), *sādhāraṇadharma* (*dharma*, or ethical principles, common to all people)[8]—were often reconstituted under the veneer of Vedic orthodoxy in the MBh.

As with the Upaniṣads, it is neither possible nor desirable to attempt to construct a single philosophical or religious system coherently presented throughout the MBh as a whole—the text reflects dialogues over time more than any cohesive monologue.[9] The various stories within the MBh, particularly those which appear to deviate from the main story line (of which there are many) very often show a variety of opinions even on a single matter.[10] "The teachings of the epic thus suggest the environment of a weakened orthodoxy being challenged and possibly overthrown by the alternative doctrines. Frequently in the text it is observed that different opinions are held even among the wise" (Sutton 2000, 7).

It is useful to point out that the new doctrines and practices that are put forth in the text are not an attempt to overthrow the prevailing orthodoxy from outside the Brahmanic tradition. Rather, as Fitzgerald (2004, 53–55) points out, it appears to be an ongoing reconstitution of a newly emerging orthodoxy from within the Brahmanical tradition in reaction to changing religious sentiments in relation to political contexts. This is not to say that whatever orthodoxy (or rather, orthodoxies) the text puts forward are consistent—this is certainly not the case. Given the nature of textual composition over many years and regions (not to mention within various Sanskritic and vernacular traditions), such consistency would be impossible. Fitzgerald (2004), Reich (1998), and others have pointed out that there is a general lack of easy answers to complex moral and social problems found within the text and, in many ways, *that is the point* (that is, as acknowledged explicitly several times in the text itself, *dharma* is *sūkṣma,* "subtle"). The text's brilliance lies in the presence of various voices: the incorporation of conflicting views regarding the nature of *dharma,* the status of Vedic sacrifices, the status of women, and so on, and ongoing (and sometimes implicit) discussions about the nature of what constitutes a good Brahmin and a good Kṣatriya. All of this is found within this popular text that must have influenced and been influenced by a radically larger audience than a group (or groups) of ritual technicians (as in the White Yajurvedic tradition). In a sense, we can say that the character of Yājñavalkya in the MBh is now on a much larger narrative stage with a much larger audience. Like the BĀU, however, the larger narrative of the MBh—which incorporates the various, sometimes conflicting, voices—does so with larger narrative (and sometimes conflicting) goals.

It is quite clear, no matter the numerous variations in the manuscripts, that at least one guiding principle of the MBh as a whole is a reconstitution of the nature of Brahmanism, by which I mean the religious tradition in which the Brahmin class is seen as authorized (*adhikāra*) to determine orthodoxy and orthopraxy. Such correct doctrine and correct practice as determined by this elite is most often (if, in some cases, only nominally) based on the Veda.[11] In some cases, this apparently conservative stance has allowed for rather radically new interpretations. For example, the *yajña* ("sacrifice"), so central to the worldview of early Brahmanism, is relativized in one passage of the MBh in relationship to one's material means to perform it (13.110.2ff.). Here the discussion hinges on determining what suitable alternative may be performed by those without the financial means to perform a sacrifice. This passage does not deny the value of sacrifice (though certain other MBh passages, such as in the Bhagavadgītā, do), but it emphasizes practical concerns and incorporates them within a larger ideal. Sutton (2000, 3), expounding on this particular passage, summarizes quite nicely: "There is clear recognition [found in the MBh] that as long as they [new beliefs and doctrines] do not oppose the most basic premises of Vedic belief and practice, alternative ideas are to be endorsed and pursued."

Though the MBh is a reconstitution of Brahmanism from within, this did not occur in a vacuum, uninfluenced by religious trends from without. On the contrary, it is quite clear that traditions such as Buddhism and Jainism[12] influenced newly emerging doctrines found within the MBh. Indeed, if it were not for ascetic traditions outside (or on the fringes) of the Vedic fold, it is unlikely that a principle like *ahiṃsā* or practices like *yoga* would have attained the status that they have within the text and become so prevalent in the larger Hindu tradition.[13]

The dating of the MBh, as with all dating of ancient texts, is highly debatable. However, rough dates of the MBh rather consistently appear to fall somewhere between the 2nd century BCE and 4th century CE which is consonant with the urbanized worldview of the texts and our current knowledge of the period.[14] The redaction that we have today probably became standardized toward the end of this period, that is, by the time of the Gupta dynasty (ca. 320 CE–480 CE).

While new religious ideas appear to have been incorporated into the MBh's notion of Brahmanism and the external influences of Jainism and Buddhism must have played a part, there is tantalizing evidence of sociological and political reasons for the core narrative of the MBh to be structured the way it is to achieve certain ends. Fitzgerald (2003; trans., 2004b) has argued that the MBh is a radical Brahmanical reaction to royal favoritism toward Buddhism during the reign of Aśoka Maurya (ca. 3rd century BCE) in an attempt to reposition Brahmanism as intimately connected to government rule (i.e., the Brahmin with the Kṣatriya). Favoritism towards Buddhism and the equation of Buddhist principles to governing principles on the part of Aśoka may have served as the negative backdrop with which the composers were contending. In this fashion, the MBh is intimately concerned with the relation of Brahmanism and the ruling classes, and much of the text is designed to show how Brahmanic principles can be applied to statecraft.

The MBh is a massive text consisting of a series of interlocking narratives held together by a larger narrative frame. It is for this reason that it can be thought of as a "mythopedia," or in a rather unflattering manner as "so dismally intractable" (van Buitenen, trans., 1973, xxxi). It is superfluous for our purposes, however, to enter into a larger discussion of the narrative of the MBh as a whole.[15] This is because Yājñavalkya appears only in a few brief references and in one longer passage. While I will discuss these passages in some detail—discussing the ways in which Yājñavalkya is portrayed and why—it is fair to say that the Yājñavalkya passages are statistically minor in the MBh.[16] This is not to say that these passages do not follow various patterns set down in the text or that the topics discussed are necessarily out of place or unimportant. Rather, these passages are neither as foundational to the larger narrative as others nor would their absence in themselves be necessarily missed in the text.[17] The Yājñavalkya passages do reinforce certain themes brought up in the text, but often simply as an augment to the narrative, rather than being central to it.

While Yājñavalkya is not in any way central to any larger narrative in the MBh, he is still central to our purposes here, and he has obviously become a part of the larger Hindu *imaginaire* outside of the White Yajurveda. The following is the list of passages where Yājñavalkya appears. I will deal with the longer passage (book 12) first as it provides a greater context from which to understand the shorter passages (books 2, 13, and 14).

2.4.10
2.7.10
2.30.35
12.298.3ff
13.4.50
14.71.3
14.72.17

MBh Book 12 (Śāntiparvan)

Yājñavalkya appears in one extended narrative in the MBh. In book 12, perhaps the most didactic of any of the books of the MBh, Yājñavalkya is cast in a dialogue with Janaka (12.298.3ff.), though a dialogue not quite like any other that Yājñavalkya has been associated with. While Yājñavalkya had not previously been associated with *yoga* directly in the earlier literature, the narrative in book 12 is an extended (and rather technical) discussion of Sāṃkhya-Yoga between Yājñavalkya and Janaka.[18] This extended narrative is placed into the distant past, rather than in the narrative present. We will see in other passages of the MBh that Yājñavalkya, like Vyāsa, moves between narrative past and present, both as an active participant in the current time and as a remembered individual through narrations of the past.

In the Śāntiparvan, Yudhiṣṭhira has been asking Bhīṣma a series of questions about the nature of the universe, virtue/sin, and transcendence, and Bhīṣma relates stories about ancient seers and their dialogues with others (particularly, Janaka or kings who are said to be from Janaka's lineage: *janakātmaja*), dialogues that are highly influenced by Sāṃkhya and Yoga doctrine. Yudhiṣṭhira frames the story of Yājñavalkya's dialogue with Janaka by posing a very elaborate question to Bhīṣma:

> *yudhiṣṭhira uvāca*
> *dharmādharmavimuktaṃ yad vimuktaṃ sarvasaṃśrayāt*
> *janmamṛtyuvimuktaṃ ca vimuktaṃ puṇyapāpayoḥ* (12.298.1)
> *yac chivaṃ nityam abhayaṃ nityaṃ cākṣaram avyayam*
> *śuci nityam anāyāsaṃ tad bhavān vaktum arhati* (12.298.2)
> *bhīṣma uvāca*
> *atra te vartayiṣye 'ham itihāsaṃ purātanam*
> *yājñavalkyasya saṃvādaṃ janakasya ca bhārata* (12.298.3)
> *yājñavalkyam ṛṣiśreṣṭhaṃ daivarātir mahāyaśāḥ*
> *papraccha janako rājā praśnaṃ praśnavidāṃ varaḥ* (12.298.4)

> Yudhiṣṭhira said, "Please tell me about what is freed from dharma and adharma, freed from attachment, freed from birth and death, and freed from sin and virtue. [Tell me about] that which is eternally auspicious and fearless, eternally indestructible and imperishable, eternally bright and effortless, O Sir!"
>
> Bhīṣma said, "Here I will engage in an ancient tale of a conversation between Yājñavalkya and Janaka, O Bhārata. King Janaka, one of great glory, the son of Devarāti and best in knowing how to ask questions, asked the great ṛṣi Yājñavalkya . . ."

Contrary to the framing of this story, the doctrine that follows does not appear to have ancient precedent in what we know of Yājñavalkya. Janaka asks a series of questions about the types of the senses (*indriya*), the types of *prakṛti*, the unmanifest (*avyakta*) and highest *brahman*, and what is beyond that. Janaka says that he is ignorant (*ajñāna*) and calls Yājñavalkya a "treasure composed of knowledge" (*jñānamayo nidhiḥ*). Apparently, Janaka has reached such a high status that Yājñavalkya agrees to answer as is eternal custom (*dharmaḥ sanātanaḥ*), though he states that no answer is unknown to Janaka (*na tavāviditaṃ kiṃ cit*). Here Janaka is introduced as the idealized interlocutor—the best in asking questions—suggesting Yājñavalkya is the idealized teacher who proceeds to answer the questions thoroughly.

What follows this short exchange is a lengthy discourse by Yājñavalkya on the nature of Sāṃkhya and Yoga. It does not seem necessary here to enter into the philosophical details at length as it is in accord with the general discussion of Sāṃkhya and Yoga found elsewhere in the Śāntiparvan and is not particularly unique to Yājñavalkya,[19] but I will highlight some of the significant aspects of the discussion and turn to the larger issue of Yājñavalkya's role in this passage.

Yājñavalkya numerically explains the different types of manifest and unmanifest things and then the sixteen modifications (*vikāra*) of those things, which consist of organs of perception and what is perceived, speech, and parts of the body (12.298.13). He goes on to explain the creation of the mind and consciousness. These are explained in relation to their *adhyātma* and *adhibhūta* (12.301.1ff.) correlates, the role of the three *guṇas* (12.302.1ff.), and the nature of having attributes (*saguṇa*) and not having attributes (*nirguṇa*).

Having discussed the "Sāṃkhya wisdom" (*sāṃkhyajñāna*), Yājñavalkya proceeds to discuss Yoga. There is an explicit attempt to integrate the two. In transition between the two topics, Yājñavalkya says:

> *nāsti sāṃkhysamaṃ jñānaṃ nāsti yogasamaṃ balam*
> *tau ubhāv ekacaryau tu ubhāv anidhanau smṛtau* (12.304.2)
> *pṛthak pṛthak tu paśyanti ye 'lpabuddhiratā narāh*
> *vayaṃ tu rājan paśyāma ekam eva tu niścayāt* (12.304.3)

> There is no knowledge equal to Sāṃkhya, nor force equal to Yoga. Those two are a single practice, they are both endless (or: continuous or all encompassing).

> Weak-minded men see them as separate, but we, O King,
> due to [our] discernment, see them as just one.[20]

Yājñavalkya goes on further to say that the person who sees them as the same is a *tattvavid* (a "knower of the truth"; 12.304.4).[21] Yājñavalkya then continues with a discussion of the breaths and means of meditation. He says that *yogins* have spoken of yoga as possessed of "eight limbs" and this can be found in the Veda (*vedeṣu cāṣṭagunitaṃ yogam āhur manīṣiṇaḥ,* 12.304.7). Yājñavalkya continues with a discussion about the signs of an impending death and states that through a combination of Yoga and Sāṃkhya one can conquer death and unite the individual soul with the supreme soul (*sasāṃkhyadhāraṇaṃ caiva viditvā manujarṣabha; jayec ca mṛtyuṃ yogena tatpareṇāntarātmanā,* 12.305.20). This is directly similar to the preceding chapters on Sāṃkhya.

> The discourse of Yājñavalkya displays the typical features noted in the earlier chapters [of the MBh] on the same subject. Yoga is linked with Sāṃkhya by the declaration that they are essentially the same, though the stress in Yoga is on the power that it brings both whilst existing in this world and in forcing one's way to salvation. The two types of *yoga,* breath control and concentration, are described briefly and the ultimate goal of the techniques is presented as mokṣa in the conclusion of the discourse. (Sutton 2000, 108)

Up until this point it is quite clear that there are self-conscious continuities and differences in this portrayal of Yājñavalkya. 12.291–12.308 is a cluster of Janaka-dialogues (albeit with different individuals likely going by that name), so including the famous of association of Yājñavalkya and Janaka is appropriate. Most clearly, the reference to a dialogue between Yājñavalkya and Janaka is a means to connect this story to the famous episodes found in the Upaniṣad and to appropriate that status. Further, Yājñavalkya being called a *ṛṣi* is a continued elaboration of his hagiography indicating an elevation of his status over time, here putting him on par with Vaisiṣtha (291–296), Bhārgava (297) and the like. The constant praising of both Janaka and Yājñavalkya indicates not only a friendly relationship between them within the narrative, but also the relative status that the two characters have attained within the larger MBh listening community as idealized priest and king.

Most importantly, what we have in this passage is the placing of (relatively) new doctrines of Sāṃkhya and Yoga into the mouth of a *ṛṣi* where the two are grouped as essentially the same. In many ways, this is a natural association not only because new doctrines, if taken as eternally true, are often placed in the mouths of already established authorities and connected to the ancient past, but also for thematic reasons. As we have seen in the BĀU, Yājñavalkya's dialogues are also focused on immortality, fearlessness, death, and the nature of what is truly indestructible. In the *Mahābhārata,* though framed differently, the thematic focus is quite similar, albeit dealt with through the view of enumerative Sāṃkhya and briefly with a discussion of yogic practices. While there is no clear evidence of established yogic practices present in the early Upaniṣads, breath is a common topic as well as (albeit to a lesser extent) self-restraint. Practices of breath control and concentration often associated with later traditions of classical *yoga* appear well established by the time of the MBh.

In the BĀU, the theme of true or correct knowledge deals with the nature of the sacrifice, death, and transcendence. In this context, this theme is expanded to include Yoga and Sāṃkhya. The teachings in this narrative are not portrayed in such a way to deny or criticize the authority of the Veda; on the contrary, these teachings of Yoga and Sāṃkhya are said to be encompassed within the Veda and are seen as its true expression. Yājñavalkya claims that all these teachings are found within the Veda itself (if one knows how to find them) establishing an already authoritative precedent. In describing Yājñavalkya's role here Sutton (2000, 44) states: "We have a teacher of Sāṃkhya claiming not to deny the Vedas but that his conclusions are the true conclusion of the Vedas, recognised within them only by those who are able to properly comprehend such wisdom."

Sutton is correct from the perspective of the tradition that propagated these teachings. However, for our purposes, it is fruitful to view this somewhat differently: as far as the larger literary history is concerned, it is not so much a "teacher of Sāṃkhya claiming not to deny the Vedas," but rather it is a character that was already well-known as a Vedic teacher of the hoary past being portrayed in a different form of literature with different ends—to argue that Sāṃkhya/Yoga teachings and the Vedic teachings are one and the same. To put it another way, it is not only Sāṃkhya accepting the authority of the Veda, but it is also the authority of the Veda being brought forth to authorize Sāṃkhya. The two are used to justify each other, though it is clear that Sāṃkhya is given a higher status of a sort as it is said to be the "true" Vedic teaching. This is pointed out directly in the subnarrative of Yājñavalkya's conversation with a Gandharva that he related to Janaka (12.306.1ff.). Yājñavalkya states rather bluntly:

> *sāṅgopāṅgān api yadi pañca vedān adhīyate*
> *vedavedyaṃ na jānīte vedabhāravaho hi saḥ* (12.306.48)
> *yo ghr̥tārthī kharīkṣīraṃ mathed gandharvasattama*
> *viṣṭhāṃ tatrānupaśyeta na maṇḍaṃ nāpi vā ghr̥tam* (12.306.49)
> *tathā vedyam avedyaṃ ca vedavidyo na vindati*
> *sa kevalaṃ mūḍhamatir jñānabhāravahaḥ smr̥taḥ* (12.306.50)
>
> Even if one studies the five Vedas with the limbs (*aṅga*) and sub-limbs (*upāṅga*), [but] does not know what is to be known through the Veda (*vedavedya*), he is simply carrying the weight of the Veda. Should one, whose object is butter, churn the milk of a she-ass, O best of the Gandharvas, he will find [something that smells like? looks like?] excrement there and not cream or butter. In the same way, one who knows the Veda [but] does not find what is related to the Veda and what is not is regarded as a mere idiot carrying the weight of knowledge.

Ganguli (1991, 10:51n1) states that the comparison being made here is between two types of fools: one ignorant enough to expect butter from ass's milk and another who does not understand the true nature of the Veda, though he has studied it. This is possible, but the passage is not entirely clear. Though Ganguli does not elaborate, if the two metaphors are symmetrical, then the Veda is being compared to the milk of a she-ass which, when churned, produces something foul. In such a reading, one wonders then if this is a negative assessment of the Veda itself. I think this is unlikely because, in the context of the larger narrative, Yājñavalkya in no way dismisses or denigrates the value of the Veda, and it is doubtful that he is doing so here.[22] However, the excrement may refer to one who knows the Veda (the milk of the she-ass) but proceeds to misinterpret its true teaching (churning which produces something like excrement). However, this interpretation is a bit clumsy, as the nature of this type of milk is that it cannot produce ghee or butter under any circumstance. Does this mean that the nature of the Veda prevents it from producing true knowledge? Such an interpretation is hard to reconcile with the rest of the passage that does value the Veda—in fact, Yājñavalkya's authority comes from that value and it is that value being given to Sāṃkhya and Yoga.

Another possibility is that the first metaphor of a person churning ass's milk is not simply stating that this person is ignorant enough to expect the impossible (which, of course, he is),[23] but it is also stating that one's goal must be appropriate to the object used to attain that goal. No butter will come from the milk of a she-ass as no true knowledge will come from inappropriate sources.[24] Here, the unexpressed correlate to the she-ass is that the Veda is the milk of a cow—as milk is the proper substance for making ghee when churned, so the Veda is the proper source for true knowledge. What I think is implied here (and reinforced in what follows) is that if one's goal is the true nature of things then study of the Veda is essential (which would be consonant with the rest of the narrative). The second statement regarding the knower of the Veda is a wordplay. It appears to be saying that once one has the appropriate goal (the true nature of things) and the appropriate object to obtain that goal (the Vedas) it is still useless unless one realizes that goal. In this context of Sāṃkhya, that goal is understanding the true nature of *prakr̥ti* and *puruṣa* which is said to be found in the Vedas. Here, rather than a simple comparison between two types of fools, is a two-step argument: (1) know where to find the truth and (2) find the truth there. The desire for something and the means to something only matter in so much as they actually lead to the attainment of the goal. In this interpretation, the novelty here is not knowing where to find that truth (in this larger passage, the Veda appears to be assumed as the place to find this truth), but rather what that truth is: the doctrine of Sāṃkhya and the practice of Yoga.

These are simply two possibilities for understanding this passage. Implicit in this passage seems to be a reference to a load animal carrying a burden whose value it does not know (i.e., it simply carries the weight of it; this is a common metaphor in later Sanskrit literature). However, by referring to milk, rather than to a load, the passage is not entirely clear. It is possible that several images are being brought together here that do not perfectly parallel each other. This passage may also be a reference to the older Yājñavalkya and his association with harsh language towards others.

What is clear in the larger narrative is that by appropriating the Veda and the status of the Veda for the ends of Sāṃkhya/Yoga, both Janaka and Yājñavalkya are here functioning as iconic of the Vedic tradition, and the earlier dialogue format that is attributed to the two in the BĀU is here easily manipulated to incorporate new teachings. As we saw in the beginning of this passage, the narrator, Bhīṣma, puts this story into the past and thus claims ancient precedent. As I will show below, the literary tradition that produced this part of the MBh was certainly aware and expressive of a general character template of whom Yājñavalkya was seen to be. This view included him being portrayed principally (though not exclusively) as an orthoprax Vedic priest. Indeed, it is based on this claim that he is called a *ṛṣi*, having moved from a simple Vedic priest to the level of iconic ancient Vedic priest, where he has the authority to discourse on such matters in this passage.

What follows this formal discussion of Yoga and Sāṃkhya is perhaps the most interesting passage regarding Yājñavalkya in all of the MBh. After explaining Yoga and Sāṃkhya directly to Janaka, Yājñavalkya switches to telling a narrative about himself—specifically, how he came to have all this knowledge that has just been relayed to Janaka.

> *avyaktasthaṃ paraṃ yat tat pṛṣṭas te 'haṃ narādhipa*
> *paraṃ guhyam imaṃ praśnaṃ śṛṇuṣvāvahito nṛpa* (12.306.1)
>
> You have asked me about the highest [*brahman*] that resides in the unmanifest, O King. This question is a great mystery. Listen closely, O King.
>
> *yathārṣeṇeha vidhinā caratāvamatena ha*
> *mayādityād avāptāni yajūṃṣi mithilādhipa* (12.306.2)
>
> By conducting myself here with humility in accordance with the rules laid down by the *ṛṣis*, the *yajus* were attained by me from the sun, O King of Mithila.

Here Yājñavalkya enters into a long explanation of how he came to have all of the knowledge that he is sharing with Janaka. This passage is the first elaborated hagiography explaining how Yājñavalkya is said to have received the White Yajurveda from the Sun, what this entailed, and how the teaching spread (or rather, how it became known as its own school of ritual interpretation). This narrative clearly has as its model Yājñavalkya's association with the Sun, perhaps dating back to the ŚB/BĀU, but this certainly must also have been a more popular understanding of the figure at the time.[25] However, as a hagiographical elaboration, this long passage brings in many unprecedented details and is an extension of known details suggesting why Yājñavalkya had to appeal to the Sun in the first place, his relation to the Black Yajurvedic tradition and his teacher, and how he propagated his teachings. Yājñavalkya concludes with a subnarrative where he tells of a questioning session between him and a Gandharva.

I will translate the first part of this narrative and highlight what appears to be the most important aspects for our purposes. We will then turn to the larger issues regarding the innovations found in this text, what may be the rationale behind the changes or continuities, and what might be the larger overall purpose of including these hagiographical details and what they do to the narrative as a whole. Yājñavalkya continues:

> *mahatā tapasā devas tapiṣṭhaḥ sevito mayā*
> *prītena cāhaṃ vibhunā sūryeṇoktas tadānagha* (12.306.3)
>
> "With great ascetic heat (*tapas*), I served the best blazing deity (*tapiṣṭha*). Then, O Sinless One, the all-pervading Sun [was] pleased [and] said to me:
>
> *varaṃ vṛṇīṣva viprarṣe yad iṣṭaṃ te sudurlabham*
> *tat te dāsyāmi prītātmā matprasādo hi durlabhaḥ* (12.306.4)
>
> 'Choose a boon, O Brahmin Ṛṣi, which you desire and is difficult for you to obtain. I will give it to you with a pleased soul, for my grace is difficult to obtain.'
>
> *tataḥ praṇamya śirasā mayoktas tapatāṃ varaḥ*
> *yajūṃṣi nopayuktāni kṣipram icchāmi veditum* (12.306.5)
>
> Then, having bowed with my head, I said to the best of those who give heat, 'I want to know immediately the *yajus* not used [or: not known].'

tato māṃ bhagavān āha vitariṣyāmi te dvija
sarasvatīha vāgbhūtā śarīraṃ te pravekṣyati (12.306.6)

Then the Lord said to me, 'I will bestow this to you, O Twice-born. [The goddess] Sarasvatī, composed of speech, will enter your body.'

tato mām āha bhagavān āsyaṃ svaṃ vivṛtaṃ kuru
vivṛtaṃ ca tato me "syaṃ praviṣṭā ca sarasvatī (12.306.7)

Then the Lord said to me, 'Open your mouth.' Thus I opened my mouth and Sarasvatī entered.

tato vidahyamāno 'haṃ praviṣṭo 'mbhas tadānagha
avijñānād amarṣāc ca bhāskarasya mahātmanaḥ (12.306.8)

Burning, I then entered the water, O Sinless one, out of ignorance and impatience with the great-souled Sun.

tato vidahyamānaṃ māṃ uvāca bhagavān raviḥ
muhūrtaṃ sahyatāṃ dāhas tataḥ śītībhaviṣyasi (12.306.9)

Then, the Sun Lord said to me while I was burning, 'Endure the burning for a moment—you will then become cool.'

śītībhūtaṃ ca māṃ dṛṣṭvā bhagavān āha bhāskaraḥ
pratiṣṭhāsyati te vedaḥ sottaraḥ sakhilo dvija (12.306.10)

And having seen me cooled, the Sun Lord said, 'The Veda will establish itself in you along with the subsequent/concluding portion and the supplement,[26] O Twice-born.

kṛtsnaṃ śatapathaṃ caiva praṇeṣyasi dvijarṣabha
tasyānte cāpunarbhāve buddhis tava bhaviṣyati (12.306.11)

'You will bring forth (√*praṇī*)[27] the whole Śatapatha, O Bull among Twice-born, and at the end of that, your mind will be [fixed upon] not being born again.

prāpsyase ca yad iṣṭaṃ tat sāṃkhyayogepsitaṃ padam
etāvad uktvā bhagavān astam evābhyavartata (12.306.12)

'And you will obtain that desire which is the place desired by Sāṃkhya and Yoga.' Having said this much, the Sun approached the Asta hill [i.e., the sun set or went home].

tato 'nuvyāhṛtaṃ śrutvā gate deve vibhāvasau
gṛham āgatya saṃhṛṣṭo 'cintayaṃ vai sarasvatīm (12.306.13)

Then I heard the speech and, when the blazing god left, I went home delighted and thought of Sarasvatī.

tataḥ pravṛttātiśubhā svaravyañjanabhūṣitā
oṃkāram āditaḥ kṛtvā mama devī sarasvatī (12.306.14)

Then the adorned one came forth to me. The goddess Sarasvatī was decorated with vowels and consonants having made OM the first.[28]

tato 'ham arghyaṃ vidhivat sarasvatyai nyavedayam
tapatāṃ ca variṣṭhāya niṣaṇṇas tatparāyaṇaḥ (12.306.15)

Then, in accordance with the rules, I offered *arghya* water to Sarasvatī and to the incendiary one (the Sun), the best of burners. Then I was seated with them as [my] last resort.

tataḥ śatapathaṃ kṛtsnaṃ sarahasyaṃ sasaṃgraham
cakre sapariśeṣaṃ ca harṣeṇa parameṇa ha (12.306.16)

Thus the whole Śatapatha together with the secret doctrine, appendix, and supplement, I made with the highest joy.

kṛtvā cādhyayanaṃ teṣāṃ śiṣyāṇāṃ śatam uttamam
vipriyārthaṃ saśiṣyasya mātulasya mahātmanaḥ (12.306.17)

And having taught these to the best one hundred of those students, displeasing for my great-souled maternal uncle with his students

tataḥ saśiṣyeṇa mayā sūryeṇeva gabhastibhiḥ
vyāpto yajño mahārāja pitus tava mahātmanaḥ (12.306.18)

then I, with [my] students, like the sun with its hands (= rays) completely took over the sacrifice of your great-souled father, O King.

miṣato devalasyāpi tato 'rdhaṃ hṛtavān aham
svavedadakṣiṇāyātha[29] *vimarde mātulena ha* (12.306.19)

Then as Devala looked on, I took half as my own reward for Veda recitation in conflict with my maternal uncle.

sumantunātha pailena tathā jaimininā ca vai
pitrā te munibhiś caiva tato 'ham anumānitaḥ (12.306.20)

Thus Sumantu, Paila, Jaimini, your father and even the other sages agreed with me.

daśa pañca ca prāptāni yajūṃṣy arkān mayānagha
tathaiva lomaharṣāc ca purāṇam avadhāritam (12.306.21)

I obtained the ten times five *yajus* from the Sun, O Sinless one and likewise studied the Purāṇa from Lomaharṣa.

bījam etat puraskṛtya devīṃ caiva sarasvatīm
sūryasya cānubhāvena pravṛtto 'haṃ narādhipa (12.306.22)

Having put the seed and the goddess Sarasvatī in front[30] and with the luster of Sūrya, I commenced, O King

kartuṃ śatapathaṃ vedam apūrvaṃ kāritaṃ ca me
yathābhilaṣitaṃ mārgaṃ tathā tac copapāditam (12.306.23)

to make the Śatapatha Veda. I made something that had not been made before. Likewise, the path (i.e., the Śatapatha), in accordance with my desire, was accomplished.

śiṣyāṇām akhilaṃ kṛtsnam anujñātaṃ sasaṃgraham
sarve ca śiṣyāḥ śucayo gatāḥ paramaharṣitāḥ (12.306.24)

> The whole [text] with the complete abstracts was taught to the students. All the students, who were pure, greatly rejoiced.
>
> *śākhāḥ pañcadaśemās tu vidyā bhāskaradarśitāḥ*
> *pratiṣṭhāpya yathākāmaṃ vedyaṃ tad anucintayam* (12.306.25)
>
> Having established the fifty branches of science that I saw from the Sun, according to my desire I meditated on that object of knowledge."

Here the text switches to a discourse between Yājñavalkya and a Gandharva who is apparently both asking about and verifying the knowledge that Yājñavalkya possesses. For our purposes, this short passage is not particularly novel: it continues the themes already discussed earlier in the conversation between Yājñavalkya and Janaka and is a simplified discussion of Sāṃkhya (perhaps an intentional reiteration of what preceded). The main purpose of this passage appears to be to put this dialogue outside of the mundane world and thus associate it with the otherworldly by means of the character of a Gandharva. It should be remembered that, in the BĀU, Yājñavalkya's knowledge was tested twice by knowledge that was held by a Gandharva in the two possession episodes (BĀU 3.3 and 3.7). In those cases, the interlocutors knew the Gandharva's proper answers, but they were testing whether Yājñavalkya's knowledge was equivalent. In this MBh passage, Yājñavalkya is going so far as to teach a celestial being about the nature of the cosmos. In this sense, Yājñavalkya's knowledge is said to be not simply for human beings on earth nor is it a truth relative to this world. It is an all-encompassing truth for beings both mundane and divine.

Characterizing Yājñavalkya

This long passage gives a particular view of whom Yājñavalkya was, what he was thought to have accomplished, and how. While this view is clearly based on the earlier literary tradition—such as Yājñavalkya being associated with the beginning of the White Yajurveda via the Sun, his connection with Janaka, as well as thematic continuities mentioned earlier—this version also has its own unique narrative expansion that varies significantly from the BĀU/ŚB.

First and most obviously, beginning with the ŚB and finding its full expression in the BĀU, Yājñavalkya's principal character trait has been his irreverent and sarcastic persona. I have outlined these instances of sarcasm in the short exchanges in the ŚB. Though it is clear that his opinion was not always accepted, when sarcasm occurs in the ŚB his position is listed as authoritative. This trait was further elaborated in the BĀU. In BĀU 1.1, Yājñavalkya claims the cows meant for the most learned before a debate could even begin—certainly an audacious act. He trades verbal barbs with the other contestants during the course of the debate, culminating in the most sharp exchanges with Śākalya (3.9). Even in private conversations with Janaka, Yājñavalkya continues to show himself superior to others (BĀU 4.1: "this is like saying a person has a mother, father, and a teacher."). Within the White Yajurvedic tradition, however, these were not negative portrayals of this figure, but quite the opposite. We have seen that it is most fruitful to view the character's sarcasm as "pride in correct knowledge." This is to say, his pride was not viewed as a character flaw or anything of the sort by the tradition; it rather was seen as justified by the fact that it was warranted—he was proper in acting superior because his knowledge proved that he was superior. The principal use of this sarcasm was to focus the narratives on *establishing* Yājñavalkya and the school that he was associated with as authoritative.

The MBh narrative, however, has a different focus—that of an *already established* Yājñavalkya as a *ṛṣi* and the founder of the White Yajurveda. As such, rather than trying to argue for the validity of the tradition or of a particular spokesman for the tradition, the narrative after the Sāṃkhya-Yoga discussion is concerned with explaining how this tradition came about and to position this within the ancient past via a myth of Yājñavalkya's interaction with the Sun. In this fashion, the pride and sarcasm that are commonly used in portraying Yājñavalkya in other narratives aren't as apparent. However, these aspects of this character's earlier portrayal were apparently known, as they occasionally break through the surface of this narrative and suggest his literary past. Indeed, in this case, it is his own telling of his past that suggests audaciousness—he claims half of the recitation fee apparently meant for his uncle.

As we have previously seen, Yājñavalkya's association with the Sun dates back to the BĀU and perhaps even to the Sun mantra we saw in the ŚB. In the MBh, the association with the Sun is given full expression by incorporating many new details into the hagiography of Yājñavalkya. Many of these details serve to fill out what could be seen as silences or gaps in the other portrayals of Yājñavalkya. Thus, while the BĀU/ŚB passages do not elaborate on the nature of Yājñavalkya's association with the Sun, it is part of the goal of the MBh narrative to explain this directly.

The narrative begins by explaining that it is Yājñavalkya who appealed to the Sun to be granted knowledge of the sacrifice. Interestingly, at least one major question is left unanswered in the framing; that is, why Yājñavalkya appealed to the Sun in the first place. This question, however, is taken up by composers of the Purāṇas in later centuries and did not apparently concern the composers of this narrative.[31] Through Yājñavalkya's appeal to the Sun, we are told that not only was he given the White Yajurveda, but the whole of the Veda as well as other oral texts.

If in the Upaniṣads there is a tendency to focus on *bandhus*—latent connections (whether etymological, narrative, or both) focused on similarity in sound and/or the nature of two entities—we find something similar in this narrative of the divine interacting on earth. Yājñavalkya is said to have used *tapas* (ascetic heat accumulated through austerities) to appeal to the *tapiṣṭha* (the "best of heat" and perhaps "the best ascetic," as the Sun burns naturally). It is said that because the Sun's grace is "difficult to achieve" (*sudurlabha*), Yājñavalkya should choose a boon that is also "difficult to achieve" (*durlabha*).[32] While Yājñavalkya used heat to appease the heated one (the Sun), it is through heat that the Sun, through the intermediary of Sarasvatī, burns Yājñavalkya. It is clear here that the Sun's *tapas* is greater than Yājñavalkya's as the Sun causes Yājñavalkya to feel great heat and pain which he attempts to quench by entering water. Further in the narrative, we find that Sarasvatī came to Yājñavalkya in the form of speech (*vāk*) thus explaining why it was that she initially entered through his mouth. The form of speech is particularly appropriate because the *mantras* (indeed all of the Vedas and the appendices) that Yājñavalkya is to receive from the Sun will be in the form of speech.[33]

The binary complementarity that we find in this story is a way to provide a natural explanation for what could otherwise seem obscure or extranormal—direct contact with a god and the subsequent boon. Etymological *bandhus* within the Upaniṣads do a similar thing—finding the "natural" (if hidden) connection between words or concepts shows the "truth" of the connection between them. Note that Yājñavalkya at the beginning of this narrative refers to Janaka's query as a "great mystery" (*paraṃ guhyam*) which suggests that only a mysterious (i.e., divine) explanation will serve.

In the MBh, the *bandhus* in question are not always etymological equations (such as *sudurlabha/durlabha* among others), but the narrative also structures itself on binary complementarities—one approaches the hot god (the sun) through heat, and the god approaches the person through the same means. Since orally recited texts are being requested, it is natural then that these would then enter through the mouth, where the goddess assumes the form of the Sanskrit syllabary itself. Indeed, the complementarity reaches its climax when Yājñavalkya refers to himself as the Sun and his students as the sunrays during the course of the sacrifice that follows (12.306.18). In a sense, the teachings of the Sun made Yājñavalkya (and his students) one and the same with the Sun.[34] This complementarity is narratively required in this story for the divine interaction to take place. This is supported by the fact that when Yājñavalkya breaks with the complementarity (by entering water to cool himself), the Sun intervenes and tells Yājñavalkya that he must endure the heat to receive his boon.[35] This association with Yājñavalkya and *tapas* may be an allusion to his association with renunciation in the BĀU as well as Janaka's own renunciation at the end of this passage. It is clear that the burning sensation and eventually its dissipation was necessary for the boon, while Yājñavalkya's entering the water broke the complementarity by bringing together apparently opposing elements (fire and water).

The inquiry relates to a "great mystery" and the story of the Sun god's interaction with Yājñavalkya serves as an explanation of how Yājñavalkya came to have all this knowledge, and the system of complementarity structures the interaction between the divine and the mundane. While *bandhus* serve to show the connectedness between words and concepts to indicate a deeper or higher truth, here such connections are narrative ones that similarly attempt to show a truth—the system by which Yājñavalkya was able to beseech the Sun for his blessings and thus the origins of the White Yajurveda.

If Yājñavalkya can be characterized by his pride in earlier portrayals, in this MBh passage we actually have something that is almost opposite.[36] Yājñavalkya here is portrayed as an idealized supplicant who not only serves the great Sun god, but does so to a degree that pleases the god—no small task as the god himself admits. At the beginning, Yājñavalkya states that he acted though "despised" (*avamata*) by others, suggesting he committed an offense towards his teacher and perhaps suggesting he was wrong in his action. He shows proper respect to the Sun god by bowing his head towards him (12.306.5), while it is said later (12.306.15) that he follows the proper hospitality rules in offering *arghya* water to Sarasvatī and the Sun when he invokes them. Rather than being prideful, Yājñavalkya admits his own human weakness by not initially withstanding the burning heat of the Sun. He claims that it was his ignorance (*avijñāna*) and impatience (*amarṣa*) which led him to do so, realizing after the fact that he should have accepted the situation on the Sun god's terms. In fact, his impatience may be an oblique reference to his character portrayed elsewhere—such as driving off the cows before the debate begins in the BĀU or his apparent frustration with various interlocutors in that debate.

The reasons for Yājñavalkya's portrayal as humble in this narrative are many—the first is the obvious hierarchical relationship established between a human being and the divine, the Sun god. As is seen in much of Hindu religious literature, a principal means to approaching a god is to show one's deference to the divine power. While the beginning of this narrative framed Yājñavalkya as a *ṛṣi*, the point of much of the narrative is to explain how he became one. This mythological narrative explains how a remarkable human being was able to beseech the great Sun god, not only in receiving the fifty *yajus* formulas, but even the entire Vedas and appendices. Certainly, Yājñavalkya's subservience, along with the structural complementarity, is a means to explain how such a boon could be attained. By establishing a mythological origin, this narrative is more concerned with explaining how things came to be than with any rivalry between different groups of priests.

Though this narrative is not directly concerned with Yājñavalkya's portrayal as a sarcastic and bold individual, this is not to say that there are not possible undercurrents in the narrative which suggest that the composers were aware of Yājñavalkya's character from other sources. I have already mentioned that his portrayal as impatient could be such an allusion. In fact, there are other passages which suggest that such aspects form part of the background of this tale, even if they are not foregrounded in the narrative itself. For example, the question is left open as to why Yājñavalkya felt compelled to beseech the Sun in the first place for *yajus* that were "not used" (*nopayukta*) in the sacrifice. This mention of previously unknown *mantras* makes clear that Yājñavalkya intends to make himself unique among Vedic sacrificers, not the least because he would position himself as the human beginning of a new teaching lineage. While not saying so directly, this suggests that Yājñavalkya was circumventing his maternal uncle, who may have been (though again it is not explicitly stated to be) Yājñavalkya's teacher. Certainly, we know that the uncle was not pleased with Yājñavalkya taking it upon himself to teach students (12.306.17), perhaps usurping his role as teacher after Yājñavalkya received this divine wisdom from the Sun. This conflict apparently comes to a head when Yājñavalkya and the students participate in the sacrifice, and Yājñavalkya claims half of the *dakṣiṇa* (sacrificial fee) apparently meant for his uncle. In doing so, Yājñavalkya is making a claim to be his uncle's equal—a claim that the other priests (Sumantu, Jaimini, and Paila) and Janaka's father agree is valid. In a fashion, if a *brahmodya* like the one in the BĀU is to establish one's superior knowledge by verbal debate, here Yājñavalkya apparently proved his knowledge of proper ritual actions (and the accompanying *mantras*) by performing them in the Vedic ritual itself. Not only then is the Sun god said to have given these texts to Yājñavalkya, but through his enactment of these teachings during the ritual the other priests acknowledge their validity and correctness. In a sense, the knowledge given to Yājñavalkya by the Sun is being independently validated by the established Vedic priests in the ritual.[37]

At this point, an important question can be raised: if the preceding discussion between Janaka and Yājñavalkya was focused solely on the nature of Sāṃkhya and Yoga, what would be the purpose of a narrative that is more concerned with the mythological background of Yājñavalkya and only secondarily with Sāṃkhya and Yoga? Further, why would this subnarrative be followed by a second subnarrative of a discussion between Yājñavalkya and a Gandharva?

There are both text-internal and text-external answers to these questions—some, of course, more convincing than others. Most obviously, as mentioned before, Janaka is asking a question that Yājñavalkya calls a "great mystery."[38] If Yājñavalkya is about to expound upon the highest *brahman*, then it serves him to explain where such secret knowledge originated. As such, Yājñavalkya is telling a story that shows why the knowledge he has is particular to him. In contrast, in the Gandharva episodes of the BĀU, where Yājñavalkya attained the knowledge that was held by celestial beings and imparted only to those Brahmins who happened to be at the home of Patañcala Kāpya, origin was not at issue. In that case, Yājñavalkya knowing the answers showed that his knowledge was equal to that of the Gandharvas and not dependent upon them. As such, it showed his knowledge as superior to the other Brahmins whose knowledge was dependent on the Gandharvas.

In the MBh, though, the situation is somewhat different. What is being asked of Yājñavalkya is not what a Gandharva may or may not know, given their apparently privileged position as celestial beings. Rather, Yājñavalkya is being asked by Janaka to explain the highest principle of all, and this apparently required narrative justification as to how he could have such knowledge. The narrative of the Gandharvas that follows shows that even they do not have such knowledge, perhaps self-consciously contrasting with the BĀU portrayal. Indeed, the Sun god is said to have told Yājñavalkya that, after he learned all these sacred texts, his mind would be focused on not being born again (i.e., final liberation, 12.306.11), which is the culminating topic of the preceding section of Sāṃkhya and Yoga thematically connected to this passage.

There is another reason for the possible inclusion of this narrative. While framing the narrative as an ancient discussion between Yājñavalkya and Janaka would itself be enough to link these doctrines to the Vedic past, the narrative is bringing the Vedas into close conjunction with Sāṃkhya and Yoga (so also with surrounding narratives; see Fitzgerald 2012). It is likely that there was an apparent tension between differing worldviews. This is supported by the fact that it is unlikely that the tradition would have argued so directly that the two views were one and the same, if such a position were self-evident or widely held. In so doing, at least in this case, it may have raised the question of why Yājñavalkya is not associated with similar Yoga/Sāṃkhya teachings elsewhere.[39] Certainly, there are thematic overlaps with the BĀU concerning the nature of death, immortality, the fearless, and so on, but nothing in the BĀU broaches the technicality one finds in these discussions of Sāṃkhya and, to a lesser degree, Yoga. While the BĀU passages are not simple, they also are not formal philosophy with very specific technical terms employed in a fashion similar to Sāṃkhya. Perhaps one reason for the inclusion of this story was to give a background to a character who may otherwise seem out of place in this context.

The main purpose of this narrative, however, is to bring the doctrines of Sāṃkhya/Yoga together with the character of Yājñavalkya. As we have seen, the previous discussion regarding Sāṃkhya and Yoga contained little or no narrative elements, except for the framing of the story. What followed was a rather dry, technical listing of principles that was more a monologue than a dialogue or story. While Yājñavalkya had directly said to Janaka that Sāṃkhya, Yoga, and the Veda were the same, here the purpose of the origin story is *to narratively show* how this is the case. The story relates how Yājñavalkya received sacred texts from the Sun, but also how he will, afterwards, focus his mind on not dying again (*apunarmr̥tyu*). In this fashion, this narrative is telling the audience that the preceding discussion on the nature of the cosmos based on Sāṃkhya and Yoga (and whose explicit goal is liberation from rebirth) is the culmination of the revelation that Yājñavalkya received from the Sun. Not only did the Sun grant Yājñavalkya the *yajus*, the ŚB, etc., but he also granted him the ability to see the truth of Sāṃkhya and Yoga within that. Thus this narrative "proves" that this doctrine is the highest because the Sun god granted it to Yājñavalkya as such. If the BĀU genealogy which mentions Yājñavalkya and the Sun is meant to explain the origins of the White Yajurveda, the MBh myth encompasses that while integrating the origin of Sāṃkhya/Yoga within that same origin.

This helps to explain certain details that appear in this narrative. In the BĀU, Yājñavalkya is said only to have received the *yajus* from the Sun. Here, on the other hand, Yājñavalkya is said to receive the *yajus*, the ŚB, and the whole Veda (with the concluding portion and supplement, 12.306.10–11). It could be argued that this is simply hagiographical hyperbole—that is, the authors may have inflated the passage to include all these sacred texts as a means of glorifying Yājñavalkya. This is, of course, quite possible and even likely as Yājñavalkya is said to be a *r̥ṣi*. However, such a response does not answer the more important question of whether doing so alters the narrative in other ways.

In fact, here I think we have another case where the narrative is making an argument similar to the one made by Yājñavalkya to Janaka about the apparent sameness of Sāṃkhya, Yoga, and the Veda. Lines 12.306.10–12 are a progressive statement about the sacred texts imparted to Yājñavalkya by the Sun (12.306.10: the Veda, the concluding portion, the supplement; 12.306.11: the ŚB) and what they will lead to (12.306.11: focus of the mind on liberation; 12.306.12: the place desired by Sāṃkhya and Yoga, i.e., liberation itself). This is to say that all of the Vedic tradition is said to be within Yājñavalkya (given to him by the Sun) and all of it leads to the goal of Sāṃkhya and Yoga. In this fashion, I think the portrayal of Yājñavalkya receiving more than simply the White Yajurveda is meant not so much to glorify Yājñavalkya, but rather to make Yājñavalkya iconic of the *whole Vedic tradition*. As such, placing the doctrines of Sāṃkhya and Yoga as the pinnacle of Yājñavalkya's teaching is a means to incorporate the established tradition into what is more recent.

Finally, this story serves, in many ways, the same function as the genealogies that we find in the BĀU. The genealogies there list the names of teachers and students as a means of not only elucidating the (not necessarily factual) history of a teaching lineage, but also as a means to claim a validity to those teachings which preceded it.[40] This narrative (and the subnarrative of the Gandharva) does the same thing here. In the BĀU, the list of largely human teachers is here a story of how one student, Yājñavalkya, was taught by the ultimate teacher—the Sun god. In this fashion, this story is a narrative genealogy which validates the teachings of Sāṃkhya and Yoga that precede it.

MBh Book 2 (Sabhāparvan)

There are a series of smaller passages where Yājñavalkya appears in the MBh. In some of these passages, there is little detail given about his character, so it is not entirely clear what the composers' conception of this figure was. However, in many, there are parallels with other stories, verbal echoes, or suggestive links to the Yājñavalkya that we have encountered so far, clearly indicating that the figure of Yājñavalkya is consciously being rewritten into different scenarios.

In passage 2.4.10 there is a single reference to Yājñavalkya. He appears amongst a list of several other famous Brahmins in attendance at Yudhiṣṭhira's assembly hall (*sabhā*, hence the name of the book). As with Janaka's gifting of cows and his kingdom in the BĀU, the trope of tremendous gift-giving appears in this passage, but it is far more elaborate. Not only does the trope of a thousand cows appear, but a thousand cows are given to every Brahmin in attendance (*dadau tebhyaḥ sahasrāṇi gavām*).[41] The text further elaborates the various foods that are given to feed the Brahmins and tells us that new clothes were given for them to wear. While the context of Janaka's gift-giving in the BĀU was to establish which particular Brahmin was most learned in *brahman* (*brahmiṣṭha*), here all the illustrious Brahmins and Kṣatriyas are fed and given gifts by Yudhiṣṭhira, presumably to show his status, righteousness, and generosity.

Yājñavalkya's name appears within a list of others in attendance with no elaboration. There is little overlap with the genealogies we have seen in the BĀU, but the reason seems obvious: the MBh passage is not a straightforward genealogy but rather a listing of the religiously important individuals who attended the grand hall. In introducing the list of individuals the text calls those in attendance *r̥ṣis* and kings from various countries.

> *sabhāyām r̥ṣayas tasyāṃ pāṇḍavaiḥ saha āsate*
> *āsāṃ cakrur narendrāś ca nānādeśasamāgatāḥ* (2.4.7)
>
> In that hall seers [r̥ṣi] and princes from many countries sat with the Pāṇḍavas (Van Buitenen, trans., 1975, 38)

Following this introduction, more than sixty *r̥ṣis* are mentioned. Within this list we find:

> *tittirir yājñavalkyaś ca sasuto lomaharṣaṇaḥ*
> *apsuhomyaś ca dhaumyaś ca āṇīmāṇḍavyakauśikau* (2.4.10)
>
> Then there were Tittiri,[42] Yājñavalkya, Lomaharṣana and his son; Apsuhomya, Dhaumya, Māṇḍavya-with-the-Stake, Kauśika . . . (Van Buitenen, trans., 1975, 38)

It should be pointed out that the names in the larger list do not appear connected to Yājñavalkya as we know him from earlier sources.[43] However, certain other important Upaniṣadic names do occur in this list: Nāciketas, probably related to Naciketas of *Kaṭha Upaniṣad*; Gautama, which is a name often used for Uddālaka Āruṇi (BĀU, *Chāndogya Upaniṣad*); Paiṅga, perhaps connected to Paiṅgya in *Kauṣītaki Brāhmaṇa*/

Kauṣītaki Upaniṣad,[44] and Śāṇḍilya, who is the principal authority in the middle books of the ŚB.[45]

It appears clear that the individuals mentioned in this passage are taken as authoritative in ritual and religious matters (they are introduced as *r̥ṣis,* Vedic "seers"), whether the ancient past, the more recent present, and as is often the case, a collapsing of the two (though in many cases it is unclear what their specific realm of authority is). The list concludes by saying

> *munayo dharmasahitā dhr̥tātmāno jitendriyāḥ*
> *ete cānye ca bahavo vedavedāṅgapāragāḥ* (2.4.16)
> *upāsate mahātmānaṃ sabhāyām r̥ṣisattamāḥ*
> *kathayantaḥ kathāḥ puṇyā dharmajñāḥ śucayo 'malāḥ* (2.4.17)

> These and many other hermits [who were] firm in Law, masters of soul and senses, learned in the Vedas and their branches, and eminent seers [r̥ṣi] attended on the great-spirited King in his assembly hall. [These munis were] wise in the Law, pure and immaculate [people who] narrated auspicious tales. (Van Buitenen, trans., 1975, 38; modified for clarity)

It should be pointed out that the individuals mentioned play no narrative role in the story (though they are said to tell auspicious narratives!) but rather serve to emphasize the greatness of the assembly hall (*sabhā*) created by the *asura,* Maya, for the Pāṇḍavas. The building of this hall prefigures Yudhiṣthira's desire (instigated by the visit of Nārada) to perform the *rājasūya,* the consecration ceremony of a king. Indeed, as Van Buitenen has pointed out in his introduction to this book, the whole structure of book 2 appears to be based on this ancient Vedic rite (1975, 5ff.).

When Yājñavalkya is mentioned, it is in the same vein as Tittiri and Lomaharṣana. But who are Tittiri and Lomaharṣana? Tittiri, as we will discuss in chapter 4, is often viewed as the compiler of the *Taittirīya Brāhmaṇa* and *Taittirīya Upaniṣad,* a leader of the Black Yajurvedic school of ritual interpretation, and in the Purāṇas is often called the teacher of Yājñavalkya. Lomaharṣana is a figure connected with Purāṇic literary production. As we saw in book 12, Yājñavalkya is said to have learned the Purāṇas from one Lomaharṣa, which is unlikely to be a coincidence.

By Tittiri's association with Yājñavalkya, it is suggested here that, at least as early as book 2 of the MBh, a connection was made between these two individuals which may foreshadow the apparent connection (and disjuncture) of the Black and the White Yajurvedic traditions found in later literature. What exactly this association means is a bit unclear as the text does not elaborate these relationships, but by placing the two in apposition it does show that the hagiographical elaboration that we find in later Purāṇas had a precedent. It is possible that this figure may have been viewed as Yājñavalkya's maternal uncle whom we encountered in book 12, though this is not explicitly stated. In any event, it is noteworthy that both are mentioned side by side, but there is no mention of a perceived split between Yajurvedic schools. It is also not entirely clear whether in this passage Yājñavalkya was seen as the founder of his own school or not. Most likely he was, as he is called a *r̥ṣi* along with the others in attendance. Whether there was any perceived animosity between different Yajurvedic schools is not stated, but, as we will see, the remainder of the story clearly sees Yājñavalkya as the paramount Yajurvedin.

Following this passage, the sage Nārada appears to both question king Yudhiṣṭhira about how he conducts his politics, as well as to emphasize that Yudhiṣṭhira should perform the *rājusūya* sacrifice. During the course of this conversation, Nārada describes the assembly halls of other kings, apparently in an attempt to equate Yudhiṣṭhira with them and to reinforce the need for Yudhiṣṭhira to perform the sacrifice as other (human and divine) kings had done.

Further, in 2.7.10, which is part of Nārada's description of other assembly halls, Yājñavalkya is again listed among prominent Brahmins attending the assembly hall of a king. Here, however, his status is higher than his status in attending Yudhiṣṭhira's hall. In this passage, Yājñavalkya is said to be attending the hall of the king of the gods, Indra (Śakra), which doubly serves to show Yājñavalkya's exalted position as well as that of Indra's celestial hall. As Nārada's story is a narrative within a narrative, we have Yājñavalkya as a character in a larger narrative about a narrative in which he is a character. Here also at least two other famous Upaniṣadic individuals are in attendance: Uddālaka and Śvetaketu. The status of all of them is elevated to the divine realm, fitting for the location.

ayonijā yonijāś ca vāyubhakṣā hutāśinaḥ
īśānaṃ sarvalokasya vajriṇaṃ samupāsate (2.7.13)

These seers, born from wombs and not born from wombs, living on the wind, maintaining the fires, all wait upon the sovereign of the entire universe, the Thunderbolt-wielder. (trans., Van Buitenen 1973, 46)

At 2.30.35, Yājñavalkya appears again. However, rather than appearing in a list with little elaboration, it is quite clear that the Yājñavalkya we have met in the ŚB and the BĀU is the individual being referred to. After Nārada has finished his conversation with Yudhiṣṭhira, the Pāṇḍavas are convinced of the need to perform the royal sacrifice. As Van Buitenen has pointed out (trans., 1975, 4), this desire for a sacrifice on Yudhiṣṭhira's part seems a bit odd, considering that Yudhiṣṭhira had already lost his kingdom at Hāstināpura, so he has little on which to base such a claim. While it appears that Yudhiṣṭhira initially wants to stake his claim as a new king, he quite clearly aspires to be no less than a world sovereign—a *samrāj*. However, it is important, at least narratively I would argue, that Yudhiṣṭhira make such a claim in this text—if he is going to lose everything later in the fateful game of dice, he has to have *everything* to lose.[46]

Within this passage, it is absolutely clear that Yājñavalkya must be the same character referred to in the BĀU, because here Yājñavalkya is said to have functioned as the principal *adhvaryu* (*adhvaryusattama*), the Yajurvedic priest, for Yudhiṣṭhira's *rājasūya*. Though earlier Yājñavalkya was mentioned in a list of individuals, here he is singled out for his ritual abilities. Further, Yājñavalkya is said to be "most learned in *brahman*" (*brahmiṣṭha*!),[47] clearly a direct reference to his role in the BĀU public debate at Janaka's court. Indeed, all of the four priests (Satyavatī's son,[48] Yājñavalkya, Susāman, Paila) who are chosen to perform the *rājasūya* are said to be "worthy Brahmans who seemed to embody the Vedas themselves" (Van Buitenen, trans., 1975, 88; *vedān iva mahābhāgān sākṣān mūrtimato dvijān*). At the least, Yājñavalkya's authority here is considered absolute along with the other three priests. That each priest is considered the leader of his particular tradition is also clear in 2.30.36:

eteṣāṃ śiṣyavargāś ca putrāś ca bharatarṣabha
babhūvur hotragāḥ sarve vedavedāṅgapāragāḥ

> The flocks of their [i.e., the ṛṣis'] pupils and their sons, who, bull of the Bharatas, were learned in the Vedas and their branches, all became acolytes. (trans., Van Buitenen 1973, 88)

Certainly this passage makes clear that they were considered leaders in their particular ritual functions, if not the founders of their respective traditions. Moreover, even their pupils and sons are said to be "learned in the Vedas and their branches" which we must assume is a valorization of the teachers themselves (i.e., if their students are so learned, yet they are still students, then the teachers must be that much more so).

A novelty arises in this passage: Was the Yājñavalkya we have encountered earlier thought to have progeny? Within the BĀU, he had a student (Sāmaśravas) whom he asked to lead the cows away from Janaka's court before the debate even took place. We have also encountered Yājñavalkya's two wives (Maitreyī and Kātyāyanī). Nowhere, however, in the early textual record is there any mention of other family members.[49] Of course, absence from the earlier literary record does not mean that Yājñavalkya was thought not to have children (indeed, the other priests mentioned must have had wives—a requirement before one can be a priest—but they are not mentioned). It was most likely assumed by the BĀU audience that Yājñavalkya had children, and it was not deemed narratively necessary to mention them, though it may have been possible that in the literary world of the BĀU, the ideal of a "good sage" did not *necessarily* require one to have children. This passage from the MBh, however, suggests that the broader Indian tradition, at least by the time of the MBh, viewed Yājñavalkya as having children whether the earlier tradition did or not. It could be that children are a novelty introduced by the MBh in Yājñavalkya's biography, but it is more likely to have been simply the common conception about Yājñavalkya's life that never entered into the earlier literary record.

Note that Yājñavalkya is a minor character in this narrative in that his personality is not elaborated, nor does he have any speaking role. His function here is limited to simply his presence. While this presence, I would argue, is integral to the narrative, it is because of the structural and thematic function of the character rather than any larger role played by the character himself. We should note here that Yājñavalkya's authority is not questioned by the author(s) of these passages; but rather it is clear that the popularity and fame of Yājñavalkya had great appeal. If book 12 of the MBh held Yājñavalkya as iconic of the Vedic tradition as a whole, here that iconic status is limited only to the role of the *adhvaryu* proper and not connected with *yoga*. In the MBh, a text that must have had a pan-Indian elite circulation (via enactment, recitation, or what have you), Yājñavalkya's authoritativeness as a *ṛṣi*, while not necessarily a given (as his status is mentioned in the text), is simply asserted as fact. Reiteration of Yājñavalkya being a *brahmiṣṭha* and his role as a Yajurvedic priest are sufficient verbal echoes of his portrayals in earlier literature.

If one takes these references to Yājñavalkya in book 2 together, however, a larger pattern emerges. Van Buitenen has suggested that the differing narratives found in the Sabhāparvan regarding the assembly halls of various gods are intended to serve a particular function—to properly place Yudhiṣṭhira and his hall within the cosmic schema. That is to say that Yudhiṣṭhira, following the model of the gods, is establishing himself as well by (re)establishing the cosmos.

As Van Buitenen points out (trans., 1975, 10), ancient subcontinental thinkers viewed space as two pyramids placed with their bases touching. The four points on the touching bases represents the four cardinal directions while the top point, the zenith, represents the "world of Brahmā" (*brahmaloka*). The earth is conceived of as the lowest point, the nadir, where Yudhiṣthira's assembly hall resides. In the course of the establishment of Yudhiṣṭhira as *samrāj*, his position on earth is established in the cosmic schema—Yudhiṣṭhira takes the ritual step from the nadir to the zenith, establishing a parallel with Brahmā's world, while his four brothers ritually connect themselves to the worlds of the gods in the four cardinal directions (Arjuna to the north, Bhīma to the east, Sahadeva to the south, and Nakula to the west). All of this places the kingdom and the king within the cosmic scheme—not as superior to the gods, but rather as equals to or perhaps homologies of them.

In looking at Yājñavalkya's function in this section, a secondary equivalence is being made between Yudhiṣṭhira and Indra, suggesting two (not necessarily contradictory) views of the cosmic hierarchy being employed simultaneously.[50] While Yudhiṣṭhira is being directly associated with Brahmā as the zenith of the cosmos—suggesting an equivalence or parallel—Yudhiṣṭhira is secondarily equated with Indra as "king of the gods."

The most obvious reference to the equation of Yudhiṣṭhira and Indra is that the capital of Yudhiṣṭhira's new kingdom is named Indraprastha ("the establishment of Indra"), suggesting directly that Yudhiṣṭhira is "Indra on earth." Interestingly, in this MBh section, Yājñavalkya functions as a connecting link between the assembly at the hall of Yudhiṣṭhira and the hall of Indra through his performance in their *rājasūyas*. Yājñavalkya is present at both sacrifices further suggesting that Yudhiṣṭhira's hall is similar in grandeur to Indra's. By portraying Yājñavalkya as the *adhvaryu* in the *rājasūya* that is said to take place in both halls there is a symbolic correspondence of Indra as the king of heaven and Yudhiṣṭhira as king of earth. Thus, Yudhiṣṭhira's claim to be *samrāj* is claiming to be parallel to Indra's position in the heavens. This is explicitly stated at the conclusion:

> *prāvartataivaṃ yajñaḥ sa pāṇḍavasya mahātmanaḥ*
> *pr̥thivyām ekavīrasya śakrasyeva triviṣṭape* (2.30.52)
>
> Thus did the sacrifice begin of the great-spirited Pāṇḍava, the One Hero on earth, as of Śakra in heaven. (trans., Van Buitenen, 1973, 89)

Why Yājñavalkya serves a mediating function must be because of the level of his authoritativeness and his revered position. Thus, he can serve in sacrifices in both the divine and the earthly worlds. Narratively, this makes sense given that the *adhvaryu* priest is, in many ways, the most important priest in the sacrifice as he does the majority of ritual acts. If there is going to be a parallel in priests made between the two performances, Yājñavalkya would be the natural choice.

While Indra as "king of the gods" is found throughout the Vedas, one may ask why there are two different correspondences (between Yudhiṣṭhira and Brahmā, and Yudhiṣṭhira and Indra) being played out in the text that could be seen, at least superficially, as contradicting each other. One can further ask, why is it that Arjuna, who is normally associated with Indra (as his offspring), is superseded by Yudhiṣṭhira in this association?[51]

While much has been written about Indra's apparent fall in status in the post-Vedic period, Gonda (1967) has clearly shown that this is an oversimplification and that Indra serves different functions in different passages across texts. Thus, while Indra is often portrayed as one of the most important deities in the *Ṛgveda,* this does not mean that later stories in the MBh or Purāṇas that may give Indra a lesser status (or even a negative one) disavow the validity of his positive portrayals. It is in this fashion, I contend, that the MBh is equating Yudhiṣṭhira and Brahmā via the spatial correspondence of zenith and nadir, but ideologically equating Yudhiṣṭhira and Indra as king of all (*samrāj* on earth and *samrāj* in heaven).

There is textual evidence that explains why these two conceptions of Yudhiṣṭhira and the divine hierarchy of the gods were not seen as at odds with each other. The standard explanation of the origins of the five Pāṇḍava brothers was that the three oldest were born to one mother (Kuntī) and the two youngest to another (Mādrī). All had different fathers: Dharma was the father of Yudhiṣṭhira, Indra was Arjuna's father, Vāyu was Bhīma's, and the twin Aśvins were the fathers of Mādrī's two boys (Nakula and Sahadeva).[52]

This maps nicely onto the explanation of Yudhiṣṭhira ritually conquering the zenith of Brahmā and the four brothers conquering the four cardinal directions as his representatives. In this sense, the five Pāṇḍavas map themselves on to the five non-earthly worlds as representatives of different gods and thus encompass the cosmos.[53]

Another explanation, however, helps to bring these two cosmic views together. We find a tale of how the five sons are all said to be Indra himself, whether directly or indirectly. MBh 1.189.27 gives an explanation of how the five brothers constitute five aspects of a single Indra or are the five Indras.[54] In this story, Indra is said to have insulted the "great god" (Mahādeva) stating that he himself was the greatest of all gods:

> *tam abravīd devarājo mamedaṃ*
> *tvaṃ viddhi viśvaṃ bhuvanaṃ vaśe sthitam*
> *īśo 'ham asmīti samanyur abravīd*
> *dṛṣṭvā tam akṣaiḥ subhṛśaṃ pramattam* (1.189.15)
>
> Quoth Indra: "I am the king of the Gods
> And all the world is under my sway!
> I am the lord!" said he in anger
> As he saw the other absorbed in the game.
> (trans., Van Buitenen 1973, 371)

Apparently, it is Indra's pride that gets the better of him and propels the story forward. The great god causes Indra to become immobile and admonishes him. He then tells Indra to push aside a great mountain and enter its center along with "four others who matched his splendor" (Van Buitenen, trans., 1973, 372; *tulyadyutīṃś caturo 'nyān dadarśa* 1.189.20). Indra pleads that he be allowed to eventually escape this fate, and the great god tells him that he, along with the four other Indras, will be reborn on earth through divine fathers. Thus, they are born as the Pāṇḍavas, where their great deeds will allow them once again to return to the world of Indra (*indraloka*; 1.189.26).

Though historically later in time (though how much later is open to debate), the *Mārkaṇḍeya Purāṇa* (MārkP) gives a different story of the relationship of Indra and the Pāṇḍavas that also serves to reconcile these apparently different views of the cosmos.[55] Gonda (1967, 245–46) summarizes a series of tales of Indra in MārkP (chapter 5) that not only attempts to reconcile varying accounts of this god, but attempts to explain his role in the MBh (which is one of the main goals of the MārkP). Through a series of transgressions, Indra loses his fiery energy (*tejas*), his strength (*balam*), and his form (*rūpam*) to various gods: his *tejas* to Dharma, his *balam* to Vāyu, and his *rūpam* to the two Aśvins. It is said then that these gods release Indra's powers as the Pāṇḍavas on earth. As such, the Pāṇḍavas are as much related to Indra (or are even Indra himself) as they are the sons of other deities.

What we have in these passages is an explanation of how two apparently different views of the cosmos are actually (made to be) viewed as complementary. While Yudhiṣṭhira encompasses Brahmā's world at the zenith of the cosmos, Indra—represented as all of the five Pāṇḍavas—encompasses the whole cosmos. Yudhiṣṭhira as Indra is synecdochic for his brothers as well. Thus, Yudhiṣṭhira's *rājasūya* simultaneously makes him equal with all the realms and gods of the cosmos but particularly equal to, even one and the same with, Indra.[56]

Mbh Books 5, 13, 14

Yājñavalkya appears in three smaller passages and in one oblique reference that can be dealt with rather briefly. This is not because these passages (or the larger stories in which they appear) are not important in themselves, but rather because there is less context in which to analyze the role of Yājñavalkya at any great length. At the least, however, these passages show Yājñavalkya's continuing importance.

There is an oblique reference to Yājñavalkya in book 5 of the MBh where he is not mentioned directly, but reference is made to the association of the Sun with the White Yajurvedic formulas. This passage is concerned with explaining the nature of the eastern (*pūrva*) direction.[57] It is first explained that this is the direction from which the Sun rises. The passage continues by elaborating the nature of the Sun.

> *atra dattāni sūryeṇa yajūṃṣi dvijasattama*
> *atra labdhavaraiḥ somaḥ suraiḥ kratuṣu pīyate* (5.106.11)

> It is here that the *yajus* formulas were given by the Sun, O best of the twice-borns. It is here that *soma*, by means of (?) auspicious boons, was drunk in the sacrifices by the Suras.

While Yājñavalkya's name is not mentioned directly, we have a direct thematic reference to the BĀU 6.5.3 and MBh 12 which points to the origin of the *yajus* in the Sun (*sūrya*/*āditya*). While this is not a direct reference, it must be an allusion to the notion that Yājñavalkya is said to have received the *yajus* from the Sun god. In no other case of which I am aware is the Sun associated with the *yajus* formulas directly.

Yājñavalkya also appears in a narrative found in book 13 of the MBh (13.4.50ff.) among, again, a list of other *ṛṣis*. He appears at the conclusion of the tale of how Viśvāmitra, though born a Kṣatriya, became (or better: *was really*) a Brahmin.[58] This story is told to Yudhiṣṭhira who has inquired about how such a transformation could take place.

While Yudhiṣṭhira in his question to Bhīṣma makes mention of many myths related to this issue, his interlocutor chooses to relate only one story about this transformation of class (*varṇa*) identity. Bhīṣma narrates the story of Satyavatī where the *caru* (an offering of rice/barley) was switched, thus causing a transformation prior to birth of the standard class ordering.[59] Thus, it is said that Viśvāmitra was truly a Brahmin, though he was born of a Kṣatriya. As Sathaye (2015) has pointed out, this is one textual means of normalizing what otherwise could be seen as socially transgressive.

Yājñavalkya appears in a list of *ṛṣis* that is at the end of this story (13.4.58). It is not clear whether this list was later appended to the story or is original to it. As we have seen with the BĀU, a genealogical list following a story is often a means by which to give validity to the story itself, even if the genealogy is part of the story (as it is in this case).

Toward the conclusion of the narration, Bhīṣma tells of the lineage that Viśvāmitra creates:

> *tato brāhmaṇatāṃ yāto viśvāmitro mahātapāḥ*
> *kṣatriyaḥ so 'py atha tathā brahmavaṃśasya kārakaḥ* (13.4.47)
> *tasya putrā mahātmāno brahmavaṃśavivardhanāḥ*
> *tapasvino brahmavido gotrakartāra eva ca* (13.4.48)
>
> Then the great ascetic Viśvāmitra attained the state of a Brahmin. Now, even though a Kṣatriya, he established a lineage of Brahmins. His great-souled sons, who furthered the lineage of Brahmins, were great ascetics, knowers of *brahma,* and even makers of clans/races (*gotra*).

Following this statement, some sixty-two names of various (apparently important) Brahmins are mentioned.[60] Yājñavalkya appears in this list as the "celebrated Yājñavalkya" (*yājñavalkyaś ca vikhyātaḥ*) further indicating the status that he is said to have attained by the time of the composition of the MBh. At the conclusion of the narration, Bhīṣma says that Viśvāmitra's progeny were *munis* versed in *brahman* (*viśvāmitrātmajāḥ sarve munayo brahmavādinaḥ,* 13.4.58).

Yājñavalkya's inclusion in this list is interesting as he is seen to be the offspring of Viśvāmitra. This is the earliest mention of any perceived larger family associated with Yājñavalkya, and there is no literary precedent for it. However, I am less inclined to read this genealogy as an attempt at any literal historical fact, but rather for the purposes that it serves in the larger narrative.[61] That said, there may have been a tradition that did view this as literal historical fact quite early.

Viśvāmitra is said to have "truly" been a Brahmin and that his transformation from Kṣatriya status to the status of Brahmin is less a matter of transgressing social *varṇa* norms and more about how he realized his inherent nature as a Brahmin. Thus, his supposed "becoming" a Brahmin is not, in the narrative, a change of state, but it is his realization of a state that was always there, albeit latent.

For some, Yājñavalkya may have been seen as a descendant of Viśvāmitra. Indeed, in Yudhiṣṭhira's initial questioning he mentioned that the fifty sons of Viśvāmitra were cursed to be *śvapacas* ("dog eaters" or outcastes) for not properly honoring their elder brother, Devarāta. It is tempting to read this concluding list as a list of those very sons, particularly since Devarāta is mentioned at the top. This interpretation is supported by the fact that they are introduced as Viśvāmitra's progeny. It may be that this list was included to make a thematic connection to the opening of the dialogue. However, it is not clear how to reconcile the numerical difference (i.e., the fifty sons of Viśvāmitra with the sixty-two *munis* mentioned). There is also no repetition in the final list of the attainment of the status of "dog eaters" (something that does not appear anywhere in the textual record with regard to Yājñavalkya).

I think we can also view this genealogical list functioning as a justification of the story, like the narrative in book 12 that I discussed. If Viśvāmitra was truly a Brahmin and, as the story elaborates, was a Brahmin of great repute, then it would be natural to associate other well-known *munis* with him. As we have seen elsewhere, being able to trace one's lineage is a means of verifying one's status.[62] Also, if these *munis* were said to have been versed in *brahma* (*brahmavādin*), then it is also natural to include a character whose central story focuses around him being the most learned in *brahman* (*brahmiṣṭha*) as well as the founder/representative of a priestly ritual tradition.

Another reason why Yājñavalkya may be associated with Viśvāmitra here is a thematic one: Viśvāmitra is said to have transcended apparently static *varṇa* boundaries. Whether Yājñavalkya is said to have done the same (as a *śvapaca*) is less than clear. However, the character of Yājñavalkya is also known for being associated with such *varṇa* transformations. As we have seen in the ŚB (11.6.2.1–10), Yājñavalkya sneaked off to learn the true meaning of the *agnihotra* from Janaka. This passage concluded by saying, "Thereafter Janaka was a Brahmin" (*táto brahmā́ janaká āsa*). Perhaps the thematic similarity of Viśvāmitra's realization of his Brahmin nature and Janaka's transformation into the same led to the association of Yājñavalkya with Viśvāmitra. It should be noted that at least one principal difference between the two exists: Janaka apparently was a Brahmin because of the knowledge he held, whereas Viśvāmitra was such because of his own nature.

Yājñavalkya appears again in book 13 in the variant readings, though not in the critical edition. Yājñavalkya's name is invoked in explaining the merits of *yoga* and the association of *yoga* with the god Śiva.

> *yājñavalkya iti khyāta ṛṣiḥ paramadhārmikaḥ*
> *ārādhya sa mahādevaṃ prāptavāñ jñānam uttamam* (*13.88.1)

> The *ṛṣi* known as Yājñavalkya was highly virtuous. By pleasing Mahādeva [through yoga] he acquired the greatest knowledge.

We will recall that Yājñavalkya was associated with *yoga* in book 12 in the discussion of Sāṃkhya and Yoga. The exact reason for this association is not made explicit here, but it is apparent that Yājñavalkya's other representations (such as in the BĀU) as a knower of the self (*ātman*) and the universal principle (*brahman*) are here melded together with the newly emerging tradition of *yoga* as it was in book 12. While it is unclear in the BĀU whether there was any established tradition of *yoga* at the time, it is clear that careful reflection and "true knowledge" were means of understanding the nature of things. In this light, as in book 12, Yoga as a tradition may have been a fairly newly emerging tradition by the time of the MBh. Interestingly, Yājñavalkya's association with *yoga* is directly connected to Śiva (Mahādeva), the god who becomes the foremost *yogin* among the gods. Note here that as in book 12, Yājñavalkya is said to have pleased the god in his acquiring the knowledge of *yoga*. It appears that Śiva is taking precedence here by replacing Yājñavalkya's association with the Sun.[63]

Yājñavalkya also appears again in book 14, the Aśvamedhaparvan, in rather cursory fashion. However, his brief mention here again confirms the status that Yājñavalkya has attained in the greater Indian *imaginaire*. When Vyāsa is addressed by Yudhiṣṭhira to perform the Aśvamedha (the "horse sacrifice"), he responds

> *ahaṃ pailo 'tha kaunteya yājñavalkyas tathaiva ca*
> *vidhānaṃ yad yathākālaṃ tat kartāro na saṃśayaḥ* (14.71.3)

> Myself, O son of Kunti, Paila and Yājñavalkya will perform, there is no doubt, the prescribed acts at the appropriate time.

Yājñavalkya is again here mentioned as a principal ritual priest in the carrying out of a sacrifice for Yudhiṣṭhira: in this case, the elaborate horse sacrifice that assures one's sovereignty over the realm. Interestingly, Yājñavalkya is placed on the same level as Vyāsa (both the narrator of the story as well as a participant in it) and Paila, a famous R̥gvedic sage said to have been a student of Vyāsa. While there is no direct elaboration on these characters, it is clear that by simply mentioning their names the status (and efficacy) of the ritual to be performed is guaranteed.

As the horse sacrifice progresses and the horse is prepared to be released to wander for a year, Arjuna has prepared himself to follow the horse, to protect it, and to conquer with the attending army the realms into which the horse wanders. A large crowd gathers to see the departure of the army and the horse. Here again Yājñavalkya's name is invoked, but indirectly.

> *yājñavalkyasya śiṣyaś ca kuśalo yajñakarmaṇi*
> *prāyāt pārthena sahitaḥ śāntyartham vedapāragaḥ* (14.72.17)

> And the student of Yājñavalkya, who was well-versed in the sacrifice and excelled in the Vedas proceeded together with Pārtha [with the rites] for the purpose of peace/happiness [for the *yajamāna*].

The name of this student of Yājñavalkya is not mentioned, and there are no textual clues if any particular individual is intended. It may be a reference to Sāmaśravas whom we have encountered in the BĀU, or, more likely, it is simply a reference to the fact that Yājñavalkya was thought to have disciples who would be attendant priests during the course of a sacrifice (as in 2.30.36).

Conclusion

Yājñavalkya in the MBh is a multifaceted figure, one whose dimensions have been elaborated or changed to meet the needs of this different literary context. Some, such as Witzel (2003), have rightly pointed to the apparent "r̥ṣification" of Yājñavalkya within the context of the MBh. This is certainly the case—we have seen Yājñavalkya introduced as a *r̥ṣi* in various settings in the MBh, even where he is said to have been the *adhvaryu* priest for Indra's *rājasūya*. Of course, such a view of Yājñavalkya was foreshadowed at the end of BĀU 6 in his association with the Sun god which is then elaborated in book 12 of the MBh.[64] Clearly, Yājñavalkya's popularity and the view of him has expanded and has led to greater hagiographical detail in the MBh, suggesting that this figure was seen by the composers and the audience as a representative of one Vedic tradition. In book 12, Yājñavalkya is made representative of the Vedic tradition as a whole.

Scholars, however, have tended to see a sharp break in the characterization of Yājñavalkya as one progresses from the ŚB, to the BĀU, to the MBh. In general, this view sees a progression of this figure from a ritual exegete, to a philosopher, to a mythologized figure with little historical grounding. In the case of the ŚB and the BĀU, however, I have argued that a sharp break from a ritual exegete to a philosopher is hard to maintain. Certainly, Yājñavalkya's portrayal in the earlier parts of the ŚB is ritualistic in nature—but then again, so is the text as a whole. Such is the nature of Brāhmaṇa literature—thus it should not come as a surprise that Yājñavalkya's character fits appropriately into the genre. The BĀU certainly does contain narratives that are more philosophically oriented (i.e., asking about abstract foundations, discussing death and immortality), but it must be remembered that these were also concerns that arose in the ŚB (particularly in the later ŚB narratives that are longer). The principal difference is that in the BĀU such concerns are given extended treatment. I am not suggesting that there is not a qualitative difference between the ŚB and the BĀU, nor am I arguing against the generally accepted relative chronology that the BĀU was composed afterward. Rather, I am suggesting that one should not conflate the development of a literary genre necessarily with a determination about the historicity of any particular individual within it. Certainly, Yājñavalkya's character has changed within the BĀU portrayal, but one should not expect a character from one genre to necessarily be the same when portrayed in another. In fact, it would be more peculiar if such changes did not occur.[65]

Further, as I pointed out earlier, the changes that are often highlighted in the characterization between the ŚB and the BĀU are overstated. While the importance of Yājñavalkya as a spokesperson for the tradition has clearly grown (we see it even in the latter books of the ŚB), there are literary continuities between the ŚB and the BĀU that clearly point to why the tradition did not see any break in such portrayals. For example, while the BĀU discussions may be more philosophically oriented (however one may define that), those narratives are still premised on the ritual context. Not only is the context of BĀU 3 a *brahmodya,* but many of the questions relate explicitly to Vedic ritual context. BĀU 4, a private conversation with King Janaka, may be argued to be more philosophically inclined, but again, I think this says more about the type of narrative rather than something fundamental or historical about the figures in it.

In the case of the MBh, some scholars have argued for a different type of shift—a progressive *ṛṣification* that goes beyond historical probability. In this case, such a break is easier to maintain as few outside of the tradition view the MBh as containing a straightforward historical narrative and tend to view the text or significant portions of it as legend or myth. However, with such a division in mind, those who have looked at the character of Yājñavalkya have either dismissed such portrayals altogether (Fišer) or give them relatively short treatment (Witzel, Bronkhorst). Certainly, if history only consisted of accumulating a list of explicit facts, the MBh portrayal of Yājñavalkya yields very limited data. However, as I have argued, if one should take the narratives seriously, both individually and collectively, they do yield important information about how individuals saw and used this figure in different contexts—that is, rather than a history of listed facts, one can see a history of reception, appropriation, and propagation of traditions centered around a particularly important figure.

If we look at the MBh portrayals of Yājñavalkya more broadly, though, we can begin to see how the tradition viewed this figure in this context, and, I would argue, it is not necessarily so shockingly different than the portrayals that we have found in the ŚB and the BĀU. As in those cases, to be sure, certain aspects of a character are highlighted, elaborated, or changed to make certain points within the narrative, but there is a continuity—a self-conscious one—in the character's redeployment. In the MBh as well, I would maintain, there is the same effort at continuity even—or especially—in the face of authorizing newer teachings.

First and foremost, in the smaller passages, Yājñavalkya is portrayed principally as a Vedic ritualist. He is described as an *adhvaryu* priest among other priests and even as the idealized *adhvaryu* priest (*adhvaryusattama*) at the *rājasūya* of Indra. In this context, he is utilized as a connection between the mundane performance of the rite of Yudhiṣṭhira and the divine performance of Indra. This connection serves the larger narrative need of linking the two together so as to create an equivalence between the king of the gods in heaven and the (soon-to-be) king of the gods on earth.[66] Though it appears that these passages are most concerned with the ritualistic background of Yājñavalkya, the composers seem aware of his other principal characterization: Yājñavalkya is called a *brahmiṣṭha,* a direct verbal echo to his portrayal in the BĀU.

In the context of book 12, Yājñavalkya functions both as a Vedic ritualist and as speculative philosopher. Yājñavalkya is initially portrayed as a learned exponent of Sāṃkhya and Yoga. Not only is this something that is a new development for his character, but the doctrines are also a relatively new development within the ancient Hindu tradition. As such, there is not much of a precedent for his association. Clearly, there are thematic overlaps in the narratives with the nature of the universe, death, and the like found in earlier portrayals of Yājñavalkya culminating in a discussion of the nature of what is indestructible and the nature of *brahma*. These overlaps, however, appear somewhat secondary to the larger goal of elucidating the Sāṃkhya doctrine, in a larger context of narratives geared towards something similar (Fitzgerald 2012).

However, what these overlaps serve to do is to recall a Yājñavalkya who must have been more popularly known. While the composers may not have been intimately knowledgeable of the BĀU and the ŚB, they certainly were aware of those portrayals in some fashion. For example, book 12 ends the discussion of Janaka and Yājñavalkya by relating a narrative of how Yājñavalkya was given the white *yajus* from the Sun. This portrayal must be based on a shared notion of who Yājñavalkya was. As a ritualist, Yājñavalkya comes to stand in for the whole of the Vedic tradition, as the Sun not only gives him the white *yajus* (as in the BĀU), but the whole Veda and appendices. He then serves as *adhvaryu* in the sacrifice of Janaka's father, enacting the oral texts that he received. As a philosopher (here meaning one concerned with the "true" meaning of the Veda beyond ritual action), Yājñavalkya is told by the Sun that he will turn his mind towards that which will lead to the end of rebirth. In this narrative, both the philosopher and the ritualist are brought together to validate the teachings of Sāṃkhya and Yoga that precede it. Yājñavalkya is made iconic of the Vedic tradition as a whole, so as to graft the speculations of Sāṃkhya and Yoga onto it as its pinnacle.

If one looks at these portrayals in the MBh as a whole, we see that Yājñavalkya consistently appears in ritual settings. Of note, Yājñavalkya appears in two of the most significant royal rituals in the MBh—the *rājasūya* and the *aśvamedha*. These two are the most important sacrifices (symbolically, at least) for the establishment of a kingdom (the *aśvamedha*) and the establishment of sovereignty over the earth (the *rājasūya*). Further, in book 12, he is associated with the ritual of Janaka's father. All of these passages show that Yājñavalkya was viewed as iconic for his ritual tradition—and in book 12, the Vedic tradition as a whole. Collectively, these passages elaborate the theme of the interdependency of the kings and Brahmin priests. In the ŚB and the BĀU, we have seen a progressive connection established between Janaka and Yājñavalkya. Yājñavalkya has become the ideal court priest willing to share his knowledge with Janaka. Janaka, the ideal king, reciprocates with the gift of cows and eventually the kingdom and himself. Yājñavalkya in the MBh further elaborates this connection between Brahmin and king. While still connected with Janaka, Yājñavalkya has moved beyond this singular association. He has become the idealized priest for different kings: Yudhiṣṭhira, Janaka's father, and even the divine king, Indra. As Fitzgerald (trans., 2003 2004) has pointed out, one of the main goals of the MBh must have been to argue for the interdependency of the Vedic priesthood and kingship in the context of the Buddhist challenge. Clearly, this idealized symbiotic relationship influenced the composers' inclusions of Yājñavalkya in the various passages discussed in this chapter.

We also find within the MBh the first clear traces of the development of a hagiography surrounding the figure of Yājñavalkya. Clearly this literary tradition has attempted to retain a continuity with Yājñavalkya's literary past as such a continuity makes the redeployment of a figure more convincing and more believable. This is particularly seen in the passage from book 12, where newer doctrines of Sāṃkhya and Yoga are attributed to Yājñavalkya, where the composers feel compelled to justify the new with the old in a rather novel fashion. In the MBh, we have seen what can be called the "hagiographical imperative"—the desire on the part of any particular community to answer those questions that have been left out, silenced, or unexpressed within a particular religious literary tradition. Within such a literary and religious drive, the figure under consideration may be elevated in status, and the stories often focus on why that person attained that status. Such an imperative appears to develop when a particular figure becomes prominent—eliciting further interest in (and speculation on) the moods, motivations, and events in the character's life.

However, in this case and likely most others, the hagiographical imperative is equally (if not more so) impelled by the needs of the composers of a particular narrative and not solely the needs of an audience. This is to say that hagiographical expansion goes hand in hand with the need to adapt a figure to the needs of the composer(s) creating the hagiography. Such a statement is not particularly novel—certainly most would agree that composers of hagiographies have particular goals in mind when creating their stories that go beyond simply the valorization of a particular figure. However, it should equally be borne in mind that there is a logic to these adaptations—a logic that intentionally redeploys (or discards) aspects of a particular figure or event not only to situate it, but also to situate what might be more subtle intents of the newly composed narrative.

4

Yājñavalkya beyond the Veda

As we have seen in the last chapter, Yājñavalkya begins to enter into the broader *imaginaire* of Hinduism beginning, at least as far as the extant textual tradition, in the *Mahābhārata* (MBh). While the extent to which Yājñavalkya was known to a larger community cannot be ascertained with any certainty in the MBh, the MBh was certainly composed for a much larger community than earlier Vedic literary productions. However, one must remember that the early epic-hearing community was probably still limited. At least as far as the Sanskrit MBh is concerned, a direct audience would have had to have been conversant with Sanskrit which would limit its size. Certainly the composers of the epics themselves must have formed semi-elite cadres who shared (directly or indirectly), refined, and passed down their work over time.[1] To claim, however, that the Sanskrit epics are a type of elite discourse is not to deny their "popularity," but rather to acknowledge that we are faced with a different type of elite discourse than one finds in the earlier Vedic literary productions—one that is more broad, but not universally accessible.[2] However, through enactment, secondary discourses or commentary (whether public or private), and through composition of vernacular forms of such religious works, these literary traditions not only received much larger audiences beyond a strictly Sanskrit-understanding audience, but propagated themselves, mutated, and took on new lives of their own over time both in the expansion of particular genres of literature and in the creation of new genres to fit new needs.[3]

Purāṇas—often translated as "legend"—was one such new Sanskrit literary genre that emerged. As a literary genre that claims religious authority in the context of already established authorities, the Purāṇas incorporate, modify, and redeploy accepted ideas, tropes, and stories to fit their own ends and contexts. This is to say that they (like the MBh in the characterization of Yājñavalkya) were, to greater and lesser degrees, beholden to their literary religious past. Such a statement in no way denies ingenuity, creative expression, or autonomy—all of which are patently evident in the Purāṇas—but rather acknowledges that in the development of new religious understandings that do not wholly disavow the past, there is a need to reconcile that past to the present. While it is clear that the Purāṇas represent a sharp break with a certain past—particularly with the spread and popularity of various forms of *bhakti*—the texts often ensconce such radical changes within rather traditional garb. These include narrations on the origins of the Vedas, discussing important Vedic sages, and so on. The Hindu Purāṇas position themselves as a necessary complement to the Veda, as required learning to fully understand religious truth found in all established texts (Rao 2004, 98).

The term *purāṇa* literally means "that which came before" or "ancient" and is often classified alongside the epics—*itihāsa*—both within secondary scholarship and within the indigenous tradition.[4] The term *itihāsa* is sometimes translated as "history" and literally means "so indeed it was." Western scholars are more likely to refer to both of these genres as "legend" and "myth" because, at least from a perspective outside of the tradition, much contained within these documents are concerned with creation, various gods, or with such a distant past that historical veracity is improbable, if not impossible.[5]

The Purāṇas are stereotypically divided into two categories: the *mahāpurāṇas* (the "Great Purāṇas") and the *upapurāṇas* (the "Secondary Purāṇas"). However, such a classification, which is found in the tradition itself, is not particularly useful from an analytical perspective. The classifications can be misleading as they appear to be a value judgment of the text in question. Indeed, certain *mahāpurāṇas* do claim their own superiority over other textual traditions, but so also do certain *upapurāṇas* (Rao [2004, 102] citing a conference paper of Nye [1985]). As Rao suggests, determining the status of a particular Purāṇa for any given community must be highly contextualized and its formal classification has little comparative value.[6]

The dates of the Purāṇas have also been a hotly contested issue, with any number of scholars offering varying criteria of how a date should be ascribed to a text or a particular part of a text. In this case (as opposed to the texts discussed earlier), there has been little consensus.[7] I follow Rocher (1986, 104) who has suggested that the Purāṇas contain material that is both ancient and relatively recent, and it is impossible to assign a single date to any particular text as a whole. This said, however, it is likely that all of the Yājñavalkya passages are either contemporaneous with or, more likely, postdate the MBh, because they build off already established models found in the earlier texts. It is possible that the Yājñavalkya narrative in book 12 of the MBh is contemporaneous with certain Purāṇic accounts as there are several overlaps.

While detailed studies of individual Purāṇas have become more popular within academic circles, particularly in the drive for appreciating and understanding the "localness" of traditions in lieu of pan-Indian generalizing,[8] this chapter is not concerned with such a detailed study of any particular Purāṇa nor its larger historical context. This is the case for two reasons. The first is that a focus on the textual history of any Purāṇa would require at least a book-length treatment in itself. The second is that since we are only concerned with the character of Yājñavalkya, such a larger approach, while useful for a number of reasons, would prove extraneous here. Instead, this chapter focuses on those stories regarding Yājñavalkya and what those stories appear to be saying in themselves and how they relate to other pre-Purāṇic and Purāṇic sources. This is not to say that historical context is irrelevant, but rather that the influence of historical context on any particular Yājñavalkya narrative would be difficult, perhaps impossible, to point out clearly without larger case studies of each and every Purāṇa.

My approach in this chapter varies to some degree from that of the previous chapters. Chapter 1 followed, in order, the passages where Yājñavalkya appeared in the *Śatapatha Brāhmaṇa* (ŚB) and was a close analysis of those passages. Chapter 2, while focusing on select passages, was concerned with particular narratives and their larger frame narrative found in chapters 3 and 4 of the *Bṛhadāraṇyaka Upaniṣad* (BĀU). Chapter 3 also shifted its orientation from the previous two. That chapter was concerned with bringing apparently disparate passages together with one larger narrative in the MBh to see how Yājñavalkya may have been viewed by an Epic audience. In this chapter, the nature of the evidence also serves to determine the angle of approach. There are several short passages mentioning Yājñavalkya and also several longer passages spread throughout many Purāṇas. In this fashion, I wish to approach these texts thematically; rather than try to trace a direct historical development in Yājñavalkya's hagiography—which I am not convinced is possible in the Purānas—I am more concerned with Purāṇic elaboration and innovation in the context of the literary past that the authors of these texts were contending with.

The following themes encompass most of the narrative passages in which Yājñavalkya appears in the Purāṇas: (1) retellings of the BĀU/ŚB; (2) a concern with names and explaining origins (specifically, the division of the Vedas and the perceived split between the White and Black Yajurveda); (3) Yājñavalkya in relation to *yoga;* (4) the relationship of kings and Brahmins; and (5) Yājñavalkya in relation to the *dharmaśāstra* tradition. These themes that I isolate are not exhaustive, but rather appear to be those themes the producers of the texts were concerned with elaborating. All of these, excluding the last, are continuations of themes that we have seen in the pre-Purāṇic material, albeit a few are rather radical reinterpretations of that material. Most of the passages assume that the Vedas and Vedic rites are authoritative, but sometimes this is used to other ends (such as with *yoga*). All passages seem to imply that Yājñavalkya was seen as a Vedic sage by the composers, though there is considerable discussion on whether Yājñavalkya is arrogant or whether moral fault lies in his teacher, Vaiśaṁpāyana.

What we see in the first four themes in regard to the figure of Yājñavalkya, however, are those literary frames of reference that have already been established in previous literature. These are themes that the *paurāṇikas* (and perhaps their audience) felt needed reiteration and/or elaboration. It is within these narratives that we see the boundaries for such elaboration; that is, those particular themes and structures upon which this particular hagiographical imperative was focused. While it should be obvious, it bears repeating that in the case of hagiographical expansion, such elaboration is often defined by "rules" which are often implicitly drawn from what is already known and accepted as true. This does not mean that rules or conventions are not broken (even intentionally so) or that individual agency is suppressed by such constraints, but rather that they serve as a frame of reference even when they are ignored or denied. Hagiography, when coupled with a rather extensive literary past, though, would tend towards the conservative in that such literary elaboration is usually neither free form nor is it simply "myth" in the sense of adding "falsehoods" or something "made up" onto what is already accepted as true. Rather, by structuring hagiographical elaboration upon that which is already established, it draws upon a memory of Yājñavalkya (who he is, what he said, and so on) which permits what is "new" in the narrative to be accepted as true and ancient by any given community.

While I have stressed the conservative nature of the above themes in that they draw on what has literary precedent for their own purposes, certainly we find great innovation. It is, for example, within this conservative frame that we find great character elaboration, particularly regarding the personality of particular individuals. We also find, for example, more elaborate details regarding the context of the *brahmodya* at Janaka's court, while simultaneously noting a condensing of the philosophical discussion almost to the point of its elimination. We find an interesting reinterpretation of Yājñavalkya's relationship with his wives and a novel story about a mongoose that Yājñavalkya is said to have offended. Thus, while I suggest the frames that guide these literary productions are conservative, they do not straightjacket the texts only to a literary past, but rather create contours for the then present.[9]

The final section of this chapter will explore the (apparently new) association of Yājñavalkya with ancient Indian law codes as found in the *Yājñavalkyasmṛti* and will explore possible reasons for this elaboration in Yājñavalkya's biography. While I have emphasized the conservative nature of hagiography earlier, this does not mean that hagiography is *necessarily* conservative. I do not wish to imply that hagiography, by definition, cannot be something wholly or mostly new—it certainly can. However, in this case, I suggest that there are aspects of Yājñavalkya's literary past that serve to make his association with the *dharma* tradition not wholly incongruous with that past. That is, while this association between Yājñavalkya and the legal tradition is apparently novel, I will offer a number of suggestive (though not definitive) reasons why such an association would be made and what it might have meant to members of the tradition.

It should be pointed out that each Yājñavalkya narrative is not necessarily limited to only one of the themes isolated above. In fact, there seems to be a cross-fertility in the texts where the themes and their developments may come from multiple, probably shared, sources simultaneously. Many contain several of these themes, incorporating them in different ways to different ends. One way of conceiving of this is to consider the framework as a web, where various strands may be more or less directly related to a previous textual tradition and others to a shared oral tradition which was not codified in the same way. In this fashion, while I will isolate what I find to be unique or interesting in a particular telling, I will also thematically juxtapose these narratives to each other in order to view them intertextually.

The following is an alphabetical list of Purāṇas in which Yājñavalkya appears:

Agni
Bhāgavata
Brahma
Brahmāṇḍa
Garuḍa
Kūrma
Liṅga
Padma
Skanda
Śiva
Varāha
Vāyu
Viṣṇu

Retellings

Most of the Yājñavalkya passages in the Purāṇas are consciously aware of the many portrayals of Yājñavalkya that we have discussed so far, though the specific sources of their inspiration may never be fully transparent. This is because any particular innovation in a given text may be an individual innovation or part of a shared oral tradition of which we do not have evidence. Though there are cases of more direct borrowing and these may allow one to determine more precise lines of transmission,[10] most of the Purāṇic stories appear to be influenced by sources at one or several steps removed. While I am open to the theoretical possibility of being able to determine the relative remove of a Purāṇic telling from earlier literary sources, I think such an endeavor is faced with obstacles—which may, in many cases, prove to be insurmountable.[11]

The main difficulty in isolating sources of a particular portrayal is determining where the literary elite view of Yājñavalkya (as found in the ŚB and BĀU and to some degree in the MBh) ends and a more widespread or popular (albeit Sanskritic) understanding begins. Such is the nature of oral texts that are no longer confined to a very small elite community (such as the White Yajurvedins). This does not, of course, mean that ritual elites do not have their own "popular" view of the figure that may have existed alongside the textual record, parts of which may have become incorporated into oral texts later.[12]

Most of our Purāṇic passages concerning Yājñavalkya (similar to the MBh, though not in degree) are neither literal restatements of a previous literary record nor a simple reworking of a known text, but for our purposes are more fruitfully understood as based on a *literary memory* of those texts which serves as building blocks for new textual productions. As such, the fluidity of memory in this case suggests that one may intend to be (to whatever degree) faithful to a literary past, but one is not necessarily strongly bound to it. Such a model helps one to understand the continuity and innovation in its variety in such literary productions, but it also helps to explain why, in the case of innovation, a tradition is able to model it on a remembered (if not textually literal) past. It is in this fashion that we find retellings of some of the narratives we have encountered in the ŚB/BĀU, though these tellings are significantly different.

Brahmodya

In the *Brahmāṇḍa Purāṇa* (BP),[13] 1.2.34.34 onward is a retelling of chapter 3 of the BĀU, though with several interesting novelties. Śāṃśapāyana, following a discussion of the origin of the Vedas that concludes by mentioning the name Śākalya, inquires how this "arrogant" (*garvita*) person was slain at the horse-sacrifice of Janaka. Note that here we once again have Yājñavalkya associated with the horse sacrifice. However, in this context, this is a detail grafted onto the BĀU narrative where the specific ritual was not mentioned. Note also that the theme is misplaced pride and anger *on the part of Śākalya* that is said to be his undoing, a characterological opposite of Yājñavalkya's earlier portrayal of well-placed pride and sarcasm.

Indeed, in this telling arrogance and greed are said to be the characteristics of each of the other priests in attendance (though not Yājñavalkya) where the Brahmins argue and all make the claim that "This wealth is mine" (1.2.34.44; *mamaitad dhanam ity uta*). Their claim for the wealth and status of *brahmiṣṭḥa* is said to be because of the "defilement of wealth" (*dhanadoṣa*); that is, out of greed. Yājñavalkya, on the other hand, is introduced as a knowledgeable and wise seer who was born of Brahmā (*vidvān brahmaṇas tu sutaḥ kaviḥ*). He is said to be possessed of great brilliance (*mahātejas*), possessed of ascetic heat (*tapasvin*) and the ultimate knower of *brahman* (*brahmavittama*).[14] Interestingly, Yājñavalkya proceeds to calm the fighting Brahmins (1.2.34.49) and carries out what is said to be an elaborate debate with each of them that culminates in his asking them individually a question which they cannot answer (1.2.34.53). The debate or the individual questions Yājñavalkya is said to ask are not stated directly in the text, but this is an inversion of his being questioned in the BĀU.

Śākalya apparently was watching this debate, yet remained silent. Yājñavalkya directly asks him why he is not participating. Apparently, this direct challenge was seen as an insult by Śākalya.

> *evaṃ sa dharṣitas tena roṣāt tāmrāsyalocanaḥ* (1.2.34.56)
>
> Thus he was ill treated (or: insulted). For that reason his eyes and face became red like copper because of his anger.

We are told that an extensive debate took place between the two (1.2.34.62), but no details are given other than that Śākalya asked Yājñavalkya more than one thousand questions and Yājñavalkya answered them. Yājñavalkya then challenges Śākalya with a single question.

> *susūkṣmajñānasaṃyuktaṃ sāṃkhyaṃ yogam athāpi vā* ||
> *adhyātmasya gatiṃ mukhyāṃ dhyānamāmārgam athāpi vā* ||
> (1.2.34.65)

> "What is connected with very subtle (i.e. the most subtle) knowledge, Yoga or Sāṃkhya? Which is primary, the path related to the self or the path of Yoga?[15]

As in the BĀU, the answer is left unexpressed. It is tempting to read an answer from Yājñavalkya's portrayal in the MBh—that neither is superior to the other and thus it is a trick question—but it is not entirely clear. Śākalya was not able to answer the question and he died because of it.

In this version of the BĀU story a number of interesting changes can be seen. If I am correct that what appears prideful or arrogant on the part of Yājñavalkya in the BĀU/ŚB was viewed positively in that it was justified by his knowledge, here that trait in the narrative is expressed quite differently. Rather than eliminate the theme of pride, the composers of this narrative *transfer* it onto the other participants and portray it negatively. While all the Brahmins appear to be spitefully arguing, Śākalya is made exceptional in his anger and it eventually leads to his death. Why Yājñavalkya's challenge to him is the cause of his anger in the BP is unclear. In the ŚB/BĀU versions, such anger would make sense—Yājñavalkya calls Śākalya a "fire-quencher" (*ulmukāvakṣáyaṇa*/ *aṅgārāvakṣayaṇa*; ŚB 11.6.3/BĀU 3.9.18) and an "idiot" (*ahallika*; BĀU 3.9.25). In fact, if anyone is portrayed as angry in the ŚB/BĀU versions, it is Yājñavalkya, though it would be a seemingly controlled anger at least in comparison. It seems that the BP version gives a "sanitized" version of the character of Yājñavalkya as a means to valorize him. Rather than remove those characteristics altogether, though the composers place these characteristics onto others (particularly Śākalya), so as to portray them in a bad light. If the ŚB/BĀU versions were about pride in correct knowledge, in the BP we have the inverse—where the theme is concerned with misplaced pride or arrogance. To maintain a positive portrayal of Yājñavalkya, the characteristics of the participants are inverted as well.

This inversion of personality traits to provide the inverse moral lesson also appears to be the case with greed. In the BĀU, Yājñavalkya laying claim to the cows could be interpreted as his greed as well as his pride. This is supported by the fact that Yājñavalkya himself says that all the Brahmins at the sacrifice are really just desirous of cows (*gokāma*), apparently including himself. In the BĀU, the conclusion, however, tells us that Yājñavalkya's claim was justified. In this BP narrative, however, all of the Brahmins try to lay claim to the wealth in a fashion similar to Yājñavalkya in the BĀU. In fact, the *purāṇic* characterization is narrative proof that they are just *gokāmas*. In the BP version, Yājñavalkya does not make a claim to the wealth, but rather calms the other priests down and persuades them to debate with him so that it can be proven which Brahmin should take away the elaborate wealth.[16]

The transference of the personality characteristics of greed and anger, I suggest, was probably because of the authority associated with Yājñavalkya as a sage by the time of this composition. It appears that those in the tradition in which this text was produced were uncomfortable with what could be interpreted as negative characteristics of Yājñavalkya's personality in the stories of BĀU/ŚB. While imparting a similar moral message (i.e., arrogance without justification is bad), the rewritings of the story prevent potential interpretive ambiguities in the earlier tellings. If Gārgī foreshadows Śākalya's death with her warning at the end of BĀU 3.8, here the intensity of Śākalya's anger (that is, red eyes and a face like copper) serves to do the same.

We should note that no Brahmin is named other than Yājñavalkya and Śakalya. It is clear that the tradition behind this narrative saw these two characters as the center of the narrative.[17] A female, such as Gārgī, is not mentioned, perhaps suggesting that she has been written out of the narrative or that the basis of this telling is the ŚB version. It may indicate an uncomfortableness with women participating in such debates on the part of the composers, though it is possible she is an implied participant.

The debate itself is practically eliminated from the narrative, but given that this story immediately follows a discussion of the lineages of well-known Vedic personages and leads to the question of how Śākalya died, they are unnecessary. While valorizing Yājñavalkya and his apparent brilliance, the explicit purpose of the narrative is to explain Śākalya's death. For this reason, the single question that Yājñavalkya asked him (as opposed to his one thousand useless ones) and that led to his death is necessary. Any other explicit detail within the rest of the debate (between other Brahmins or that Śākalya posed to Yājñavalkya) would be superfluous.[18]

Maitreyī and Kātyāyanī

In the *Skanda Purāṇa* (SP),[19] we encounter a narrative that is not a retelling per se, but a narrative elaboration at least nominally based on what we find in BĀU 2.4/4.5, the dialogue between Yājñavalkya and his wives. After a fairly long discussion (6.129; examined below) about the origin of the White Yajurveda and the BĀU, Sūta (the character who is answering questions from assembled sages) concludes by mentioning that Yājñavalkya had a son named Kātyāyana who composed the well-known *śrautasūtras* (6.129.71). The assembled sages, rather than asking about Kātyāyana directly, ask about his mother. This narrative is thematically concerned with the issue of names and origins; that is, how Kātyāyanī came to have a son by the name of Kātyāyana. As such this serves as a transition into the next thematic section. However, it is included here because the story is also an elaborate expansion upon perceived gaps in the narratives found in the BĀU. There are areas in the BĀU narrative, I would argue, that were seen as open enough to lead to multiple readings, and the composers of this narrative are apparently limiting those readings through their own retelling. While the composers of the passage in the BP transferred what could be read as negative characteristics of Yājñavalkya from the ŚB/BĀU onto the other Brahmins, here the narrative, rather than removing or transferring aspects of the narrative, fills out the story to "solve" a perceived problem—Yājñavalkya's apparent favoritism towards one wife.

Like the MBh passage (2.30.36) that mentioned that Yājñavalkya had children, here too that claim is made, but it is made more directly by attributing a name and textual tradition to Yājñavalkya's son. However, the gathered sages (and presumably the audience) wonder about where this child came from, perhaps even because of the lack of mention in the earlier textual record. The narrative that follows is based on a perceived rivalry between Yājñavalkya's two wives from the BĀU. It is probably based more directly on BĀU 4.5 than on 2.4 because it is in 4.5 where there is greater narrative interest placed on the wives.

This story begins by narrating that Kātyāyanī and Maitreyī were both the wives of Yājñavalkya. It further adds the detail that Maitreyī was senior, although Kātyāyanī is said to have "good features" (*kalyāṇī*). Kātyāyanī becomes jealous of Maitreyī as she appears to be Yājñavalkya's favorite. This notion of Yājñavalkya preferring one wife over the other is probably linked to the fact that in the BĀU episode (2.4/4.5) Maitreyī is the one to whom Yājñavalkya gives instruction on the nature of immortality. It is also in BĀU 4.5 that Kātyāyanī is marked as different from Maitreyī—Kātyāyanī was *strīprajñā* rather than a *brahmavādinī*. In both BĀU versions, Yājñavalkya refers to Maitreyī as dear (*priyā*) to him, and she becomes more dear due to her interest in immortality. In the BĀU, nothing is said about Kātyāyanī outside of the narrative frame, suggesting at least to the composers of the SP that she could be interpreted as less important than Maitreyī. This SP narrative, however, is arguing that Kātyāyanī was not less important (nor that she was of a fundamentally different nature), and she is moved to the center of the narrative while Maitreyī remains largely in the frame. This text argues that the problem was an issue of seniority that determined Yājñavalkya's affections.[20] Maitreyī was preferred by Yājñavalkya because she was the first wife, and the text assumes that this is natural. The possible favoritism in the BĀU episode is what the SP is apparently elaborating on when it says that Kātyāyanī was severely distressed by Yājñavalkya's favoritism. "She stopped taking baths and eating food. She never indulged in jokes and fun. She always heaved sighs and kept her eyes filled with tears" (6.130.12).

Kātyāyanī then comes across Śāṇḍilī, said to be the daughter of the sage Śāṇḍilya, whose husband (the great sage Jaimini!) appears to be doting over her. Most importantly, he is said to "expound on matters good and bad" (6.130.16) to his wife. Clearly, this is a reference to Yājñavalkya choosing to expound on immortality to Maitreyī in the BĀU which this particular Purāṇic tradition clearly viewed as preferential treatment. Kātyāyanī asks Śāṇḍilī to explain to her how she has such a devoted husband, and Śāṇḍilī proceeds to tell her a story about the power of worshipping Pārvatī. She explains how Pārvatī was able, through one year of resisting Śiva, to cause him to give up his association with the goddess Gāṅgā. While Śiva felt compelled to hold the Gāṅgā in his hair, Pārvatī says that she will not be a second wife to another woman and will continue her austerities separately from Śiva until he breaks off the association. Pārvatī prevails in the end and the two are reunited.

The text continues by saying that if Kātyāyanī properly worships the goddess for a year at the pilgrimage site of Hāṭakeśvara and maintains a vow of celibacy for that time, she will attain an equal status in regards to Yājñavalkya's affections. The narrative concludes that this is precisely what she did, and Yājñavalkya came to her and later they bore a son by the name of Kātyāyana.

Clearly this narrative is concerned with the possible problems inherent in one individual having multiple spouses—what must have been a real-world problem and not only a textual one. Yājñavalkya is one of the few characters in the early literature who is said to have more than one spouse. It makes sense that his relationships are used as examples of a possible rivalry. In fact, the BĀU accounts lend themselves to such a reading and this text then provides a ritual solution to a perceived problem. As Yājñavalkya is seen as favoring one spouse over the other, the most effective way to insure that he treats both wives equally is by appealing to the goddess Pārvatī who herself is said to have had a similar problem with Śiva.[21]

Of course, the main reason for this passage as a whole is to valorize a particular vow and ritual that women can undertake at a particular pilgrimage site, Hāṭakeśvara. While stories of Śiva's and Pārvatī's relationship (including jealousy) are common, this story is here paralleled with Yājñavalkya and his two wives to establish a ritual women can employ to assure the affection of their husbands. There is no direct reference to other narrative details from earlier textual sources except for Yājñavalkya's relationship with his wives. However, it is clear that he is accepted as a sage on par with Jaimini.

Yājñavalkya and Gārgī

One narrative that is particularly unique is found in the SP (1.2.13.62ff). Yājñavalkya is said to be staying in the city of Mithi (Mithilā?), and upon seeing a mongoose (*nakula*), he tells Gārgī to be sure to guard the milk. It is unclear who Gārgī is in relation to Yājñavalkya. Is she his wife, a student in his *āśrama*, or both? No answer is given, but it is clear that this later textual tradition viewed these two figures as intimately connected.[22] This is probably because, as I have discussed in chapter 2, the inclusion of women in a *brahmodya* was at least unusual, where the composers of the narratives intentionally constructed the gender of these two characters so as to not be representative of women in ancient India.[23] Here that concern is "solved" by suggesting their relationship was more than just priests arguing at a *brahmodya*. Whether as a wife or student, Gārgī is seen here only in relation to Yājñavalkya, which is distinct in context from her portrayal in the BĀU, where her uniqueness of gender was used a literary weapon against rivals.

After Gārgī is introduced, she disappears from the narrative. The character is principally serving a narrative function—of introducing the mongoose who proceeds to take offense at being called a *nakula* by Yājñavalkya. While *nakula* properly means "mongoose," the mongoose himself interprets the word as *na kula,* that is, "one who does not have a noble family." The mongoose takes offense, chastises Yājñavalkya, and curses him to be born in the next life into a lowly family (1.2.13.98–99). Yājñavalkya is said to have been reborn in Merudeśa[24] to a Brahmin family that conducts itself in a dishonorable manner. Yājñavalkya (now named Bhartr̥yajña) becomes a follower of Śiva, and the narrative argues that one who properly worships Śiva can transcend being born into an ignoble family (1.2.13.104ff).

Names and Origins

Many of the textual references to Yājñavalkya found in the Purāṇas are concerned with two overlapping themes—the origin of the name Vājasaneya and the origin of the White Yajurveda as distinct from the Black Yajurveda. Given that in the ancient Hindu view the name of something is fundamentally connected to its nature (hence the importance of Upaniṣadic *bandhus*), it is not surprising that these themes show up together in the narratives.

I have suggested that in the ŚB and the BĀU there is a tension between the White Yajurvedic tradition and the already established Vedic traditions found in more western regions. I have argued that Yājñavalkya's sarcasm was one rhetorical means for establishing the authority of what must have been a newly emerging tradition in the BĀU and ŚB. In the MBh (12.306), we have one narrative that explores, albeit reservedly, the split between the traditions. We have seen in the MBh that Yājñavalkya appealed to the Sun god to be given his own Veda that was "not used" (*nopayukta*) in the sacrifice. In that story, we do not know why Yājñavalkya felt that he needed to appeal to the Sun. The only dispute that is explicitly mentioned took place between Yājñavalkya and Vaiśaṁpāyana. That dispute was about whether Vaiśaṁpāyana accepted the validity of what Yājñavalkya received from the Sun by sharing the payment for the sacrifice with him.

Many of the Purāṇic narratives, however, are concerned with exploring the relationship of the White and Black Yajurveda. In these narratives, we find answers to unexpressed questions or gaps in the earlier narratives. Such questions include: Why would Yājñavalkya appeal to the Sun, thus circumventing his own teacher? Was there a moral flaw involved on either Yājñavalkya's or Vaiśaṁpāyana's part?

If so, how does this affect the narrative? In many of these stories, both Yājñavalkya and Vaiśaṁpāyana are clearly seen as sages (if only after the fact in the case of Yājñavalkya), so what could lead to such a split between two apparently *dharmic* men? Some narratives are concerned with making sure that the reader understands that they are still both authoritative sages, while others leave Vaiśaṁpāyana's status ambiguous, perhaps suggesting stronger White Yajurvedic influence.

What should be pointed out is that these later narratives which focus on the split between the two traditions are elaborating upon what is not directly expressed in the earlier tradition. While I suggested that we can point to a tension between the White Yajurvedic tradition and other already established traditions, we should not read the Purāṇic accounts as necessarily representing a reality on the ground either in previous times or during the time these accounts were written. Krishnamurti (1984) overemphasizes, I think, this split and the animosity between the two traditions as a historical reality dating back to the origins of the White Yajurveda. However, he principally draws this conclusion based on the later texts. These texts are more concerned with explaining what could be seen as complex moral ambiguities, I contend, and are less concerned with accurately describing how the two traditions actually interacted with each other. For example, how and when is a student justified in defying a teacher? Such questions are important when one realizes that this is a discussion about sages who are often seen as paradigmatic examples of proper behavior. In this sense, the composers are exploiting a trope about the division between these two schools of ritual interpretation. Certainly, both the White and Black tradition viewed themselves as more orthodox and authoritative than the other, and the rhetoric within the traditions appear to support that. This, however, is an internal *rhetorical* position that does not necessarily support a conclusion of direct animosity between them at any particular historical point in time.

Brahmāṇḍa Purāṇa

BP contains a lengthy story about Yājñavalkya (1.2.35). Prior to this passage he is mentioned simply as one of eighty-six *śrutarṣis*, or sages of the Yajurveda.[25] In the first instance, he is neither given greater attention than the other sages mentioned along with him nor when he is mentioned again at 1.2.33.16 where he is listed as an *adhvaryu* priest among many. However, this discussion is what leads into the BP dialogue between Śākalya and Yājñavalkya discussed above. Following this debate, Sūta continues with a description of the origins of the Veda as a whole and Yājñavalkya's role within that, in particular. Similar to the MBh, here Yājñavalkya is associated with Vyāsa, though he is said to be a student of Vaiśaṁpāyana, one of four students of Vyāsa (along with Jaimini, Sumantu, and Paila). This group of four students of Vyāsa becomes a standard trope in the Purāṇas for understanding the division of four Vedas—each is entrusted by Vyāsa with propagating a single Veda via his students.[26] This notion was probably implicit in the narrative found in book 12 of the MBh (given the implied ritual role of each at Janaka's sacrifice), but here it is stated explicitly.

The text states (1.2.35.8) that a student of Vaiśaṁpāyana composed the Yajurveda itself (*vaiśaṁpāyanaśiṣyo 'sau yajurvedam akalpayat*). This was then taught to Vaiśaṁpāyana's students, but "one [student] there, Yājñavalkya, who was of great *tapas*, was excluded" (1.2.35.9; *ekas tatra parityakto yājñavalkyo mahātapāḥ*). It is not entirely clear what is intended here because in the narrative that follows, Yājñavalkya possessed the Yajurveda and is said to have vomited it to return it to his teacher. For this reason, I think the exclusion mentioned in this passage is not that Yājñavalkya was excluded from learning the Black Yajurveda, but rather that he was at some point excluded from the Black Yajurvedic tradition as the story continues to explain.

The sages proceed to ask Sūta where the name *caraka adhvaryu* comes from as a designation of those who follow the Black Yajurveda (1.2.35.14). The story is told that certain sages required the attendance of all the sages of the Veda on Mount Meru. Whoever did not show up within a specified time would incur the sin of "killing a Brahmin" (*brahmahatyā*) and would be required to carry out the appropriate expiation. For a reason that is not explained in the text, Vaiśaṁpāyana was unable to attend. Because he was not able to attend, he called his students together to perform the appropriate expiation. At this point, Yājñavalkya said that he would perform it alone (*aham ekaś cariṣyāmi*) and did not need the assistance or skills of the other students. Vaiśaṁpāyana got angry (*kruddha*) at Yājñavalkya and told him to return everything he had learned from him: "Thus the most knowledgeable in *brahman* vomited [the *yajus's*] smeared with blood" (1.2.35.20; *rudhireṇa tathāktāni charditvā brahmavittamāḥ*). Yājñavalkya then is said to appeal to the Sun to receive the Veda, but little detail is given. The Sun, in the form of a horse, gives Yājñavalkya the White Yajurveda. It is here (1.2.35.25–27) that the names for the traditions are explained—the Vājasaneya are so named because the Sun took the form of a horse (*vājin*), whereas the *carakas* are named such because of the expiation that they had to perform (*caraṇa*).

Along with the obvious purpose of this passage to explain the names used to designate members of each tradition, this narrative also fleshes out parts of Yājñavalkya's biography in rather novel ways. First and foremost, this narrative explains *why* Yājñavalkya would have to appeal to the Sun for another Veda. We are told that Yājñavalkya offered to carry out the expiation without the assistance of the other students. Why exactly this made Vaiśaṁpāyana angry is not stated, but it is probably because of perceived arrogance on the part of Yājñavalkya in that he does not think he needs assistance. This would fit with our portrayal of Yājñavalkya in other texts as arrogant, only here he is not given the option to prove in the ritual that his arrogance is justified. In this reading, the Sun giving him the White Yajurveda is the justification of his pride.

It may also be that Yājñavalkya wishes to exclude the other students in what may be seen as their proper duty towards their teacher, perhaps keeping any merit accumulated for himself. Vaiśaṁpāyana's anger could also be because he had asked all of his students to perform the expiation, and Yājñavalkya saying that he would do so alone is directly contradicting his teacher's order. In the context of the great value placed on the teacher/student relationship, particularly here in the semi-mythological realm of the earliest sages of the Veda, the last interpretation also seems likely in this passage.

This passage is interesting in its portrayal of Vaiśaṁpāyana. The story mentions that Vaiśaṁpāyana failed to appear at a meeting of the other sages. No reason is given as to why he could not attend, but it is clear that he acquired the sin of killing a Brahmin for not doing so. Clearly, this is the most grievous sin possible, but there is a narrative gap regarding moral culpability. Did Vaiśaṁpāyana do something that caused him to miss the meeting? Was it intentional? This narrative suggests moral culpability on the part of Vaiśaṁpāyana, but it is muted as there is no elaboration upon the cause. But such is often the case for being on the receiving end of a curse in such texts: the outcome is the outcome, no matter the reasons.

In this narrative, it is not clear why Yājñavalkya would vomit back the text and why it would be "smeared with blood." For some, however, this is a way to explain how the Black Yajurveda texts are "mixed"—that is, Brāhmaṇa-style commentary intermingled with *mantras*. This type of explanation also appears to be from a White Yajurvedic perspective: the implication is that the Black Yajurvedic texts are impure or less worthy as vomit is generally reviled, so also blood. Here, though, this explanation is implied.

Bhāgavata Purāṇa

A story very similar to the one above is found in the *Bhāgavata Purāṇa* (BhP). In the course of explaining the origin of the Vedas, Vaiśaṁpāyana, the principal sage of the *caraka adhvaryus*, is said to have incurred the sin of *brahmahatyā* (12.6.61). In this version, unlike the SP version, the exact transgression is not explicitly stated. Further, this narrative makes clear that it is arrogance on the part of Yājñavalkya that leads to his having to return his knowledge of the Yajurveda to Vaiśaṁpāyana. Yājñavalkya mocks the other students of Vaiśaṁpāyana and offers to carry out the performance himself.

> *yājñavalkyaś ca tacchiṣya āhāho bhagavan kiyat* ||
> *caritenālpasārāṇāṃ cariṣye 'haṃ suduścaram* || (12.6.62)
>
> Yājñavalkya, a student of his (Vaiśaṁpāyana) said, "O distinguished one, how much [is to be gained] by the performance of these [students] of little value? I [alone] will perform the difficult practice."

Vaiśaṁpāyana is said to become angry or offended (*kupita*) at being addressed in this fashion and tells Yājñavalkya (12.6.63), "Leave! Enough of a student like you who despises the sages" (*yāhy alaṃ tvayā viprāvamantrā śiṣyeṇa*) and asks for him to return the knowledge that he has attained. Interestingly, in 12.6.64, Yājñavalkya is referred to as Devarāta. It is clear that this name must refer to Yājñavalkya, but there is no explanation given for this alternative name. It is said that Devarāta vomits the text back (though not mixed with blood in this case). The students of Vaiśaṁpāyana become enamored with the vomited texts, and they take the form of Tittira birds (perhaps to avoid any pollution associated with vomit or perhaps because it is in pieces) and gather it up. This passage thus explains the origin of the Taittirīya of the Black Yajurveda as connected with the Tittira bird. Note that a Tittiri (perhaps an alternative name for Vaiśaṁpāyana) was mentioned at Yudhiṣṭhira's court in the MBh along with Yājñavalkya (MBh 2.4).

The text continues that Yājñavalkya praised the Sun in an elaborate manner (12.6.67–72). The Sun, in the form of a horse (*vājirupa*), came to Yājñavalkya and imparted the White Yajurveda to him out of his grace (*prasāda*). Because of the mention of grace, the emphasis here appears to be on the Sun's own determination and less so on Yājñavalkya earning it through penance.

Again, in this passage we clearly have a concern for explaining the name of the tradition in connection to its origin. Here, however, it is explained that Yājñavalkya was seen to speak ill of the sages and incurred the wrath of his teacher. In the praising of the Sun, we are told that it was the grace of the Sun that allowed Yājñavalkya to learn the texts of the White Yajurveda. In conclusion, the text mentions that students such as Kāṇva and Mādhyandina (among others) learned from Yājñavalkya, thereby also giving an origin of the two recensions of the ŚB known today.

Viṣṇu Purāṇa

Chapter 5 of the *Viṣṇu Purāṇa* (VP) contains a story similar to that found in BhP, but adds a number of details. I will concern myself here with only those significant differences found in the text.[27] The first interesting addition is that Yājñavalkya is said to have been particularly devoted to his teacher (trans., Wilson 1972, 225). This addition indicates that Vaiśaṁpāyana somehow misunderstood Yājñavalkya and does not place any moral blame on either of them for what ensues.

The VP also indicates that Vaiśaṁpāyana's rage is caused by Yājñavalkya's arrogance, but adds further that, according to Vaiśaṁpāyana, Yājñavalkya has disobeyed his teacher's command (trans., Wilson 1972, 226). It appears that both possible readings that we have encountered in the BhP—of arrogance and of contravening the teacher's order—are combined here. Vaiśaṁpāyana's anger is directed at Yājñavalkya who insulted the others present, but he also says that Yājñavalkya disobeyed his command. Yājñavalkya retorts that he spoke in good faith, but that since his teacher asked for his teachings to be returned, Yājñavalkya was obliged to do so. He vomits the text back, but like the SP these are stained with blood. This version appears to include multiple explanations for the disagreement between Yājñavalkya and his teacher, but it also suggests that any rift between the two is ultimately a misunderstanding.

Another added detail is that Vaiśaṁpāyana is said to have accidentally killed the child of his sister after incurring the sin of Brahmin-killing for not attending the meeting of the sages. Here again the text is filling out narrative gaps that we have seen in other stories. The story explains how the sin of *brahmahatyā* is incurred in a concrete fashion. It still appears that moral culpability is muted, as the killing is accidental and due to the curse, but this version suggests that a Brahmin was actually killed. The text concludes with the same explanation of the name Taittirīya and Vājasaneya where Yājñavalkya receives the White Yajurveda texts that are *ayātayāma*, "not used" or "unknown."

Yājñavalkya and Yoga

The association of Yājñavalkya with *yoga* that we first saw in the MBh appears in a number of scattered passages in various Purāṇas. The references to Yājñavalkya and a *yoga* tradition are usually only one or two lines of text without any elaboration. Therefore I will only discuss them briefly. In all passages where Yājñavalkya is associated with yoga, the concern appears to be with explaining (albeit briefly) from where Yājñavalkya may have learned it. This is probably because there is little precedent for this association in the earlier tradition (with the exception of the MBh) and the concern of the composers of these passages is to establish a lineage of the *yoga* practices associated with Yājñavalkya.

In the BhP (9.12.4) a list of the kings of the Ikṣvāku race is given. One king, by the name of Hiraṇyanābha ("one whose navel is golden") is mentioned, and it elaborates that "Yājñavalkya of Kośala" is said to have studied *yoga* from him. Further, it is said that Hiraṇyanābha was a pupil of Jaimini and the *yoga* that he taught was *yoga* that leads to *siddhis* (magical powers) and destroys ignorance. Other forms of *yoga* that may have different goals are not mentioned, so it is unclear whether or not this was seen as a particular school of yoga. In the Śiva Purāṇa (39.26) we have an almost identical account associating

Yājñavalkya with Hiraṇyanābha. Though many of the names of individuals in the solar race differ, there is substantial overlap. Again, Yājñavalkya is said to have learned *yoga* from him.[28]

What these short passages do, however, is give a genealogy to a *yoga* tradition that is associated with Yājñavalkya. Whether or not these references refer to late yogic texts[29] attributed to Yājñavalkya is uncertain, as there is not enough detail given. Given that the early texts do not associate Yājñavalkya with *yoga*, these passages are an attempt to fill out such a genealogy. Why *yoga* teachings are said to come from a king is unclear, but the passages which discuss the lineages of solar kings are more concerned with valorizing particular kings than with tracing the actual origins of *yoga*. As we will see, Yājñavalkya is often seen as an ideal priest associated with many kings.

Kings and Brahmins

The relationship of kings and Brahmins has been a leitmotif of all the Yājñavalkya narratives. In the ŚB, Yājñavalkya is first associated with Janaka. In the BĀU, Janaka is an ideal king of sorts—he offers wealth for the most learned in *brahman*, he learns directly from Yājñavalkya after approaching him for knowledge, and he is said to even give away his people and himself to Yājñavalkya. In the MBh, Yājñavalkya is a priest for Indra and also for Yudhiṣṭhira, the two most important kings on heaven and earth. He is said to have taught Janaka the subtleties of Sāṃkhya and Yoga as well as tell a story about how he came to receive all this knowledge from the Sun.

In the Purāṇas as well, Yājñavalkya is associated with a number of kings.[30] While Janaka reappears with Yājñavalkya in certain passages, other kings are also associated with him. While Fitzgerald has pointed out that there is an implicit argument in the MBh to associate a Brahmin elite intimately with the ruling elite, in the case of Yājñavalkya this is a leitmotif to his character across different literary genres. This is to say that Yājñavalkya has become an idealized Vedic priest, particularly in his idealized relationships with the ruling elite. This ideal has its roots in the ŚB, but gains full expression from the BĀU onward and continues throughout the Epic and Purāṇic literature.

A story that is meant to valorize a particular pilgrimage spot on the Gāṅgā River is found in the *Brahma Purāṇa*. Chapter 17 is devoted to extolling the virtues of the pilgrimage site of Janasthāna. The text (17.1ff) relates that in the past, a king Janaka was born of the solar dynasty and was married to Guṇārṇavā ("ocean of qualities"). He goes to his leading priest, Yājñavalkya, asking how one is to attain enlightenment while still attached to the worldly life. It is clear that Janaka does not think that he could give up attachment (specifically, symbolized by the inclusion of a wife in this narrative). Thus, he seeks an alternative way to salvation; one that is said to be easier as "eschewal of attachment is a strenuous task."[31]

Interestingly, Yājñavalkya is not the one to answer the question, but Yājñavalkya tells Janaka that they should visit Janaka's father-in-law, the god Varuṇa (17.8). In earlier narratives including Yājñavalkya and Janaka, Yājñavalkya has answered the queries that Janaka has put to him. However, he does not do so here. The main reason for this appears to be based on the nature of the question. The personage of Yājñavalkya that is known from the other literature is not associated with worldly life, particularly not espousing doctrines that reconcile life in this world and salvation. Indeed, in the Maitreyī episodes (BĀU 2.4/4.5), Yājñavalkya explicitly argues that detaching oneself from worldly things (particularly family) is the means to immortality. In fact, his leaving Maitreyī at the end of these episodes is an enactment of the doctrine that preceded it—one should detach oneself from what is dear (*priya*), and Yājñavalkya does so by leaving.

In this regard, taking into account the collective portrayal of Yājñavalkya from various sources, the question posed by Janaka is probably not one that the composers saw as appropriate for the character of Yājñavalkya to answer directly. As we have seen, Yājñavalkya's teachings have been anything but easy in trying to understand the nature of existence and enlightenment, so Yājñavalkya suggests that they visit someone more fitting—the father of Janaka's wife. In this regard, given that Varuṇa is said to be Janaka's father-in-law, Varuṇa's character in a sense embodies the notion of enjoyment (he had a daughter—Janaka's wife—yet is a great deity) and thus is more appropriate to ask the question regarding combining enjoyment and larger religious goals.

Varuṇa (17.10) proceeds to explain that both attachment and non-attachment can lead to liberation. He argues that the householder is the ideal position that one should have in life, and through the merit acquired in this stage, one can attain liberation. Varuṇa then tells them that performing their ritual duties (*karma*) on the banks of the Gāṅgā will lead to liberation. Unlike the MBh story where Janaka ultimately renounces, he follows Varuṇa's advice and the story concludes (17.22) that Janaka attained liberation there and that the particular place is known as Janasthāna.

While this passage is concerned with names and origins (of Janasthāna), it also elaborates the theme of the relationship of kings and Brahmins. Clearly, this is a remembered association with Yājñavalkya and Janaka, but outside of their association, there is little elaboration. I have suggested that there may be a remembrance of Yājñavalkya from other sources in that he does not answer Janaka's question, but the association of the two is the basis of the narrative.

While Janaka appears to have a privileged relationship with Yājñavalkya, other kings are associated with him as well. One passage of the *Varāha Purāṇa* (44.1ff) is concerned with a particular worship ceremony of Viṣṇu on the twelfth day of the month. A story is narrated to show the power of a particular *vrata* (vow) that is undertaken. A king by the name of Vīrasena ("one whose army is strong") is said to lack sons, and so he undertakes a vow to guarantee male offspring (44.10). Yājñavalkya comes to this king and asks him the aim of his penance, and the King suggests that he is about to die and does not have a male heir. Yājñavalkya stops him from continuing his penance and tells him about the *dvadaśavrata* to guarantee male offspring. While the narrative does not offer the possibility of attaining liberation through having sons, it does state that individuals with sons will spend a *kalpa* in the world of Brahmā.

Yājñavalkya and *Dharmaśāstra*

Yājñavalkya becomes associated with the *dharma* ("proper conduct") tradition that, at least as far as our literary evidence can be dated, begins roughly in the 3rd century BCE (Olivelle, trans., 2000; trans., 2019). While it is clear that this expert tradition must have existed prior to this, it does not seem possible to determine with any specificity how far back the tradition may go.

Outside of the *dharmaśāstras* proper, we find a few, albeit scattered, references in the Purāṇas to Yājñavalkya as a participant in the legal expert tradition. There is little discussion in these passages to shed light on this association, but he is listed along with well-known individuals in the legal tradition and, in one case, to serve in establishing *dharma* at the end of the Kali yuga. For example, the *Padma Purāṇa* (PP 3.19.9), while not specifically mentioning the *smṛti* tradition, lists Yājñavalkya among a number of prominent sages, many associated with *dharmaśāstra* text production (Manu, Āpastamba, Nārada, Gautama). Alternatively, PP 6.236.22–27 classifies different *smṛti* compositions based on their quality (*guṇa*). It lists, among others, Yājñavalkya Ātreya, Taittira, and Kātyāyana as composers of texts which are *rājasa* in quality and lead to heaven. In the *Agni Purāṇa* (AP 162.1–2), he is listed as the third of twenty lawgivers after Manu and Viṣṇu. This list, albeit with a different ordering, contains the same names mentioned in the *Yājñavalkyasmṛti* (YS 1.4–5). While not directly mentioned as a law giver, Yājñavalkya is said in another *Agni Purāṇa* (AP) passage (16.8–13) to accompany Kalki as his priest, when this final manifestation of Viṣṇu comes to eradicate unrighteousness in the world and to establish *dharma* once again.

These passages (though perhaps with the exception of AP 16.8–13) are references to a legal tradition associated with Yājñavalkya. Since there are so few details in these contexts, one cannot say with any confidence what the view of any individual tradition might have entailed nor the source of that view. However, we do have the *Yājñavalkyasmṛti* (YS)—a legal text in the *dharmaśāstra* tradition—that has come down to us, probably from the 4th or 5th century CE (Olivelle, trans., 2019).

While a large amount of scholarship has been devoted to the *dharma* tradition, both in translation (most recently, trans., Olivelle 2000; 2005; trans., 2019) and as it has been applied in British law in India and its aftermath (Dirks 2001), only very recently has work considered more seriously why Yājñavalkya has become associated with a particular legal text, the YS.[32]

The main reason for this lacuna is the apparent enigmatic association of Yājñavalkya with the text. While the purported author throughout, there are only two places in the text (in the beginning frame and at 3.110) where there is any clear or direct reference to this figure. Like the *Manusmṛti* (trans., Olivelle 2005a, 26–27), the character to whom this text is ascribed is a figure who recedes into the background of legal discussions and is almost forgotten. This is not to say that the text may not be principally the work of a single author, but rather that authorship, outside of naming and introducing the text, did not appear to be of particular concern for the composers. In a way, this makes complete sense—the *dharma* texts are not concerned with characters and narratives, but with *dharma* and its application.

Olivelle (trans., 2019, xiii–xv) has suggested some reasons why the text was attributed to Yājñavalkya, in particular its clear association with the White Yajurveda. "The ascription to Yajnavalkya in the frame narrative is confirmed by the internal evidence showing that the historical author of the text belonged to the *Śukla Yajur Veda* reputedly founded by Yajnavalkya. Scholars have noted that most of the *mantras* in the text are derived from the *Vājasaneyī Saṃhītā* and that it follows the *Pāraskaragṛhyasūtra*, both belonging to the *Śukla Yajur Veda*" (Olivelle, trans., 2019, ix). Olivelle further argues that geographical location, dynastic legitimization, and the importance of yoga at the time (x) are complimentary reasons justifying Yājñavalkya's ascription to the text. The YS appears to be a product of the Gupta dynasty, also centered in the eastern heartland Pataliputra like Yājñavalkya himself, and Olivelle suggests that it was perhaps composed under Gupta patronage to bolster their own legitimacy.

All of that said, however, the later tradition saw something of a disconnect with this attribution and the Yājñavalkya of the BĀU. Even the composer of the most famous commentary on the YS, Vijñāneśvara, was not willing to take the attribution to Yājñavalkya at face value. He claims that the text must have been organized and edited by a student of Yājñavalkya, clearly recognizing Yājñavalkya as an authoritative figure of the past, but not the historical composer. Before commenting directly on the YS, Vijñāneśvara states in his foreword:

> *yājñavalkyaśiṣyaḥ kaścit praśnottararūpaṃ yājñavalkyamunipraṇītam dharmaśāstraṃ saṃkṣipya kathayām āsa yathā manupraṇītaṃ bhṛgu . . .*

> Some pupil of Yājñavalkya, having abridged the dharmaśāstra produced by the muni Yājñavalkya, recited it in the form of question and answer, as Bhṛgu (does of) that produced by Manu.

It appears here that the tradition was not willing to accept that the text as it had it was the unedited product of Yājñavalkya. Rather, the text places the ultimate source of what is to follow as Yājñavalkya's teaching, but places the text as we have it into the hands of one of his students. While this passage clearly places the text on the level of Manu's text, it also suggests authorial remove in the same manner as Manu. It moreover implies that an "original" must have existed, but is no longer available to the tradition.

While scholars have not universally agreed on the date of the YS, it clearly was composed after and modeled on the text of Manu, likely during the Gupta period (Olivelle, trans., 2019). The beginning lines of the text are clearly an echo of the beginning of the laws of Manu.

> *yogīśvaram yājñavalkyam saṃpūjya munayo 'bruvan*
> *varṇāśrametarāṇām no brūhi dharmān aśeṣataḥ* (1.1)
>
> The sages, having worshipped Yājñavalkya, the best of yogis, said, "Tell us completely the dharma of *varṇas* (classes), *āśramas* (stages) and of others. (cf. Manu 1.1)

Yājñavalkya is said to be seated in Mithilā (1.2), the capital of Videha, where he thinks deeply before he begins his discourse. He proceeds to list the sources of *dharma* (such as the Vedas, other *dharmaśāstras*, etc.) and lists twenty composers of the *dharmaśāstras* that include himself, suggesting this frame may have been added after the composition of a core text.

Yājñavalkya disappears from the narrative as a character (though always present as an author) only to appear again in the middle of the text (YS 3.110). The purported author says that he received the Āraṇyaka from the Sun and that he is the composer of a *yogaśāstra*.[33] This status as a composer of a *yogaśāstra* text suggests that *yoga* was well-established, and the text is paralleling Yājñavalkya's earlier association as a master of *yoga*—known also from the MBh and Purāṇas, but now apparently also a *yoga* text—to grant further authority to a *smṛti*.

This passage does not appear to make sense in its immediate context, and Kane suggests that it is simply inserted to glorify the text (Kane 1968, vol. 1, pt. 1, 422–23). One should note, though, that while this passage is similar to the beginning of the text (where Yājñavalkya is introduced as a *yogin*), it states that Yājñavalkya received the Āraṇyaka, almost certainly meaning the BĀU, from the Sun and not the White Yajurveda as a whole. It is interesting that this text does not refer to the *Bṛhadāraṇyaka* as an Upaniṣad, suggesting a fluidity of these genre classifications (which the name of the BĀU itself suggests).

Why the tradition associates this *smṛti* with Yājñavalkya is still something of an enigma, especially since his earlier biography doesn't obviously lend itself to this, where his association with abstract thought, ritual, and transcending the world is more apparent. It may simply be the case that Yājñavalkya had attained such a status as a great *ṛṣi* that he was naturally associated with the *dharma* tradition. It is also likely, as Kane, Olivelle, and others have suggested, that this text is intimately connected to the White Yajurvedic tradition and to assign the text the status attained by the tradition's earliest spokesman would make sense, especially given the geographical situatedness of the Guptas (Olivelle, trans., 2019).

But I think there are other suggestive reasons why Yājñavalkya may be a natural spokesman for a particular *dharma* tradition based on the comparison with Manu. Such a comparison especially makes sense, both in that the YS appears to be based directly on the Laws of Manu and in that Yājñavalkya's life story is thematically defined an ideal relationship of kings with Brahmins.

As Olivelle (trans. 2005a, 18ff.) has pointed out, Manu is an idealized author of the legal text attributed to him. Manu is said to be the first man (hence, his name means "man") of the solar dynasty and the first king. Mythologically, it works nicely that the first person and the first ruler be one and the same and that he is the one to lay down law codes that (future) men are to follow—society is at its very beginning, and thus there is a need to institute social rules; who better than the beginning of mankind himself? Attaching this name to the text serves to naturalize the rules that are to follow: the paradigmatic man laid down the paradigm for men to follow. As such, these rules are not constructed by a concrete historical person at a particular time, but rather positioned back into the golden age at the beginning of creation. While it is clear that *The Laws of Manu* was composed by Brahmins, placing the authorship onto a mythological king further argues for an interdependency between the ruling class and the religious elite.

In the case of the YS, I think we have something similar occurring, likely with the goal of bolstering the Gupta's dynastic standing in support of Olivelle's argument. While Manu is an idealized king,

Yājñavalkya, as we have seen, had become an idealized priest, *particularly in his association with kings*. In the ŚB and the BĀU, Yājñavalkya is closely associated with king Janaka (himself an idealized king) and is portrayed as an idealized friend of kings, willing to share his knowledge (and receive proper payment). In the MBh and the Purāṇas, Yājñavalkya is associated with other idealized kings—Indra, Yudhiṣṭhira, and Rāma, among others. In many of these contexts, the Vedic sacrifices that are said to take place are those that particularly call for a symbiotic relationship between Brahmins and Kṣatriyas: the *aśvamedha* and the *rājasūya*, grand royal rituals highlighting a symbiotic relationship of priests and rulers.[34]

In a manner similar to how Olivelle argues that the figure of Manu "works" for that legal tradition, Yājñavalkya—as a royal adviser!—does so as well.[35] Yājñavalkya himself, given the proliferation of the kingly narrative contexts in which he appears, may have been seen as symbolic of the symbiotic relation between kings and priests. As such, I think the association of Yājñavalkya with a *smṛti* text is not simply to raise the status of the text (which, of course, it also does), but it also resonates with one of the larger goals of *dharma* texts in establishing the king and the priest at the top of the socio-religious order.[36] As such, the Guptas appear to have been positioning themselves as the ideal kings in a symbiotic relationship with Brahmins priests, embodied here by Yājñavalkya, the idealized priest of that region.

Conclusion

We have seen that Yājñavalkya appears in a number of contexts in the Purāṇic literature and to a limited degree in the legal text attributed to him. In the case of the Purāṇas, hagiographical elaboration of Yājñavalkya has generally followed these patterns: (1) retellings of previously known stories (even in creating new stories based on these); (2) a discussion of the origins and names of the White and Black Yajurveda; (3) Yājñavalkya's relation to the *yoga* tradition; (4) an elaboration of the relationship of kings and Brahmins; and finally (5) the attribution of Yājñavalkya to a legal tradition.

In each of these cases, a number of novelties have arisen such as the nature of the dispute between Vaiśampāyana and Yājñavalkya, the personality of Kātyāyanī, and so on. What these stories tell us is not only what the various composers of the Purāṇas knew of from the earlier literary tradition, but more importantly, what they thought of as important, what they repeat or recompose, and/or what they expand upon or constrict. For example, Yājñavalkya's apparent arrogance was clearly an issue for later composers. In one case, the composers transferred Yājñavalkya's pride and his supposed greed for cows onto the other Brahmins present in the *brahmodya*, taking what was a positive character trait in the earlier literature and turning it into a negative one of other participants. Such a move was clearly to recharacterize and valorize Yājñavalkya as a reasonable and even-tempered sage. In another case, one Purāṇa identifies Yājñavalkya's arrogance as the reason for his split with his teacher, Vaiśaṁpāyana. In another Purāṇa, Vaiśaṁpāyana says that Yājñavalkya had directly ignored a teacher's command and this was the cause for the split, while another version leaves the cause open-ended. In another, the mongoose says that Yājñavalkya is arrogant in saying that the animal does not have a noble family. This was clearly a misunderstanding (and one that Yājñavalkya tries to correct), but it certainly resonates with the portrayal of Yājñavalkya we find elsewhere. In other passages, we are told that Yājñavalkya acquired his knowledge of *yoga* so as to establish a lineage of this knowledge not present in the earliest texts.

While many of these longer passages have larger goals (such as valorizing a particular pilgrimage, a particular ritual, or explaining the origin of the Vedas), what these passages also do is show us how various composers "read" Yājñavalkya in the Hindu tradition in the process of creating and validating their own traditions. For example, in the case of the Kātyāyanī story, it is clear that the composers "read" the Maitreyī episodes as showing favoritism towards one wife. The narrative then is an attempt to fill out that story, to suggest that by performing particular rituals one can guarantee the affections of a spouse as well as to explain Kātyāyana's origins.

I have also suggested that a composite view of Yājñavalkya shows that he is seen as intimately associated with kings and kingly rule. He has been associated with Janaka, Rāma, and others. Most often he has been associated with sacrifices that serve to establish kingly rule, such as the *aśvamedha* and the *rājāsūya*. Clearly, for many, Yājñavalkya was an idealized sage, but one who had an idealized relationship with kings, both human and divine.

It is this composite view that also helps us to further understand the association with Yājñavalkya and the *smṛti* tradition. As an idealized priest with idealized relationships with kings, Yājñavalkya functions like Manu, albeit from the other side of the purported Brahmin/Kṣatriya model of codependency. Yājñavalkya, narratively known as one who discourses *with* kings on matters of religious significance, becomes known as one who has laid down rules in the *smṛti* texts *for* historical kings.

Conclusion

Yājñavalkya and Ancient Indian Literary Memory

In the preceding chapters I have traced the figure of Yājñavalkya through the early religious Sanskrit literature in a variety of genres across time: the early Brāhmaṇas, the Upaniṣads, the Epic *Mahābhārata,* and into the Purāṇas. What I have done is to present and analyze the passages and narratives associated with this literary figure so as to trace the development of a White Yajurvedic ritualist/philosopher into an iconic figure of India's past. This synchronic and diachronic presentation is done intentionally to emphasize not only a particular method of close reading, but also as a means to watch a literary tradition surrounding a particular figure evolve across time.

This book has focused on the development of this figure within the larger Sanskrit literary tradition and has emphasized how various Sanskrit literary productions, while positioning themselves as faithful to a literary past, contend with that past in incorporating what is new and novel. We have seen that in the case of Yājñavalkya most newly produced narratives regarding this individual utilized similar themes, ideas, and character traits that are found in the earlier tradition to their own ends. Clearly, they were aware of the earlier stories and felt a need to incorporate the new with the old and thus give what is new a precedent.

We have seen, for example, the development and redeployment of Yājñavalkya's sarcastic wit as it developed across literary traditions. In the *Śatapatha Brāhmaṇa* (ŚB), sarcasm appears only when Yājñavalkya's opinion is taken as authoritative in ritual matters. I have suggested that this character trait ideally positioned Yājñavalkya to be the spokesman for the White Yajurvedic tradition (as shown especially in the *Bṛhadāraṇyaka Upaniṣad* [BĀU]), a tradition that apparently felt the need to justify itself against the prevailing orthodoxy of the western regions. It is in the BĀU that we find sarcasm used strategically as a means to bolster the authority of Yājñavalkya and therefore the tradition as a whole that he represents. From the viewpoint of the White Yajurvedic tradition, this sarcasm can be understood as "pride in correct knowledge," where Yājñavalkya's wit and sarcasm are justified by the fact that he is portrayed as the most learned in *brahman*.

While sarcasm is not found in the *Mahābhārata* (MBh) portrayals of Yājñavalkya, we find the sarcasm attributed to Yājñavalkya put to different uses in the Purāṇas. One of the reasons for these different uses is based on the ambiguity of sarcasm itself. While dependent upon the context and the intent, sarcasm can be variously interpreted: it may be seen as justified, arrogant, humorous, or rude. As such, this is the ambiguity that the Purāṇic stories are exploring. In one narrative, this ambiguity is mentioned directly, where Vaiśaṁpāyana is said to misunderstand Yājñavalkya's statement about doing the sacrifice alone. In another case, in a Brāhmaṇa-style wordplay, Yājñavalkya calling a mongoose a *nakula* is misinterpreted by the mongoose as an insult, and he calls Yājñavalkya arrogant for assuming to know the nature of his family. We have also seen in another passage where Yājñavalkya is said to have spoken rudely to his teacher, but his penance towards the Sun apparently absolves him of any indiscretion.

In another Purāṇic passage, the narrators explore the ambiguity of sarcasm, arrogance, and greed, but deny that it is a trait of Yājñavalkya. Here the composers transfer what theoretically could be interpreted as "negative" character traits of Yājñavalkya onto the other Brahmins said to be in attendance. The composers explicitly portray such traits as negative while portraying Yājñavalkya as the opposite—the level-headed Brahmin calming the others and convincing them to debate with him. Here, Śākalya is portrayed as arrogant, but without the proper knowledge to justify it. Of course, Yājñavalkya wins in the end not because of his pride and sarcasm, but because of a lack of those traits.

As new traditions developed in ancient India (i.e., Sāṃkhya, Yoga, venerating particular pilgrimage sites, and so on) and with the rise of the importance of certain deities (Rāma, Śiva) within the broader expanse of Hinduism, the various traditions find creative ways to associate Yājñavalkya with them. Yājñavalkya was said to attend the *aśvamedha* of Janaka, but also the *rājasūya* of Yudhiṣṭhira and Indra. He is said to have attended the *aśvamedha* of Rāma, yet to have learned *yoga* from Śiva. Śiva, in another Purāṇa, is said to have helped Yājñavalkya overcome an ignoble birth which was the result of Yājñavalkya's insult to a mongoose.

While previous scholarship on Yājñavalkya generally has dismissed the evolving character of Yājñavalkya in the larger tradition, I have argued that there are discernable patterns in the compositions of the "Yājñavalkya narratives," patterns that suggest how earlier stories were understood. For example, such patterns include explaining what is *not said* in particular texts (such as elaborating the character of Kātyāyanī or telling in more detail Yājñavalkya's relationship with his purported teacher and the Sun god). In such cases, we can see where composers (and probably the audience) had questions that they wanted answers to: Why is Kātyāyanī treated differently in the BĀU story? What is her relationship with Yājñavalkya and how did they come to have a son? What is the nature of the split of the White Yajurveda and the Black Yajurveda? How can one explain the existence of two Yajurvedic traditions, but accept that both are authoritative in their own way? I have shown that such questions can be discerned from the "answers" we find in the narratives; that is, that the creation of certain new stories are based on perceived gaps in earlier stories. In this sense, new compositions are hagiographical elaborations based on earlier ones and are a form of community commentary.

Another pattern or theme that repeatedly returns in the passages associated with Yājñavalkya is his association with kings. The ŚB and the BĀU lay the groundwork, but as the status of Yājñavalkya expands outside of the White Yajurvedic tradition, Yājñavalkya becomes associated with many kings, whether human or divine. Clearly, the later literary traditions are telling us that Yājñavalkya has become an icon of an ideal priest/king relationship, and in tracing these passages we can see that process occurring. Not only does Yājñavalkya share his knowledge with willing kings, but he accepts knowledge from kings in both ritual matters (the *agnihotra* in the ŚB) and ascetic discipline (*yoga* in various Purāṇas). This theme is, I have suggested, one plausible explanation for Yājñavalkya being associated with the *smṛti* tradition. As Manu is an idealized king who composes a legal text, Yājñavalkya, who is said to do the same, is an idealized priest in his relationships with kings, albeit from the opposite side of the dominant *varṇa* coin.

This complex characterization of Yājñavalkya across texts forces us to question the standard demarcation that scholars have used in the past in discussing Yājñavalkya. To talk about a "split Yājñavalkya" as "ritualist" in the ŚB and as "philosopher" in the BĀU and position this distinction as a shift from "history" to "myth" is, I have shown, an oversimplification, not only of how genre functions, but also of the stories themselves. The stories of Yājñavalkya in the literary traditions of the MBh and the Purāṇas show us that this *is not* how Yājñavalkya was viewed by those traditions. In fact, many of these later characterizations of Yājñavalkya show that he was viewed as a complex character who was both a ritualist and a philosopher depending on the context under discussion and that this complexity had early precedent. An audience probably assumed this complex background even if a particular narrative appeared to emphasize one aspect of his character. Given the many portrayals of multiple aspects of this character, there does not appear to be a straightforward development from one to the other in the literature.[1]

In this regard, I have suggested that it is useful to think of the production of stories surrounding particular early literary figures as their "lives." The life of a figure is not simply the conglomeration of stories about that figure, but the interrelationship of those stories and what this tells us about how a tradition develops in view of that figure. We can speak of the "life" of a figure within a particular text, but also between texts and across time. Clearly, these are interrelated, and I hope I have shown that looking at both the synchronic and diachronic evolution of a figure in the texts is one of our best means to query the early reception of those texts.

Hence, by watching the development of the stories surrounding Yājñavalkya—first within the White Yajurveda proper and then for the growing audiences of the MBh and the Purāṇas—we can watch how later religious literary productions contend with their past in creating the present. In this way, we can see what stories are important to them, what character traits are emphasized or elided, or what gaps or silences in the narrative are filled out. Such a view of the production of religious literary texts grants a means to probe how these stories were understood within a larger context or, in a sense, to examine how they were "read" by looking at how they were recomposed.

I have suggested, particularly in regard to the Purāṇas, but equally of the MBh, that it is often fruitful to think of these sorts of literary productions as based on a literary "memory." That is, that the original texts (whether in the form that we have them today or otherwise) may not have been known intimately (such as they would be within a particular literary tradition responsible for maintaining them), but the stories from such texts were known more popularly. This suggests that what scholars have often seen as fixed "literary" traditions also have more popular (or "folk") counterparts—stories more broadly known, but not necessarily in a fixed or canonized form. Such a view of Yājñavalkya also helps us in understanding how in reinterpreting the stories, themes, and characters there is a certain amount of flexibility to the new literary creations that still draw on previous templates of a well-known figure.

Although this diachronic study allows for an internal insight into how various traditions over time may have viewed this figure, it also allows for external insights previously not available to scholars. For example, while it is certainly Brahmins who were composing the MBh and the various Purāṇas, how is it that they seem quite aware of Yājñavalkya's portrayal in an Upaniṣad of a specific ritual school? Secondary literature overwhelmingly refers to the Upaniṣads as composed of "secret teachings," and many scholars emphasize the "guardedness" of this early oral tradition (the Vedas and Upaniṣads) from those who are not direct participants in their own particular literary tradition.[2] If this is true in the case of the Upaniṣads, how is it that the composers of the MBh and the Purāṇas, texts that had a much wider audience, were familiar enough with these stories so as to elaborate their own narratives based on characteristics, themes, structures, and so on from the earlier narratives?

In the Brāhmaṇas we have myriad intertextual references that show that different *śākhas* were clearly aware of the particularities of ritual practice of different schools. What I am suggesting, however, is that the stories found in the Brāhmaṇas and Upaniṣads had greater extra-*śākha* transmission of the figures, ideas, beliefs, and practices found in those texts wider and wider audiences than generally acknowledged. Stories travel, and claims of secrecy say more about the value attributed to them than about their actual restrictiveness.

A project that remains to be done is to find where various Upaniṣadic stories from different sources and the personages within them appear in the later literature. However, in light of what we have seen in the case of Yājñavalkya, the stories surrounding him appear to have been more broadly known. As such, we need to rethink our characterization of the Upaniṣads as closely guarded, "secret" teachings and to take seriously the possibility that they (at least the narrative parts of them) must have circulated more widely, perhaps intentionally to *popularize* certain doctrines and practices amongst a larger Brahmanical community. This is to say that some secrets are "badly held secrets," even intentionally so.

Finally, this project has been an attempt to problematize the overly simplistic division between "historical fact" from "fiction" made by those studying famous personages in ancient India. As I have argued explicitly, such a sharp divide becomes complicated when it comes to religious narratives. Narratives of any type are always motivated beyond simply a listing of what had actually occurred. Those motivations may be to glorify an individual, a particular rite, or to fill out gaps in a story, but none of this makes a story a priori "false" in a historical sense. When any particular narrative is told, rhetorical strategies, emphases, or elaborations may be added to make a story interesting, add new dimensions to it, and so on, but the presence of such narrative strategies does not necessarily determine what may be factually true or invented. Instead, they can be used to interrogate *the process* of literary creation. Certainly, we are on surer historical ground in claiming that when a story tells us Yājñavalkya was in the abode of Indra performing a sacrifice that this is hagiographical elaboration. But throughout this book, my emphasis has been on what those elaborations and elisions tell us about how certain people viewed a figure at different times and how the figure of Yājñavalkya began to expand into more popular forms of what becomes known as Hinduism. This is to say that history is not simply limited to the factually true, but also must include what those historical people, in the reception and recomposition of Yājñavalkya in different narratives, thought was true and attempted in their compositions to make true. Such a methodological standpoint, in the case of Yājñavalkya, has allowed us to bypass such sharp distinctions of "fact" and "fiction" and focus on the historical and cultural processes of the creation of a sage across time.

Appendix

Text and Translation of *Bṛhadāraṇyaka Upaniṣad* (Kāṇva) Chapters 3 and 4

Chapter 3

3.1

janako ha vaideho bahudakṣiṇena yajñeneje | tatra ha kurupañcālānāṃ brāhmaṇā abhisametā babhūvuḥ | tasya ha janakasya vaidehasya vijijñāsā babhūva kaḥ svid eṣāṃ brāhmaṇānām anūcānatama iti | sa ha gavāṃ sahasram avarurodha | daśadaśa pādā ekaikasyāḥ śṛṅgayor ābaddhā babhūvuḥ ||1||

1. Janaka, [the king] of Videha performed a sacrifice entailing large sacrificial fees.[1] Brahmins of Kuru-Pañcāla were gathered together there. That Janaka of Videha had a desire to know, "Who of these Brahmins is most learned in Vedic knowledge?"[2] He corralled a thousand cows; to the horns of each of them were bound ten quarter-units of gold.

tān hovāca | brāhmaṇā bhagavanto yo vo brahmiṣṭhaḥ sa etā gā udajatām iti | te ha brāhmaṇā na dadhṛṣuḥ | atha ha yājñavalkyaḥ svam eva brahmacārim uvāca | etāḥ somyodaja sāmaśravā3 iti | tā hodācakāra | te ha brāhmaṇāś cukrudhuḥ kathaṃ no brahmiṣṭho bruvīteti | atha ha janakasya vaidehasya hotāśvalo babhūva | sa hainaṃ papraccha | tvaṃ nu khalu no yājñavalkya brahmiṣṭho 'sī3 iti | sa hovāca | namo vayaṃ brahmiṣṭhāya kurmo gokāmā eva vayaṃ sma iti | tam ha tata eva praṣṭum dadhre hotāśvalaḥ ||2||

2. He said to them, "Distinguished Brahmins! Let him who is most learned in *brahman* among you drive away these cows." Those Brahmins did not dare [to drive them off].

Now Yājñavalkya said to his pupil (*brahmacārin*), "Sāmaśravas, dear one, drive these away!" He drove them away.

Those Brahmins were outraged [and said], "How does he say he is the most learned in *brahman* among us?"

Now Janaka of Videha had a Hotr̥ priest [named] Aśvala. He [Aśvala] asked him, "Are you indeed, Yājñavalkya, the most learned among us?"

He replied, "We pay homage to the most learned, [but] we just want cows." At this, indeed, the Hotr̥ Aśvala dared to question him.

yājñavalkyeti hovāca | yad idaṁ sarvaṃ mr̥tyunāptaṁ sarvaṃ mr̥tyunābhipannaṃ kena yajamāno mr̥tyor āptim atimucyata iti | hotrartvijāgninā vācā | vāg vai yajñasya hotā | tad yeyaṃ vāk so 'yam agniḥ sa hotā sā muktiḥ sātimuktiḥ ||3||

3. "Yājñavalkya," [Aśvala] said, "when this all [i.e., whole world] is reached by death, when all is overtaken by death, by what means does a *yajamāna* free himself completely from the reach of death?"

"By means of the Hotr̥-priest, by means of the fire, by means of speech. Indeed, the Hotr̥ of the sacrifice is speech. This speech—it is this fire here, it is the Hotr̥, it is freedom, it is complete freedom."[3]

yājñavalkyeti hovāca | yad idaṁ sarvam ahorātrābhyām āptaṁ sarvam ahorātrābhyām abhipannaṃ kena yajamāno 'horātrayor āptim atimucyata iti | adhvaryuṇartvijā cakṣuṣādityena | cakṣur vai yajñasyādhvaryuḥ | tad yad idaṃ cakṣuḥ so 'sāv ādityaḥ so 'dhvaryuḥ sā muktiḥ sātimuktiḥ ||4||

4. "Yājñavalkya," he said, "when this all is reached by night and day, when all is overtaken by night and day, by what means does a *yajamāna* free himself completely from the reach of night and day?"

"By means of the Adhvaryu priest, by means of sight, by means of the sun. Indeed, the Adhvaryu of the sacrifice is sight. This sight—it is the sun there, it is the Adhvaryu, it is freedom, it is complete freedom."

yājñavalkyeti hovāca | yad idaṁ sarvaṃ pūrvapakṣāparapakṣābhyām āptaṁ sarvaṃ pūrvapakṣāparapakṣābhyām abhipannaṃ kena yajamānaḥ pūrvapakṣāparapakṣayor āptim atimucyata iti | udgātrartvijā vāyunā prāṇena | prāṇo vai yajñasyodgātā | tad yo 'yaṃ prāṇaḥ sa vāyuḥ sa udgātā sā muktiḥ sātimuktiḥ ||5||

5. "Yājñavalkya," he said, "when this all is reached by the fortnights of the waxing and waning moon, when all is overtaken by the fortnights of the waxing and waning moon, by what means does the *yajamāna* free himself completely from the reach of the fortnights of waxing and waning moon?"

"By means of the Udgātṛ priest, by means of wind, by means of the breath. Indeed, the Udgātṛ of the sacrifice is breath. This breath—it is the wind, it is the Udgātṛ, it is freedom, it is complete freedom."

yājñavalkyeti hovāca | yad idam antarikṣam anārambaṇam iva kenākrameṇa yajamānaḥ svargaṃ lokam ākramata iti | brahmaṇartvijā manasā candreṇa | mano vai yajñasya brahmā | tad yad idaṃ manaḥ so 'sau candraḥ sa brahmā sā muktiḥ sātimuktiḥ | ity atimokṣāḥ | atha saṃpadaḥ ||6||

6. "Yājñavalkya," he said, "when this middle region appears to be (*iva*) without support, by what path does the *yajamāna* ascend to the heavenly world?"

"By means of the Brahmin priest, by means of the mind, by means of the moon. Indeed, the Brahmin of the sacrifice is the mind. The mind—it is the moon there, it is the Brahmin, it is freedom, it is complete freedom."

Those are the complete freedoms. Now the correspondences.[4]

yājñavalkyeti hovāca | katibhir ayam adya ṛgbhir hotāsmin yajñe kariṣyatīti | tisṛbhir iti | katamās tās tisra iti | puronuvākyā ca yājyā ca śasyaiva tṛtīyā | kiṃ tābhir jayatīti | yat kiṃcedaṃ prāṇabhṛd iti ||7||

7. "Yājñavalkya," he said, "with how many verses will the Hotṛ perform today in this sacrifice?"

"With three."

"Which are those three?"

"The before-offering verse, the verse concomitant with the sacrifice, and the third, the verse of praise."

"What does he win with those?"

"Whatever supports life in this world.[5]

yājñavalkyeti hovāca | katy ayam adyādhvaryur asmin yajña āhutīr hoṣyatīti | tisra iti | katamās tās tisra iti | yā hutā ujjvalanti yā hutā atinedante yā hutā adhiśerate | kiṃ tābhir jayatīti | yā hutā ujjvalanti devalokam eva tābhir jayati | dīpyata iva hi devalokaḥ | yā hutā atinedante pitṛlokam eva tābhir jayati | atīva hi pitṛlokaḥ | yā hutā adhiśerate manuṣyalokam eva tābhir jayati | adha iva hi manuṣyalokaḥ ||8||

8. "Yājñavalkya," he said, "how many oblations will the Adhvaryu offer today in this sacrifice?"

"Three."

"Which are those three?"

"The oblations that blaze up, the oblations that bubble over, and the oblations that down."[6]

"What does he win with those?"

"Those offerings which blaze up—with those, he wins just the world of the gods because, in a way, the world of the gods shines. The offerings that bubble over (*ati*)—with those he wins just the world of the fathers because, in a way, the world of the fathers is over above (*ati*). The offerings that lie down (*adhi*)—with those he wins just the world of men because, in a way, the world of men is below (*adha*)."

yājñavalkyeti hovāca | katibhir ayam adya brahmā yajñaṃ dakṣiṇato devatābhir gopāyatīti | ekayeti | katamā saiketi | mana eveti | anantaṃ vai mano 'nantā viśve devāḥ | anantam eva sa tena lokaṃ jayati ||9||

9. "Yājñavalkya," he said, "with how many deities will the *brahman* on the southern side protect the sacrifice today?"

"With one."

"Which is that one?"

"It is just the mind; the mind, indeed, is unending [and] the All Gods (*viśve devāḥ*) are unending. Unending, indeed, is the world he wins with this."[7]

yājñavalkyeti hovāca | katy ayam adyogātāsmin yajñe stotriyāḥ stoṣyatīti | tisra iti | katamās tās tisra iti | puronuvākyā ca yājyā ca śasyaiva tṛtīyā | katamās tā yā adhyātmam iti | prāṇa eva puronuvākyāpāno yājyā vyānaḥ śasyā | kiṃ tābhir jayatīti | pṛthivīlokam eva puronuvākyayā jayaty antarikṣalokaṃ yājyayā dyulokaṁ śasyayā | tato ha hotāśvala upararāma ||10||
|| iti prathamaṃ brāhmaṇam ||

10. "Yājñavalkya," he said, "how many hymns of praise will the Ugātṛ sing in this sacrifice today?"

"Three."

"Which are those three?"

"The fore-offering verse, the verse concomitant with the sacrifice, and the third, the verse of praise."

"Which are they in relation to the body?"

"The fore-offering verse is the out-breath, the verse concomitant with the sacrifice is the in-breath, and the verse of praise is the inter-breath."

"What does he win with those?"

"By means of the fore-offering he wins just the earthly world; by means of the verse concomitant with the sacrifice, the middle world; and by means of the verse of praise, the heavenly world."

Thereupon, Hotṛ Aśvala ceased [questioning him].

3.2

atha hainaṃ jāratkārava ārtabhāgaḥ papraccha | yājñavalkyeti hovāca | kati grahā katy atigrahāḥ iti | aṣṭau grahā aṣṭāv atigrahā iti | ye te 'ṣṭau grahā aṣṭāv atigrahāḥ katame ta iti ||1||

1. Next Jāratkārava Ārtabāga questioned him. "Yājñavalkya," he said, "how many graspers are there and how many over-graspers?"[8]

"Eight graspers and eight over-graspers."

"Which are those eight graspers and eight over-graspers?"

prāṇo vai grahaḥ | so 'pānenātigrāheṇa gṛhītaḥ | apānena hi gandhāñ jigrati ||2|| vāg vai grahaḥ | sa nāmnātigrāheṇa gṛhītaḥ | vācā hi nāmāny abhivadati ||3|| jihvā vai grahaḥ | sa rasenātigrāheṇa gṛhītaḥ | jihvayā hi rasān vijānāti ||4|| cakṣur vai grahaḥ | sa rūpeṇātigrāheṇa gṛhītaḥ | cakṣuṣā hi rūpāṇi paśyati ||5|| śrotraṃ vai grahaḥ | sa śabdenātigrāheṇa gṛhītaḥ | śrotreṇa hi sabdāñ chṛṇoti ||6|| mano vai grahaḥ | sa kāmenātigrāheṇa gṛhītaḥ | manasā hi kāmān kāmayate ||7|| hastau vai grahaḥ | sa karmaṇātigrāheṇa gṛhītaḥ | hastābhyāṁ hi karma karoti ||8|| tvag vai grahaḥ | sa sparśenātigrāheṇa gṛhītaḥ | tvacā hi sparśān vedayate | ity ete 'ṣṭau grahā aṣṭāv atigrahāḥ ||9||

2. "One grasper is the out-breath. It is grasped by means of the in-breath, which is the over-grasper, for by means of the in-breath[9] one smells odors.

3. "One grasper is speech. It is grasped by means of name, which is the over-grasper, for by means of speech one speaks the names [of things].

4. "One grasper is the tongue. It is grasped by means of taste, which is the over-grasper, for by means of the tongue one comprehends tastes.

5. "One grasper is sight. It is grasped by means of visible form, which is the over-grasper, for by means of sight one sees visible forms.

6. "One grasper is hearing. It is grasped by means of sound, which is the over-grasper, for by means of hearing one hears sounds.

7. "One grasper is mind. It is grasped by means of desire, which is the over-grasper, for by means of mind one experiences desires.

8. "One grasper is the two hands. [They] are grasped by means of action, which is the over-grasper, for by means of the hands one performs action.

9. "One grasper is skin. It is grasped by means of touch, which is the over-grasper, for by means of skin one comprehends types of touch.

"These are the eight graspers and eight over-graspers."

yājñavalkyeti hovāca | yad idaṁ sarvaṃ mr̥tyor annaṃ kā svit sā devatā yasyā mr̥tyur annam iti | agnir vai mr̥tyuḥ | so 'pām annam | apa punar-mr̥tyuṃ jayati ||10||

10. "Yājñavalkya," he said, "this all [i.e., whole world] is the food of death, of which deity is death the food?"

"Death, indeed, is fire. It [fire] is the food of water. [By this][10] one eschews repeated death."

yājñavalkyeti hovāca | yatrāyaṃ puruṣo mriyata ud asmāt prāṇāḥ krāmanty āho3 neti | neti hovāca yājñavalkyaḥ | atraiva samavanīyante | sa ucchvayati | ādhmāyati | ādhmāto mr̥taḥ śete ||11||

11. "Yājñavalkya," he said, "where a man dies, do the breaths depart from him or not?"

"No,"Yājñavalkya replied. "They accumulate right here [i.e., in the body]; It swells, becomes bloated. [Thus] a dead man lies bloated."[11]

yājñavalkyeti hovāca | yatrāyaṃ puruṣo mriyate kim enaṃ na jahātīti | nāmeti | anantaṃ vai nāmānantā viśve devāḥ | anantam eva sa tena lokaṃ jayati ||12||

12. "Yājñavalkya," he said, "where a man dies, what does not leave him?"[12]

"Name. Indeed, without end is name and without end are the All Gods. The unending world he wins by this."

yājñavalkyeti hovāca | yatrāsya puruṣasya mr̥tasyāgniṃ vāg apy eti vātaṃ prāṇaś cakṣur ādityaṃ manaś candraṃ diśaḥ śrotraṃ pr̥thivīṁ śarīram ākāśam ātmauṣadhir lomāni vanaspatīn keśā apsu lohitaṃ ca retaś ca nidhīyate kvāyaṃ tadā puruṣo bhavatīti | āhar somya hastam ārtabhāga | āvām evaitasya vediṣyāvo na nāv etat sajana iti | tau hotkramya mantrayāṃ cakrāte | tau ha yad ūcatuḥ karma haiva tad ūcatuḥ | atha yat praśaśaṁsatuḥ karma haiva tat praśaśaṁsatuḥ | puṇyo vai puṇyena karmaṇā bhavati pāpaḥ pāpeneti | tato ha jāratkārava ārtabhāga uprarāma ||13||

|| iti dvitīyaṃ brāhmaṇam ||

13. "Yājñavalkya," he said, "where a man dies, his speech goes into fire, breath into wind, sight into sun, mind into the moon, hearing into the quarters, the body into the earth, his self (*ātman*) into space, the body hairs into plants, the head hairs into trees, and his blood and semen are deposited in the waters, then where does that person come to be?"

"Take my hand, dear Ārtabhāga. We will discuss this, but not in public."

The two stepped out and discussed it. What they discussed was only action. Now, what they praised was only action. One comes to good by good action and bad by bad action.

Thereupon, Jāratkārava Ārtabhaga ceased [questiong him].

3.3

atha hainaṃ bhujyur lāhyāyaniḥ papraccha | yājñavalkyeti hovāca | madreṣu carakāḥ paryavrajāma | te patañcalasya kāpyasya gr̥hān aima | tasyāsīd duhitā gandharvagr̥hītā | tam apr̥cchāma ko 'sīti | so 'bravīt sudhanvāṅgirasa iti | taṃ yadā lokānām antān apr̥cchāmāthainam abrūma kva pārikṣitā abhavann iti kva pārikṣitā abhavan | sa tvā pr̥cchāmi yājñavalkya kva pārikṣitā abhavann iti ||1||

1. Next, Bhujyu Lāhyāyani questioned him. "Yājñavalkya," he said, "[once] we wandered as itinerants[13] among the Madras. We went to the home of Patañcala Kāpya. He had a daughter seized by a Gandharva.

"We asked him, 'Who are you?'

"He said, 'Sudhanvan Āṅgirasa.'

"When we were asking him about the ends of the worlds, we asked, 'Where did the Pārikṣitas come to be?' Just where did they come to be? I ask you, Yājñavalkya, where did the Pārikṣitas come to be?"

sa hovāca | uvāca vai saḥ | agacchan vai te tad yatrāśvamedhayājino gacchantīti | kva nv aśvamedhayājino gacchantīti | dvātriṁśataṃ vai devarathāhnyāny ayaṃ lokaḥ | taṁ samantaṃ pr̥thivī dvis tāvat paryeti | tāṁ samantaṃ pr̥thivīṃ dvis tāvat samudraḥ paryeti | tad yāvatī kṣurasya dhārā yāvad vā makṣikāyāḥ patraṃ tāvān antareṇākāśas tān indraḥ suparṇo bhūtvā vāyave prāyacchat | tān vayur ātmani dhitvā tatrāgamayad yatrāśvamedhayājino 'bhavann iti | evam iva vai sa vāyum eva praśaśaṁsa | tasmād vāyur eva vyaṣṭir vāyuḥ samaṣṭiḥ | apa punarmr̥tyuṃ jayati ya evaṃ veda | tato ha bhujyur lāhyāyanir upararāma ||2||

|| *iti tritīyam brāhmaṇam* ||

2. He said, "He, indeed, told you: they went to where the offerers of the horse sacrifice go."[14]

"But where do the offerers of the horse sacrifice go?"

"This world is [the size of the traversing of] the chariot of the gods for thirty-two days.[15] The earth, which is twice that size, encompasses it on all sides. The ocean, which is twice that size, encompasses the earth on all sides. There is a space between as thin as a razor's edge or a bug's wing. Indra became a bird and delivered them [the Pārikṣitas] to the wind. The wind put them in itself and went to where the offerers of the horse sacrifice were. In a similar way, he [the Gandharva] praised only wind. Therefore the 'individual' is simply the wind and the 'collective' is [simply] the wind. Whosoever know this in this way eschews repeated death."

Thereupon, Bhujyu Lāhyāyani ceased questioning him.

3.4

atha hainam uṣastaś cākrāyaṇaḥ papraccha | yājñavalkyeti hovāca | yat sākṣād aparokṣād brahma ya ātmā sarvāntaras taṃ me vyācakṣveti | eṣa ta ātmā sarvāntaraḥ | katamo yājñavalkya sarvāntaraḥ | yaḥ prāṇena prāṇiti sa ta ātmā sarvāntaraḥ | yo 'pānenāpānīti sa ta ātmā sarvāntaraḥ | yo vyānena vyānīti sa ta ātmā sarvāntaraḥ | ya udānenodāniti sa ta ātmā sarvāntaraḥ | eṣa ta ātmā sarvāntaraḥ ||1||

1. Next Uṣusta Cākrāyaṇa questioned him. "Yājñavalkya," he said, "explain to me the *brahman* that is clear and not obscure, which is the self [*ātman*] within all."

"That which is within all is your self."

"Which one is [the self] within all, Yājñavalkya?"

"The one who exhales with the out-breath, that is your self within all. The one who inhales with the in-breath, that is your self within all. The one who breathes between with the middle-breath, that is your self within all. That one who breathes up with the up-breath, that is your self within all. That which is within all is your self."

sa hovācoṣastaś cākrāyaṇaḥ | yathā vibrūyād asau gaur asāv aśva ity evam evaitad vyapadiṣṭaṃ bhavati | yad eva sākṣād aparokṣād brahma ya ātmā sarvāntaras taṃ me vyācakṣveti | eṣa ta ātmā sarvāntaraḥ | katamo yājñavalkya sarvāntaraḥ | na dr̥ṣṭer draṣṭāraṃ paśyeḥ | na śruteḥ śrotāraṁ śr̥ṇuyāḥ | na mater mantāraṃ manvīthāḥ | na vijñāter vijñātāraṃ vijānīyāḥ | eṣa ta ātmā sarvāntaraḥ | ato 'nyad ārtam | tato hoṣastaś cākrāyaṇa upararāma ||2||

|| iti caturthaṁ brāhmaṇam ||

2. Uṣasta Cākrāyaṇa replied, "If one says like this, it is like pointing out that 'This a cow and this a horse.' Explain to me *just* the *brahman* that is clear and not obscure, that is the self [*ātman*] within all."

"That which is within all is your self."

"Which one is [the self] within all, Yājñavalkya?"

"You wouldn't see the seer of seeing. You wouldn't hear the hearer of hearing. You wouldn't think of the thinker of thinking. You wouldn't perceive the perceiver of perceiving. That is your self within all. Anything other than this is pain."

Thereupon, Uṣasta Cākrāyaṇa ceased [questioning him].

3.5

atha hainaṃ kaholaḥ kauṣītakeyaḥ papraccha | yājñavalkyeti hovāca | yad eva sākṣād aparokṣād brahma ya ātmā sarvāntaras taṃ me vyācakṣveti | eṣa ta ātmā sarvāntaraḥ | katamo yājñavalkya sarvāntaraḥ | yo 'śanāyāpipāse śokaṃ mohaṃ jarāṃ mr̥tyum atyeti | etaṃ vai tam ātmānaṃ viditvā brāhmaṇāḥ putraiṣaṇāyāś ca vittaiṣaṇāyāś ca lokaiṣaṇāyāś ca vyutthāyātha bhikṣācaryaṃ caranti | yā hy eva putraiṣaṇā sā vittaiṣaṇā yā vittaiṣaṇā sā lokaiṣaṇā | ubhe hy ete eṣaṇe eva bhavataḥ | tasmād brāhmaṇaḥ pāṇḍityaṃ nirvidya bālyena tiṣṭhāset | bālyaṃ ca pāṇḍityaṃ ca nirvidyātha muniḥ | amaunaṃ ca maunaṃ ca nirvidyātha brāhmaṇaḥ | sa brāhmaṇaḥ kena syād yena syāt tenedṛśa eva | ato 'nyad ārtam | tato ha kaholaḥ kauṣītakeya upararāma ||1||

|| iti pañcamaṃ brāhmaṇam ||

1. Next Kahola Kauṣītakeya questioned him. "Yājñavalkya," he said, "explain to me just the *brahman* that is clear and not obscure, that is the self [*ātman*] within all."

"That which is within all is your self."

"Which one is [the self] within all, Yājñavalkya?"

"He is the one who goes beyond hunger and thirst, suffering and delusion, old age and death. Having come to know that this is the self, Brahmins abandon the desire for sons, the desire for wealth, and the desire for [various] worlds and wander as a mendicant. The desire for sons is the desire for wealth and the desire for wealth is the desire for [various] worlds—both are simply desires. Therefore, a Brahmin rids himself of the pandit's life and would be like a child. Having given up the pandit's life and the child's life, he is a sage. Then, having given up the non-sagely and sagely lives, he is a Brahmin.[16] He, in whatever manner he may live, is still such a Brahmin.[17] Anything other than this is pain."

Thereupon, Kahola Kauṣītakeya ceased [questioning him].

3.6

atha hainaṃ gārgī vācaknavī papraccha | yājñavalkyeti hovāca | yad idaṁ sarvam apsv otaṃ ca protaṃ ca kasmin nu khalv āpa otāś ca protāś ceti | vāyau gārgīti |

kasmin nu khalu vāyur otaś ca protaś ceti | antarikṣalokeṣu gārgīti |

kasmin nu khalv antarikṣalokā otāś ca protāś ceti | gandharvalokeṣu gārgīti |

kasmin nu khalu gandharvalokā otāś ca protāś ceti | ādityalokeṣu gārgīti |

kasmin nu khalv ādityalokā otāś ca protāś ceti | candralokeṣu gārgīti |

kasmin nu khalu candralokā otāś ca protāś ceti | nakṣatralokeṣu gārgīti |

kasmin nu khalu nakṣatralokā otāś ca protāś ceti | devalokeṣu gārgīti |

kasmin nu khalu devalokā otāś ca protāś ceti | indralokeṣu gārgīti |

kasmin nu khalv indralokā otāś ca protāś ceti | prajāpatilokeṣu gārgīti |

kasmin nu khalu prajāpatilokā otāś ca protāś ceti | brahmalokeṣu gārgīti | kasmin nu khalu brahmalokā otāś ca protāś ceti |

sa hovāca gārgi mātiprākṣīḥ | mā te mūrdhā vyapaptat | anatipraśnyāṃ vai devatām atipr̥cchasi | gārgi mātiprākṣīr iti | tato ha gārgī vācaknavy upararāma ||1||

|| iti ṣaṣṭhaṃ brāhmaṇam ||

1. Next Gārgī Vācaknavī questioned him. "Yājñavalkya," she said, "This all [i.e., whole world] is woven to and fro on the waters, but on what are the waters woven to and fro?"

"On air, Gārgī."

"But on what is the air woven to and fro?"

"On the middle worlds, Gārgī."

"But on what are the middle worlds woven to and fro?"

"On the worlds of the Gandharvas, Gārgī."

"But on what are the worlds of the Gandharvas woven to and fro?"

"On the worlds of the sun, Gārgī."

"But on what are the worlds of the sun woven to and fro?"

"On the worlds of the moon, Gārgī."

"But on what are the worlds of the moon woven to and fro?"

"On the worlds of the stars, Gārgī."

"But on what are the worlds of the stars woven to and fro?"

"On the worlds of the gods, Gārgī."

"But on what are the worlds of the gods woven to and fro?"

"On the worlds of Indra, Gārgī."

"But on what are the worlds of Indra woven to and fro?"

"On the worlds of Prajāpati, Gārgī."

"But on what are the worlds of Prajāpati woven to and fro?"

"On the worlds of *brahman*, Gārgī."

"But on what are the worlds of *brahman* woven to and fro?"

Yājñavalkya said, "Gārgī, don't ask about what is beyond this, lest your head shatter apart! You are asking beyond the deity that should not be asked beyond. Gārgī, don't ask beyond [this]!"

Thereupon, Gārgī Vācaknavī ceased [questioning him].

3.7

atha hainam uddālaka āruṇiḥ papraccha | yājñavalkyeti hovāca | madreṣv avasāma patañcalasya kāpyasya gṛheṣu yajñam adhīyānāḥ | tasyāsīd bhāryā gandharvagṛhītā | tam apṛcchāma ko 'sīti | so 'bravīt kabandha ātharvaṇa iti | so 'bravīt patañcalaṃ kāpyaṃ yājñikāṁś ca vettha nu tvaṃ kāpya tat sūtraṃ yenāyaṃ ca lokaḥ paraś ca lokaḥ sarvāṇi ca bhūtāni saṃdṛbdhāni bhavantīti | so 'bravīt patañcalaḥ kāpyo nāhaṃ tad bhagavan vedeti | so 'bravīt patañcalaṃ kāpyaṃ yājñikāṁś ca vettha nu tvaṃ kāpya tam antaryāmiṇaṃ ya imaṃ ca lokaṃ paraṃ ca lokaṁ sarvāṇi ca bhūtāni yo 'ntaro yamayatīti | so 'bravīt patañcalaḥ kāpyo nāhaṃ taṃ bhagavan vedeti | so 'bravīt patañcalaṃ kāpyaṃ yājñikāṁś ca yo vai tat kāpya sūtraṃ vidyāt taṃ cāntaryāmiṇam iti sa brahmavit sa lokavit sa devavit sa vedavit sa bhūtavit sa ātmavit sa sarvavit | iti tebhyo 'bravīt | tad ahaṃ veda | tac cet tvaṃ yājñavalkya sūtram avidvāṁs tam cāntaryāmiṇaṃ brahmagavīr udajase mūrdhā te vipatiṣyatīti | veda vā ahaṃ gautama tat sūtraṃ taṃ cāntaryāmiṇam iti | yo vā idaṃ kaścid brūyād veda vedeti yathā vettha tathā brūhīti ||1||

1. Next Uddālaka Āruṇi questioned him. "Yājñavalkya," he said,"[once] we lived among the Madras studying sacrifice in the house of Patañcala Kāpya. He had a wife possessed by a Gandharva."

"We asked him, 'Who are you?'

"He said, 'Kabandha Ātharvaṇa.'

"He then asked Patañcala Kāpya and the students learning the sacrifice, 'Do you know, Kāpya, the string by which this world, the next world, and all beings are strung together?'[18]

"Patañcala Kāpya said, 'Distinguished one, I do not know that.'

"He said to Patañcala Kāpya and the students learning the sacrifice, 'Do you know the inner controller who controls this world, the next world, and all beings from within?'

"Patañcala Kāpya said, 'Distinguished one, I do not know that.'

"He said to Patañcala Kāpya and the students learning the sacrifice, 'Indeed, Kāpya, one who would know that thread and that inner controller, he is a knower of *brahman*, he is a knower of the worlds, he is a knower of gods, he is a knower of the Vedas, he is a knower of beings, he is a knower of the self, he is a knower of all!' That is what he said to them.

"I know this. If you, Yājñavalkya, drive away the cows meant for the *brahman* [knower among us] not knowing the thread and the inner controller, your head will shatter apart!"

"I know, Gautama, that string and that inner controller."

"Anyone can say 'I know, I know'—tell us what you know."

sa hovāca | vāyur vai gautama tat sūtram | vāyunā vai gautama sūtreṇāyaṃ ca lokaḥ paraś ca lokaḥ sarvāṇi ca bhūtāni saṃdr̥bdhāni bhavanti | tasmād vai gautama puruṣaṃ pretam āhur vyasraṁsiṣatāsyāṅgānīti | vāyunā hi gautama sūtreṇa samdr̥bdhāni bhavantīti | evam evaitat yājñavalkya | antaryāmiṇaṃ brūhīti ||2||

2. Yājñavalkya said, "The thread, Gautama, is indeed the air. By means of the thread that is air,[19] this world, the next world, and all beings are strung together. This is why, Gautama, they say of a dead man, 'His body parts are unstrung'—because by the thread that is the air they are strung together."

"It is so, Yājñavalkya. Tell [us] about the inner controller."

yaḥ pr̥thivyāṃ tiṣṭhan pr̥thivyā antaro yaṃ pr̥thivī na veda yasya pr̥thivī śarīraṃ yaḥ pr̥thivīm antaro yamayaty eṣa ta ātmāntaryāmy amr̥taḥ ||3||

3. "The one remaining in the earth, yet is separate from the earth, whom the earth does not know, whose body is the earth, who controls the earth from within—that is your self, the inner controller, the immortal.

yo 'psu tiṣṭhann adbhyo 'ntaro yam āpo na vidur yasyāpaḥ śarīraṃ yo 'po 'ntaro yamayaty eṣa ta ātmāntaryāmy amr̥taḥ ||4||

4. "The one remaining in the waters, yet is separate from the waters, whom the waters do not know, whose body is the water, who controls the waters from within—that is your self, the inner controller, the immortal.

yo 'gnau tiṣṭhann agner antaro yam agnir na veda yasyāgnīḥ śarīraṃ yo 'gnim antaro yamayaty eṣa ta ātmāntaryāmy amr̥tah ||5||

5. "The one remaining in fire, yet is separate from fire, whom fire does not know, whose body is fire, who controls fire from within—that is your self, the inner controller, the immortal.

yo 'ntarikṣe tiṣṭhann antarikṣād antaro yam antarikṣaṃ na veda yasyāntarikṣaṁ śarīraṃ yo 'ntarikṣam antaro yamayaty eṣa ta ātmāntaryāmy amr̥taḥ ||6||

6. "The one remaining in the middle region, yet is separate from the middle region, whom the middle region does not know, who controls the middle region from within—that is your self, the inner controller, the immortal.

yo vāyau tiṣthan vāyor antaro yaṃ vāyur na veda yasya vāyuḥ śarīraṃ yo vāyum antaro yamayaty eṣa ta ātmāntaryāmy amr̥taḥ ||7||

7. "The one remaining in the wind, yet is separate from the wind, whom the wind does not know, whose body is the wind, who controls the wind from within—that is your self, the inner controller, the immortal.

yo divi tiṣṭhan divo 'ntaro yaṃ dyaur na veda yasya dyauḥ śarīraṃ yo divam antaro yamayaty eṣa ta ātmāntaryāmy amr̥taḥ ||8||

8. "The one remaining in the sky, yet is separate from the sky, whom the sky does not know, whose body is the wind, who controls the wind from within—that is your self, the inner controller, the immortal.

ya āditye tiṣṭhan ādityād antaro yam ādityo na veda yasyādityaḥ śarīraṃ ya ādityam antaro yamayaty eṣa ta ātmāntaryāmy amr̥taḥ ||9||

9. "The one remaining in the sun, yet is separate from the sun, whom the sun does not know, whose body is the sun, who controls the sun from within—that is your self, the inner controller, the immortal.

yo dikṣu tiṣṭhan digbhyo 'ntaro yaṃ diśo na vidur yasya diśaḥ śarīraṃ yo diśo 'ntaro yamayaty eṣa ta ātmāntaryāmy amṛtaḥ ||10||

10. "The one remaining in the quarters, yet is separate from the quarters, whom the quarters do not know, whose body is the quarters, who controls the quarters from within—that is your self, the inner controller, the immortal.

yaś candratārake tiṣṭhaṁś candratārakād antaro yaṃ candratārakaṃ na veda yasya candratārakaṁ śarīraṃ yaś candratārakam antaro yamayaty eṣa ta ātmāntaryāmy amṛtaḥ ||11||

11. "The one remaining in the moon and the stars, yet is separate from the moon and the stars, of whom the moon and the stars do not know, whose body is the moon and the stars, who controls the moon and the stars from within—that is your self, the inner controller, the immortal.

ya ākāśe tiṣṭhann ākāśād antaro yam ākāśe na veda yasyākāśaḥ śarīraṃ ya ākāśam antaro yamayaty eṣa ta ātmāntaryāmy amṛtaḥ ||12||

12. "The one remaining in space, yet is separate from space, whom space does not know, whose body is space, who controls space from within—that is your self, the inner controller, the immortal.

yas tamasi tiṣṭhaṁs tamaso 'ntaro yaṃ tamo na veda yasya tamaḥ śarīraṃ yas tamo 'ntaro yamayaty eṣa ta ātmāntaryāmy amṛtaḥ ||13||

13. "The one remaining in darkness, yet is separate from darkness, whom darkness does not know, whose body is darkness, who controls darkness from within—that is your self, the inner controller, the immortal.

yas tejasi tiṣṭhaṁs tejaso 'ntaro yaṃ tejo na veda yasya tejaḥ śarīraṃ yas tejo 'ntaro yamayaty eṣa ta ātmāntaryāmy amṛtaḥ || ity adhidaivatam ||14||

14. "The one remaining in the light, yet is separate from the light, whom light does not know, whose body is light, who controls light from within—that is your self, the inner controller, the immortal."

That is in respect to the divine.

athādhibhūtam | yaḥ sarveṣu bhūteṣu tiṣṭhan sarvebhyo bhūtebhyo 'ntaro yaṁ sarvāṇi bhūtāni na vidur yasya sarvāṇi bhūtāni śarīraṃ yaḥ sarvāṇi bhūtāny antaro yamayaty eṣa ta ātmāntaryāmy amṛtaḥ | ityadhibūtam ||15||

15. Now, in respect to beings . . .

"The one remaining in all beings, yet is separate from all beings, whom all beings do not know, whose body is all beings, who controls all beings from within—that is your self, the inner controller, the immortal."

That is in respect to beings.

athādhyātmam | yaḥ prāṇe tiṣṭhan prāṇād antaro yaṃ prāṇo na veda yasya prāṇaḥ śarīraṃ yaḥ prāṇam antaro yamayaty eṣa ātmāntaryāmy amṛtaḥ ||16||

16. "Now, in respect to the self . . .

"The one remaining in breath, yet is separate from breath, whom breath does not know, whose body is breath, who controls breath from within—that is your self, the inner controller, the immortal.

yo vāci tiṣṭhan vāco 'ntaro yaṃ vāṅ na veda yasya vāk śarīraṃ yo vācam antaro yamayaty eṣa ta ātmāntaryāmy amṛtaḥ ||17||

17. "The one remaining in speech, yet is separate from speech, whom speech does not know, whose body is speech, who controls speech from within—that is your self, the inner controller, the immortal.

yaś cakṣuṣi tiṣṭhaṁś cakṣuṣo 'ntaro yaṃ cakṣur na veda yasya cakṣuḥ śarīraṃ yaś cakṣur antaro yamayaty eṣa ta ātmāntaryāmy amṛtaḥ ||18||

18. "The one remaining in sight, yet is separate from sight, whom sight does not know, whose body is sight, who controls sight from within—that is your self, the inner controller, the immortal.

yaḥ śrotre tiṣṭhañ chrotrād antaro yaṁ śrotram na veda yasya śrotraṁ śarīraṃ yaḥ śrotram antaro yamayaty eṣa ta ātmāntaryāmy amṛtaḥ ||19||

19. "The one remaining in hearing, yet is separate from hearing, whom hearing does not know, whose body is hearing, who controls hearing from within—that is your self, the inner controller, the immortal.

yo manasi tiṣṭhan manaso 'ntaro yaṃ mano na veda yasya manaḥ śarīraṃ yo mano 'ntaro yamayaty eṣa ta ātmāntaryāmy amṛtaḥ ||20||

20. "The one remaining in the mind, yet is separate from the mind, whom the mind does not know, whose body is the mind, who controls the mind from within—that is your self, the inner controller, the immortal.

yas tvaci tiṣṭhaṁs tvaco 'ntaro yaṃ tvaṅ na veda yasya tvak śarīraṃ yas tvacam antaro yamayaty eṣa ta ātmāntaryāmy amṛtaḥ ||21||

21. "The one remaining in skin, yet is separate from skin, whom skin does not know, whose body is the skin, who controls the skin from within—that is your self, the inner controller, the immortal.

yo vijñāne tiṣṭhan vijñānād antaro yaṃ vijñānaṃ na veda yasya vijñānaṁ śarīraṃ yo vijñānam antaro yamayaty eṣa ta ātmāntaryāmy āmṛtaḥ ||22||

22. "The one remaining in perception, yet is separate from perception, whom perception does not know, whose body is perception, who controls perception from within—that is your self, the inner controller, the immortal.

yo retasi tiṣṭhan retaso 'ntaro yaṁ reto na veda yasya retaḥ śarīraṃ yo reto 'ntaro yamayaty eṣa ta ātmāntaryāmy amṛtaḥ || adṛṣṭo draṣṭāśrutaḥ śrotāmato mantāvijñāto vijñātā | nānyo 'to 'sti draṣṭā nānyo 'to 'sti śrotā nānyo 'to 'sti mantā nānyo 'to 'sti vijñātā | eṣa ta ātmāntaryāmy amṛtaḥ | ato 'nyad ārtam | tato hoddālaka āruṇir upararāma ||23||

|| iti saptamaṃ brāhmaṇam ||

23. "The one remaining in semen, yet is separate from semen, whom semen does not know, whose body is semen, who controls semen from within—that is your self, the inner controller, the immortal.[20]

He is the unseen seer; the unheard hearer; the unthought thinker; the unperceived perceiver. Other than that, there is no seer. Other than that, there is no hearer. Other than that, there is no thinker. Other than that, there is no perceiver. That is your self, the inner controller, the immortal. Anything other than this is pain."

Thereupon, Uddālaka Āruṇi ceased [questioning him].

3.8

atha ha vācknavy uvāca | brāhmaṇā bhagavanto hantāham imaṃ dvau praśnau prakṣyāmi | tau cen me vakṣyati na vai jātu yuṣmākam imaṃ kaścid brahmodyaṃ jeteti | pṛccha gārgīti ||1||

1. Next (Gārgī) Vācaknavī said, "Distinguished Brahmins! I will ask him two questions. If he gives me the answers, none of you will ever beat him in this debate about *brahman*."

"Ask, Gārgī."

sā hovāca | ahaṃ vai tvā yājñavalkya yathā kāśyo vā vaideho vograputra ujjyaṃ dhanur adhijyaṃ kṛtvā dvau bāṇavantau sapatnātivyādhinau haste kṛtvopottiṣṭhed evam evāhaṃ tvā dvābhyāṃ praśnābhyām upodasthām | tau me brūhīti | pṛccha gārgīti ||2||

2. She said, "As a warrior-son of Kāśī or Videha strings his unstrung bow, takes two enemy-piercing arrows in hand, and rises up [in battle], Yājñavalkya, so I rise up against you with two questions. Answer me these two!"

"Ask, Gārgī."

sā hovāca | yad urdhvaṃ yājñavalkya divo yad avāk pṛthivyā yad antarā dyāvāpṛthivī ime yad bhūtaṃ ca bhavac ca bhaviṣyac cety ācakṣate kasmiṃs tad otaṃ ca protaṃ ceti ||3||

3. She said, "That which is above the sky, that which is below the earth, that which is between the sky and the earth, and that which people call the past, present, and future—on what are these woven to and fro?"

sa hovāca | yad urdhvaṃ gārgi divo yad avāk pṛthivyā yad antarā dyāvāpṛthivī ime yad bhūtaṃ ca bhavac ca bhaviṣyac cety ācakṣata ākāśe tad otaṃ ca protaṃ ceti ||4||

4. He said, "That which is above the sky, that which is below the earth, that which is between the sky and the earth, and that which people call the past, present, and future—on space, Gārgī, these are woven to and fro."

sā hovāca | namaste 'stu yājñavalkya yo ma etaṃ vyavoco 'parasmai dhārayasveti | pṛccha gārgī ||5||

5. She said, "Honor to you, Yājñavalkya, you sure solved that one for me. Brace yourself for the second!"[21]

"Ask, Gārgī."

sā hovāca | yad urdhvaṃ yājñavalkya divo yad avāk pṛthivyā yad antarā dyāvāpṛthivī ime yad bhūtaṃ ca bhavac ca bhaviṣyac cety ācakṣate kasmiṃs tad otaṃ ca protaṃ ceti ||6||

6. She said, "That which is above the sky, that which is below the earth, that which is between the sky and the earth, and that which people call the past, present, and future—on what are these woven to and fro?"

sa hovāca | yad urdhvaṃ gārgi divo yad avāk pṛthivyā yad antarā dyāvāpṛthivī ime yad bhūtaṃ ca bhavac ca bhaviṣyac cety ācakṣata ākāśa eva tad otaṃ ca protaṃ ceti | kasmin nu khalv ākāśa otaś ca protaś ceti ||7||

7. He said, "That which is above the sky, that which is below the earth, that which is between the sky and the earth, and that which people call the past, present, and future—just on space, Gārgī, these are woven to and fro."

"But *on what* is space woven to and fro?"[22]

sa hovāca | etad vai tad akṣaraṃ gārgi brāhmaṇā abhivadanty asthūlam anaṇv ahrasvam adīrgham alohitam asneham acchāyam atamo 'vāyv anākāśam asaṅgam arasam agandham acakṣuṣkam aśrotram avāg amano 'tejaskam aprāṇam amukham amātram anantaram abāhyam | na tad aśnāti kiṃcana | na tad aśnāti kaścana ||8||

8. He said, "That, Gārgī, is the imperishable, and Brahmins revere/call it as neither gross nor fine, neither short nor long, without blood or fat, without shadow[23] or darkness, without air or space, without contact,[24] without taste or smell, without sight or hearing, without speech or mind, without energy or life-breath, without mouth or measure,[25] without inside or out, it does not eat anything and nothing eats it.

etasya vā akṣarasya praśāsane gārgi sūryācandramasau vidhr̥tau tiṣṭhataḥ | etasya vā akṣarasya praśāsane gārgi dyāvāpr̥thivyau vidhr̥te tiṣṭhataḥ | etasya vā akṣarasya praśāsane gārgi nimeṣā muhūrtā ahorātrāṇy ardhamāsā māsā r̥tavaḥ saṃvatsarā iti vidhr̥tās tiṣṭhanti | etasya vā akṣarasya praśāsane gārgi prācyo 'nyā nadyaḥ syandante śvetebhyaḥ parvatebhyaḥ pratīcyo 'nyā yāṃ yāṃ ca diśamanu | etasya vā akṣarasya praśāsane gārgi dadato manuṣyāḥ praśaṁsanti yajamānaṃ devā darvīṃ pitaro 'nvāyattāḥ ||9||

9. "At the command of this imperishable, Gārgī, the sun and the moon stand separate. At the command of this imperishable, Gārgī, the sky and the earth stand separate. At the command of this imperishable, Gārgī, the seconds and hours, the days and nights, the fortnights and months, and the seasons and years stand separate. At the command of this imperishable, Gārgī, some rivers flow east from the snowy mountains and others west, each in their appropriate directions. At the command of this imperishable, Gārgī, men praise donors, gods are dependent on *yajamānas*, and the forefathers on the ancestral offering-ladle.[26]

yo vā etad akṣaraṃ gārgy aviditvāsmiṁl loke juhoti yajate tapas tapyate bahūni varṣasahsrāṇy antavad evāsya tad bhavati | yo vā etad akṣaraṃ gārgy aviditvāsmāl lokāt praiti sa kr̥paṇaḥ | atha ya etad akṣaraṃ gārgi viditvāsmāl lokāt praiti sa brāhmaṇaḥ ||10||

10. "Without knowing this imperishable, if one makes offerings, carries out sacrifices, and performs austerities in this world for many thousand years, Gārgī, his deeds would amount to nothing. One who departs from this world without knowing this imperishable, Gārgī, is wretched. Now, one who departs from this world knowing this imperishable, Gārgī, he is a Brahmin.[27]

tad vā etad akṣaram gārgy adr̥ṣṭaṃ draṣṭr aśrutaṃ śrotr amataṃ mantr avijñātaṃ vijñātr̥ | nānyad ato 'sti dr̥ṣṭr̥ | nānyad ato śrotr̥ | nānyad ato 'sti mantr̥ | nānyad ato 'sti vijñātr̥ | etasmin nu khalv akṣare gārgy ākāśa otaś ca protaś ceti ||11||

11. "This imperishable, Gārgī, is the unseen seer; is the unheard hearer; is the unthought thinker, is the unperceived perceiver. Other than this, there is no seer. Other than this, there is no hearer. Other than this, there is no thinker. Other than this, there is no perceiver. On this imperishable, Gārgī, space is woven to and fro."

sā hovāca | brāhmaṇā bhagavantas tad eva bahu manyedhvaṃ yad asmān namaskāreṇa mucyedhvam | na vai jātu yuṣmākam imaṃ kaścid brahmodyaṃ jeteti | tato ha vācaknavy upararāma ||12||

|| iti aṣṭamaṃ brāhmaṇam ||

12. She said, "Distinguished Brahmins, you should think yourself big men to have escaped from him by [only] paying homage. None of you will ever beat him in this religious debate!"

Thereupon (Gārgī) Vācaknavī ceased [questioning him].

3.9

atha hainaṃ vidagdhaḥ śākalyaḥ papraccha | kati devā yājñavalkyeti | sa haitayaiva nividā pratipede yāvanto vaiśvadevasya nividy ucyante | trayaś ca trī ca śatā trayaś ca trī ca sahasreti | om iti hovāca | katy eva devā yājñavalkyeti

| trayas triṁśad iti | om iti hovāca | katy eva devā yājñavalkyeti | ṣaḍ iti | om iti hovāca | katy eva devā yājñavalkyeti | traya iti | om iti hovāca | katy eva devā yājñavalkyeti | dvāv iti | om iti hovāca | katy eva devā yājñavalkyeti | adhyardha | om iti hovāca | katy eva devā yājñavalkyeti | eka iti | om iti hovāca | katame te trayaś ca trī ca śatā trayaś ca trī ca sahasreti ||1||

1. Next Vidagdha Śākalya questioned him. "How many gods are there, Yājñavalkya?"

In accordance with the ritual invocation, he replied, "As many as are mentioned in the invocation to the All-Gods: 'three and three hundred, and three and three thousand.'"

"Yes," he said, "but how many are there really?"

"Thirty-three."

"Yes," he said, "but how many are there really?"

"Six."

"Yes," he said, "but how many are there really?"

"Three."

"Yes," he said, "but how many are there really?"

"Two."

"Yes," he said, "but how many are there really?"

"One and a half."

"Yes," he said, "but how many are there really?"

"One."

"Yes," he said, "but which are those three and three hundred, and three and three thousand?"

sa hovāca | mahimāna evaiṣām ete | trayas triṁśat tv eva devā iti| katame te trayas triṁśad iti | aṣṭau vasava ekādaśa rudrā dvādaśādityās ta ekatriṁśad indraś caiva prajāpatiś ca trayas triṁśāv iti ||2||

2. Yājñavalkya said, "They are simply their powers—but the gods are only thirty-three."

He said, "Which are those thirty-three?"

"The eight Vasus, the eleven Rudras, and the twelve Ādityas—this is thirty one. And then there are Indra and Prajāpati which is thirty three."

katame vasava iti | agniś ca pṛthivī ca vāyuś cāntarikṣaṃ cādityaś ca dyauś ca candramāś ca nakṣatrāṇi caite vasavaḥ | eteṣu hīdaṁ sarvaṃ vasu hitam iti tasmād vasava iti ||3||

3. "Which are the Vasus?"

"Fire, earth, wind, the middle region, sun, sky, moon, and stars—those are the Vasus; this whole treasure (*vasu*) is deposited in them, therefore they are called Vasus."

katame rudrā iti | daśeme puruṣe prāṇā ātmaikādaśaḥ | te yadāsmāc charīrān martyād utkrāmanty atha rodayanti | tad yad rodayanti tasmād rudrā iti ||4||

4. "Which are the Rudras?"

"The ten breaths in a man, and the self (*ātman*) in the eleventh. When they depart from the mortal body, they cause people to weep. People are caused to weep (*rud-*), therefore they are the Rudras."

katama ādityā iti | dvādaśa vai māsāḥ saṁvatsarasyaita ādityāḥ | ete hīdaṁ sarvam ādadānā yanti | te yad idaṁ sarvam ādadānā yanti tasmād ādityā iti ||5||

5. "Which are the Ādityas?"

"The twelve months of the year, indeed, are the Ādityas; they proceed (*yanti*) taking (*ādadānāḥ*) all this (along with them)."

katama indraḥ katamaḥ prajāpatir iti | stanayitnur evendro yajñaḥ prajāpatir iti |katamaḥ stanayitnur iti | aśanir iti | katamo yajña iti | paśava iti ||6||

6. "Which is Indra and which is Prajāpati?"

"Indra is the thunder, and Prajāpati is the sacrifice."

"What is thunder?"

"The thunderbolt."

"What is the sacrifice?"

"The domestic animals."

katame ṣaḍ iti | agniś ca pr̥thivī ca vāyuś cāntarikṣaṃ cādityaś ca dyauś caite ṣaṭ | ete hīdaṁ sarvaṁ ṣaḍ iti ||7||

7. "Which are the six?"

"Fire, earth, the wind, the middle region, sun, and sky—those are the six; they are all this."[28]

katame te trayo devā iti | ima eva trayo lokāḥ | eṣu hīme sarve devā iti | katamau tau dvau devāv iti | annaṃ caiva prāṇaś ceti | katamo 'dhyardha iti | ya 'yaṃ pavata iti ||8|| tad āhur yad ayam eka ivaiva pavate | atha katham adhyardha iti | yad asminn idaṁ sarvam adhyārdhnot tenādhyardha iti | katama eko deva iti | prāṇa iti | sa brahma tyad ity ācakṣate ||9||

8. "Which are the three gods?"
"Only these three worlds; all the gods are within them."
"Which are the two gods?"
"Only food and breath."
"Which is the one and one-half?"
"The one that wafts.

9. Some say, 'He that wafts is, in a manner, only one. Now, how is it one and one-half?' Therefore he is one and one-half (*adhyardh-*); all this has grown (*adhyārdhnot*) in him."
"Which is the one god?"
"Breath. He is called *Brahman* and *Tyad*."

pṛthvy eva yasyāyatanam agnir loko mano jyotir yo vai taṃ puruṣaṃ vidyāt sarvasyātmanaḥ parāyaṇaṁ sa vai veditā syād yājñavalkya | veda vā ahaṃ taṃ puruṣaṁ sarvasyātmanaḥ parāyaṇaṃ yam āttha | ya evāyaṁ śārīraḥ puruṣaḥ sa eṣaḥ | vadaiva śākalya tasya kā devateti | amṛtam iti hovāca ||10||

10. "Should a person know that person whose abode is earth, whose world is fire, [and] whose light is the mind—that person who is the ultimate goal of every self (*ātman*)—then he, indeed, would be a knower, Yājñavalkya."

"I know that person, the ultimate goal of every self (*ātman*), of whom you speak. That person is this very body. Tell me, Śākalya, who is his deity?"
"The immortal," he said.

kāma eva yasyāyatanaṁ hṛdayaṃ loko mano jyotir yo vai taṃ puruṣaṃ vidyāt sarvasyātmanaḥ parāyaṇaṁ sa vai veditā syād yājñavalkya | veda vā ahaṃ taṃ puruṣaṃ sarvasyātmanaḥ parāyaṇaṃ yam āttha | ya evāyaṃ kāma-mayaḥ puruṣaḥ sa eṣaḥ | vadaiva śākalya tasya kā devateti | striya iti hovāca ||11||

11. "Should a person know that person whose abode is desire, whose world is the heart, [and] whose light is the mind—that person who is the ultimate goal of every self (*ātman*)—then he, indeed, would be a knower, Yājñavalkya."

"I know that person, the ultimate goal of every self (*ātman*), of whom you speak. That person is the one composed of desire. Tell me, Śākalya, who is his deity?"

"Women," he said.

rūpāṇy eva yasyāyatanaṃ cakṣur loko mano jyotir yo vai taṃ puruṣaṃ vidyāt sarvasyātmanaḥ parāyaṇaṁ sa vai veditā syād yājñavalkya | veda vā ahaṃ taṃ puruṣaṁ sarvasyātmanaḥ parāyaṇaṃ yam āttha | ya evāsāv āditye puruṣaḥ sa eṣaḥ | vadaiva śākalya tasya kā devateti | satyam iti hovāca ||12||

12. "Should a person know that person whose abode is visible forms, whose world is sight, [and] whose light is the mind—that person who is the ultimate goal of every self (*ātman*)—then he, indeed, would be a knower, Yājñavalkya."

"I know that person, the ultimate goal of every self (*ātman*), of whom you speak. That person is the one in the sun. Tell me, Śākalya, who is his deity?"

"Truth," he said.

ākāśa eva yasyāyatanaṁ śrotraṃ loko mano jyotir yo vai taṃ puruṣaṃ vidyāt sarvasyātmanaḥ parāyaṇaṁ sa vai veditā syād yājñavalkya | veda vā ahaṃ taṃ puruṣaṁ sarvasyātmanaḥ parāyaṇaṃ yam āttha | ya evāyaṁ śrotraḥ prātiśrutkaḥ puruṣaḥ sa eṣaḥ | vadaiva śākalya tasya kā devateti | diśa iti hovāca ||13||

13. "Should a person know that person whose abode is space, whose world is hearing, [and] whose light is the mind—that person who is the ultimate goal of every self (*ātman*)—then he, indeed, would be a knower, Yājñavalkya."

"I know that person, the ultimate goal of every self (*ātman*), of whom you speak. That person is the one [connected to/consisting of] hearing and echo. Tell me, Śākalya, who is his deity?"

"The quarters," he said.

tama eva yasyāyatanaṁ hṛdayaṃ loko mano jyotir yo vai taṃ puruṣaṃ vidyāt sarvasyātmanaḥ parāyaṇaṁ sa vai veditā syād yājñavalkya | veda vā ahaṃ taṃ puruṣaṃ sarvasyātmanaḥ parāyaṇaṃ yam āttha | ya evāyaṃ chāyāmayaḥ puruṣaḥ sa eṣaḥ | vadaiva śākalya tasya kā devateti | mṛtyur iti hovāca ||14||

14. "Should a person know that person whose abode is darkness, whose world is the heart, [and] whose light is the mind—that person who is the ultimate goal of every self (*ātman*)—then he, indeed, would be a knower, Yājñavalkya."

"I know that person, the ultimate goal of every self (*ātman*), of whom you speak. That person is the one composed of shadow. Tell me, Śākalya, who is his deity?"

"Death," he said.

rupāṇy eva yasyāyatanaṁ cakṣur loko mano jyotir yo vai taṃ puruṣaṃ vidyāt sarvasyātmanaḥ parāyaṇaṁ sa vai veditā syād yājñavalkya | veda vā ahaṃ taṃ puruṣaṁ sarvasyātmanaḥ parāyaṇaṃ yam āttha | ya evāyam ādarśe puruṣaḥ sa eṣaḥ | vadaiva śākalya tasya kā devateti | asur iti hovāca ||15||

15. "Should a person know that person whose abode is visible forms, whose world is sight, [and] whose light is the mind—that person who is the ultimate goal of every self (*ātman*)—then he, indeed, would be a knower, Yājñavalkya."

"I know that person, the ultimate goal of every self (*ātman*), of whom you speak. That person is the one seen in the mirror. Tell me, Śākalya, who is his deity?"

"Life," he said.

āpa eva yasyāyatanaṁ hṛdayaṃ loko mano jyotir yo vai taṃ puruṣaṃ vidyāt sarvasyātmanaḥ parāyaṇaṁ sa vai veditā syād yājñavalkya | veda vā ahaṃ taṃ puruṣaṁ sarvasyātmanaḥ parāyaṇaṃ yam āttha | ya evāyam apsu puruṣaḥ sa eṣaḥ | vadaiva śākalya tasya kā devateti | varuṇa iti hovāca ||16||

16. "Should a person know that person whose abode is the waters, whose world is the heart, [and] whose light is the mind—that person who is the ultimate goal of every self (*ātman*)—then he, indeed, would be a knower, Yājñavalkya."

"I know that person, the ultimate goal of every self (*ātman*), of whom you speak. That person is the one in the waters. Tell me, Śākalya, who is his deity?"

"Varuṇa," he said.

reta eva yasyāyatanaṁ hr̥dayaṃ loko mano jyotir yo vai taṃ puruṣaṃ vidyāt sarvasyātmanaḥ parāyaṇaṁ sa vai veditā syād yājñavalkya | veda vā ahaṃ taṃ puruṣaṁ sarvasyātmanaḥ parāyaṇaṃ yam āttha | ya evāyaṃ putramayaḥ puruṣaḥ sa eṣaḥ | vadaiva śākalya tasya kā devateti | prajāpatir iti hovāca ||17||

17. "Should a person know that person whose abode is semen, whose world is the heart, [and] whose light is the mind—that person who is the ultimate goal of every self (*ātman*)—then he, indeed, would be a knower, Yājñavalkya."

"I know that person, the ultimate goal of every self (*ātman*), of whom you speak. That person is the one composed of a son. Tell me, Śākalya, who is his deity?"

"Prajāpati," he said.

śākalyeti hovāca yājñavalkyaḥ | tvāṁ svid ime brāhmaṇā aṅgārāvakṣayaṇam akratā3 iti ||18||

18. "O Śākalya," Yājñavalkya said, "have these Brahmins made you their fire-quencher?"

yājñavalkyeti hovāca śākalyaḥ | yad idaṃ kurupañcālānāṃ brāhmaṇān atyavādīḥ kiṃ brahma vidvān iti | diśo veda sadevāḥ sapratiṣṭhā iti | yad diśo vettha sadevāḥ sapratiṣṭhāḥ ||19|| kiṃdevato 'syāṃ prācyāṃ diśyasīti | ādityadevata iti | sa ādityaḥ kasmin pratiṣṭhita iti | cakṣuṣīti | kasmin nu cakṣuḥ pratiṣṭhitam iti | rūpeṣv iti | cakṣuṣā hi rūpāṇi paśyati | kasmin nu rūpāṇi pratiṣṭhitānīti | hr̥daya iti hovāca | hr̥dayena hi rūpāṇi jānāti | hr̥daye hy eva rūpāṇi pratiṣṭhitāni bhavantīti | evam evaitad yājñavalkya ||20||

19. "Yājñavalkya," said Śākalya, "What is the *brahman* that you know [that allows] you to out-talk these Brahmans of Kuru-Pañcāla?"

"I know the quarters with their deities and foundations."

"So, you know the quarters with their gods and foundations.

20. Then who is the deity in the eastern quarter?"

"The sun."

"On what is the sun founded?"

"On sight."

"On what is sight founded?"

"On visible forms, because one sees visible forms with sight."

"On what are visible forms founded?"

"On the heart, because one knows visible forms with the heart. Indeed, visible forms are founded on the heart."

"It is so, Yājñavalkya.

kiṃdevato 'syāṃ dakṣiṇāyām diśyasīti | yamadevata iti | sa yamaḥ kasmin pratiṣṭhita iti | yajña iti | kasmin nu yajñaḥ pratiṣṭhata iti | dakṣiṇāyām iti | kasmin nu dakṣiṇā pratiṣṭhiteti | śraddhāyām iti | yadā hy eva śraddhatte 'tha dakṣiṇāṃ dadāti | śraddhāyāṁ hy eva dakṣiṇā pratiṣṭhiteti | kasmin nu śraddhā pratiṣṭhiteti | hr̥daya iti hovāca | hr̥dayena hi śraddhāṃ jānāti | hr̥daye hy eva sraddhā pratiṣṭhitā bhavatīti | evam evaitad yājñavalkya ||21||

21. Who is the deity of the southern quarter?" [Śākalya asked].

"Yama."

"On what is Yama founded?"

"On the sacrifice."

"On what is the sacrifice founded?"

"On the sacrificial fee."

"On what is the sacrificial fee founded?"

"On trust, because when one trusts, they give the sacrificial fee. Indeed, the sacrificial fee is founded on trust."

"On what is trust founded?"

"On the heart," he said, "for one knows trust with the heart. Indeed, trust is founded on the heart."

"It is so, Yājñavalkya.

kiṃdevato 'syāṃ pratīcyāṃ diśyasīti | varuṇadevata iti | sa varuṇaḥ kasmin pratiṣṭhita iti | apsv iti | kasmin nv āpaḥ pratiṣṭhitā iti | retasīti | kasmin nu retaḥ pratiṣṭhitam iti | hr̥daya iti | tasmād api pratirūpaṃ jātam āhur hr̥dayā diva sr̥pto hr̥dayād iva nirmita iti | hr̥daye hy eva retaḥ pratiṣṭhitaṃ bhavatīti | evam evaitad yājñavalkya ||22||

22. "Who is the deity of the western quarter?" [Śākalya asked].

"Varuṇa."

"On what is Varuṇa founded?"

"On the waters."

"On what are the waters founded?"

"On semen."

"On what is semen founded?"

"On the heart," he said, "because when a newborn is a mirror-image of him [i.e., the father], people say 'He has slid out of his heart! He was built from his heart!' Indeed, semen is founded on the heart."

"It is so, Yājñavalkya.

kiṃdevato 'syām udīcyāṃ diśyasīti | somadevata iti | sa somaḥ kasmin pratiṣṭhita iti | dīkṣāyām iti | kasmin nu dīkṣā pratiṣṭhiteti | satya iti | tasmād api dīkṣītam āhuḥ satyaṃ vadeti | satye hy eva dīkṣā pratiṣṭhiteti | kasmin nu satyaṃ pratiṣṭhitam iti | hṛdaya iti hovāca | hṛdayena hi satyaṃ jānāti | hṛdaye hy eva satyaṃ pratiṣṭhitaṃ bhavatīti | evam evaitad yājñavalkya ||23||

23. "Who is the deity of the northern quarter?" [Śākalya asked]

"Soma."[29]

"On what is Soma founded?"

"On the sacrificial consecration."

"On what is the sacrificial consecration founded?"

"On truth," he said, "because they tell the man consecrated for sacrifice, 'Speak the truth.' Indeed the sacrificial consecration is founded on truth."

"On what is truth founded?"

"On the heart," he said, "because one knows truth with the heart. Indeed, truth is founded on the heart."

"It is so, Yājñavalkya.

kiṃdevato 'syāṃ druvāyāṃ diśyasīti | agnidevata iti | so 'gniḥ kasmin pratiṣṭhita iti vācīti | kasmin nu vāk pratiṣṭhiteti | hṛdaya iti | kasminn u hṛdayaṃ pratiṣṭhitam iti ||24||

24. "Who is the god of the fixed direction?" [Śākalya asked]

"Fire."

"On what is fire founded?"
"On speech."
"On what is speech founded?"
"On the heart."
"On what is the heart founded?"

ahalliketi hovāca yājñavalkyaḥ | yatraitad anyatrāsman manyāsai | yad dhy etad anyatrāsmat syāc chvāno vainadadyur vayāṁsi vainadvimathnīrann iti ||25||

25. "You are an idiot!" Yājñavalkya said, "should you think it is founded on something other than ourselves! Were it founded on something other than ourselves, dogs would eat it or birds would tear it up!"

kasmin nu tvaṃ cātmā ca pratiṣṭhitau stha iti | prāṇa iti | kasmin nu prāṇaḥ pratiṣṭhita iti | apāna iti | kasmin nv apānaḥ pratiṣṭhita iti | vyāna iti | kasmin nu vyānaḥ pratiṣthita iti | udāna iti | kasmin nu udāna pratiṣṭhita iti | samāna iti | sa eṣa neti nety ātmā | agṛhyo na hi gṛhyate | aśīryo na hi sīryate | asaṅgo na hi sajyate | asito na vyathate | na riṣyati | etāny aṣṭāv āyatanāny aṣṭau lokā aṣṭau devā aṣṭau puruṣāḥ | sa yas tān puruṣān niruhya pratyuhyāty akrāmat taṃ tvaupaniṣadaṃ puruṣaṃ pṛcchāmi | taṃ cen me na vivakṣyasi mūrdhā te vipatiṣyatīti | taṁ ha na mene śākalyaḥ | tasya ha mūrdhā vipapāta | api hāsya parimoṣiṇo 'sthīny apajahrur anyan manyamānāḥ ||26||

26. "On what are you and your self (*ātman*) founded?"
"On the out-breath."
"On what is the out-breath founded?"
"On the in-breath."
"On what is the in-breath founded?"
"On the inter-breath."
"On what is the inter-breath founded?"
"On the up-breath."
"On what is the up-breath founded?"
"On the link-breath. The self is 'not this, not that.' He is ungraspable because he is not grasped. He is undecaying because he does not decay. He is not clinging because he is not clung to.[30] He is unbound [because?] he does not tremble. He is not hurt. Those are the eight abodes, the eight worlds, the eight deities, the eight persons. I ask you

about that person who is the hidden connection (*upaniṣad*), who carries away, returns, and goes beyond those persons? If you will not tell me, your head will shatter apart!"

Alas, Śākalya did not know him. His head did, indeed, shatter apart. Robbers also stole his bones, thinking they were something else.

atha hovāca brāhmaṇā bhagavanto yo vaḥ kāmayate sa mā pṛcchatu | sarve vā mā pṛcchata | yo vaḥ kāmayate taṃ vaḥ pṛcchāmi sarvān vā vaḥ pṛcchāmīti | te ha brāhmaṇā na dadhṛṣuḥ ||27||

27. Now Yājñavalkya said, "Distinguished Brahmins, Let whomever of you who desires question me or let all of you question me. Let whomever desires me to, question him or let me question all of you." Those Brahmins did not dare.

tān haitaiḥ ślokaiḥ papraccha | yathā vṛkṣo vanaspatis tathaiva puruṣo 'mṛṣā | tasya lomāni parṇāni tvag asyotpāṭikā bahiḥ || tvaca evāsya rudhiraṃ prasyandi tvaca utpaṭaḥ | tasmāt tad ātṛṇṇāt praiti raso vṛkṣād ivāhatāt || māṁsāny asya śakarāṇi kināṭaṁ snāva tat sthiram || asthīny antarato dārūṇi majjā majjopamā kṛtā || yad vṛkṣo vṛkṇo rohati mūlān navataraḥ punaḥ | martyaḥ svin mṛtyunā vṛkṇaḥ kasmān mūlāt prarohati || retasa iti mā vocata jīvatas tat prajāyate | dhānāruha iva vai vṛkṣo 'ñjasāpretya sambhavaḥ || yat samūlam āvṛheyur vṛkṣaṃ na punar ābhavet | martyaḥ svin mṛtyunā vṛkṇaḥ kasmān mūlāt prarohati || jāta eva na jāyate ko nv enaṃ janayet punaḥ | vijñānam ānandaṃ brahma rātir dātuḥ parāyaṇaṃ tiṣṭhamānasya tadvida iti ||28||

|| iti navamaṃ brāhmaṇam ||

|| iti tṛtīyo 'dhyāyaḥ ||

28. [Yājñavalkya] questioned them with these verses.

As is a mighty tree,
so truly is man.
His body hairs are leaves,
his skin the outer bark.

Blood flows from his skin,
[as] sap flowing from [the tree's] skin.
From the pricked skin [blood] comes,
[as] sap from a cut tree.

His flesh is the sapwood,
the tendons are the fibers—that's certain.
His bones are the heartwood,
his marrow made equal to [its] marrow (i.e. pith).

A tree, when cut down, grows
again from the root in newer form.
A mortal man who is cut down by death,
from what root will he grow?

Do not say "from semen,"
that is produced from him while he is alive.
Just as a tree sprouts from a seed,
It takes birth at once, even before he dies.[31]

When torn up with its root,
a tree will not be born again.
A mortal man who is cut down by death,
from what root will he grow?

He is [already] born, and not being born,
who would give birth to him again?
Perception, bliss, *brahman*,
That is the gift of the givers, the highest goal.
—for the one who knows this and stands firm."

Chapter 4

4.1

janako ha vaideha āsāṃ cakre | atha ha yājñavalkya āvavrāja | taṁ hovāca yājñavalkya kim artham acārīḥ paśūn icchann aṇvantān iti | ubhayam eva samrāḍ iti hovāca ||1||

1. Janaka of Videha was seated and Yājñavalkya came [to him]. He said to him, "Yājñavalkya, for what reason do you come? Are you seeking cows or subtle discussion?"[32]

He replied, "Both, O King."

yat te kaścid abravīt tac chṛṇavāmeti | abravīn me jitvā śailinir vāg vai brahmeti | yathā mātṛmān pitṛmān ācāryavān brūyāt tathā tac chailinir abravīd vāg vai brahmeti | avadato hi kiṁ syād iti | abravīt tu te tasyāyatanaṃ pratiṣṭhām | na me 'bravīd iti | ekapād vā etat samrāḍ iti | sa vai no brūhi yājñavalkya | vāg evāyatanam ākāśaḥ pratiṣṭhā prajñety enad upāsīta | kā prajñatā yājñavalkya | vāg eva samrāḍ iti hovāca | vācā vai samrāḍ bandhuḥ prajñāyate | ṛgvedo yajurvedaḥ sāmavedo 'tharvāṅgirasa itihāsaḥ purāṇaṃ vidyā upaniṣadaḥ ślokāḥ sūtrāṇy anuvyākhyānāni vyākhyānānīṣṭaṁ hutam āśitaṃ pāyitam ayaṃ ca lokaḥ paraś ca lokaḥ sarvāṇi ca bhūtāni vācaiva samrāṭ prajñāyante | vāg vai samrāṭ paramaṃ brahma | nainaṃ vāg jahāti sarvāṇy enaṃ bhūtāny abhikṣaranti devo bhūtvā devān apy eti ya evaṃ vidvān etad upāste | hastyṛṣabhaṁ sahasraṃ dadāmīti hovāca janako vaidehaḥ | sa hovāca yājñavalkyaḥ pitā me 'manyata nānanuśiṣya hareteti ||2||

2. [Yājñavalkya said,] "Someone told you something [already]. Let me hear it."

"Jitvan Śailini told me that *brahman* is speech."

"Śailini saying *brahman* is speech is like saying a person has a mother, father, and a teacher—because what could a person have without speech? But did he tell you its abode and foundation?"

"No, he did not tell me."

"Then it is [a] one-legged [*brahman*], O King."

"Then you tell me, Yājñavalkya."

"The abode is speech itself, the foundation is space, and it should be revered as 'knowledge.'"

"What is the nature of this knowledge, Yājñavalkya?"

"Speech itself, O King," he said. "By means of speech, O King, a connection[33] is known. The Ṛgveda, Yajurveda, Sāmaveda, Atharva-Aṅgirasa, history, legend, science, the hidden teaching, verses, aphorisms, explanations, glosses, the oblation, the offering, the giving of food and water;[34] this world and the next world; and all beings—we know these only through speech, O King. The highest *brahman*, O King, is speech. If one knows this and reveres it in this way, speech never leaves him and all beings flock to him. He becomes a god among the gods."

Janaka of Videha said, "I give you a thousand cows with bulls and elephants!"

Yājñavalkya said, "My father believed that one should not take [a gift] without having taught [the giver something]."

yad eva te kaścid abravīt tac chr̥ṇavāmeti | abravīn ma udaṅkaḥ śaulbāyanaḥ prāṇo vai brahmeti | yathā mātr̥mān pitr̥mān ācāryavān brūyāt tathā tac chaulbāyano 'bravīt prāṇo vai brahmeti | aprāṇato hi kiṁ syād iti | abravīt tu te tasyāyatanaṃ pratiṣṭhām | na me 'bravīd iti | ekapād vā etat samrāḍ iti | sa vai no brūhi yājñavalkya | prāṇa evāyatanam ākāśaḥ pratiṣṭhā priyam ity enad upāsīta | kā priyatā yājñavalkya | prāṇa eva samrāḍ iti hovāca | prāṇasya vai samrāṭ kāmāyāyājyaṃ yājayaty apratigr̥hasya pratigr̥hṇāti | api tatra vadhāśaṅkaṃ bhavati yāṃ diśam eti prāṇasyaiva samrāṭ kāmāya | prāṇo vai samrāṭ paramaṃ brahma | nainaṃ prāṇo jahāti sarvāṇy enaṃ bhūtāny abhikṣaranti devo bhūtvā devān apy eti ya evaṃ vidvān etad upāste | hasty-r̥ṣabhaṁ sahasraṃ dadāmīti hovāca janako vaidehaḥ | sa hovāca yājñavalkyaḥ pitā me 'manyata nānanuśiṣya hareteti ||3||

3. [Yājñavalkya said,] "Someone told you something [already]. Let me hear it."

"Udaṅka Śaulbāyana told me that *brahman* is breath."

"Śaubāyana saying *brahman* is breath is like saying that a person has a mother, father, and a teacher—because what could a person have without breath? But did he tell you its abode and foundation?"

"No, he did not tell me."

"Then it is [a] one-legged [*brahman*], O King."

"Then you tell me, Yājñavalkya."

"The abode is breath itself, the foundation is space, and it should be revered as 'dear.'"

"What is the nature of 'dear,' Yājñavalkya?"

"Breath itself, O King," he said. "Indeed, it is for the love of the breath, O King, that one sacrifices for whom one should not have sacrifices done or accepts gifts from one whom one should not receive gifts. O King, for the love of breath there is a fear of death wherever he goes. The highest *brahman*, O king, is the breath. If one knows this and reveres it in this way, breath never leaves him and all beings flock to him. He becomes a god among the gods."

Janaka of Videha said, "I give you a thousand cows with bulls and elephants!"

Yājñavalkya said, "My father believed that one should not take a [gift] without having taught [the giver something]."

yad eva te kaścid abravīt tac chr̥ṇavāmeti | abravīn me barkur vārṣṇaś cakṣur vai brahmeti | yathā mātr̥mān pitr̥mān ācāryavān brūyāt tathā tad vārṣṇo bravīc cakṣur vai brahmeti | apaśyato hi kiṁ syād iti | abravīt tu te tasyāyataṃ pratiṣṭhām | na me 'bravīd iti | ekapād vā etat samrāḍ iti | sa vai no brūhi yājñavalkya | cakṣur evāyatanam ākāśaḥ pratiṣṭhā satyam ity enad upāsīta | kā satyatā yājñavalkya | cakṣur eva samrāḍ iti hovāca | cakṣuṣā vai samrāṭ paśyantam āhur adrākṣīr iti sa āhādrākṣam iti tat satyaṃ bhavati | cakṣur vai samrāṭ paramaṃ brahma | nainaṃ cakṣur jahāti sarvāṇy enaṃ bhūtāny abhikṣaranti devo bhūtvā devān apy eti ya evaṃ vidvān etad upāste | hastyr̥ṣabhaṁ sahasraṃ dadāmīti hovāca janako vaidehaḥ | sa hovāca yājñavalkyaḥ pitā me 'manyata nānanuśiṣya hareteti ||4||

4. [Yājñavalkya said,] "Someone told you something [already]. Let me hear it."

"Barku Vārṣṇa told me that *brahman* is sight."

"Vārṣṇa saying *brahman* is sight is like saying that a person has a mother, father, and a teacher—because what could a person have without sight? But did he tell you its abode and foundation?

"No, he did not tell me."

"Then it is [a] one-legged [*brahman*], O King."

"Then you tell me, Yājñavalkya."

"The abode is sight itself, the foundation is space, and it should be revered as 'truth.'"

"What is the nature of 'truth,' Yājñavalkya?"

"Sight itself, O King," he said. "O King, when they ask someone who saw with sight, 'Have you seen?' and he responds 'I saw'—that is truth. The highest *brahman* is sight, O King. If one knows this and reveres it in this way, sight never leaves him and all beings flock to him. He becomes a god among the gods."

Janaka of Videha said, "I give you a thousand cows with bulls and elephants!"

Yājñavalkya said, "My father believed that one should not take [a gift] without having taught [the giver something]."

yad eva te kaścid abravīt tac chr̥ṇavāmeti | abravīn me gardabhīvipīto bhāradvājaḥ śrotraṃ vai brahmeti | yathā mātr̥mān pitr̥mān ācāryavān brūyāt tathā tad bhāradvājo 'bravīc chrotraṃ vai brahmeti | aśr̥ṇvato hi kiṁ syād iti | abravīt tu te tasyāyatanaṃ pratiṣṭhām | na me 'bravīd iti | ekapād vā etat samrāḍ iti | sa vai no brūhi yājñavalkya | śrotram evāyatanam ākāśaḥ pratiṣṭhān anta ity enad upāsīta | kānantatā yājñavalkya | diśa eva samrāḍ iti hovāca | tasmād vai samrāḍ api yāṃ kāṃ ca diśaṃ gacchati naivāsyā antaṃ gacchati | anantā hi diśaḥ | diśo vai samrāṭ śrotram | śrotraṃ vai samrāṭ paramaṃ brahma | nainaṃ śrotraṃ jahāti sarvāṇy enaṃ bhūtāny abhikṣaranti devo bhūtvā devān apy eti ya evaṃ vidvān etad upāste | hastyr̥ṣabhaṁ sahasraṃ dadāmīti hovāca janako vaidehaḥ | sa hovāca yājñavalkyaḥ pitā me 'manyata nānanuśiṣya hareteti ||5||

5. [Yājñavalkya said,] "Someone told you something [already]. Let me hear it."

"Gardabhīvipīta Bhāradvāja told me that *brahman* is hearing."

"Bhāradvāja saying *brahman* is hearing is like saying that a person has a mother, father, and a teacher—because what could a person have without hearing? But did he tell you its abode and foundation?

"No, he did not tell me."

"Then it is [a] one-legged [*brahman*], O King."

"Then you tell me, Yājñavalkya."

"The abode is hearing itself, the foundation is space, and it should be revered as 'endless.'"

"What is the nature of 'endless,' Yājñavalkya?"

"The directions themselves,[35] O King," he said. "Because, O King, in whatever direction a man may go, he does not reach the end because the directions are endless. Hearing, O King, are the directions. The highest *brahman* is hearing. If one knows this and reveres it in this way, hearing never leaves him and all beings flock to him. He becomes a god among the gods."

Janaka of Videha said, "I give you a thousand cows with bulls and elephants!"

Yājñavalkya said, "My father believed that one should not take [a gift] without having taught [the giver something]."

yad eva te kaścid abravīt tac chr̥ṇavāmeti | abravīn me satyakāmo jābālo mano vai brahmeti | yathā mātr̥mān pitr̥mān ācāryavān brūyāt tathā taj jābālo 'bravīn mano vai brahmeti | amanaso hi kiṁ syād iti | abravīt tu te tasyāyatanaṃ pratiṣṭhām | na me 'bravīd iti | ekapād vā etat samrāḍ iti | sa vai no brūhi yājñavalkya | mana evāyatanam ākāśaḥ pratiṣṭhānanda ity enad upāsīta | kānandatā yājñavalkya | mana eva samrāṭ iti hovāca | manasā vai samrāṭ striyam abhihāryate tasyāṃ pratirūpaḥ putro jāyate sa ānandaḥ | mano vai samrāṭ paramaṃ brahma | nainaṃ mano jahāti sarvāṇy enaṃ bhūtāny abhikṣaranti devo bhūtvā devān apy eti ya evaṃ vidvān etad upāste | hastyr̥ṣabhaṃ sahasraṃ dadāmīti hovāca janako vaidehaḥ | sa hovāca yājñavalkya pitā me 'manyata nānanuśiṣya hareteti ||6||

6. [Yājñavalkya said,] "Someone told you something [already]. Let me hear it."

"Satyakāma Jābāla told me that *brahman* is mind."

"Jābāla saying *brahman* is mind is like saying that a person has a mother, father, and a teacher—because what could a person have without the mind? But did he tell you its abode and foundation?

"No, he did not tell me."

"Then it is [a] one-legged [*brahman*], O King."

"Then you tell me, Yājñavalkya."

"The abode is mind itself, the foundation is space, and it should be revered as 'bliss.'"

"What is the nature of 'bliss,' Yājñavalkya?"

"The mind itself, O King," he said. "Indeed, O King, it is with the mind that a man brings near a woman and in her begets a son who is a mirror-image [of him]. The highest *brahman,* O King, is mind. If one knows this and reveres it in this way, the mind never leaves him and all beings flock to him. He becomes a god among the gods."

Janaka of Videha said, "I give you a thousand cows with bulls and elephants!"

Yājñavalkya said, "My father believed that one should not take [a gift] without having taught [the giver something]."

yad eva te kaścid abravīt tac chr̥ṇavāmeti | abravīn me vidagdhaḥ śākalyo hr̥dayaṃ vai brahmeti | yathā mātr̥mān pitr̥mān ācāryavān brūyāt tathā tac chākālyo 'bravīd hr̥dayaṃ vai brahmeti | ahr̥dayasya hi kiṁ syād iti | abravīt tu te tasyāyatanaṃ pratiṣṭhām | na me 'bravīd iti | ekapād vā etat samrāḍ iti | sa vai no brūhi yājñavalkya | hṛdayam evāyatanam ākāśaḥ pratiṣṭhā sthitir ity enad upāsīta | kā sthitatā yājñavalkya | hṛdayam eva samrāḍ iti hovāca | hṛdayaṃ vai samrāṭ sarveṣāṃ bhūtānām āyatanam | hṛdayaṃ vai samrāṭ sarveṣāṃ bhūtānāṃ pratiṣṭhā | hṛdaye hy eva samrāṭ sarvāṇi bhūtāni pratiṣṭhitāni bhavanti | hṛdayaṃ vai samrāṭ paramaṃ brahma | nainaṁ hṛdayaṃ jahāti sarvāṇy enaṃ bhūtāny abhikṣaranti devo bhūtvā devān apy eti ya evaṃ vidvān etad upāste | hastyṛṣabhaṃ sahasraṃ dadāmīti hovāca janako vaidehaḥ | sa hovāca yājñavalkyaḥ pitā me 'manyata nānanuśiṣya hareteti ||7|

|| iti prathamaṃ brāhmaṇam ||

7. [Yājñavalkya said,] "Someone told you something [already]. Let me hear it."

"Vidagdha Śākalya told me that *brahman* is the heart."

"Śākalya saying *brahman* is the heart is like saying that a person has a mother, father, and a teacher—because what could a person have without the heart? But did he tell you its abode and foundation?

"No, he did not tell me."

"Then it is [a] one-legged [*brahman*], O King."

"Then you tell me, Yājñavalkya."

"The abode is the heart itself, the foundation is space, and it should be revered as 'stability.'"

"What is the nature of 'stability,' Yājñavalkya?"

"The heart itself, O King," he said. "Indeed, O King, the abode of all beings is the heart; the foundation of all beings is the heart—because, O King, all beings are founded on the heart. The highest *brahman*, O King, is the heart. If one knows this and reveres it in this way, the heart never leaves him and all beings flock to him. He becomes a god among the gods."

Janaka of Videha said, "I give you a thousand cows with bulls and elephants!"

Yājñavalkya said, "My father believed that one should not take [a gift] without having taught [the giver something]."

4.2

janako ha vaideha kūrcād upāvasarpann uvāca namaste 'stu yājñavalkya | anu mā śādhīti | sa hovāca yathā vai samrāṇ mahāntam adhvānam eṣyan ratham vā nāvaṃ vā samādadītaivam evaitābhir upaniṣadbhiḥ samāhitātmāsi | evaṃ vr̥ndāraka āḍhyaḥ sannadhītaveda uktopaniṣat ka ito vimucyamānaḥ kva gamiṣyasīti | nāhaṃ tad bhagavan veda yatra gamiṣyāmīti | atha vai te 'haṃ tad vakṣyāmi yatra gamiṣyasīti | bravītu bhagavān iti ||1||

1. Now Janaka of Videha stepping down from his grass seat said, "Homage to you, Yājñalkya. Instruct me."

Yājñavalkya said, "O King, as one going on a great road [or journey] equips himself with a chariot or ship, so are you yourself (*ātman*) equipped with the hidden teachings (*upaniṣad*). In this way being a leader of men and wealthy, you have learned the Vedas, and are versed in the hidden teachings (*upaniṣad*). [Can you tell me] where you will go when you are released from here [i.e., death]?"

"No, distinguished one, I do not know where I will go."

"Now, indeed, I will tell you where you will go."

"Tell me, distinguished one."

indho ha vai nāmaiṣa yo 'yaṃ dakṣine 'kṣan puruṣaḥ | taṃ vā etam indhaṁ santam indra ity ācakṣate parokṣeṇaiva | parokṣapriyā iva hi devāḥ pratyakṣadviṣaḥ ||2||

2. "Truly, Indha is the name of the person in the right eye. Though being Indha, they [people] rather obscurely call him Indra, because the gods are fond of the rather obscure and dislike the obvious.

athaitad vāme 'kṣaṇi puruṣarūpam eṣāsya patnī virāṭ | tayor eṣa saṃstāvo ya eṣo 'ntarhr̥daye ākāśaḥ | athainayor etad annaṃ ya eṣo 'ntarhr̥daye lohitapiṇḍaḥ | athainayor etat prāvaraṇaṃ yad etad antarhr̥daye jālakam iva | athainayor eṣā sr̥tiḥ saṃcaraṇī yaiṣā hr̥dayād ūrdhvā nāḍy uccarati | yathā keśaḥ sahasradhā bhinna evam asyaitā hitā nāma nāḍyo 'ntarhr̥daye pratiṣṭhitā bhavanti | etābhir vā etad āsravad āsravati | tasmād eṣa praviviktāhāratara ivaiva bhavaty asmāc chārīrād ātmanaḥ ||3||

3. "Now that having the human form in the left eye is his wife, Virāj. Their joining place is that space in the heart. Their food is the lump of blood in the heart and their covering is a sort of net inside the heart. The channel that they traverse is the vein that leads up from the heart. Like a hair is divided a thousand fold, its veins, named Hitā, are established inside the heart. That which flows, flows through them. Therefore this [self?] has somewhat more refined food than this bodily self (*ātman*).

tasya prācī dik prāñcaḥ prāṇā dakṣiṇā dig dakṣiṇe prāṇāḥ pratīcī dik pratyañcaḥ prāṇā udīcī dig udañcaḥ prāṇā ūrdhvā dig ūrdhvāḥ prāṇā avācī dig avāñcaḥ prāṇāḥ sarvā diśaḥ sarve prāṇāḥ | sa eṣa neti nety ātmā | agṛhyo na hi gṛhyate | aśīr yo na hi śīryate | asaṅgo na hi sajyate | asito na vyathate | na riṣyati | abhayaṃ vai janaka prāpto 'sīti hovāca yājñavalkyaḥ | sa hovāca janako vaideho 'bhayaṃ tvā gacchatād yājñavalkya yo no bhagavann abhayaṃ vedayase | namas te 'stu | ime videhā ayam aham asmi ||4||

|| iti dvitīyaṃ brāhmaṇam ||

4. "His eastern breaths (*prāṇa*) are on the eastern side, his southern breaths on the southern side, his western breaths on the western side, his northern breaths on the northern side, his upper breaths on the upper part, his lower breaths on the lower part; all his breaths are all the directions.

"The self is "Not this, not that." Ungraspable for he is not grasped. Undecaying for he does not decay. Not clinging for he is not clung to. Unbound [because] he does not tremble. He is not hurt,"[36] Yājñavalkya said. "Truly, Janaka, you have obtained the fearless."

Janaka said, "Homage to you! Let the fearless come to you, Yājñavalkya, who has taught us the fearless. The people of Videha and I also are yours!"[37]

4.3

janakaṁ ha vaidehaṃ yājñavalkyo jagāma | sa mene na vadiṣya iti | atha ha yaj janakaś ca vaideho yājñavalkyaś cāgnihotre samūdāte | tasmai ha yājñavalkyo varaṃ dadau | sa ha kāmapraśnam eva vavre | taṁ hāsmai dadau | taṁ ha samrāḍ eva pūrvaṃ papracha ||1||

1. Now [one day] Yājñavalkya went to Janaka of Videha. He thought, "I will not tell him."[38] Janaka of Videha and Yājñavalkya were talking about the daily fire sacrifice.

Yājñavalkya granted him a boon [in the past].[39] Janaka chose the right to question him at will and Yājñavalkya granted it to him. The king asked first:

yājñavalkya kiṃjyotir ayaṃ puruṣa iti | ādityajotiḥ samrāḍ iti hovāca | ādityenaivāyaṃ jyotiṣāste palyayate karma kurute vipalyetīti | evam evaitad yājñavalkya ||2||

2. "Yājñavalkya, this person has what as his light?"

"He has the sun as his light, O King," he said. "By the light which is the sun he sits down, goes, performs actions, and returns."

"It is so, Yājñavalkya.

astamita āditye yājñavalkya kiṃjyotir evāyaṃ puruṣa iti | candramā evāsya jyotir bhavatīti | candramasaivāyaṃ jyotiṣāste palyayate karma kurute vipalyetīti | evam evaitad yājñavalkya ||3||

3. But when the sun sets, this person has what as his light?"

"He has the moon as his light," he said. "By the light which is the moon that a man sits down, goes, performs actions, and returns."

"It is so, Yājñavalkya.

astamita āditye yājñavalkya candramasy astamite kiṃjyotir evāyaṃ puruṣa iti | agnir evāsya jyotir bhavatīti | agninaivāyaṃ jyotiṣāste palyayate karma kurute vipalyetīti | evam evaitad yājñavalkya ||4||

4. But when the sun and the moon set, this person has what as his light?"

"He has the fire as his light," he said. "By the light which is the fire that a man sits down, goes, performs actions, and returns."

"It is so, Yājñavalkya.

astamita āditye yājñavalkya candramasy astamite śānte 'gnau kiṃjyotir evāyaṃ puruṣa iti | vāg evāsya jyotir bhavatīti | vācaivāyaṃ jyotiṣāste palyayate karma kurute vipalyetīti tasmād | vai samrāḍ api yatra svaḥ pāṇir na vinirjñāyate 'tha yatra vāg uccaraty upaiva tatra nyetīti | evam evaitad yājñavalkya ||5||

5. But when the sun and the moon set and the fire has gone out, this person has what as his light?"

"He has the speech as his light," he said. "By the light which is the speech that a man sits down, goes, performs actions, and returns. Thus when someone cannot see one's own hand, O King, he goes to where speech arises."

"It is so, Yājñavalkya.

astamita āditye yājñavalkya candramasy astam ite śānte 'gnau śāntāyāṃ vāci kiṃjyotir evāyaṃ puruṣa iti | ātmaivāsya jyotir bhavatīti | ātmanaivāyaṃ jyotiṣāste palyayate karma kurute vipalyetīti ||6||

6. But when the sun and the moon set and the fire has gone out and speech is quieted, this person has what as his light?"

"He has the *ātman* (self) as his light," he said. "By the light which is the self that a man sits down, goes, performs actions, and returns."

katama ātmeti | yo 'yaṃ vijñānamayaḥ prāṇeṣu hṛdyantarjyotiḥ puruṣaḥ sa samānaḥ sann ubhau lokāv anusaṃcarati dhyāyatīva lelāyatīva | sa hi[40] *svapno bhūtvemaṃ lokam atikrāmati mṛtyo rūpāṇi* ||7||

7. "Which self is that?"

"This person is the one who consists of perception[41] among the breaths, the inner light in the heart. Being one and the same [he] travels to both worlds, sometimes contemplating, sometimes flickering[42]—because when he falls asleep he goes beyond this world, these visible forms of death.

sa vā ayaṃ puruṣo jāyamānaḥ śarīram abhisaṃpadyamānaḥ pāpmabhiḥ saṁsṛjyate | sa utkrāman mriyamāṇah pāpmano vijahāti ||8||

8. When being born and entering into a body, [this person] is joined with evils. When rising up and dying, he leaves the evils.

tasya vā etasya puruṣasya dve eva sthāne bhavata idaṃ ca paralokasthānaṃ ca | sandhyaṃ tṛtīyaṁ svapnasthānam | tasmin sandhye sthāne tiṣṭhann ete ubhe sthāne paśyatīdaṃ ca paralokasthānaṃ ca | atha yathākramo 'yaṃ paralokasthāne bhavati tam ākramam ākramyobhayān pāpmana ānandāṁś ca paśyati | sa yatra prasvapity asya lokasya sarvāvato mātrām apādāya svayaṃ vihatya svayaṃ nirmāya svena bhāsā svena jyotiṣā prasvapiti | atrāyaṃ puruṣaḥ svayaṃjyotir bhavati ||9||

9. "This very person has just two places—this world and the place of the next world. The third is the meeting place of dream-sleep. When residing in that meeting place, he sees both states—this world and the place of the next world. Now he is like a doorway into the place of the next world and having entered this doorway, he sees troubles and joys. Where he dreams, he takes a part of from the whole world, breaks it down himself, and creates it himself with his own lustre, his own light. In this place, he becomes one whose light is himself.

na tatra rathā na rathayogā na panthāno bhavanti | atha rathān rathayogān pathaḥ sr̥jate | na tatrānandā mudaḥ pramudo bhavanti | athānandān mudaḥ pramudaḥ sr̥jate | na tatra veśāntāḥ puṣkariṇyaḥ sravantyo bhavanti | atha veśāntān puṣkariṇīḥ sravantīḥ sr̥jate | sa hi kartā ||10||

10. "In that place there are no chariots, no chariot-horses, and no roads, but he creates chariots, chariot-horses, and roads. In that place, there are no joys, pleasures, and delights, but he creates joys, pleasures, and delights. In that place there are no pools, lotus-ponds, or rivers, but he creates pools, lotus-ponds, and rivers because he is the creator.

tad ete ślokā bhavanti |
svapena śārīram abhiprahatyāsuptaḥ suptān abhicākaśīti | śukram ādāya punar aiti sthānaṁ hiraṇmayaḥ puruṣa ekahaṁsaḥ ||11|| prāṇena rakṣan navaraṃ kulāyaṃ bahiṣkulāyād amr̥taś caritvā | sa īyate 'mr̥to yatrakāmaṁ hiraṇmayaḥ puruṣa ekahaṁsaḥ ||12|| svapnānta uccāvacamīyamāno rūpāṇi devaḥ kurute bahūni | uteva strībhiḥ saha modamāno jakṣad utevāpi bhayāni paśyan ||13|| ārāmam asya paśyanti na taṃ paśyati kaścaneti |

11. Now there are these verses.

Having struck down the bodily [self] by sleep,
The non-sleeping one surveys the sleeping [senses].

Having taken the light he goes again to his place,
The golden person, the single goose.

12. Guarding his nest below with his breath,
The immortal wanders outside the nest.
The immortal goes where he desires
The golden person, the single goose.

13. In the state of sleep, going to places high and low,
The god [non-bodily self] makes the visible forms.
Seemingly rejoicing with women,
and laughing, seemingly now seeing fearful things.

14. They see his pleasure-place,
but no one sees him.

taṃ nāyataṃ bodhayed ity āhuḥ | durbhiṣajyaṁ hāsmai bhavati yam eṣa na pratipadyate | atho khalv āhur jāgaritadeśa evāsyaiṣa iti | yāni hy eva jāgrat paśyati tāni supta iti | atrāyaṃ puruṣaḥ svayaṃjyotir bhavati | so 'haṃ bhagavate sahasraṃ dadāmi | ata ūrdhvaṃ vimokṣāya brūhīti ||14||

"People say, 'You should not wake someone who has gone to sleep because curing him is difficult if he has not returned.' Now people also say, 'This is his waking place' because the things one sees while awake are what one sees while asleep. Here, this person is his own light."

Janaka said, "Distinguished one, I give you a thousand cows. Tell me more about release."[43]

sa vā eṣa etasmin saṃprasāde ratvā caritvā dṛṣṭvaiva puṇyaṃ ca pāpaṃ ca punaḥ pratinyāyaṃ pratiyony ādravati svapnāyaiva | sa yat tatra kiṃcit paśyaty ananvāgatas tena bhavati | asaṅgo hy ayaṃ puruṣa iti | evam evaitad yājñavalkya | so 'haṃ bhagavate sahasraṃ dadāmi | ata ūrdhvaṃ vimokṣāyaiva brūhīti ||15||

15. "Having experienced and moved about in the serene [state] and having seen the good and the bad, he runs back along the same path and through the same opening right back to dream-sleep. Whatever he sees in that [serene state] does not follow him because there is no attachment to this person."

"It is so, Yājñavalkya. I give you a thousand cows. Tell me more about release."[44]

sa vā eṣa etasmin svapne ratvā caritvā dr̥ṣṭvaiva puṇyaṃ ca pāpaṃ ca punaḥ pratinyāyaṃ pratiyony ādravati buddhāntāyaiva | sa yat tatra kiṃcit paśyaty ananvāgatas tena bhavati | asaṅgo hy ayaṃ puruṣa iti | evam evaitad yājñavalkya | so 'haṃ bhagavate sahasraṃ dadāmi | ata ūrdhvaṃ vimokṣāyaiva brūhīti ||16||

16. "Having experienced and moved about in dream-sleep and having seen the good and the bad, he runs back along the same path and through the opening right back to the waking state. Whatever he sees in that (dream-state) does not follow him because there is no attachment to this person."

"It is so, Yājñavalkya. I give you a thousand cows. Tell me more about release."

sa vā eṣa etasmin buddhānte ratvā caritvā dr̥ṣṭvaiva puṇyaṃ ca pāpaṃ ca punaḥ pratinyāyaṃ pratiyony ādravati svapnāntāyaiva ||17||

17. "Having experienced and moved about in the waking state and having seen the good and the bad, he runs back along the same path and through the opening right back to the dream state.

tad yathā mahāmatsya ubhe kūle anusaṃcarati pūrvaṃ cāparaṃ ca | evam evāyaṃ puruṣa etāv ubhāv antāv anusaṃcarati svapnāntaṃ ca budhāntaṃ ca ||18||

18. "It's like this—as a great fish travels between two banks,[45] this side and that side, in the same way this person travels to both the waking state and dream state.

tad yathāsminn ākāśe śyeno vā suparṇo vā viparipatya śrāntaḥ saṁhatya pakṣau saṃlayāyaiva dhriyate | evam evāyaṃ puruṣa etasmā antāya dhāvati yatra supto na kaṃcana kāmaṃ kāmayate na kaṃcana svapnaṃ paśyati ||19||

19. "It's like this—as a hawk or a falcon in the sky flies around and once tired stretches its wings to sail to its nest,[46] in the same way a man runs to this realm (for sleep), where, while sleeping, desires nothing and sees no dreams.

tā vā asyaitā hitā nāma nāḍyo yathā keśaḥ sahasradhā bhinnas tāvatāṇimnā tiṣṭhanti śuklasya nīlasya piṅgalasya haritasya lohitasya pūrṇāḥ | atha yatrainaṃ ghnantīva jinantīva hastīva vicchāyayati gartam iva patati yad eva jāgradbhayaṃ paśyati tad atrāvidyayā manyate | atha yatra deva iva rājevāham evedaṁ sarvo 'smīti manyate so 'sya paramo lokaḥ ||20||

20. "His veins named Hitā which are like a hair divided a thousand fold are established [in the heart?] filled with white, blue, orange, green and red fluid. Here (dream-sleep) he sees the terrors of the waking world because of ignorant thinking—as if killed or conquered, as if an elephant chased him or he fell into a hole. Now where he thinks, like a god or a king, 'I am this whole world,' that is his highest world.

tad vā asyaitad aticchandā apahatapāpmābhayaṁ rūpam | tad yathā priyayā striyā saṃpariṣvakto na bāhyaṃ kiṃcana veda nāntaram | evam evāyaṃ puruṣaḥ prājñenātmanā saṃpariṣvakto na bāhyaṃ kiṃcana veda nāntaram | tad vā asyaitad āptakāmam ātmakāmam akāmaṁ rūpaṁ śokāntaram ||21||

21. "That is his form that is beyond desire, freed from the bad, and without fear. It is like this—as a man embraced by a loved woman knows neither outside nor in, in this way this person embraced by self (*ātman*) which is knowledge knows neither inside or out. Clearly, that is his form—where desire is fullfilled [because] desire is the self (*ātman*); he is without desire, he is far from sorrow.

atra pitāpitā bhavati mātāmātā lokā alokā devā adevā vedā avedāḥ | atra steno 'steno bhavati bhrūṇahābhrūṇahā cāṇḍālo 'cāṇḍālaḥ paulkaso 'paulkasaḥ śramaṇo 'śramaṇas tāpaso 'tāpasaḥ | ananvāgataṃ puṇyenānanvāgataṃ pāpena | tīrṇo hi tadā sarvāñ chokān hṛdayasya bhavati ||22||

22. "Here a father is not a father, a mother not a mother, the worlds not worlds, the gods not gods, the Vedas not

Vedas. Here a thief is not a thief, an abortionist not an abortionist, a *cāṇḍāla* not a *cāṇḍāla*, a *paulkasa* not a *paulkasa*,[47] a recluse not a recluse, an ascetic not an ascetic. The good and the bad do not follow him. For he has gone beyond all sorrows of the heart.

yad vai tan na paśyati paśyan vai tan na paśyati | na hi draṣṭur dṛṣṭer viparilopo vidyate 'vināśitvāt | na tu tad dvitīyam asti tato 'nyad vibhaktaṃ yat paśyet ||23||

23. "He does not see; though [capable of] seeing he does not see—since there is no separation of the seeing from the seer because it is indestructible. But there is no second, no other that is distinct from him, that he could see.

yad vai tan na jighrati jighran vai tan na jighrati | na hi ghrātur ghrāter viparilopo vidyate 'vināśitvāt | na tu tad dvitīyam asti tato 'nyad vibhaktaṃ yaj jighret ||24||

24. "He does not smell; though [capable of] smelling, he does not smell—since there is no separation of the smelling from the smeller because it is indestructible. But there is no second, no other that is distinct from him, that he could smell.

yad vai tan na rasayate rasayan vai tan na rasayate | na hi rasayitū rasayater viparilopo vidyate 'vināśitvāt | na tu tad dvitīyam asti tato 'nyad vibhaktaṃ yad rasayet ||25||

25. "He does not taste; though [capable of] tasting, he does not taste—since there is no separation of the tasting from the taster because it is indestructible. But there is no second, no other that is distinct from him, that he could taste.

yad vai tan na vadati vadan vai tan na vadati | na hi vaktur vakter viparilopo vidyate 'vināśitvāt | na tu tad dvitīyam asti tato 'nyad vibhaktaṃ yad vadet ||26||

26. "He does not speak; though [capable of] speaking, he does not speak—since there is no separation of speaking from the speaker because it is indestructible. But there is no second, no other that is distinct from him, that he could speak to.

yad vai tan na śr̥ṇoti śr̥ṇvan vai tan na śr̥ṇoti | na hi śrotuḥ śruter viparilopo vidyate 'vināśitvāt | na tu tad dvitīyam asti tato 'nyad vibhaktaṃ yac chr̥ṇuyāt ||27||

27. "He does not hear; though [capable of] hearing, he does not hear—since there is no separation of hearing from the hearer because it is indestructible. But there is no second, no other that is distinct from him, that he could hear.

yad vai tan na manute manvāno vai tan na manute | na hi mantur mater viparilopo vidyate 'vināśitvāt | na tu tad dvitīyam asti tato 'nyad vibhaktaṃ yan manvīta ||28||

28. "He does not think; though [capable of] thinking, he does not think—since there is no separation of thinking from the thinker because it is indestructible. But there is no second, no other that is distinct from him, that he could think of.

yad vai tan na spr̥śati spr̥śan vai tan na spr̥śati | na hi spraṣṭuḥ spr̥ṣṭer viparilopo vidyate 'vināśitvāt | na tu tad dvitīyam asti tato 'nyad vibhaktaṃ yat spr̥śet ||29||

29. "He does not touch; though [capable of] touching, he does not touch—since there is no separation of touching from the toucher because it is indestructible. But there is no second, no other that is distinct from him, that he could touch.

yad vai tan na vijānāti vijānan vai tan na vijānāti | na hi vijñātur vijñāter viparilopo vidyate 'vināśitvāt | na tu tad dvitīyam asti tato 'nyad vibhaktaṃ yad vijānīyāt ||30||

30. "He does not perceive; though [capable of] perceiving, he does not perceive,—since there is no separation of perception from the perceiver because it is indestructible. But there is no second, no other that is distinct from him, that he could perceive.

yatra vā anyad iva syāt tatrānyo 'nyat paśyed anyo 'nyaj jighred anyo 'nyad rasayed anyo 'nyad vaded anyo 'nyac chr̥ṇuyād anyo 'nyan manvītānyo 'nyat spr̥śed anyo 'nyad vijānīyāt ||31||

31. "Where there is something of an other,[48] one can see the other, one can smell the other, one can taste the other, one can speak to the other, one can hear the other, one can think the other, one can touch the other, and one can perceive the other.

salila eko draṣṭādvaito bhavati | eṣa brahmalokaḥ samrāṭ | iti hainam anuśaśāsa yājñavalkya | eṣāsya paramā gatiḥ | eṣāsya paramā saṃpat | eṣo 'sya paramo lokaḥ | eṣo 'sya parama ānandaḥ etasyaivānandasyānyāni bhūtāni mātrām upajīvanti ||32||

32. "He becomes the one water, the non-dual seer. That is the world of *brahman,* O King." So did Yājñavalkya instruct him. "This is his highest path. This is his highest attainment. This is his highest world. This is his highest joy. On a fraction of just this bliss do other creatures live.

sa yo manuṣyāṇāṃ rāddhaḥ samr̥ddho bhavaty anyeṣām adhipatiḥ sarvair mānuṣyakair bhogaiḥ sampannatamaḥ sa manuṣyāṇāṃ parama ānandaḥ | atha ye śataṃ manuṣyāṇām ānandāḥ sa ekaḥ pitr̥̄ṇāṃ jitalokānām ānandaḥ | atha ye śatam pitr̥̄ṇām jitalokānām ānandāḥ sa eko gandharvaloka ānandaḥ | atha ye śataṃ gandharvaloka ānandāḥ sa ekaḥ karmadevānām ānando ye karmaṇā devatvam abhisaṃpadyante | atha ye śatam karmadevānām ānandāḥ sa eka ājānadevānām ānandaḥ | yaś ca śrotriyo 'vr̥jino 'kāmahataḥ | atha ye śatam ājānadevānām ānandāḥ sa ekaḥ prajāpatiloka ānandaḥ | yaś ca śrotriyo 'vr̥jino 'kāmahataḥ | atha ye śataṃ prajāpatiloka ānandāḥ sa eko brahmaloka ānandaḥ | yaś ca śrotriyo 'vr̥jino 'kāmahataḥ | athaiṣa eva parama ānandaḥ | eṣa brahmalokaḥ samrāḍ iti hovāca yājñavalkyaḥ | so 'haṃ bhagavate sahasraṃ dadāmi | ata ūrdhvaṃ vimokṣāyaiva brūhīti | atra ha yājñavalkyo bibhayāṃ cakāra medhāvī rājā sarvebhyo māntebhya udarautsīd iti ||33||

33. "That [joy] which is accomplished and rich among men, ruling others [i.e., other joys] and fully endowed with all human delights, that is the highest joy of men. Now, one hundred joys of men is but the single joy of the ancestors who have won their world. And one hundred joys of the ancestors who have won their world is a single joy in the world of the Gandharvas. One hundred joys in the world of the Gandharvas is a single joy of gods-by-rites, that is one who attains godhood through rites. One hundred joys of gods-by-rites is the single joy of gods-by-birth and also the one learned in the Vedas, who is not crooked and not overcome by desire. One hundred joys of gods-by-birth is the single joy in the world of Prajāpati and also the one learned in the Vedas, who is not crooked and not overcome by desire. One hundred joys in the world of Prajāpati is the single joy in the world of *brahman* and also the one learned in the Vedas, who is not crooked and not overcome by desire. Now certainly that is the highest joy, that is the world of *brahman,* O King." So said Yājñavalkya.

"Distinguished one, I give you a thousand cows. Tell me further about release!"

At this point Yājñavalkya became afraid thinking, "This king is smart. He has driven me from every conclusion.

sa vā eṣa etasmin svapnānte ratvā caritvā dr̥ṣṭvaiva puṇyam ca pāpaṃ ca punaḥ pratinyāyaṃ pratiyony ādravati buddhāntāyaiva ||34||

34. "Having experienced and moved about in dream-sleep and having seen the good and the bad, he runs back along the same path and through the same opening right back to the waking state.

tad yathānaḥ susamāhitam utsarjad yāyād evam evāyaṁ śarīra ātmā prājñenātmanānvārūḍha utsarjan yāti | yatraitad ūrdhvocchvāsī bhavati ||35||

35. "As a heavily loaded cart goes along creaking, in this way this bodily self (*ātman*) burdened with the self (*ātman*) which is knowledge, goes along creaking when he breathes his last breath.

sa yatrāyam aṇimānaṃ nyeti jarayā vopatapatā vāṇimānaṃ nigacchati | tad yathāmraṃ vodumbaraṃ vā pippalaṃ vā bandhanāt pramucyate evam evāyaṃ puruṣa ebhyo 'ṅgebhyaḥ saṃpramucya punaḥ pratinyāyaṃ pratiyony ādravati prāṇāyaiva ||36||

> **36.** "A man falls into frailness by sickness or old age. As a mango, fig, or a pipal-fruit comes free from the stem, in this way a person comes free from his limbs and again goes back along the same path and through the same opening right back to the breath.

tad yathā rājānam āyāntam ugrāḥ pratyenasaḥ sūtagrāmaṇyo 'nnaiḥ pānair āvasathaiḥ pratikalpante 'yam āyātyayam āgacchatīti | evaṁ haivaṃ vidaṁ sarvāṇi bhūtāni pratikalpanta idaṃ brahmāyātīdam āgacchatīti ||37||

> **37.** "As when a king arrives, warriors, judges, heralds and village chiefs welcome with [gifts of] food, drink, and lodging shout 'He's arriving! He's coming!' So in this way when a knowing person arrives, all beings[49] shout "This *brahman* comes! This *brahman* comes!"

tad yathā rājānaṃ prayiyāsantam ugrāḥ pratyenasaḥ sūtagrāmaṇyo 'bhis-amāyanti | evam evemam ātmānam antakāle sarve prāṇā abhisamāyanti | yatraitad ūrdhvocchvāsī bhavati ||38||

|| *iti tṛtīyaṃ brāhmaṇaṃ* ||

> **38.** "As a king is about to depart, warriors, judges, charioteers, and village chiefs gather around, in this way all the breaths gather around a man at his end time when he breathes his last breath.

4.4

sa yatrāyam ātmābalyaṃ nyetya saṃmoham iva nyeti | athainam ete prāṇā abhisamāyanti | sa etās tejomātrāḥ samabhyādadāno hṛdayam evānvavakrāmati | sa yatraiṣa cākṣuṣaḥ puruṣaḥ parāṅ paryāvartate | athārūpajño bhavati ||1||

> **1.** "When the body (*ātman*) becomes weak and he is in some sort of delusion, the breaths gather around. Taking these bits of splendor with him he descends back into the heart. When the person that is the eye turns back [into the heart], he has no knowledge of visible forms.

ekībhavati na paśyatīty āhuḥ | ekībhavati na jighratīty āhuḥ | ekībhavati na rasayata ity āhuḥ | ekībhavati na vadatīty āhuḥ | ekībhavati na śṛṇotīty āhuḥ | ekībhavati na manuta ity āhuḥ | ekībhavati na spṛśatīty āhuḥ | ekībhavati na vijānātīy āhuḥ | tasya haitasya hṛdayasyāgraṃ pradyotate | tena pradyotenaiṣa ātmā niṣkrāmati cakśuṣṭo vā mūrdhno vānyebhyo vā sarīradeśebhyaḥ | tam utkrāmantaṃ prāṇo 'nūtkrāmati | prāṇam anūtkrāmantaṁ sarve prāṇā anūtkrāmanti | savijñāno bhavati | savijñānam evānvavakrāmati taṃ vidyākarmaṇī samanvārabhete pūrvaprajñā ca ||2||

2. "They say, 'He's becoming one,[50] he cannot see.' 'He's becoming one, he cannot taste.' 'He's becoming one, he cannot speak.' 'He's becoming one, he cannot hear.' 'He's becoming one, he cannot think.' 'He's becoming one, he cannot feel touch.' 'He's becoming one, he cannot perceive.' The top of his heart lights up and by that light he exits from the eye, or the head, or some other part of the body. When departing, the breath departs with him. When the breath is departing, all the breaths depart with him. He becomes only awareness and he descends into awareness. Knowledge, actions, and memory surround him completely.

tad yathā tṛṇajalāyukā tṛṇasyāntaṃ gatvānyam ākramam ākramyātmānam upasaṁharati | evam evāyam ātmedaṁ śarīraṃ nihatyāvidyāṃ gamayitvānyam ākramyātmānam upasaṁharati ||3||

3. "It is like this—as a caterpillar goes to the tip of a blade of grass, takes the next step [by stretching onto the next blade of grass] and then draws itself (*ātman*) together, in this way the self (*ātman*), having felled the body and sent (itself) to non-knowing, takes the next step and then draws itself (*ātman*) together.

tad yathā peśaskārī peśaso mātrām apādāyānyan navataraṃ kalyāṇataraṁ rūpaṃ tanute | evam evāyam ātmedaṁ śarīraṃ nihatyāvidyāṃ gamayitvānyan navataraṃ kalyāṇataraṁ rūpaṃ kurute pitryaṃ vā gāndharvaṃ vā daivaṃ vā prājāpatyaṃ vā brāhmaṃ vānyeṣāṃ vā bhūtānām ||4||

4. "It is like this—as a weaver-woman takes off a measure of colored yarn and weaves a newer and prettier form, in this way the self (*ātman*), having felled the body and sent himself to non-knowing, makes itself a newer, prettier form—of an ancestor, or a Gandharva, or a god, or Prājapati, or Brahmā,[51] or of other beings.[52]

sa vā ayam ātmā brahma vijñānamayo manomayaḥ prāṇamayaś cakṣurmayaḥ śrotramayaḥ pṛthivīmaya āpomaya vāyumaya ākāśamayas tejomayo 'tejomayaḥ kāmamayo 'kāmamayaḥ krodhamayo 'krodhamayo dharmamayo 'dharmamayaḥ sarvamayaḥ | tad yad etad idaṃmayo 'domaya iti | yathākārī yathācārī tathā bhavati | sādhukārī sadhur bhavati | pāpakārī pāpo bhavati | puṇyaḥ puṇyena karmaṇā pāpaḥ pāpena | atho khalv āhuḥ kāmamaya evāyaṃ puruṣa iti | sa yathākāmo bhavati tat kratur bhavati | yat kratur bhavati tat karma kurute | yat karma kurute tad abhisaṃpadyate ||5||

5. "Now certainly this self is *brahman* which consists of perception, mind, breaths, sight, hearing, the earth, the waters, the wind, space, brightness, darkness, desire, non-desire, anger, non-anger, *dharma, adharma,* the self made of everything. [Thus they say,] 'He is made of this. He is made of that.' According to his action and his conduct a man becomes [what he becomes]. One who does good action becomes good and one who does bad action becomes bad. By good actions one becomes good and bad by action one becomes bad. Now they say, 'This person is just composed of desire.' His desire is in accordance with his intention and he performs action in accordance with his intention. His actions determine him.

tad eṣa śloko bhavati | tad eva saktaḥ saha karmanaiti liṅgaṃ mano yatra niṣaktam asya | prāpyāntaṃ karmaṇas tasya yat kiṃceha karoty ayam | tasmāl lokāt punar aityasymai lokāya karmaṇe || iti nu kāmayamānaḥ | athākāmayamāno yo 'kāmo niṣkāma āptakāma ātmakāmo na tasy prāṇā utkrāmanti | brahmaiva san brahmāpy eti ||6||

6. "Now there is this verse:

A man attached with action goes,
To where his character, his mind, is affixed.
Having reached the end of his actions
Whatever he performs here—
He comes again from that world,
to this world, to action.

"But that is regarding a man who desires. Now a person who does not desire—that is one without desires, free from desire, whose desires are fulfilled, whose desire is the self, his breaths do not depart. He is just *brahman* and to *brahman* he goes.

tad eṣa śloko bhavati | yadā sarve pramucyante kāmā ye 'sya hṛdi śritāḥ | atha martyo 'mṛto bhavaty atra brahma samaśnuta iti || tad yathāhinirlvayanī valmīke mṛtā pratyas tā śayīta | evam evedaṁ śarīraṁ śete | athāyam aśarīro 'mṛtaḥ prāṇo brahmaiva teja eva | so 'haṃ bhagavate sahasraṃ dadāmīti hovāca janako vaidehaḥ ||7||

7. "Now there is this verse:
When they are all let go,
those desires affixed in the heart;
Then a mortal becomes immortal,
and has attained *brahman* here.

"It is like this—as a snakeskin lay dead and discarded on an anthill, in just this way the corpse lies. Now this immortal, incorporeal body is the breath—only *brahman*, only light."

Janaka of Videha said, "Distinguished one, I give you a thousand cows."

tad ete ślokā bhavanti | aṇuḥ panthā vitataḥ purāṇo māṁ spṛṣṭo 'nuvitto mayaiva | tena dhīrā apiyanti brahmavidaḥ svargaṃ lokam ita ūrdhvaṃ vimuktāḥ ||8||

8. "Now there is this verse:
A fine, long, and ancient path,
I have touched it to me, I have found it;
By it intelligent men, knowers of *brahman*
go to the heavenly world, released from here.

tasmiñ chuklam uta nīlam āhuḥ piṅgalaṁ haritaṃ lohitaṃ ca | eṣa panthā brahmaṇā hānuvittas tenaiti brahmavit puṇyakṛt taijasaś ca ||9||

9. "In it are the white and the blue, they say,
And the orange, the red, and the yellow;
This path was found by *brahman*,

By it goes the knower of *brahman*,
the doer of good, the person of light.

andhaṃ tamaḥ praviśanti yo 'vidyām upāsate | tato bhūya iva te tamo ya u vidyāyāṁ ratāḥ ||10||

10. "They enter into blind darkness,
Those who venerate ignorance/ignorantly;
And a somewhat greater darkness,
[Enter] those who delight in knowledge.

anandā nāma te lokā andhena tamas āvr̥tāḥ | tāṁs te pretyābhigacchanty avidvāṁso 'budho janāḥ ||11||

11. "'Joyless,' by name, are those worlds,
Encompassed in blind darkness;
To them they go when they die,
People who are unlearned and the unwise.

ātmānaṃ ced vijānīyād ayam asmīti pūruṣaḥ | kim icchan kasya kāmāya śarīram anusaṃjvaret ||12||

12. "Should a person perceive the self (*ātman*),
Knowing 'I am he;'
What could he want? Whom could he desire,
That he would distress [himself] about this body.

yasyānuvittaḥ pratibuddha ātmāsmin saṃdehye gahane praviṣṭaḥ | sa viśvakr̥t sa hi sarvasya kartā tasya lokaḥ sa u loka eva ||13||

13. "For the one who found and perceived
the self (*ātman*) that has entered the dense body;
He is the maker of all, the creator of everything,
This is his world, indeed he is the world.

ihaiva santo 'tha vidmas tad vayaṃ na ced avedir mahatī vinaṣṭiḥ | ye tad vidur amr̥tās te bhavanty athetare duḥkham evāpiyanti ||14||

14. "While even being here we know it,
If you don't, you are ignorant—it is your great destruction;
Those who know become immortal,
And the others go to sorrow.

yadaitam anupaśyaty ātmānaṃ devam añjasā | īśānaṃ bhūtabhavasya na tato vijugupsate ||15||

15. "When someone truly sees
The self (*ātman*) as god;
He is the ruler of the past and the future,
He will not want to hide from him.

yasmād arvāk saṃvatsaro 'hobhiḥ parivartate | tad devā jyotiṣāṃ jyotir āyur hopāsate 'mr̥tam ||16||

16. "Below him, the year revolves
Together with the days;
The gods venerate that light of lights,
As life, as immortality.

yasmin pañca pañcajanā ākāśaś ca pratiṣṭhitaḥ | tam eva manya ātmānaṃ vidvān brahmāmr̥to 'mr̥tam ||17||

17. "In it, the five groups of five
and space are established.
I think this as the self (*ātman*),
I who know this immortal *brahman* am immortal.

prāṇasya prāṇam uta cakṣuṣaś cakṣur uta śrotrasya śrotraṃ manaso ye mano viduḥ | te nicikyur brahma purāṇam agryam ||18||

18. "Those who know the breath of the breath,
The hearing of the hearing,
The thinking of the thinking;
They perceive *brahman*,
The ancient,
The first.

manasaivānudraṣṭavyaṃ neha nānāsti kiṃcana | mr̥tyoḥ sa mr̥tyum āpnoti ya iha nāneva paśyati ||19||

19. "It is to be perceived with the mind alone
That there is nothing diverse at all;
From death he attains (another) death,
He who sees any diversity here.

ekadhaivānudraṣṭavyam etad apramayaṃ dhruvam | virajaḥ para ākāśād aja ātmā mahān dhruvaḥ ||20||

20. "It is to be perceived as just one,
Without measure and fixed.
The self (*ātman*) is stainless, beyond space,
great, unborn, and fixed.

tam eva dhīro vijñāya prajñāṃ kurvīta brāhmaṇaḥ | nānudhyāyād bahūñ chabdān vāco viglāpanaṁ hi tad iti ||21||

21. "The learned Brahmin, having known just this,
should cultivate wisdom;
He should not contemplate many words,
As it is just the weariness of speech.

sa vā eṣa mahān aja ātmā yo 'yaṃ vijñānamayaḥ prāṇeṣu | ya eṣo 'ntar hr̥daya ākāśas tasmiñ chete sarvasya vaśī sarvasyeśānaḥ sarvasyādhipatiḥ sa na sādhunā karmaṇā bhuyān no evāsādhunā kanīyān | eṣa sarveśvaraḥ | eṣa bhūtādhipatiḥ | eṣa bhūtapālaḥ | eṣa setur vidharaṇa eṣāṃ lokānām asaṃbhedāya | tam etaṃ vedānuvacanena brāhmaṇā vividiṣanti yajñena dānena tapasānāśakena | etam eva viditvā munir bhavati | etam eva pravrājino lokam icchantaḥ pravrajanti | etad dha sma vai tat pūrve vidvāṁsaḥ prajāṃ na kāmayante | kiṃ prajayā kariṣyāmo yeṣāṃ no 'yam ātmāyaṃ loka iti | te ha sma putraiṣaṇāyāś ca vittaiṣaṇāyāś ca lokaiṣaṇāyāś ca vyutthāyātha bhikṣācaryaṃ caranti | yā hy eva putraiṣaṇā sā vittaiṣaṇā | yā vittaiṣaṇā sā lokaiṣaṇā | ubhe hy ete eṣaṇe eva bhavataḥ | sa eṣa neti nety ātmā | agr̥hyo na hi gr̥hyate | aśīryo na hi śīryate | asaṅgo na hi sajyate | asito na vyathate | na riṣyati | etam u haivaite na tarata iti | ataḥ pāpam akaravam iti | ataḥ kalyāṇam akaravam iti | ubhe u haivaiṣa ete tarati | nainaṃ kr̥tākr̥te tapataḥ ||22||

22. "This great unborn self (*ātman*) is he who consists of perception among the breaths. He lies in that space within the heart—the Ruler of all! Controller of all! Lord of all! He does not become more by good actions nor less by bad actions. Just he is the controller! He is the ruler of creatures! He is the protector of creatures! He is the dike separating these worlds so that they don't mingle. He is the one who the Brahmins desire to know through Vedic recitation, by sacrifice, by giving, austerity, and fasting. Coming to know just him, one becomes a sage. Only out of a desire for him do wandering ascetics go wandering.

"Knowing this, men of old did not desire offspring, thinking: 'What is the use of offspring for us? Ours is this self, it is the world.' Now they gave up desire for sons, desire for wealth, and desire for (various) worlds and went about as mendicants because the desire for sons is the desire for wealth, and desire for wealth the desire for worlds. Both are just desires.

"This self is 'Not this, not that.' He is ungraspable because he is not grasped. He is undecaying because he does not decay. He is not clinging because he is not clung to. He is unbound [because] he does not tremble. He is not hurt.

"Two thoughts do not pass across him [the self], 'Thus I did something bad,' and 'Thus I did something good.' But he passes across those two. He is not burnt by what is done or not done.

tad etad r̥cābhyuktam | eṣa nityo mahimā brāhmaṇasya na vardhate karmaṇā no kanīyān | tasyaiva syāt padavittaṃ viditvā na lipyate karmaṇā pāpakeneti || tasmād evaṃvic chānto dānta uparatas titikṣuḥ samāhito bhutvātmany evātmānaṃ paśyati sarvam ātmānaṃ paśyati | nainaṃ pāpmā tarati | sarvaṃ pāpmānaṃ tarati | nainaṃ pāpmā tapati | sarvaṃ pāpmānaṃ tapati | vipāpo virajo 'vicikitso brāhmaṇo bhavati | eṣa brahmalokaḥ samrāṭ | enaṃ prāpito 'sīti hovāca yājñavalkyaḥ | so' haṃ bhagavate videhān dadāmi māṃ cāpi saha dāsyāyeti ||23||

23. "This is said in the R̥gveda:

He is a Brahmin's imperishable greatness,
He does not grow nor diminish by action.

Should one know his path to knowledge,
He is not stained by bad acts.

"Thus a man who knows in this way becomes calm, withdrawn, forbearing, and collected. He sees the self (*ātman*) in himself (*ātman*); and sees the self (*ātman*) as everything. Evil does not pass across him, [but] he passes across all evil. Evil does not burn him, [but] he burns all evil. He becomes a Brahmin who is free from evil, free from stain, and free from doubt. This is the world of *brahman*, O King, and you have been brought there by me."

"Distinguished one, I give you the people of Videha and myself as your slaves!"

sa vā eṣa mahān aja ātmānnādo vasudānaḥ | vindate vasu ya evaṃ veda ||24||

24. This great unborn self (*ātman*) is the eater of food, the giver of wealth. One who knows in this way, finds wealth.

sa vā eṣa mahān aja ātmājaro 'maro 'mr̥to 'bhayo brahma | abhayaṃ vai brahma | abhayaṁ hi vai brahma bhavati ya evaṃ veda ||25||
|| iti caturthaṃ brāhmaṇam ||

25. This great unborn self (*ātman*) is unaging, undying, immortal, free from fear, and it is *brahman*. Clearly *brahman* is fearless. One who knows in this way becomes the fearless *brahman*.

4.5

atha ha yājñavalkyasya dve bhārye babhūvatur maitreyī ca kātyāyanī ca | tayor ha maitreyī brahmavādinī babhūva | strīprajñaiva tarhi kātyāyanī | atha ha yājñavalkyo 'nyad vr̥ttam upākariṣyan ||1||

1. Now Yājñavalkya had two wives, Maitreyī and Kātyāyanī. Of the two, Maitreyī was given to talk about *brahman*[53] while Kātyāyanī was concerned with only womanly matters. One day, Yājñavalkya was preparing to enter another mode of life.[54]

maitreyīti hovāca yājñavalkyaḥ | pravrajiṣyan vā are 'ham asmāt sthānād asmi | hanta te 'nayā kātyāyanyāntaṃ karavāṇīti ||2||

2. "Maitreyī," Yājñavalkya said, "I am going to depart from this place. You see, I must make a final settlement with you and Kātyāyanī.

sā hovāca maitreyī yan nu ma iyaṃ bhagoḥ sarvā pṛthivī vittena pūrṇā syāṭ syāṃ nv ahaṃ tenāmṛtāho3 neti | neti hovāca yājñavalkyaḥ | yathaivopakaraṇa-vatāṃ jīvitaṃ tathaiva te jīvitaṁ syāt | amṛtatvasya tu nāśāsti vitteneti ||3||

3. Maitreyī said, "Revered one, should I possess this earth filled with riches would it make me immortal or not?"

"It would not," Yājñavalkya said. "Your life would be that of a wealthy person, but there is no hope of immortality through riches."

sā hovāca maitreyī yenāhaṃ nāmṛtā syāṃ kim ahaṃ tena kuryām | yad eva bhagavān veda tad eva me brūhīti ||4||

4. Maitreyī said, "What would I do with something that doesn't make me immortal? Revered one, tell me what you know."

sa hovāca yājñavalkyaḥ priyā vai khalu no bhavatī satī priyam avṛdhat | hanta tarhi bhavaty etad vyākhyāsyāmi te | vyācakṣāṇasya tu me nididhyāsasveti ||5||

5. Yājñavalkya said, "Indeed you are dear to me and now you have grown more dear. Come, then I will explain it to you. But try to pay close attention when I am speaking."

sa hovāca | na vā are patyuḥ kāmāya patiḥ priyo bhavaty ātmanas tu kāmāya patiḥ priyo bhavati | na vā are jāyāyai kāmāya jāyā priyā bhavaty ātmanas tu kāmāya jāyā priyā bhavati | na vā are putrāṇāṃ kāmāya putrāḥ priyā bhavanty ātmanas tu kāmāya putrāḥ priyā bhavanti | na vā are vittasya kāmāya vittaṃ priyaṃ bhavaty ātmanas tu kāmāya vittaṃ priyaṃ bhavati | na vā are paśūnāṃ kāmāya paśavaḥ priyā bhavanty ātmanas tu kāmāya paśavaḥ priyā bhavanti | na vā are brahmanaḥ kāmāya brahma priyaṃ bhavaty ātmanas tu kāmāya brahma priyaṃ bhavati | na vā are kṣatrasya kāmāya kṣatraṃ priyaṃ bhavaty ātmanas tu kāmāya kṣatraṃ priyaṃ bhavati | na vā are lokānāṃ kāmāya lokāḥ priyā bhavanty ātmanas tu kāmāya lokāḥ priyā bhavanti | na vā are devānāṃ kāmāya devāḥ priyā bhavanty ātmanas tu kāmāya devāḥ priyā bhavanti | na vā are vedānāṃ kāmāya vedāḥ priyā bhavanty ātmanas tu kāmāya vedāḥ priyā bhavanti | na vā are bhūtānāṃ kāmāya bhūtāni priyāṇi bhavanty ātmanas tu kāmāya bhūtāni priyāṇi bhavanti | na vā are sarvasya kāmāya sarvaṃ priyaṃ bhavaty ātmanas tu kāmāya sarvaṃ priyaṃ bhavati | ātmā vā are draṣṭavyaḥ śrotavyo mantavyo nididhyāsitavyo maitreyi | ātmani khalv are dṛṣṭe śrute mate vijñāta idaṁ sarvaṃ viditam ||6||

6. He said, "It is not out of love for the husband that the husband is held dear, but it is out of love for the self (*ātman*) that the husband is held dear. It is not out of love for the wife that the wife is held dear, but it is out of love for the self that the wife is held dear. It is not out of love for children that the children are held dear, but it is out of love for the self that the children are held dear. It is not out of love for wealth that wealth is held dear, but it is out of love for the self that wealth is held dear. It is not out of love for livestock that livestock is held dear, but it is out of love for the self that livestock is held dear. It is not out of love for priestly status that priestly status is held dear, but it is out of love for the self that priestly status is held dear. It is not out of love for royal status that royal status is held dear, but it is out of love for the self that royal status is held dear. It is not out of love for the worlds that worlds are held dear, but it is out of love for the self that the worlds are held dear. It is not out of love for the gods that the gods are held dear, but it is out of love for the self that the gods are held dear. It is not out of love for the Vedas that the Vedas are held dear, but it is out of love for the self that the Vedas are held dear. It is not out of love for beings that beings are held dear, but it out of love for the self that beings are held dear. It is not out of love for the All that the All is held dear, but it is out of love for the self that the All is held dear.

"Maitreyī, it is the self (*ātman*) which one should see, hear, think about, and concentrate on. When one has seen, heard, thought about, and concentrated on the self, one knows this All.

brahma taṃ parādād yo 'nyatrātmano brahma veda | kṣatraṃ taṃ parādād yo 'nyatrātmanaḥ kṣatram veda | lokās taṃ parādur yo 'nyatrātmano lokān veda | devās taṃ parādur yo 'nytrātmano devān veda | vedās taṃ parādur yo 'nytrātmano vedān veda | bhūtāni taṃ parādur yo 'nyatrātmano bhūtāni veda | sarvaṃ taṃ parādād yo 'nytrātmanaḥ sarvaṃ veda | idaṃ brahmedaṃ kṣatram ime lokā ime devā ime vedā imāni bhūtānīdaṁ sarvaṃ yad ayam ātmā ||7||

7. "May priestly status abandon him who thinks priestly status as other than the self. May royal status abandon him who thinks royal status as other than the self. May the worlds abandon him who thinks the worlds as other than the self. May the gods abandon him who thinks the gods as other than the self. May the Vedas abandon him who thinks the Vedas as other than the self. May the beings abandon him who thinks the beings as other than the self. May the All abandon him who thinks the All as other than the self. Priestly status, royal status, the worlds, the gods, the Vedas, these beings, the All—all this is this self.

sa yathā dundubher hanyamānasya na bāhyāñ chabdāñ chaknuyād grahaṇāya | dundubhes tu grahaṇena dundubhyāghātasya vā śabdo gṛhītaḥ ||8||

8. "One cannot grab the external sound of a drum which is being beaten, but by grabbing the drum or the drum-player one grabs the sound.

sa yathā śaṅkhasya dhmāyamānasya na bāhyāñ chabdāñ chaknuyād grahaṇāya | śañkhasya tu grahaṇena śañkhadhmasya vā śabdo gṛhītaḥ ||9||

9. "One cannot grab the external sound of a conch which is being blown, but by grabbing the conch or the conch-player one grabs the sound.

sa yathā vīṇāyai vādyamānāyai na bāhyāñ chabdāñ chaknuyād grahaṇāya | vīṇāyai tu grahaṇena vīṇāvādasya vā śabdo gṛhītaḥ ||10||

10. "One cannot grab the external sound of a *vīṇa* which is being played, but by grabbing the *vīṇa* or the *vīṇa* player one grabs the sound.

sa yathārdraidhāgner abhyāhitasya pṛthagdhūmā viniścaranty evaṃ vā are 'sya mahato bhūtasya niḥśvasitam etad yad ṛgvedo yajurvedaḥ sāmavedo 'tharvāṅgirasa itihāsaḥ purāṇaṃ vidyā upaniṣadaḥ ślokāḥ sūtrāṇy anuvyākhyānāni vyākhyānānīṣṭaṁ hutam āśitaṃ pāyitam ayaṃ ca lokaḥ paraś ca lokaḥ sarvāṇi ca bhūtāni | asyaivaitāni sarvāṇi niśvasitāni ||11||

11. "As clouds of smoke rise from a fire when damp wood is placed on it, in this way this great being's exhalation is the Ṛgveda, Yajurveda, Sāmaveda, Atharva-Āṅgirasa, history, legend, science, the hidden teachings, verses, aphorisms, explanations, glosses, the oblation, the offering, the giving of food and water; this world and the next world; and all beings. These are all his exhalations.

sa yathā sarvāsām apāṁ samudra ekāyanam | evaṁ sarveṣāṁ sparśānāṃ tvag ekāyanam | evaṁ sarveṣāṁ gandhānāṃ nāsike ekāyanam | evaṁ sarveṣāṁ rasānāṃ jihvaikāyanam | evaṁ sarveṣāṁ rūpāṇāṃ cakṣur ekāyanam | evaṁ sarveṣāṁ śabdānāṃ śrotram ekāyanam | evaṁ sarveṣāṁ saṅkalpānāṃ mana ekāyanam | evaṁ sarveṣāṁ vidyānāṁ hṛdayam ekāyanam | evaṁ sarveṣāṁ karmaṇāṁ hastāv ekāyanam | evaṁ sarveṣām ānandānām upastha ekāyanam | evaṁ sarveṣāṁ visargāṇāṃ pāyur ekāyanam | evaṁ sarveṣam adhvanāṃ pādāv ekāyanam | evaṁ sarveṣāṃ vedānāṃ vāg ekāyanam ||12||

12. "As the ocean is the single meeting place of all waters, in this way the skin is the single meeting place of all touch; the two nostils, of all odors; the tongue, of all tastes; sight, of all visible forms; hearing, of all sounds; the mind, of all thoughts; the heart of all sciences; the two hands, of all actions; the sexual organ, of all pleasures; the anus, of all excretions; the two feet, of all travel; speech, of all Vedas.

sa yathā saindhavaghano 'nantaro 'bāhyaḥ kṛtsno rasaghana eva | evaṃ vā are 'yam ātmānantaro 'bāhyaḥ kṛtsnaḥ prajñānaghana eva | etebhyo bhūtebhyo samutthāya tāny evānu vinaśyati | na pretya saṃjñāstīty are bravīmi | iti hovāca yājñavalkyaḥ ||13||

13. "As a lump of salt, having no distinctive interior or exterior, is just a whole mass of flavor, in this way, the self (*ātman*), having no distinctive interior or exterior, is just a whole mass of cognition. It arises with them and is destroyed (*vinaśyati*)[55] after them. I am saying that after death, there is no consciousness." This is what Yājñavalkya said.

sā hovāca maitreyī | atraiva mā bhagvān mohāntam āpīpipat | na vā aham imaṃ vijānāmīti | sa hovāca na vā are 'haṃ mohaṃ bravīmi | avināśī vā are 'yam ātmānucchittidharmā ||14||

14. Maitreyī said, "You have tossed me into total confusion. I don't conceptualize this at all."

He said, "I did not say anything confusing. The self (*ātman*) is indestructable (*avīnāśin*), its nature imperishable.

yatra hi dvaitam iva bhavati tad itara itaraṃ paśyati tad itara itaraṃ jighrati tad itara itaraṁ rasayate tad itara itaram abhivadati tad itara itaraṁ śr̥ṇoti tad itara itaraṃ manute tad itara itaraṁ spr̥śati tad itara itaraṃ vijānāti | yatra tv asya sarvam ātmaivābhūt tat kena kaṃ paśyet tat kena kaṃ jighret tat kena kaṁ rasayet tat kena kam abhivadet tat kena kaṁ śr̥nuyāt tat kena kaṃ manvīta tat kena kaṁ spr̥ṣet tat kena kaṃ vijānīyāt | yenedaṁ sarvaṃ vijānāti taṃ kena vijānīyāt | sa eṣa neti nety ātmā | agr̥hyo na hi gr̥hyate | aśīryo na hi śīryate | asaṅgo na hi sajyate | asito na vyathate | na riṣyati | vijñātāram are kena vijānīyād ity uktānuśāsanāsi maitreyi | etāvad are khalv amr̥tatvam iti hoktvā yājñavalkya vijahāra ||15||

|| *iti pañcamaṃ brāhmaṇam* ||

15. "Because where there is something of an other one can see the other, one can smell the other, one can taste the other, one can greet the other, one can hear the other, and can think of the other, and one can touch the other, one can cognize the other. But this All has become just the self, then who is there to see and by what means? Who is there to smell and by what means? Who is tasted and by what means? Who is there to greet and by what means? Who is there to hear and by what means? Who is there to think about and by what means? Who is there to touch and by what means?

"By what means is one to perceive by which the whole is perceived?

"This self is 'Not this, Not that.' He is ungraspable because he is not grasped. He is undecaying because he does not decay. He is not clinging because he is not clung to. He is unbound [because] he does not tremble. He is not hurt. By what means can one perceive the perceiver?—that's the instruction. That's the extent of immortality."

Having said this, Yājñavalkya left.

atha vaṁśaḥ | pautimāṣyo gaupavanāt | gaupavanaḥ pautimāṣyāt | pautimāṣyo gaupavanāt | gaupavanaḥ kauśikāt | kauśikaḥ kauṇḍinyāt | kauṇḍinyaḥ śāṇḍilyāt | śāṇḍilyaḥ kauśikāc ca gautamāc ca | gautamaḥ ||1|| āgniveśyāt | āgniveśyo gārgyāt | gārygo gārgyāt | gārgyo gautamāt | gautamaḥ saitavāt | saitavaḥ pārāśaryāyaṇāt | pārāśaryāyaṇo gārgyāyaṇāt | gārgyāyaṇa uddālakāyanāt | uddālakāyano jābālāyanāt | jābālāyano mādhyandināyanāt | mādhyandināyanaḥ saukarāyaṇāt | saukarāyaṇaḥ kāṣāyaṇāt | kāṣāyaṇaḥ sāyakāyanāt | sāyakāyanaḥ kauśikāyaneḥ | kauśikāyaniḥ ||2|| ghṛtakauśikāt | ghṛtakauśikaḥ pārāśaryāyaṇāt | pārāśaryāyaṇaḥ pārāśaryāt | pārāśaryo jātūkarṇyāt | jātukarṇya āsurāyaṇāc ca yāskāc ca | āsurāyaṇas traivaneḥ | traivaṇir aupajandhaneḥ | aupajandhanir āsureḥ | āsurir bhāradvājāt | bhāradvāja ātreyāṭ | ātreyo māṇṭeḥ | māṇṭir gautamāt | gautamo gautamāt | gautamo vātsyāt | vātsyaḥ śāṇḍilyāt | śāṇḍilyaḥ kaiśoryāt kāpyāt | kaiśoryaḥ kāpyaḥ kumārahāritāt | kumārahārito gālavāt | gālavo vidarbhīkauṇḍinyāt | vidarbhīkauṇḍinyo vatsanapāto bābhravāt | vatsanapād bābhravaḥ pathaḥ saubharāt | panthāḥ saubharo 'yāsyād āṅgirasāt | ayāsya āṅgirasa ābhūtes tvāṣṭrāt | ābhūtis tvāṣṭro viśvarūpāt tvāṣṭrāt | viśvarūpas tvāṣṭro 'śvibhyām | aśvinau dadhīca ātharvaṇāt | dadhyaṅṅ ātharvaṇo 'tharvaṇo daivāt | atharva daivo mṛtyo prādhvaṁsanāt | mṛtyuḥ prādhvaṁsanaḥ pradhvaṁsanāt | pradhvaṁsana ekarṣeḥ | ekarṣir vipracitteḥ | vipracittir vyaṣṭeḥ | vyaṣṭiḥ sanāroḥ | sanāruḥ sanātanāt | sanātanaḥ sanagāt | sanagaḥ parameṣṭhinaḥ | parameṣṭhī brahmaṇaḥ | brahma svayaṃbhu | brahmaṇe namaḥ

|| iti ṣaṣṭham brāhmaṇam ||

|| iti caturtho 'dhyāyaḥ ||

Now the lineage: Pautimāṣya from Gaupavana; Gaupavana from Pautimāṣya; Pautimāṣya from Gaupavana; Gaupavana from Kauśika; Kauśika from Kauṇḍinya; Kauṇḍinya from Śāṇḍilya; Śāṇḍilya from Kauśika and Gautama; Gautama from Āgniveśya; Āgniveśya from Gārgya; Gārgya from Gārgya; Gārgya from Gautama; Gautama from Saitava; Saitava from Pārāśaryāyaṇa; Pārāśaryāyaṇa from Gārgyāyaṇa; Gārgyāyaṇa from Uddālakāyana; Uddālakāyana from Jābālāyana; Jābālāyana from Mādhyandināyana; Mādhyandināyana from Saukarāyaṇa; Saukarāyaṇa from Kāṣāyaṇa; Kāṣāyaṇa from Sāyakāyana; Sāyakāyana from Kauśikāyani; Kauśikāyani from Ghṛtakauśika; Ghṛtakauśika from Pārāśaryāyaṇa; Pārāśaryāyaṇa from Pārāśarya; Pārāśarya from Jātūkarṇya; Jātūkarṇya from Āsurāyaṇa and Yāska; Āsurāyaṇa from Traivaṇi; Traivaṇi from Aupajandhani; Aupajandhani from Āsuri; Āsuri from Bhāradvāja; Bhāradvāja from Ātreya; Ātreya from Māṇṭi; Māṇṭi from Gautama; Gautama from Gautama; Gautama from Vātsya; Vātsya from Śāṇḍilya; Śāṇḍilya from Kaiśorya Kāpya; Kaiśorya Kāpya from Kumārahārita; Kumārahārita from Gālava; Gālava from Vidarbhīkauṇḍinya; Vidarbhīkauṇḍinya from Vatsanapāt Bābhrava; Vatsanapāt Bābhrava from Pathin Saubhara; Pathin Saubhara from Ayāsya Āṅgirasa; Ayāsya Āṅgirasa from Ābhūti Tvāṣṭra; Ābhūti Tvāṣṭra from Viśvarūpa Tvāṣṭra; Viśvarūpa Tvāṣṭra from the two Aśvins, the two Aśvins from Dadhyañc Ātharvaṇa; Dadhyañc Ātharvaṇa from Atharvan Daiva; Atharvan Daiva from Mṛtyu Prādhvaṃsana; Mṛtyu Prādhvaṃsana from Pradhvaṃsana; Pradhvaṃsana from Eka Ṛṣi; Eka Ṛṣi from Vipracitti; Vipracitti from Vyaṣṭi; Vyaṣṭi from Sanāru; Sanāru from Sanātana; Sanātana from Sanaga; Sanaga from Parameṣṭhin; Parameṣṭhin from *brahman*. *Brahman* is self-existent. Homage to *brahman*!

Notes

Introduction

1. By "literary-historical" my claim is simply from an academic perspective concerned with reconstructing one thread of Indian religious history and is *not* from any particular theological or sectarian perspective. It is a claim about the available data (textual and material) and the import that data have had in the academic construction of Indian religious history.

2. BĀU 6.5.

3. On the problems of isolating a single or multiple historical individuals, see Lindquist (2011b). The only works of which I am aware that take a larger view of Yājñavalkya in various contexts are E. R. Krishnamurti's devotional (and somewhat polemical) study (1984) and Jha's uncritical work (1988).

4. It is also ironic that *Bṛhadāraṇyaka Upaniṣad* chapters 3 and 4 (Kāṇva) have not been critically edited. However, a start has been made by Maue (BĀU 1; unpub. diss.; University of Geißen, 1976) and Perez-Coffie (BĀU 2; unpub. diss., Harvard, 1994).

5. Such a history could also include Yājñavalkya's appearance in the later material (particularly in Vedāntic texts, Jain texts, and certain late yoga texts ascribed to him) and even modern India (see, for example, Nakamura 1967, Wujastyk 2017, and Nadkarni 2001). The tradition of the White Yajurveda still persists in northern India and at least two socio-religious institutions are dedicated to Yājñavalkya in the south (in Madras and Pune). However, such a comprehensive history would require another volume and is beyond the scope of the present monograph.

6. For a general introduction to the Upaniṣads, see Olivelle (1998) and Lindquist (2016, 2020).

7. However, see Hiltebeitel (2001) who argues that the compositional period for this text is much shorter.

8. Irascibility, short-temperedness, or even questionable morals are certainly not unknown amongst the stories about sages. In their various

contexts, these can be seen as a critique of caste (see, for example, Sathaye 2015), a form of humor, an expression of anxiety connected with the rigid practices and social "otherness" of ascetics, or even all of these simultaneously. Yājñavalkya is, however, unique in that his sarcasm towards established orthodoxy comes to define his character and his rise to being considered the founding sage of a Vedic tradition.

9. Lindquist (2011b).

10. Black (2007, 63–100) is, to a degree, an exception in this regard, though he is also only concerned with the early Yājñavalkya. While I greatly appreciate his work on Yājñavalkya, our interpretations vary, often significantly (see especially chapter 2 and Lindquist 2008, 2009).

11. Davis (1999).

12. This is not a revolutionary claim in religious studies more broadly, but it remains underappreciated in the study of ancient South Asia (notable exceptions include Sathaye 2015 and Sullivan 1999).

Chapter 1

1. Also in the correlate *Jaiminīya Brāhmaṇa* passages, which are likely later (see below).

2. "It is remarkable that Yājñavalkya is never mentioned in any other text outside of the *Śatapatha Brāhmaṇa* except in the *Śāṅkhāyana Āraṇyaka*, where, however, both references are merely transcripts from the Śatapatha" (Macdonell and Keith 1912, 189). As we will see below, however, Macdonell and Keith are mistaken in stating that "there are no references to Yājñavalkya in books v–ix . . ." of ŚB.

3. See Lindquist (2011b) for the nefariously undefined use of the term *legend* in scholarship on Yājñavalkya.

4. As with Vidagdha Śākalya (the "clever" Śākalya) where his name stands in contrast to his ultimate lack of "cleverness" exemplified in BĀU 3.9.27. The name also indicates that this Śākalya is probably the same person who composed the *padapāṭha* of the R̥V (see chapter 2). Whether this is historically accurate or not is not my concern; what is significant is that the tradition viewed them as the same. Names may also secondarily indicate something about a character, such as Śaṅkara interpreting Yājñavalkya's student's name as indicating a characteristic of Yājñavalkya—"'Sāmaśravas' means one who learns how to chant the Sāman. Hence by implication Yājñavalkya is made out to be versed in all four Vedas" (BĀUBhā 3.1.2, trans., Madhavananda 1997, 287).

5. Difficulty interpreting names is not uncommon. While names in Sanskrit often have an obvious linguistic history, the ones that do not often

remain forever in obscurity. The principal reason is that while names may carry an obvious matronymic or patronymic relation, they are also relatively free of linguistic restraints and often rely on the aesthetic or taste of the parent that is not linguistically analyzable. My thanks to Michael Witzel and Stephanie Jamison who corresponded separately with me regarding the issue of names.

6. For an accessible account of Vedic Hinduism and *yajña*, see Jamison and Witzel (2003).

7. "Vṛddhi-Bildung eines mit *yajña-* zusammengesetzten Namen-Kompositums" (Mayrhofer 1986, 410).

8. Based on the r/l variation, Witzel (2003, n113) has suggested that "the name as such probably is a popular nickname." As for Yājñavalkya's family name, Vājasaneya, Witzel suggests that this name is based on older Brahmanical names, such as Bharadvāja.

9. "Thus said Yājñavalkya, the son of *Yajñavalka,* lit. the expounder of a sacrifice, i.e., the son of Devarāta. Or it may mean a descendant of Hiraṇyagarbha (who is the expounder)"(trans. Madhavananda 1997, 70). Hiraṇyagarbha here may be an overinterpretation as the original simply reads *brahmaṇa vāptyam,* "descendant of *brahman*."

10. See J. S. Helfer's entry on Yājñavalkya in Crim (1989, 810), among others.

11. There are any number of good summaries of the Vedic texts, their interrelations, and the development of various liturgical schools. The reader is referred to Gonda (1975/1977), Jamison and Witzel (2003), Renou (1965), Santucci (1976), and Witzel (1997).

12. For example, the *Bṛhadāraṇyaka Upaniṣad* ("The Great Forest Upaniṣad") is titled both as an Āraṇyaka and an Upaniṣad and is the concluding section (book 14) of the ŚBM. Or, for example, the Taittirīya of the Black YV is a supplement of the *Taittirīya Brāhmaṇa* with books 7–9 forming the Upaniṣad. Further, certain *śākhās* do not have particular genres of texts at all: the Sāmaveda and Atharvaveda, for example, do not have Āraṇyaka texts attached to their respective corpora. The situation for the whole of the Vedic corpus is far more complex than can be described here (see note 6 above).

13. Also known as the *Vājasaneya Saṃhitā* (VS).

14. This derision is largely one-sided. The Brahmins of the White YV/ŚB apparently had more reason to openly ridicule or critique the established order of the western region in an effort to establish themselves.

15. There is also a secondary Brāhmaṇa, the *Taittirīya Brāhmaṇa,* which consists mainly of Brāhmaṇa-style text with some *mantras* (Jamison and Witzel 2003).

16. A critical edition of the *Śatapatha Brāhmaṇa* in the Mādhyandina recension was made by Weber ([1855] 1997) and was translated by Eggeling in five volumes ([1882–1900] 1993–1994). Caland ([1926] 1998) edited the books

of ŚBK up to book 7 ≈ ŚBM 5. An edition and translation of ŚBK based on Caland was produced by C. R. Swaminathan, (1994–2015).

17. cf. Bronkhorst (2007) on the cultural area of greater Magadha.

18. Compare the numerous maps and charts found throughout Witzel (1989). For a more accessible summary, see Witzel (1997, 314ff.). For a simplified map of the literary production, see Witzel (1987a, 212). For the Upaniṣads, see Olivelle (trans., 1998, 14).

19. This is contrary to Ruben (1947) who argues for precise dates of various important early thinkers. While creative and interesting, such dating is simply conjecture.

20. For a differing opinion which suggests that the final redaction of the BĀU may date to the Gupta period, see Reinvang (2000). Late dating of books 11–13 of the ŚB has also been suggested by Bronkhorst (2000, esp. 2007). While both of these arguments are intriguing, I do not find them necessarily convincing (see Lindquist 2011b and Wynne 2011).

21. However, see Bronkhorst (2007).

22. Witzel (1987a and 1997).

23. For an expansion of this argument, see Lindquist (2011b).

24. Certain personality traits of Yājñavalkya, particularly his sarcastic wit, are expanded upon in the later Purāṇas, a more appropriate genre for such elaboration. Also, in such texts as the *Jīvanmuktiviveka* (for example, 2.9), Yājñavalkya's arrogance is discussed as a hindrance towards his liberation (see Gooding 2002: 46–47, 132, and esp. 159–164).

25. The Kāṇva concludes *íti hovāca* to mark the end of Yājñavalkya's speech.

26. Following Schrapel (1970. 25).

27. See Witzel (2003) on the compound.

28. "Yājñavalkya, however, said, 'Let him place it within the altar!' thus he said. 'Let it be so as it has been prescribed for the wife,' thus (thinking) let him place it, whether or not she consort with other men" (Eggeling [1882–1900] 1993. 1: 76, n2).

29. Eggeling, I think, mistakenly puts a quotation mark here.

30. Or perhaps, "He shuts /the fire/ out from the view on the eastern side" (Fišer 1984, 68).

31. Here the concealing is done by means of a small wooden screen.

32. Eggeling ignores the desiderative, as pointed out by Fišer (1984) and Witzel (2003).

33. The Sanskrit is truncated, but the meaning seems clear.

34. Fišer suggests that √*ghas*, when not used for human females, is used primarily with divine beings (1984, 69).

35. This is the first passage in M where "Yājñavalkya" is at the end, perhaps suggesting a latter addition.

36. There are no significant variations in K for our purposes.

37. Or "stepping outside" (Eggeling).

38. In both recensions, "the kingdom will fall into confusion," *mohiṣyáti* [K *mohiṣyátīdáṃ*] *rāṣṭram íti.*

39. M *daśa kŕtvaḥ paryāvárteta,* K *daśakŕtvaḥ púnaḥ punaḥ paryāvárteta.*

40. The variant phrasing could be a dialectical preference.

41. Or "the goddess earth."

42. Eggeling ([1882–1900] 1994, 26: 2) notes the variation, but does not discuss it.

43. *nir √vadh* (K)

44. The Sanskrit here is confusing. Eggeling ([1882–1900] 1994, 26:11) translates: "Such a one indeed would be likely to be born (again) as a strange being, (as one of whom there is) evil report, such as 'he has expelled an embryo from a woman,' 'he has committed a sin . . .'" In this reading, the sin is equivalent to that of causing an abortion; my reading—to which I am not committed—suggests the sin is meted out on one's offspring. In either case, "destruction of everything" here appears to be equivalent to destroying one's lineage.

45. Note, however, that meat-eating—even of beef—wasn't uncommon in the ancient period (Jha 2002).

46. I wish to thank Joel Brereton (personal communication) for pointing out the possibility of this clever pun.

47. Following Eggeling ([1882–1900] 1994, 26:197).

48. Eggeling ([1882–1900] 1994, 26: 279–280n3) suggests that *nò svid* might be read separately as its own clause and be translated "By no means! for deities we should draw them . . ." However, this seems unlikely given that Yājñavalkya, in both recensions, simply is said to contemplate/consider the idea and such forceful rhetoric would be out of place.

49. Fišer (1984,73) suggests that this passage "criticized" Yājñavalkya. That interpretation, however, is less than apparent.

50. Swaminathan's translation (2000 III:383), however, seems to misinterpret this passage by overlooking the final *íti,* which indicates the whole passage is attributed to Yājñavalkya in K as well.

51. Passage 3.1.3.10: This passage is "prideful" but may also be read as "sarcastic." Passage 1.9.2.12 in Kāṇva omits Yājñavalkya's name.

52. I.e., such as *ávīrya* and *devā́n vásato* in ŚBM 1.1.1.9 ≈ ŚBK 2.1.1.7 or, in the case of other's practices, that it is the *yajamāna* who requests rewards from the gods (ŚBM 1.3.1.26 ≈ ŚBK 2.2.4.19), etc.

53. *katháṃ nv eṣā́m átraivá śraddhā́ bhavatī́ti*

54. Swaminathan seems to confuse the entire passage, making Yājñavalkya the questioner of Janaka (perhaps influenced by the other episode where Yājñavalkya is questioned by Janaka about the *agnihotra*). While this

interpretation is possible given the lack of expressed subjects (the questions and answers are simply marked with *íti* or *íti hovāca*), it forces us to ignore the *íti* immediately after the answers and also rather unnaturally to read the last question *and* the answer as attributed to Yājñavalkya (see his translation, 1997, 243).

55. JB: *u hūyata iva* (Oertel 1926, 329 wants to amend to *ahūyataiva*, following ŚB).

56. JB reads: *taṃ hovāca vethāgnihotraṃ yājñavalkya namas te 'stu sahasraṃ bhagavo dadma iti* | K reads: *sá hovāca námas te 'stu yājñavalkya vétthāgnihotráṁ sahásraṃ dadāmī́ti* |

57. ŚBK and JB: "one thousand" (*sahásra*) unexpressed objects, but obviously cows.

58. I prefer "cow trope" instead of "theme" as the latter suggests the subject of the discourse or a unifying idea. The "giving of cows" does not add substantively to the dialogue (it generally means "you are right, go on . . ."). It is, as Hock also mentions, largely a discourse marker.

59. Payment is apparently made *only* after the teaching (see BĀU 4).

60. Caland points to the exception of the use of *sahaśram* at the end as a Kānva expression (ed. [1926] 1998, 102). The reader is also referred to Caland's article (1915, in Dutch) cited by Bodewitz (trans., 1973, 62).

61. Note that K even includes an explanation of the etymology: *satyena hīme lokā ājityāḥ*.

62. In the BĀU, it is explicit (6.3.7, *vājasaneyāya yājñavalkyāya*; 6.3.8, *vājasaneyo yājñavalkyaḥ*; 6.5.6, *vājasaneyena yājñavalkyena*).

63. Note that while the principle of *lectio difficilior* (giving primacy to the more difficult reading) must be considered first, this principle works best with individual words or phrasing, and quite the opposite may be the case with larger text units.

64. "Satisfies" here must refer to the offerings being "replete" or perhaps "refreshed."

65. . . . *ayasthūṇagr̥hapatīnāṃ vai śaulbāyano 'dhvaryur āsa* |

66. According to Witzel (1997, 308), Gotama is a R̥gvedic poet.

67. This follows Fišer's suggestion (1984, 71–72) of reading the hapax *aṅgajit* as *aṅgavit*. However, *aṅgajit* could mean "one who has conquered their limbs" in the sense of "composed" or "virtuous." Thus Yājñavalkya would be said to know more than other, virtuous Brahmins.

68. Both recensions are in near perfect agreement.

69. Śvetaketu, son of Uddālaka Āruṇi, appears also in BĀU 6.2.1, *Chāndogya Upaniṣad* 5.3.1–6 and 6.1–16, *Kauṣītaki Upaniṣad* 1.1.

70. Perhaps the same Sātyayajña (M)/Sātyayajñi (K) encountered in ŚBM 3.1.1.4–5 ≈ ŚBK 4.1.1.3–4?

71. The Brahmins call Janaka a *rājanyabandhu*, lit. "connected to royalty." This phrasing is used as an insult, meaning something akin to "a royal person in name only." Here, however, there is also a double meaning suggesting an interstitial *varṇa* role, that because of his knowledge of the *agnihotra*, he is also like a Brahmin. This suggests a foreshadowing of the conclusion, where Janaka is said to "be a Brahmin."

72. This logical play is similar to what we saw above with eating the "not-eaten" food (ŚBM 1.1.1.9 ≈ ŚBK 2.1.1.7).

73. Bodewitz (trans., 1973, 215ff.) puts forth a number of reasons that we should not overestimate the theme of the *kṣatriya* teaching a Brahmin more generally. Most importantly, the doctrines that the *kṣatriya*s teach are not as new or as secret as they are portrayed (see chapter 5).

74. See in chapter 2 for a discussion regarding gender and knowledge possession.

75. *sa no 'tivadann iva manyate*

76. JB *taṃ hocus tvaṃ nu no brahmiṣṭho 'sī3 iti* | *sa hovāca namo vo brahmiṣṭhāyāstu* | *gokāmā eva vayaṃ sma iti* |

77. The JB varies in line order from the ŚB (and only slightly in content). For example, the discussion of Indra and Prajāpati comes after the discussion of three or two gods. Also, the "one and one half deity" is omitted in JB.

78. See chapter 2 for why this interpretation in that context is probably incorrect.

79. The "one and one half deity" presents something of an anomaly in this passage. The enumeration of gods goes from "three and three hundred and three and three thousand" to thirty-three, three, two, one and a half and, finally, to one. All of them, with the exception of one and a half, are whole numbers. Each are then listed and described, but "one and a half" is answered indirectly without an expressed subject ("What is the one and a half?" "The one that wafts [i.e., the wind])." I think, though, this interstitial positioning is intentional for two reasons: First, it indicates that while the enumeration laid out previously is based on a reduction and repetition of threes, that reduction can go further: to two and then even to fractions. This further reduction, however, can only continue up to a point where it must stop, i.e., at one. Upon reaching the one, no further reduction is possible, and hence Śākalya is told he is "asking beyond" and has sealed his fate. "One and a half" is a logical extension—even a narrative exclamation point—of the reduction that speeds up before it stops (as opposed to the preceding whole numbers) and thus highlights that the one deity is the ultimate, the irreducible.

The second reason is that we have a hierarchy of breaths (*prāṇa*) between the two deities and the one deity. The two deities are *prāṇa* and food, referring to those concrete things which keep people alive, whereas breath (*prāṇa*) as the "one deity" appears to refer to an underlying life principle in the universe, similar to *brahman* elsewhere. What lies between two such "movements of air?" The air in the atmosphere, i.e., the wind. The "one and one half" as "the one that blows" then creates an interstitial "breath" that is both in between numerically *and* in-between in the world. The term for wind that is implied cannot be said for certain, but wind as *antarikṣa* (literally, the "space between" heaven and earth—also a tripartite division!) must have been resonant with a hearing audience.

80. ŚBK and JB offer no significant variations for our purposes and are not dealt with separately here.

81. JB *vājasaneyo.*

82. JB *avṛttyā hi tam.*

83. JB *daṇḍam eva labdhvā tenaināṃ.*

84. Of course, it is difficult to say whether these were recited as a unit. The chapter division, along with the thematic links, however, suggests that they are to be considered as a unit.

85. Especially in the BĀU narrative, the claim to knowledge on Śākalya's part is a claim to immortality. The falsity of this claim is proven in his graphic death (see Lindquist 2011a).

Chapter 2

1. Renou (1948, 76) mentions that the name Yājñavalkya occurs no less than 108 times in the BĀU. This should not, however, be confused with the number of stories attributed to him nor the general sacred nature of the number 108 in the Hindu tradition. Renou is simply referring to the number of times that the name Yājñavalkya appears.

2. ŚBM and ŚBK are overwhelmingly similar in this regard, clustering together longer narratives in a single book. One passage that straddles "narrative" and "pronouncement" as I have used them is ŚBM 11.3.1.2–4. This passage is a series of questions, not unlike the longer narratives in form, but it is markedly shorter in length. This is found outside of book 13 in ŚBK (3.1.4.3–4).

3. As Olivelle notes: "Of the three, the first two sections exhibit greater internal consistency, while the third, which even the native tradition regards as supplementary, consists of disparate and often unconnected fragments" (trans., 1998, 29).

4. However, for an alternate dating, see Bronkhorst (2007).

5. For simplicity's sake, citations for BĀU are based on the K recension unless otherwise indicated. The reader is referred to Olivelle's concordance of passages (trans., 1998, 33–35) for a complete tabulation.

6. This passage is dealt with separately in the section on gender in the BĀU in this chapter.

7. My translation follows the K recension (given fully in the appendix). The variations in M are often minimal but are listed in the notes. Accent is here included following Mau (1976), but not in BĀU 3–6 as there is no critical edition of these chapters.

8. variant in Mau (trans., 1976) *-bṛ̥gaḷ̥am iva, -vṛ̥galam iva.*

9. Possibly plural here as the genealogy of 6.5 does not coincide in other regards to this passage.

10. M *cūḍa.*

11. Though he is called "Vājasaneya" a few times in the JB (see previous chapter), a text which probably postdates this text.

12. The metaphoric meaning here seems to be that even if a teacher applies (teaches) knowledge (the "mixture") onto a (particularly dull?) student (the "dried up stump"), the student and the lineage would flourish.

13. M varies considerably, but not for our purposes. See Olivelle (trans., 1998) for these variations.

14. For a textual rationale for the inclusion of matronymics, see Lindquist (2011c).

15. The genealogies of BĀU are discussed by Bronkhorst (2007) and Lindquist (2011c).

16. Roebuck (trans., 2000, 127) translates "were taught by Vājasaneya Yājñavalkya." This is certainly a possible translation of *ā* + *√khyā,* but it seems to miss the sense of the passage. We are told earlier in the genealogy that Yājñavalkya taught Āsuri, and translating as Roebuck does would make this passage appear redundant. Because of this and in light of how the later tradition views this passage (that Yājñavalkya literally received the White Yajus from the Sun), I translate differently.

17. Fišer and Bronkhorst take *hagiography* to mean simply "fiction." When I refer to their work, this is the sense I intend as well. When I myself refer to hagiography, I am referring to a narrative biographical form that is created after the death of a famous religious personage, one which may embellish the life of the individual in nonhistorical ways, but may also contain historical truths.

18. It could, for example, be the case that Yājñavalkya's family/favorite deity was the Sun. Given that he is taken as sole authority for the tradition here, it would be quite natural (even for him!) to associate his status as connected to a preferred deity.

19. On characters in Upaniṣadic narrative more broadly, see Lindquist (2018b).

20. In this case, the ring is both formal and thematic. "The *atimokṣas* and their equivalents are an ascent after death to an immortal world; the *grahas*

and *atigrahas* are a descent into life and into the perception of this world. Thus, formal correspondence, created by verbal repetition (the preverb *ati*) and by the proximity of the two passages, leads to the recognition of their contrasting elements and themes" (Brereton 1997, 8).

21. This chart should be seen as supplementary to Brereton's chart and not an attempt to supersede it. See also Lindquist (2011a) for further discussion, albeit with a different focus. Within the chart, please note: at (2) (B.1), 3.4 and 3.5 are transposed in M. In these two passages, *brahman* probably means "the formulation of truth" about "the self within all," rather than that self being equated with *brahman*. The *brahman* as "foundation" occurs first in 3.6.

22. The Gārgī passage (3.6) is not split but consists of a series of reductive questions. As Brereton (1997) has pointed out, this passage follows the ascent to heaven.

23. C.3 is more concerned with the latter foundational element, the immortal (*amr̥taḥ*), but the questions of the "string of the body" is related to the former theme.

24. The Parikṣitas are a famed Kuru family whose lineage disappeared in the distant past.

25. M *yatra tatra* for *tad yatra.*

26. This suggests that the imperishable being described is *brahman*, the foundational truth of everything.

27. Though not addressing this doubling, see Black (2007, 74ff.) on parallel tactics employed in debate.

28. For a detailed discussion of head-shattering in this episode, see Lindquist (2011a).

29. For a more detailed elaboration of this concluding structure and the nature of head-shattering, see Lindquist (2011a).

30. Previously published as Lindquist (2004), though with minor corrections here.

31. *atha hovāca brāhmaṇā bhagavanto yo vaḥ kāmayate sa mā pr̥cchatu | sarve vā mā pr̥cchata | yo vaḥ kāmayate taṃ vaḥ pr̥cchāmi sarvān vā vaḥ pr̥cchāmīti |*

32. BĀUK 3.9.27

33. I do not wish to privilege an "original" as superior to the received texts. In fact, much of this work has been concerned with the Yājñavalkyakāṇḍa as it is received. My point here, though, is that scholars have dismissed traditional commentaries on this riddle, yet the tradition, though interpretively manipulating the text in rather unconvincing ways, has by and large retained the proper meaning. A reconstruction of the original and the ways in which this riddle evolved elucidates this.

34. Notes for the BĀUK 3.9.28: (1): Numbering is my own to facilitate the argument below. (5d): Olivelle (trans., 1998) and Roebuck (trans., 2000) read the text as containing a *sandhi*, where there is a negative prefix

a- attached to *pretya,* and the translation is "before/without having died" (as Sanskrit manuscripts do not separate words, this is a possible interpretation). I, however, follow the traditional reading, particularly because the *sandhi* they suggest for K is not possible in M (see below). (7a): The translation of this line is discussed below. (8c): It is not entirely clear whether this line is part of the verses or not. Though it consists of eight beats, it is two *pādas* short of a full verse.

35. On the parts of the body, see Jamison (1986, 167–78).

36. Though the notion of a son being the "immortality" of a man may have older origins, it persists (particularly as a son is required for carrying out the *śrāddha* rites) and is often intertwined or conflated with the notion that a man's immortality can only occur in his final death (see Doniger O'Flaherty [1983, 1ff.]; also Knipe [1977, 111ff.] on death/birth rites and their interrelation).

37. (6a) *yat samūlam āvr̥heyur*
(6b) *vr̥kṣaṃ na punar ābhavet* |
(6c) *martyaḥ svin mr̥tyunā vr̥kṇaḥ*
(6d) *kasmān mūlāt prarohati* ||

38. *puṇyo vai puṇyena karmaṇā bhavati pāpaḥ pāpeneti.* Regarding the development of an "ethics" of action and its reward, see Tull (1989).

39. None of this is to say that texts, even those edited, commented on, and traditionally received cannot contradict themselves directly. Rather, I do argue that if there is an explanatorily compelling alternative that avoids direct contradiction, it should be considered first.

40. It is common that a riddle contains, most often in a latent form, its own answer. It is this form that often gives a riddle rhetorical power—the answer is simple, it appears obvious after the fact, and it is aesthetically pleasing. Here, though, the answer would seem too apparent, and the Brahmins would have been rather daft not to understand it and rise to Yājñavalkya's challenge.

41. Brereton (1997) analyzes M, but this passage was not the focus of his inquiry.

42. "Wer einmal geboren wurde, wird nicht (wieder) geboren" (Horsch 1966,159).

43. The verbal sense of the present or the progressive are both included in the present indicative form (as in many other Indo-European languages), and the interpretive line is fluid.

44. I am also here suggesting that the M literary tradition retained the more correct version of the text.

45. *parṇāni lomāni* for *lomāni parṇāni; ātunnāt* for *ātr̥ṇṇāt.*

46. *u* for *iva.*

47. *anyataḥ* for *añjasā.*

48. *udvr̥heyur* for *āvr̥heyur*—the meaning is essentially the same.

49. *rateḥ dātuḥ* for *ratiḥ dātuḥ*—the former is the grammatically proper form.

50. Note that this interpretation is consonant with Hock's (2002) reading of Vasudeva. However, for reasons external to the commentary of why this interpretation appears correct, see below in this chapter.

51. cf. R̥V 1.165.9.

52. The word *eva* in classical Sanskrit has taken over the function of the Vedic *id* (see Böhtlingk and Roth 1990, 1:1099) and is used "especially in strengthening an antithesis" (Monier-Williams 1999, 165).

53. The passive form could also imply an unexpressed instrumental agent, again suggesting that birth and rebirth does happen at the hand of some principle.

54. Underlined words are ablative:

4ab *yad vr̥kṣo vr̥kṇo rohati mūlān navataraḥ punaḥ*
4cd *martyaḥ svin mr̥tyunā vr̥kṇaḥ kasmāt mūlāt prarohati*
5ab *retasa iti mā vocata jīvatas tat prajāyate*
5cd *jāta eva na jāyate ko nv enaṃ janayet punaḥ*
6ab *dhānāruha u vai vr̥kṣo 'nyataḥ pretya sambhavaḥ*

55. Śaṅkara, to avoid the interpretive difficulty of *iva*, claims that the particle is "without meaning" here (*anarthaka*). See note 58.

56. For a discussion of these two, see the conclusion of this chapter.

57. That this is a later change may be supported by the fact that it breaks the meter.

58. *ivaśabdo 'narthakaḥ* (*Īśādidaśopaniṣadaḥ* 1992, 848).

59. Note here that Śaṅkara himself does not see the final lines as part of the poem (see trans., Madhavananda 1997, 393).

60. Olivelle (trans., 1998, 100–101, also n513) takes *aupaniṣad* as "that person providing the hidden connection" and notes that traditionally it is taken as "the person taught in the Upaniṣads." Roebuck (trans., 2000, 69n144) takes it as the connecting person between the persons mentioned in 10–17 of this section and translates as "the person of the secret teaching." I am inclined to understand it not as "that person providing the hidden connection" but as "that person who is the hidden connection itself."

61. *etāny aṣṭāv āyatanāny aṣṭau lokā aṣṭau devā aṣṭau puruṣāḥ | sa yas tān puruṣān niruhya pratyuhyāty akrāmat taṃ tvaupaniṣadaṃ puruṣaṃ pr̥cchāmi | taṃ cen me na vivakṣyasi mūrdhā te vipatiṣyatīti |*

62. Note that Śākalya's own death is directly connected to the theme of the text—death and immortality (Lindquist 2011a).

63. This is to say that the principle itself transcends this world and mankind.

64. "Light is the mind" is left out of the list of 3.9.26 perhaps because it is the same throughout all of 3.9.10–17 or perhaps suggesting that it was a

later addition. This section above is also demarcated by Yājñavalkya's interjection that the Brahmins have been using Śākalya (3.9.18).

65. In ŚB 11.6.3 *prāṇa* also probably refers to the fundamental principle of existence, both microcosmically (as in the answer of "food and breath") and macrocosmically in Yājñavalkya's final answer which leads to the "head shattering" threat.

66. This interpretation is different from Hock (2002) who sees the Yājñavalkyakāṇḍa as *advaitic*. I am inclined to the opinion that, while there is enough textual ambiguity in BĀU 3–4 to allow for such an interpretation in the later commentarial tradition, it is not original to the text.

67. There are two major points of difference between Hock's understanding of the text and my own. The first is mentioned in the note above. Second, Hock argues for "literary rings" outside of BĀU 3–4. He suggests that BĀU 2.1 is a "prelude" to the discussion of deep sleep in BĀU 4. He also sees the initial Maitreyī dialogue (2.4) as forming a ring with the elaborated version of the same narrative at 4.5. This, however, goes against the standard definition of literary ring, that is, a verbal or thematic echo binding a *single* narrative. While 2.1 and 2.4 are thematically connected to the Yājñavalkyakāṇḍa, there is no reason to view them as rings binding one larger narrative (particularly, as Hock himself notes, there is unrelated material in between). The more likely scenario is that both Maitreyī episodes were already canonized in their respective sections before chapters 1–2 and 3–4 were combined.

68. Notes for Table 2.5: (4.1) "feet": This appears to refer to a four-footed animal (i.e., a sacrificial animal) as the model of stability; (4.2) I think Hock (2002, 280) is right that this passage marks a shift towards "more esoteric discussion"; (4.2) "Janaka offers himself and his kingdom to Yājñavalkya": Note the pun that Yājñavalkya teaches Janaka about the self (in a sense, giving Janaka's own "self" to him by revelation), while Janaka offers himself in return; (4.3–4) I follow Olivelle (trans., 1998, 515) in reading *sa mene na vadiṣye* ("I will not tell him"), rather than *sam enena vadiṣye* ("I will converse with him"). This is supported by Saṅkara's reading of the text as well as manuscript evidence. On accent, see Weber (trans., 1997, 1183), Edgerton (1965, 153n2); and Hanefeld (1976, 21n1).

69. It is not clear exactly what this phrase means (one can assume it is hyperbole), but it does serve as the climax to this particular passage. Given that Janaka wishes *abhaya* for Yājñavalkya, who has given it to him, we can assume that the *abhaya* Yājñavalkya receives is because all his material needs have been met.

70. This theme is reinforced by thematic reminders in the text, such as in 3.2.13 where Yājñavalkya takes Ārtabhāga away privately to discuss *karma* and also in 3.6 where Gārgī is silenced for inquiring too far.

71. For some examples of such etiquette, see Black (2007).

72. BĀU 3.1 and 3.2 may be exceptions because the interlocutors' questions are more elaborate and shift topic. However, while these two may or may not be similar in form to the ŚB proclamations, they are the most thematically linked to those proclamations (e.g., discussing the priests and the sacrifice).

73. This further supports that BĀU 3.9 is modeled on the ŚB version in both form and content.

74. M *yatraitad* for *yad dhy etad*.

75. *ahallika* is of uncertain origin. Fišer (1984) has suggested it may be an ancient Indian curse word, hence its rarity in texts where such terms are often not appropriate. But see Jamison (1996) on cursing during the *aśvamedha*.

76. Roebuck takes a translation such as mine to be "a little forced" (trans., 2000, 71n147). However, I see nothing in the syntax that supports her position. Rather, it appears that both are proper renderings of the Sanskrit. I am, however, trying to reconcile it with the larger meaning of the passage.

77. See Olivelle (1998).

78. Similar to "this a cow and this a horse" which was mentioned earlier.

79. Previously published as Lindquist (2008). After a draft of this section was written and an abbreviated version was presented at the American Oriental Society Annual Meeting in 2003, a separate treatment of women in the *Bṛhadāraṇyaka* was published by Black (2007, 148–66). When necessary, overlap or disagreements are noted.

80. Exceptions, to greater or lesser degrees, are Findly (1985), Witzel (1987b), and Black (2007).

81. For a list of many, often rather extreme interpretations, see Findly (1985).

82. Note here that my argument is *not* against Hindu philosophical or theological interpretations of this text, which is its own domain and has its own criteria, but is rather against academic historical interpretations (as well as the dismissal of the narrative elements by philosophers) of one piece of literature.

83. That certain women spoke and/or composed in rarified, predominantly male arenas is not completely unheard of in older sources, but it is quite rare: Lopāmudrā along with her husband, Agastya, is said to have composed ṚV 1.179; Ghoṣā, daughter of Kakṣīvat, is said to have composed two long hymns (ṚV 10.39, 40); Viśvavārā composed ṚV 5.28, and Apālā, ṚV 8.91. Regarding women's role in the sacrifice itself, the most complete and even-handed account is Jamison (1996).

84. Such as the mother of Satyakāma Jābāla, Jabālā (CU 4.4), one of whose functions is to introduce the theme of lineage as a criterion for Vedic study (Lindquist 2018b).

85. Bold speech or action on the part of women is a literary theme that can be found in the earliest literature—e.g., ṚV 10.10 where Yamī pleads with

her brother to have sexual relations; R̥V 1.179 where Lopamudrā convinces her husband to break off his asceticism (see Patton 1996); and also in a reversal of the pattern, R̥V 10.95 where Urvaśī spurns her husband's advances. Jamison (1996, 15–17) suggests that the theme of woman as "independent agent" is related to conflicting male religious goals (asceticism and procreation) which can be seen in these and later narratives.

86. There is evidence of women speaking in a *brahmodya* such as the Aśvamedha (ŚB 13.5.2.1ff, *Taittirīya Saṃhitā* 7.4.19ff.), but we know that speech is ritually scripted and probably did not vary in repeated performance. Given the rather vulgar nature of that particular discourse, it may have originally been a means of psychologically offsetting the apparent distaste for the queen's copulation with the horse. See Jamison's translation (1996, 65ff.); regarding the ritual logic of the copulation see Lindquist (2003). In the BĀU, it is unclear whether or how any dialogue was ritually performed in a scripted manner.

87. "There will be no forgotten diaries unearthed in the attic, no cache of letters that can serve as a private and direct channel into women's experience" (Jamison 1996, 8). Of course, there is no such thing as "unmediated" speech, but what is important here is the matter of degree of mediation.

88. For example, see Patton (1996) and Doniger (2000).

89. Albeit contrived in its editorial phases; see Olivelle (trans., 1998, 29–30).

90. It should be pointed out that I do not wish to essentialize a "male" voice either, but the concern of this section is to deal directly with what has been the concern of secondary scholarship—the role of women in this text. Certainly, a similar study could be done on male gendered discourse, but the necessary points of comparison with other Upaniṣads, Brāhmaṇas, etc. would take us too far from our subject.

91. See Witzel (1987b).

92. However, Gārgī and Maitreyī attain an important place within the tradition relatively early: see *Aśvalāyana Gr̥hyasūtra* 3.4.4 which lists them with a female *r̥ṣi*, Prātitheyī, to whom daily tribute is paid.

93. See also its variant in *Kauṣītaki Upaniṣad* (KṣU) 4.1. This story is interesting as it inverts the normative narrative structure of the Yājñavalkya-Janaka tales (as also does ŚB 11.6.2.5–10, where Yājñavalkya learns about the *agnihotra* from Janaka). King Ajātaśatru is the impatient and irreverent Kṣatriya teacher, while Dr̥pta Bālāki is the passive Brahmin student.

94. Witzel (1987b, 403) points out that a Gārga appears at *Kāṭhaka Saṃhitā* 13.12 with other ritualists, suggesting a western origin of the school. See also (1987b, 401n82) on *-i-putra* matronymics.

95. There is no male relative of a Gārgī in the corresponding M lineage.

96. 6.4.29. The corresponding K lineage has no reference to a Gārgī.

97. This suggests that the lists may be in the form of student seniority, as there is no mention of Uddālaka being the teacher of Yājñavalkya when he is defeated by him (BĀU 3.7). Uddālaka may simply be a senior student of the Black Yajurveda. Later tradition holds Vaiśaṁpāyana of the Black Yajurveda to be Yājñavalkya's teacher.

98. That Gārgī had some seniority is perhaps indicated by the placement of her dialogues (see below).

99. Note that the majority of the final lists in both M and K use matronymics. However, the emphasis, like the other lists, appears to be on the "sons" and not on the "mothers." It is also interesting to note that in BĀUK 4.6.1 Gārgī/Gārgya is associated with Uddālaka's (i.e., Gautama's) family and that Gārgī both precedes (3.6) and follows Uddālaka's questioning (3.8) in our text. It seems possible that K viewed Gārgī as interconnected with Uddālaka's family while M viewed her as interconnected with Pārāśarīkauṇḍinī's family. See Lindqusit (2011c) on matronymics.

100. cf. Deussen (1995, 389ff.) for a not particularly successful attempt to analyze these genealogies.

101. I think Deussen (1995, 461–62) must be wrong in thinking that Gārgī's questions are fundamentally the same in both episodes (see below on the nature of the questions and how these episodes function in the text).

102. 3.4 and 3.5 are transposed in M.

103. M omits.

104. M *ākāśa eva.*

105. Translation following Rau's work on weaving in Vedic India (1970, 17).

106. The order in M is *ākāśa, antarikṣaloka, dyaurloka, ādityaloka, candraloka, nakṣatraloka, devaloka, gandharvaloka, prajāpatiloka,* and *brahmaloka.*

107. M omits.

108. M omits.

109. Böhtlingk (trans., 1889) *vipaptat.*

110. M *anatipraśnyā vai devatā atipr̥cchasi.*

111. Noted earlier, see Findly (1985).

112. Eggeling (trans., 1993–94, 5:117n2) takes the deity that is asked beyond in ŚBM 11.6.3.11 as Prajāpati and interprets similarly here. However, while that may be the case in 11.6.3.11 (which is not particularly clear; it is more likely *prāṇa* that is asked beyond. cf. *Taittirīya Brāhmaṇa* 3.10.9.5, *Praśna Upaniṣad* 3.2), it seems unlikely the case here: (1) Prajāpati is far more important in the Brāhmaṇas and plays a very minor role in Yājñavalkya's teachings (in fact, Prajāpati plays a larger role in Śākalya's teaching on the "heart"); (2) Gārgī is stopped from going "beyond the deity" (and the warning would have most appropriately come after her asking on what the worlds of Prajāpati

are woven if Prajāpati was the concern); and (3) Śākalya goes far "beyond Prajāpati" in 3.9 before the threat is given.

113. cf. CU 7.15.4, 7.16.1. Note, however, that this is not the case in PrU 3.2 (*ati praśnān pṛcchasi*), where *ati √praś* does seem to mean "to ask too many questions." However, the context is quite different there and could be translated in a more value neutral fashion as "You are asking questions beyond [decorum?]." Such a translation would fit the context of what follows (*brahmiṣṭo 'sīti tasmād te ahaṃ bravīmi*—"But you are a learned Brahmin, therefore I will answer you").

114. *yad idaṃ kurupañcālānāṃ brāhmaṇān atyavādīḥ kiṃ brahma vidvān iti.*

115. This appears to agree with Witzel (1987b: 364 n. 5).

116. Śaṅkara sees Gārgī as violating the rules of inquiry by asking an inferential question: asking about a deity that can only be learned of through private instruction. In this interpretation, Gārgī is trying to get knowledge of something that she does not possess in an inappropriate setting. This is similar to Insler's interpretation (1989–90, 99) who suggests Gārgī is asking beyond her own knowledge. This may be, but I am still inclined to see Gārgī as asking beyond knowledge as a whole.

117. Śaṅkara also notes a shift in topic. Findly (1985) sees Gārgī as introducing more heterodox ideas into the debate, but I see no reason why her questions and Yājñavalkya's subsequent answers are heterodox in any fashion, particularly in comparison with the precedents found in the *brāhmaṇa* literature.

118. Death, however, is a connected theme throughout the text and binds it into a cohesive narrative (Lindquist 2011a).

119. Witzel (1987b) has suggested that "head shattering" is often an automatic consequence of asking beyond one's knowledge. In this case, however, Yājñavalkya warns of the consequence even though the question has already been asked and yet the outcome is still averted.

120. The Sanskrit is not included here due to the size of the passage; see appendix.

121. I think "without mouth" here means without an aperture that could allow something in or out. This is paired with "without measure" indicating that the imperishable cannot be determined by either a point of entry or its size, two means of showing its distinctness. Cf. Olivelle's translation (1998, 91).

122. This is a clear foreshadowing of Śākalya's fate.

123. Such antagonism in *brahmodya* settings is found even in the ṚV (Thompson, 1997), such as ṚV 10.108 where "questions" are "arrows." It is significant, however, that this antagonistic rhetoric is in the speech of a woman in our context and that it is more forceful than any others' discourses so far.

124. See Lindquist 2018b.

125. Of course, this theme can be traced back to the ṚV, but my point here is not one of a new invention, but of an increased emphasis. It is also possible that a diversification of characters is related to the fact that these texts quite likely had an audience that was not only composed of Brahmin males.

126. CU 4.1–3.

127. CU 4.4–9.

128. Ajātaśatru (BĀU 2.1ff, KṣU 4.1ff.); Aśvapati Kaikeya (ŚB 10.6.1ff., CU 5.11ff.); Citra Gāṅgyāyani (KṣU 1.1ff.); Janaka teaching Yājñavalkya (ŚB 11.6.2); and Pravāhaṇa Jaivali (BĀU 6.2ff., CU 1.8.1).

129. It is important to note that I am not saying women did not participate in such debates (see below).

130. Black (2007, 152) says that Gārgī "does not have the authority to threaten Yājñavalkya directly." This strikes me as unlikely, even the opposite of what is intended. The reading of the head-shattering threat in M, which often contains the better and more likely original reading, makes it clear that K's "arrows" are not an empty threat. Such a reading also fits more closely with the conclusion of BĀU 3 (see Lindquist 2004).

131. Note that Olivelle (1997) comes to a similar conclusion but for different reasons. Black (2007, 151) notes the masculine form and refers to it as a "debating tactic" to "take on the rhetoric of a brahmin male subject" (152). Though noting the Kṣatriya imagery, I think Black overlooks that there is nothing Brahmin about Gārgī's use of metaphor—the male Kṣatriya imagery is a direct critique of Brahmin-ness and the male Brahmins in attendance. To my mind, Gārgī is attempting to outdo the Brahmins, not imitate them (except in gender).

It is worth noting that some have taken issue with this interpretation after its original publication, suggesting I am dismantling an important historical female role model from early texts by suggesting such a masculinization. This is, in my opinion, a mistaken reading of the argument which conflates a historical individual with a literary one. My concern here is the *literary* portrayal, a textual production by particular male Brahmin composers at a particular time—in other words, what *the composers* are doing in their word choices, etc.—and not with how particular faith communities may choose to interpret her and definitely not with who a historical Gārgī may or may not have been.

132. Note also that Gārgī is glorifying the patron, Janaka, by mentioning Videha.

133. M reads *sapatnādhivyādhinau.*

134. Note that this follows the pattern of other Yājñavalkya passages that are geared towards asserting his authority over and above others.

135. See appendix for a translation of the Maitreyī episode at 4.5.

136. *pra √vraj.* In 2.4.1 *ud √yā* is more neutral. Brereton (2006), however, has suggested that these verbs, particularly *ud √yā,* may indicate that Yājñavalkya is dying (i.e., similar to the English idiom "passing away"). Such

an interpretation would fit well with Yājñavalkya's discourse on immortality where the chapter culminates in his impending death.

137. At 4.5.15 he leaves (*vi* √*hr̥*). BAU(M) *pra* √*vraj* (which verbally echoes the beginning of the episode).

138. See Lindquist (2011a, b).

139. This may be a technical term for a person who participates in public debate (of which we have no direct evidence for Maitreyī), or it may simply mean that she had a direct interest in discussing religious and philosophical matters.

140. Or perhaps, following M (*strīprajñeva*), she is a knower of things "like womanly knowledge."

141. I cannot agree with Grinshpon's (2003) strong argument and Black's (2007) milder suggestion that the lack of a son in this episode is significant. As I see it, a son is simply irrelevant in this context as the doctrinal starting point is the nature of what is "dear" (i.e., the wife is the most dear relationship), works its way outwards, and then ends with severing the dearness of the wife when Yājñavalkya leaves her. This forms a straightforward literary ring (see Lindquist 2005, 141–43).

142. "Knowledge of womanly things" may also include those rules of conduct not dealt with in the *dharmaśāstra* texts (e.g., *Āpastamba Dharmasūtra* [ĀpDhS] 2.29.11 *sā niṣṭhā yā vidyā strīṣu śūdreṣu ca* and ĀpDhS 2.29.15 *strībhyaḥ sarvavarṇebhyaś ca dharmaśeṣān pratīyādity eka ity eke*).

143. Dharmasūtra material tells of the right of a man to parcel out his estate in advance of his death (ĀpDhS 2.14.1, *Gautama Dharmasūtra* 28.2, BaudhDhS 3.2–8).

144. Knowledge is often included in lists of different types of transferable property (ĀpDhS 1.20.15, *Vasiṣṭha Dharmasūtra* 29.19, *Baudhāyana Dharmasūtra* [BaudhDhS] 2.39).

145. Black (2007, 167) suggests maybe it is Kātyāyanī who "wins" by taking the wealth as it is not clear whether Maitreyī understands such a difficult teaching. Such an interpretation, though possible, is unlikely as it goes against one of the larger soteriological goals of this text. Black, though, is right in suggesting that there appears to be a negative undertone towards women understanding such matters here.

146. A recent notable exception is Black (2007). Roebuck (trans., 2000, 472) and Keith (1925, 506) note the following women but do not discuss them at any length.

147. *gandharva* possession is particular to young women (due to their supposed "sexual" nature).

148. Though a lack of names is significant here, Black (2007) does not discuss this issue. Compare, however, his discussion of Satyakāma's wife (160).

149. I am grateful to Caley Charles Smith for suggesting this provocative extension of the privacy theme.

Chapter 3

1. Estimated at perhaps 200–100 BCE (Witzel 2003, 135).

2. On Vyāsa, see Sullivan (1999).

3. Here I am referring specifically to the Sanskrit *Mahābhārata* attributed to Vyāsa.

4. I omit here an outline of the MBh as a whole or descriptions of the more important episodes, both of which are available elsewhere in accessible form (trans., Van Buitenen 1973, 1975; Fitzgerald 2003, 2004a, and Hiltebeitel 1976, 2001).

5. These traditions are not referred to by name, but rather by the term *nāstika*, often translated as "heretic." This term refers to those who did not hold the Veda as the central authority of religious doctrine and practice (e.g., Buddhists, Jains, etc.).

6. For a summary of these traditions, see Jaini (2001, 47–96).

7. On urbanization and its possible impact on religious thinking, see Gombrich (1988, 2009) and Olivelle (1993, trans. 1998). Particularly important here is that urbanization often facilitates the breakdown of the familial system in favor of an impersonal system of commerce (which, out of necessity, forces modifications to the notion of purity and impurity, the individual, etc.) and increases the possibilities of disease and epidemics. These changes would have happened within a context of radically increased contact and communication between communities who previously had limited or no direct contact, thus fostering dialogue, debate, and new religious expression. Such a sociological context is ripe for the rise of alternative versions of religious truth, particularly those which ultimately (if not always practically) deny the value of this worldly life.

8. This particular sense of *dharma* "was the result of the new religious perspectives and values of yoga that gradually emerged alongside older Vedic ones in the middle third of the first millennium B.C. in northern India" (Fitzgerald 2003, 109).

9. An encyclopedic-type work on religious doctrines in the *Mahābhārata* is Sutton (2000).

10. For example, on the structure and various arguments of the *aśvamedhaparvan*, see Reich (1998).

11. "The Veda" or "Vedas" is often best understood not as a reference to the four or five genres of texts that go by this name, but rather as a conceptual category of orthodox "Truth" that retains a certain fluidity (for a related discussion, see Davis 2010).

12. This includes lesser known ascetic traditions, such as the Ājīvikas, who followed the teachings of Gośāla Maskarīputra (see Basham 1951).

13. Olivelle (2005) suggests that a key notion in early Hinduism—*dharma*—only became so as Brahmins reappropriated the term from the Buddhist usage.

14. For example, Fitzgerald (2003; trans., 2004) and Reich (1998). Hiltebeitel (2001) has suggested a radically short composition period, but Fitzgerald (2003, 810ff.) has pointed out several difficulties with this scenario. That said, Hiltebeitel's suggestion is an intriguing one that needs to be considered.

15. However, I agree with Reich (1998) that when one thinks of the MBh, it is often more meaningful to think of it as a "literary tradition," rather than as a single text.

16. See Black's treatment (2018) of Yājñavalkya in the MBh based partially on a draft version of this chapter.

17. Such an argument, given the nature of the text, could be applied to other episodes as well. However, while Reich (1998) is correct that the value of the MBh is often in its dialogic mode that does not follow "Euro-centric" (her word) expectations, it is clear that Yājñavalkya's role as a character is relatively minor. Note here Fitzgerald's important argument (2012) of how the longer Yājñavalkya narrative in the Śāntiparvan functions in tandem with others in regard to Sāṃkhya-Yoga.

18. Note that Yājñavalkya is associated with *yoga* in a variant reading found in book 5 (see below in this chapter).

19. See Fitzgerald (2012) for a compelling interpretation of the presentation of Sāṃkhya and Yoga in a series of dialogues—a subset of which are Janaka dialogues with different interlocutors—in the Śāntiparvan. I am in general agreement with his argument, though I confine myself to a single dialogue and only tangentially discuss Sāṃkhya and Yoga as it pertains to Yājñavalkya's biography.

20. Note the similarity to BhG 5.4 (6.27.4): *sāṃkhyayogau pr̥thag bālāḥ pravadanti na paṇḍitāḥ | ekam apy āsthitaḥ samyag ubhayor vindate phalam* || "Fools hold that the way of Sankhya and the practice of yogic action are different, but not those who know. Through either one of them, carried out properly, one attains the reward of both" (Johnson, trans., 1994, 23).

21. Rhetorically, *tattvavid* is functioning here similarly to *sa evaṃ veda* that we encounter in the BĀU as a statement about the "true nature" of the teaching. Such statements either come immediately before or immediately after the teaching.

22. To dismiss the value of the Veda would be counterproductive to the apparent narrative intent as Yājñavalkya's authority comes from that same authority.

23. Note that ass's milk is too low in fat to produce butter. I am not sure, however, whether the reference to excrement refers to appearance or odor.

24. This may refer to sources outside of the Veda but also probably refers more specifically to *nāstika* traditions.

25. I do not wish to imply that the composers of this text were directly familiar with the ŚB/BĀU in any particular recension as we have them, but rather that they were clearly aware of the same or rather similar stories regarding Yājñavalkya whether in a fixed form or not.

26. What these sections entail is unclear: it may be the Upaniṣads, Brāhmaṇas, the Vedāṅgas, or all three. Given that it is later said that Yājñavalkya learns the Purāṇas from another teacher, these are probably not intended.

27. I translate as "bring forth" because it is not entirely clear whether the meaning here is "to compose," "to compile," or simply "to institute" the teachings. As the teachings are given from the Sun, it is unlikely that this passage is meant to attribute independent authorship to Yājñavalkya, but rather it is to explain why some may see him as an editor or author of sorts as these were not "known/used" previously.

28. This means that the auspicious syllable OM is properly positioned as the first of all sounds.

29. Irregular double sandhi of *dakṣiṇāyāḥ atha*.

30. Or: "having honored the seed and the goddess . . ."

31. See chapter 4.

32. It is unclear whether there is a different connotation intended with the added prefix *su*. This word may also mean "dear" or "beloved" but here probably indicated "*really* difficult."

33. This is probably the reason for the inclusion of Sarasvatī (speech personified) functioning as the intermediary for the Sun.

34. This may be one reason why Yājñavalkya had to endure great heat—so as to become like the Sun itself.

35. This suggests that the heat that Yājñavalkya endures is for purificatory purposes.

36. With the exception of the suggesting of a dispute with his maternal uncle. However, it is not clear in this passage what that dispute was thought to entail.

37. These human participants were not present during the period when the Sun caused Sarasvatī to enter into him and when he received all this sacred knowledge. However, as enacting the Vedic texts and knowing them are, in a significant sense, one and the same, others could verify the validity by observing the performance.

38. See Fitzgerald (2012) on 12.289–290 for larger textual reasons related to Sāṃkhya and Yoga.

39. This is not to say that there may not have been a contemporaneous oral tradition not recorded in the extant texts which associated Yājñavalkya with Sāṃkhya and Yoga, but rather that this discussion in the MBh is a nov-

elty in the larger literary record and an oral tradition associating Yājñavalkya with these doctrines cannot be particularly old.

40. The nature of authority in those genealogies is discussed at length in Lindquist (2011c).

41. cf. BĀU 2.4.3.

42. Van Buitenen (trans., 1975, 38): "Tittira."

43. In fact, only two names seem to have any connection with the genealogy in chapter 6 of BĀU where Yājñavalkya appears ("son of Śāṇḍilī" may be Śāṇḍilya mentioned in the MBh and also connected with books 6–10 of the ŚB, and Kauṣika may be connected with the "son of Kauṣikī" in MBh). Perhaps also Asita in MBh is connected to Asita Vārṣagaṇa in BĀU.

44. Macdonell and Keith ([1912]1967, 2:23)

45. Towards the end of the list a person named Kaṭha is mentioned, perhaps attributable to the *Kaṭha Upaniṣad*. However, this name does not appear there.

46. I think Van Buitenen is correct that the necessity of gambling within the *rājasūya* explains the necessity of this episode in the MBh.

47. Van Buitenen translates this as "most profoundly grounded in *brahman*" (trans., 1975, 88).

48. Note the similarity of Sumantu, Paila, and Jaimini of 12.306.20.

49. Grinshpon (2003) argues that the lack of sons is implied in BĀU 2.4/4.5 and key to the narrative. Black (2007) argues something similar, though in a less emphatic fashion. See my review of Grinshpon as to why mention of children would be narratively unimportant (Lindquist 2005).

50. Whether one is more original to the text appears impossible to say, but for our purposes it is irrelevant.

51. Indra is seen as the father of Arjuna while Yudhiṣṭhira's father is said to be Dharma.

52. This narration is found in MBh 1.114–115. Shorter summary versions are found at MBh 1.61.84 and 1.90.69.

53. On the issue of the number five in the MBh, see Murty (2003).

54. It is sometimes difficult (and probably intentionally so) to determine whether these beings are seen as "equal to Indra" and are thus called Indra or whether they are aspects of a single Indra.

55. Dating Purāṇas is extremely difficult, if not impossible. Certainly there has been little consensus in most cases (Rocher 1986, 133ff). Doniger O'Flaherty, while suggesting the dates may be based on the "misguided conjectures of scholars" (1988, 5), gives the possible date of 250 AD for MārkP. There is general consensus, though, that the MārkP is probably one of the oldest Purāṇas (Rocher 1986, 191ff.), perhaps composed soon after the redaction of the MBh.

56. In this light, the death of the Pāṇḍavas in book 17 of the MBh carries another level of meaning. After all the brothers have passed away on their

sojourn to Indra's heaven, only Yudhiṣṭhira remains to attain heaven by his own volition (rather than through dying). When confronted by Indra at the gate of heaven, Yudhiṣṭhira refuses to enter heaven if his dog companion cannot enter with him. While Indra tries to convince Yudhiṣṭhira that there is nothing wrong with abandoning the dog at this stage, he refuses. The dog shows himself to be the incarnation of Dharma and tells him that this was a test and he has passed it. In this passage, then, not only has Yudhiṣṭhira proven himself to be an upholder of *dharma* by not abandoning the dog, the dog is himself Dharma. Further, in light of the above passages, the conclusion of the MBh is also the returning of the five Indras (in the form of the Pāṇḍavas) back to Indraloka. In this sense, Yudhiṣṭhira in dialogue with the two gods, Dharma and Indra, is also a conversation between Yudhiṣṭhira and his two "fathers." Taking these passages collectively, this is also a dialogue of sorts surrounding Yudhiṣṭhira's (and his brothers') creation and role in the cosmos.

57. *pūrva* also means "being in front" as Vedic offerings are made towards the east, so the sacrificer faces east.

58. For a detailed and interesting account of the Viśvāmitra stories and their performance see Sathaye (2015).

59. Satyavatī is distressed at the outcome of this switch and asks that the "curse" of sorts be allowed to skip a generation so that her immediate progeny are not affected.

60. The southern recension contains a similar list, but many of the names are spelled differently and a few are altogether different (Ganguli, 1991, vol. 10, p. 14).

61. That this becomes perceived as fact is clear in the time of the Purāṇas, but I wish here to explore other narrative reasons that help to explain this relationship.

62. Note that in the BĀU we have a "backward looking" genealogy, justifying Yājñavalkya's position by looking at where he came from, whereas here we have a "forward looking" one which justifies Viśvāmitra's position via his descendents.

63. See chapter 4 for other connections between Yājñavalkya and Śiva.

64. Witzel sees such lines in BĀU 6 (and also Janaka giving his whole kingdom to Yājñavalkya in BĀU 4) as late additions—that is, as hagiography being tacked on to more factual accounts. While this is possible, there is no reason to assume that it *must* be the case. Such a reading presupposes that any "original" composer was only concerned with historical fact and that which is historically unlikely must be an accretion.

65. Bronkhorst (2000, 2007) has suggested that all late ŚB passages (including the BĀU) be seen as hagiography and not useful for historical reconstruction (similar to Fišer 1984).

66. Yudhiṣṭhira's brothers serve the same function in ritually connecting the king to the six directions.

Chapter 4

1. I largely agree with Rao (1993, 95–96) who suggests that we must distinguish between a "folk" orality and a "literate" orality. This is to say, that a literate orality that is part of a scholarly, elite tradition may also incorporate "folk" perspectives. While Rao is concerned particularly with the Purāṇas, this distinction is useful in other traditions as well.

2. Sathaye (2015: 30) suggests a model of how, for example, Brahmins may be classified a "folk group" in any number of configurations and yet, I would add, still constitute an "elite."

3. For this book, I am only concerned with the early Sanskritic tradition. However, it is a desideratum that various important figures also be studied in the vernacular traditions.

4. See for exanple, BĀU 4.1 where the two are listed together.

5. Whether and how the Purāṇas contain "history" in the Western sense has been a highly debated matter with greatly divergent positions being taken by different scholars (Rocher 1986, 115ff.). I have no doubt that the Purāṇic texts contain much historical information, but the determination of historical veracity must take place within the context of the larger purposes of any narrative, dynastic list, etc.

6. The same can be said for the Amarakośa's *purānaṃ pañcalakṣanam* ("the Purāṇa consisting of five classifications") that are said to define the Purāṇas as a genre. Certainly, this classification schema is of little use in determining which Purāṇas are older or closer to an original (Rocher 1986, 24–25).

7. For various and conflicting attempts at dating schemas, see Rocher (1986, 100–104, 133ff.).

8. For example, Chakrabarti (2001).

9. In all cases, it is clear that the Purāṇic composers were aware of the stories regarding Yājñavalkya. This, however, does not mean that these stories were known in a fixed form which would more likely have restricted the great innovation that we find in their compositions.

10. Such a situation would have to be determined on a case-by-case basis and would have to show intimate familiarity with a source: such as exact verbal parallels, structural mimicry, etc.

11. Questions that would need to be addressed include: How much is a composer intentionally mimicking another oral text? If one telling seems less familiar with the details of another, but still familiar with certain aspects of it, what criteria can be used to determine whether there is a shared source or whether there is an intentional manipulation of certain detail?

12. It is this aspect that some, such as Fišer, appear to be pointing to when discussing what he sees as the less-than-historical aspects of the BĀU.

13. *Brahmāṇḍapurāṇa* (ed. Shashtri: 1983).

14. BP 1.2.34.45

15. The sense of *adhyātma* here appears to be a reflection on the abstract nature of the self through a Sāṃkhya philosophical lens.

16. One should note here that the wealth described is much more elaborate (including cows, gold, jewels, women, and so on) than that found in the BĀU (one thousand cows with gold attached to their horns). The expansion here is most likely done to emphasize the greed of the Brahmins present.

17. In a fashion, this narrative almost appears to be a blending or collapsing of the ŚB and BĀU versions. In the ŚB, only Yājñavalkya and Śākalya debate with each other. In the BĀU, there are several interlocutors and we are told the content of the debate, while in the BP we have several Brahmins debating without any detail of what that debate entailed.

18. Almost the exact same story is found in the VāP (60.33ff). The main difference there is that we are not told the question that Yājñavalkya asks Śākalya that leads to his death. Also, Yājñavalkya insults Śākalya directly (60.50) explaining the cause of his anger.

19. All citations and translations of the SP are from Tagare's translation (1970, vols. 49–51).

20. This text does not suggest that Yājñavalkya is the cause of the problem, but rather that Kātyāyanī is responsible as she did not employ the proper rituals (see below in this chapter).

21. Note that it is not the exact same problem as Kātyāyanī is said to acquire equal affection from Yājñavalkya and not exclusive affection.

22. Gārgī appears with Yājñavalkya in a very brief passage in the *Liṅga Purāṇa* (LP) that is also concerned with valorizing Śiva. In 9.53–54 Yājñavalkya explains to Gārgī the nature of the supreme being which is very similar to his description of the "imperishable" found at BĀU 3.8.8.

23. Note that in the late *yoga* text attributed to Yājñavalkya, Gārgī is Yājñavalkya's wife and the tradition explains that Gārgī is simply another name for Maitreyī (*Yogayājñavalkya,* trans. Mohan, n.d.).

24. Tagare (1970, 50:109) suggests that *merudeśa* may be a reference to a desert or to Mārwār.

25. Vaiśaṁpāyana, however, is listed for his knowledge of the Vedas and perhaps specifically the *R̥gveda* (1.2.33.5–6). Tagare (trans., 1982: 325, n. 2) points out that this passage appears to contain errors in line ordering.

26. Note, however, that Yājñavalkya is said to be a student of Bāṣkala in other places and is associated with the division of the *R̥gveda* into two schools (BhP 12.6.55; 9.22.38; VP 3.4) or four (*Vāyu Purāṇa* 60.26).

27. For a translation of VP, see Wilson (1972).

28. In the *Kūrma Purāṇa* (1.24.45) there is a brief mention of Yājñavalkya as the composer of a Yogaśāstra (*yājñavalkyo mahāyogī dr̥ṣṭvā 'tra tapasā haram | cakāra tan niyogena yogaśāstram anuttamam;* "The great yogin, Yājñavalkya, having seen Hara by means of his ascetic heat, made the excellent Yogaśāstra

by his command"). Note that this may be modeled after the creation stories of the White Yajurveda, but here the principal deity is Hara (Śiva).

29. The *Yogayājñavalkya* [saṃhitā] and the *Bṛhadyogiyājñavalkyasmṛti.* Very little work has been done on these texts. However, see Divanji (1953); Kuvalayananda and Kokaje (1956); Kenghe (1971); and Kane's summary of some of the issues (1968, vol. 1, pt. 1, 449–459, and vol. 5, pt. 2, 1403–1408).

30. One passage that is not discussed due to its brevity is *Padma Purāṇa* 5.9.31. However, it is important to note that Yājñavalkya is listed there as a sage who attends Rāma's *aśvamedha* sacrifice.

31. *Brahma Purāṇa,* 825. Translations of the *Brahma Purāṇa* (1986) are from the Ancient Indian Tradition and Mythology Series where the author is listed as "A Board of Scholars."

32. While the amount of scholarship on the legal work attributed to Yājñavalkya is great, work on the attribution of this work to Yājñavalkya is limited. Overwhelmingly, scholarship has dismissed this attribution as "late" or "spurious" (for example, Kane 1968, vol. 1, pt. 1., 422–23). From a factual perspective, they are certainly correct that it cannot historically be the Yājñavalkya of the Upaniṣads, but this does little to explain the attribution in the first place. Olivelle 2019 (trans., xiii–xv) is the most detailed treatment that considers attribution as well as historical veracity.

33. *jñeyaṃ cāraṇyakam ahaṃ yadādityād avāptavān | yogaśāstraṃ ca mat-proktaṃ jñeyaṃ yogam abhīpsatā* (3.110)

34. Perhaps the close relationship between Yājñavalkya and the Sun god could have been seen as a parallel with Manu being of the solar race.

35. One could suggest that Janaka, as an idealized king, would be an obvious candidate for attribution of a *smṛti* in the White Yajurvedic tradition. However, Janaka is idealized as subservient to Yājñavalkya in issues of religious knowledge (with ŚBM 11.6.2.1–10 as a notable exception), and his principal narrative role is as an inquisitive king with deep pockets.

36. Given that Yājñavalkya is associated with the first discussion of *karma* in the BĀU, associating him with the *dharma* tradition does not seem an unnatural step.

Conclusion

1. Indeed, much that is "philosophical" in the Upaniṣads is difficult to interpret if one does not assume a ritualistic background, and I am arguing that the same holds true for characters found therein as well.

2. See Black's brief, but useful, discussion (2017) of a few of the Upa-niṣadic characters who make an appearance in the MBh.

Appendix

1. *Dakṣina* is somewhere between "gift" and "fee." It is ritually required (even the amount is often stipulated), but it is often said that it should be given generously and with trust (*śraddhā*). I prefer "fee" as the giving is never wholly optional (although additional amounts may be optional).

2. Roebuck (trans., 2000, 49) takes *brahmiṣṭha* as "truest Brāhmaṇa" or "literally '*brahman*-est.'" This is appropriate, as long as one understands that *brahman* refers less to class than to the knowledge or the ability to formulate the knowledge that is often attributed to the priestly class.

3. Note here that thc first question relates to the role of the questioner, while the second relates to the role of the respondent—a narrative device to begin the discussion. Further, I think this structure indicates that the questions being asked are initially direct and simple (i.e., "What is my role?"; "What is your role?").

4. *Saṃpadaḥ* can mean both "numerical equivalents" as well as "attainments." I translate more vaguely as "correspondences" as I think both meanings are meant here as both are stated in the following passage.

5. See Wezler (1992, 406–7). Zysk (1993, 207) mentions that *prāṇabhr̥t* is also a name for the middle bricks of the fire altar set to the east.

6. These are likely ghee, milk, and sacrificial bread (*parodāśa*).

7. This is not a particular world acknowledged by the tradition, but may indicate that whatever world he gets (gods, gandharvas, fathers, or men) will be unending.

8. Olivelle (trans., 1998, 506) here notes the double-entendre of grasper (*graha*) and over-grasper (*atigraha*) as mutually indicating two Soma cups in the ritual as well as the sense organ and sense object. The *graha* is a wooden cup for collecting soma. The *atigraha* is a clay cup used for offering extra (*ati*) cups of soma or, alternatively, because the clay cup is placed above (*ati*) the wooden one during the sacrifice. The dual meaning between cups and senses is not simply a clever word play. Given that the *vedi* in such sacrifices is referred to as a "body" (its corners are "hips" and "shoulders"), it seems clear that there is a mutual dependence in understanding the sacrifice in relation to the person and the person in relation to the sacrifice. Such double meanings should serve as a reminder of the dependence of early "philosophy" on ritual understanding and that this *brahmodya* is still very much in the context of sacrifice.

9. We expect *prāṇa* here as Böhtlingk (trans., 1889) emmends, but this is against manuscript evidence.

10. Olivelle reads (trans., 1998. 81), I think correctly, an implicit "by knowing this" (cf. 3.3.2). It should be pointed out that in the previous section it is by *actually using* the verses in the sacrifice that one attains various worlds—thus there is a shift from the ritual use to the primacy of knowledge in 3.2.

11. Cf. BĀU 1.2.6 where the breaths do depart, yet the horse still bloats.

12. This appears to extend the meaning of the previous question. Immediately prior, the passage establishes that it is the breaths that do not leave him. Here, what does not leave him appears to be more abstract ("name").

13. *Caraka* here could incidate that this priest, and whoever "we" refers to, are Black Yajurvedins (cf. ŚBM 3.8.2.24–25).

14. Note that Yājñavalkya's answer is elliptical, if not evasive, requiring the question to be put to him again in another form.

15. Thirty-two days is the longest possible month in the Indian calendar.

16. I disagree with Thieme (trans., 1965, 95) in the translation of *bālyam*. I think we have an upwards gradation of knowledge in which translating *bālyam* as "stupidity" misses the point. The text appears to be saying that one should move from the pretense of learnedness or perhaps simply functional learnedness (*pāṇḍityam*), to the "ignorance of a child" (i.e., an unmolded intellect or perhaps a state of inquisitiveness), to the sagely "search for true knowledge," and finally to attain the state of a true Brahmin (i.e., a Brahmin by birth, by knowledge, and by practice).

17. Olivelle (trans., 1998, 508) must be correct in his reading of *kena syāt yena syāt tena* as a variant of *yena kena syāt*. Taking *kena syāt* as a question ("how does one become a Brahmin?"), as others have taken it (cf. trans., Roebuck 2000, 55), is not only a tautology (though not uncommon in Sanskrit literature), but misses the point that how one becomes a Brahmin was *just described*.

18. The implied metaphor here appears to be a garland.

19. Roebuck and Olivelle translate "on air / wind." Here I take the instrumental in its most obvious meaning, "by means of," because the issue is what connects "this world, the next world, etc." and not their foundation. What everything is "on" is already implied in the previous section (i.e., *brahman*).

20. Note how this passage ends in the rather practical "semen" as a means for the perpetuation of the self (perhaps displacing a notion of immortality through one's children). Cf. 3.9.28.

21. This passage must be sarcastic. Cf. 3.4.2.

22. One senses that "*u khalu*" is meant to express Gārgī's frustration with Yājñavalkya responding again with the same answer.

23. "Without shadow" may mean without light to cast a shadow or without a form to be cast. I lean towards the former interpretation as a contrast to darkness.

24. *Asaṅgam* is somewhat out of place here, as all previous properties of the imperishable are logically paired and one would expect the same here. Unlike other translators, I think the rest of the list following *asaṅgam* are also "natural" sets.

25. I think "without mouth" here means an aperture which could allow something in or out. This is paired with "without measure" indicating that

the imperishable cannot be determined by either a point of entry or its size, two means of showing its distinctness.

26. *Darvī* (*darvyam*, M) is the technical term for a temporary ladle made out of a leaf. The offering to the ancestors is made with this leaf.

27. Note here that *brāhmaṇa* is used instead of *brahman*. However, I am inclined to believe that, again, the emphasis here is on proper knowledge and not class.

28. Śaṅkara takes *idaṃ sarvam* to be the whole list of deities mentioned: "*Because all those* (thirty-three and other gods) that have been spoken of *are* just *these six*" (Madhavananda 1997, 373).

29. Or "moon."

30. Note that M collapses this sentence with the next omitting *hi*.

31. This translation here follows Olivelle (trans., 1998, 101). For a reinterptation in the M recension, see chapter 2.

32. Or "things with less tangible ends" (Brereton, personal communication).

33. I translate *bandhu* as connection because I do not think it relates only to a counterpart, as much as to the reasoning that brings the part and counterpart into relation.

34. Others translate as just "food and water" and not the giving of it. I take this to be logically connected to oblations and offerings, and I think it indicates the ritual responsibility to a guest where *ca* is read as the break in these logical sets. All these items are apparently connected to speech due to the requirement of speaking to understand and transmit them. The giving of offerings and oblations as well as food and water to a guest may be accompanied by verses or statements or are related because of a general connection with the mouth.

35. Roebuck (trans., 2000, 74): as "hearing itself."

36. Note the obvious verbal echo, linking the end of this discussion to the end of the discussion with Śākalya (3.9.26).

37. Olivelle (trans., 1998, 111) and Roebuck add as "at your service." While this is reasonable, I think this phrase needs to be connected to the dialogue marker of the thousand cows, which marks the conclusion of a particular topic. Here, though, it is the end of the whole discussion, so the thousand cows is modified and intensified. In this fashion I choose a slightly stronger translation connecting "possession" of cows with "possession" of the kingdom. Note the irony of Yājñavalkya teaching Janaka about the self, and Janaka returns the gift by giving himself to Yājñavalkya (Brereton, personal communication). Also, the "fearless" given to Yājñavalkya is not clear. Brereton (personal communication) suggests the "fearless" might be of another type—that of not fearing for money or livelihood.

38. Following the manuscript tradition which retains double-accent. Alternatively, others have read this as *sam enena vadiṣye*, "I will talk with him."

39. Cf. ŚB XI.6.2.10

40. M *sadhīḥ*.

41. Note that this matches M's reading where previously M drops perception and adds *ātman* at 3.7.22–23.

42. These two in apposition seem to indicate "calmness" versus "activity."

43. This could mean "for release from the boon" (trans., Olivelle 1998, 113ff.). However, one would expect some mention of the release being accomplished. I am inclined to take this as "Tell me more about release [from this world, i.e., death]" paralleling *vimucyamānaḥ* in 4.1.7 and *ūrdhvaṃ vimuktāḥ* in 4.4.8 (which would mark that the series of verses is the final answer). Yājñavalkya's later frustration would be the fact that he was unable to dodge the actual question.

44. 15 is omitted in M, which is probably the better reading.

45. Roebuck (trans., 2000, 80) translates as "travels along both banks." However, I think the metaphor is related to movement to and from the states of dreaming and waking so the fish here must be travelling from one bank to the other.

46. Unlike Roebuck (trans., 2000, 80) and Olivelle (trans., 1998, 115), I take *saṁ √han* here to mean "to be put in unison" by stretching out both wings horizontally to sail (rather than "folding" the wings in) as this is what these types of birds do when they are approaching their nests. Swooping, by means of folding the wings in, is an attack posture. See Burton (1990).

47. In these two cases, it is not clear what these terms mean. They are likely tribal terms that were Sanskritized (Brereton, personal communication).

48. I follow Brereton's (1986) interpretation of *iva* which I think is particularly important here: "something (*iva*) of an other" is to indicate that *in reality* there is no other, but there is the perception of an other in phenomenal existence.

49. There appears to be an intentional double meaning of "people" and the "senses."

50. *√ekībhū* probably refers to his senses gathering around and becoming indistinguishable.

51. Or: of *brahman*.

52. Note here that it is not that he takes over a body of his ancestor, but rather that he takes on a body appropriate of an ancestor, and so on.

53. I suspect implicit in this is "with her husband" as there is no textual evidence of her participating in any debate.

54. There are possible sacrificial implications here—*upa* + *ā* + *√kṛ* is used in the animal sacrifice for sending the animal to "dedication"; it is also used to indicate that the priest should begin (G.U. Thite, personal communication).

55. Olivelle (trans., 1998, 131) translates *vinaśyati* as "disappears after them," which is probably what Yājñavalkya intends. I translate this as "is

destroyed" (the primary meaning of the verb) because I think this is where Maitreyī's confusion lies—that is, Yājñavalkya *appears* to be saying that the *ātman* is *actually* destroyed, something that would be rather confusing given the context of a discussion about immortality. Yājñavalkya recognizes her misunderstanding and clarifies that the soul is indestructable (*avināśin*). Maitreyī's confusion in 2.4 is different—her confusion there is not understanding how there is no awareness after death after which Yājñavalkya explains the nature of non-awareness.

References

Primary Texts and Translations

Agni Purāṇa. 1970. Translated by N. Gangadharan. In *Ancient Indian Tradition and Mythology*, vols. 27–28. Delhi: Motilal Banarsidass.

The Bhagavad Gita. 1994. Translated by W. J. Johnson. In Oxford World Classics series. New York: Oxford University Press.

Bhāgavaṭa Purāṇa. 1976–1978. Translated by G. V. Tagare. In *Ancient Indian Tradition and Mythology*, vols. 7–11. Delhi: Motilal Banarsidass.

Brahmāṇḍa Purāṇa, Part I. 1982. Translated by G. V. Tagare. Delhi: Motilal Banarsidass.

Brahmāṇḍapurāṇam of Kṛṣṇa Dvaipāyana Vyāsa. 1983. Edited by J. L. Shastri. Reprint, Delhi: Motilal Banarsidass,.

Brahma Purāṇa. 1985–1986. Translated by a Board of Scholars, In *Ancient Indian Tradition and Mythology*, vols. 33–36. Delhi: Motilal Banarsidass.

The Bṛhadāraṇyaka Upaniṣad with the Commentary of Śaṇkaracārya. 1997. Translated by Swami Madhavanda. Reprint, Calcutta: Advaita Ashrama.

Bṛhadāraṇyakopanishad in der Mādhjaṁdina-Recension. 1889. Edited and translated by O. Böhtlingk. St. Petersburg: Kaiserliche Akademie der Wissenschaften.

Bṛhadāraṇyakopaniṣad I: Versuch einer kritischen Ausgabe nach akzentuierten Handschriften der Kāṇva-Rezension mit einer Einleitung und Anerkungen. 1976. Edited by D. Maue. Unpublished dissertation, University of Geißen.

Bṛhadāraṇyakopaniṣad II: Critical Edition of the Second Chapter of the Kāṇva Recension according to Accented Manuscripts with a Critical-Exegetical Commentary. 1994. Edited by C. A. Pérez-Coffie. Unpublished disssertation, Harvard University.

The Dharmaśāstras of Āpastamba, Gautama, Baudhāyana, and Vasiṣṭha: Sanskrit Editions and Annotated Translations. 2000. In *Sources of Indian Law*. Edited and translated by P. Olivelle. Delhi: Motilal Banarsidass.

The Early Upaniṣads: Annotated Text and Translation. 1998. Edited and translated by P. Olivelle. New York: Oxford University Press.

Eighteen Principal Upaniṣads. 1958. Edited by V. P. Limaye and R. D. Vadekar. Poona: Vaidika Saṁśodhana Maṇḍala.

Īśādidaśopaniṣadaḥ: The Ten Principle Upaniṣads with Śāṅkarabhāṣya (no editor given). 1992. Reprint, Delhi: Motilal Banarsidass.

"Īśopaṇiṣad (= Vājasaneyi-Saṃhitā 40) 1–14." Translated by P. Thieme. *Journal of the American Oriental Society* 85, no. 1 (1965): 89–99.

Iśibasiyam Suttaim. 1988. Edited and translated in Hindi by M. Vinayasagar and English translation by K. Shastri and D. C. Sharma. Jaipur: Prakrit Bharati Academy.

Isibhasiyaim. 1973. Edited by Walter Schubring. Reprint, Hamburg: De Gruyter, 1969.

Jaiminīya Brāhmaṇa I, 1–65: Translation and Commentary with a Study—Agnihotra and Prāṇāgnihotra. 1973. Edited and translated by H. W. Bodewitz. Leiden: E. J. Brill.

The Jyotiṣṭoma Ritual: Jaiminīya Brāhmaṇa I, 66–364. 1990. Edited and translated by H. W. Bodewitz. Leiden: E. J. Brill.

Kāṇvaśatapathabrāhmaṇam (I.G.N.C.A. series, 7 vols.). 1994–2015. Edited and translated by C. R. Swaminathan. Delhi: Motilal Banarsidass.

Kūrma Purāṇa, Part 1. 1972. Edited and translated by A. Bhattacharya. Fort Ramnagar: All-India Kashi Trust.

Kūrma Purāṇa. 1981. Translated by G. V. Tagare. In *Ancient Indian Tradition and Mythology*, vol. 20. Delhi: Motilal Banarsidass.

The Liṅga Purāṇa, Part II, vol. 6. 1970. Translated by a board of scholars. Delhi: Motilal Banarsidass.

Mahābhārata, 4 vols. 1971–1975. Edited by V. S. Sukthankar et al. Poona: Bhandarkar Oriental Research Institute. The electronic version of the critical edition of the text is available at http://bombay.oriental.cam.ac.uk/john/mahabharata/statement.html.

The Mahābhārata: 1 The Book of the Beginning. 1973. Translated by J. A. B. van Buitenen. Chicago: University of Chicago Press.

The Mahābhārata: 2 The Book of the Assembly Hall; 3 The Book of the Forest. 1975. Translated by J. A. B. van Buitenen. Chicago: University of Chicago Press.

The Mahābhārata: 11 The Book of the Women; 12 The Book of Peace, Part 1. 2004a. Translated by J. Fitzgerald. Chicago: University of Chicago Press.

The Mahabharata of Krishna-Dwaipayana, 12 vols. 1991. Translated by K. M. Ganguli. New Delhi: Manoharlal Munshiram.

Manu's Code of Law: A Critical Edition and Translation of the Mānavadharmaśāstra. 2005a. Edited and translated by P. Olivelle. New York: Oxford University Press.

Padma Purāṇa. 1970. Translated by N. A. Deshpande. In *Ancient Indian Tradition and Mythology*, vols. 39–47. Delhi: Motilal Banarsidass.

The Rigveda: The Earliest Religious Poetry of India. 2014. Translated by S. Jamison and J. Brereton. New York: Oxford University Press.

The Śatapatha Brāhmaṇa in the Kāṇvīya Recension. (1926) 1998. Edited by W. Caland and revised by Raghu Vira. Reprint, Delhi: Motilal Banarsidass

Śatapatha Brāhmaṇa in the Mādhyandina Śākhā with Extracts from the Commentaries of Sāyaṇa, Harisvāmin, and Dvivedaṅga. (1855) 1997. Edited by A. Weber. Reprint, Varanasi: Chowkhamba Sanskrit Series 96.

The Śatapatha Brāhmaṇa According to the Text of the Mādhyandina School. (1882–1900). Translated by J. Eggeling. In *Sacred Books of the East*, vols. 12, 26, 41, 43, 44, ed. M. Müller. Reprint, Delhi: Motilal Banarsidass, 1993–1994.

Sechzig Upanishads des Veda. (1897) 1995. Translated by P. Deussen. Leipzig: F. A. Brockhaus. English translation by V. M. Bedekar and G. B. Palsule. *Sixty Upaniṣads of the Veda*, 2 vols. Reprint, Delhi: Motilal Banarsidass.

Shatapatha Brahmana, Electronic Text, [Re-engineered in HTML with hyperlinks to RV Quotations and Context]. 1997. Encoding and editing by J. R. Gardner. TITUS Project CD ROM, Frankfurt.

Śiva Purāṇa. 1992. Translated by a board of scholars. In *Ancient Indian Tradition and Mythology*, vol. 4. Reprint, Delhi: Motilal Banarsidass.

The Skanda-Purāṇa. 1970. Translated by G. V. Tagare. In *Ancient Indian Tradition and Mythology*, vol. 49–51. Delhi: Motilal Banarsidass.

Śrimadbhāgavatapurāṇam with Commentary of Śrīdhara Svāmin. 1988. Edited by J. L. Shastri. Reprint, Varanasi: Motilal Banarsidass.

The Treatise on Liberation-in-Life: Critical Edition and Annotated Translation of Jivanmuktiviveka of Vidyāraṇya. 2002. Edited by Robert Gooding. Unpublished dissertation, University of Texas at Austin.

The Upaniṣads. 2000. Translated by V. Roebuck. New Delhi: Penguin Books.

The Varāha Purāṇa. 1985. Translated by S. Venkitasubramonia Iyer. In *Ancient Indian Tradition and Mythology*, vol. 31. Delhi: Motilal Banarsidass.

The Vishnu Purana: A System of Hindu Mythology and Tradition. 1972. Translated by H. H. Wilson. Calcutta: Punthi Pustak.

Yājñavalkya: A Treatise on Dharma. 2019. Edited and translated by Patrick Olivelle. Murty Classical Library of India 20. Cambridge, MA: Harvard University Press.

Yājñavalkyasmr̥tiḥ. 2000. Edited with Hindi translation by U. Pāṇḍeya and Ś. Nārāyaṇa Miśra. Reprint, Vārāṇasī: Caukhambhā Saṃskr̥t Saṃsthān.

Yājñavalkyasmriti with the Commentary of Vijnanesvara. 1918. Translated by S. C. Vidyaranya. In *The Sacred Books of the Hindus*, vol. 21. Allahabad: Indian Press.

Yajurveda Saṁhitā: Sanskrit Text with English Translation. 1997. Edited and translated by R. T. H. Griffiths, and revised by R. P. Arya. Delhi: Parimal Publications.

Yogayājñavalkya. Translated by A. G. Mohan. Madras: Ganesh and Company, n.d.

Secondary Sources

Allchin, F. R., ed. 1995. *The Archaeology of Early Historic South Asia: The Emergence of Cities and States*. New York: Cambridge University Press.

Barthes, R. 1972. *Mythologies*. Selected and translated by A. Lavers. New York: Hill and Wang.

Basham, A. L. 1951. *History and Doctrines of the Ajivikas: A Vanished Indian Religion*, London: Luzac.

Black, B. 2007. *The Character of the Self in Ancient India: Kings, Priests, and Women in the Early Upaniṣads*. Albany: State University of New York Press.

Black, B. 2018. "The Upaniṣads and the Mahābhārata." In *The Upaniṣads: A Complete Guide*, edited by Signe Cohen. New York: Routledge.

Böhtlingk, O., and Roth. (1855–1875) 1990. *Sanskrit-Wörterbuch herausgegeben von der Kaiserlichen Akademie der Wissenschaften*, 7 vols. St. Petersburg: Buchdr. der K. Akademie der Wissenschaften.

Brereton, J. 1982. "The Particle *iva* in Vedic Prose." *Journal of the American Oriental Society* 102: 443–50.

Brereton, J. 1986. "*Tat Tvam Asi* in Context." *Zeitschrift der Deutschen Morgenländischen Gesellschaft* 13: 98–109.

Brereton, J. 1996. "Yājñavalkya's Curse." *Studien zur Indologie und Iranistik* 20: 47–57.

Brereton, J. 1997. "Why Is a Sleeping Dog Like a Vedic Sacrifice?" In Witzel, *Inside the Texts Beyond the Texts: New Approaches to the Study of the Vedas*, edited by M. Witzel, 1–14. Harvard Oriental Series Opera Minora, 2. Cambridge, MA: Department of Sanskrit and Indian Studies.

Brereton, J. 2006. "The Composition of the Maitreyī Dialogue in the Bṛhadāraṇyaka Upaniṣad." *Journal of the American Oriental Society*, 126, no. 3: 323–45.

Bronkhorst, J. 2000. *The Two Traditions of Meditation in Ancient India*. Reprint, New Delhi: Motilal Banarsidass.

Bronkhorst, J. 2007. *Greater Magadha: Studies in the Culture of Early India*. Leiden: Brill.

Bronkhorst, J. 2011. *Buddhism in the Shadow of Brahmanism*. Leiden: Brill.

Bronkhorst, J. 2016. *How the Brahmins Won: From Alexander to the Guptas*. Leiden: Brill.

Burton, R. 1990. *Bird Flight: An Illustrated Study of Birds' Aerial Mastery*. New York: Facts On File, Inc.

Chakrabarti, K. 2001. *Religious Process: The Purāṇas and the Making of a Regional Tradition*. New Delhi: Oxford University Press.

Caland, W. 1915. "Over en uit het Jaiminīya-Brāhmaṇa." *Versl. Meded. Kon. Akad. v. Wetensch., Afd. Letterk.* Vijfde Reejs I, Amsterdam, 1–106 [cited in Bodewitz 1973].

Caland, W. 1932. "A Note on the Śatapatha Brāhmaṇa." *Acta Orientalia* 10: 126–34.

Davis, D. 2010. *The Spirit of Hindu Law*. Cambridge: Cambridge University Press.

Davis, R. 1999. *Lives of Indian Images*. Reprint, Delhi: Motilal Banarsidass.

Deussen, Paul. 1995. *The Philosophy of the Upaniṣads*. Authorized translation by A. S. Weden. New York: Dover Publications.

Dirks, N. 2001. *Castes of Mind: Colonialism and the Making of Modern India*. Princeton, NJ: Princeton University Press.

Divanji, P. C. 1953. "Bṛhad Yogi Yājñavalkya-Smṛti and Yoga Yājñavalkya." *Annals of the Bhandarkar Oriental Research Institute*, 34, 1–29.

Doniger, W. 2000. *The Bedtrick: Tales of Sex and Masquerade*. Chicago: University of Chicago Press.

Doniger, W., and L. Patton, eds. 1996. *Myth and Method*. Charlottesville: University Press of Virginia.

Doniger O'Flaherty, W., ed. 1983. *Karma and Rebirth in Classical Indian Traditions*. Delhi: Motilal Banarsidass.

Doniger O'Flaherty, W., ed. 1988. *Textual Sources for the Study of Hinduism*. Chicago: University of Chicago Press.

Edgerton, F. 1965. *The Beginnings of Indian Philosophy*. Cambridge, MA: Harvard University Press.

Erdosy, G. 1988. *Urbanization in Early Historic India*. Oxford: BAR.

Findly, E. B. 1985. "Gargi at the King's Court: Women and Philosophic Innovation in Ancient India." In *Women, Religion, and Social Change*, 37–58. New York: State University of New York Press.

Fišer, I. 1984. "Yājñavalkya in the Śruti Tradition of the Veda." *Acta Orientalia* 10: 55–87.

Fitzgerald, J. 2003. "The Many Voices of the Mahābhārata." *Journal of the American Oriental Society* 123, no. 4: 803–18.

Fitzgerald, J. 2004b. "Mahābhārata." In *The Hindu World*. edited by S. Mittal and G. Thursby, 52–74. New York: Routledge.

Fitzgerald, J. 2012. "The Sāṃkhya-Yoga 'Manifesto' at *MBh* 12.289.290." In *Battle, Bards, and Brāhmins: Papers of the 13th World Sanskrit Conference*, vol. II. Delhi: Motilal Banarsidass.

Gombrich, R. 1988. *Theravāda Buddhism: A Social History from Ancient Benares to Modern Columbo*. New York: Routledge.

Gombrich, R. 2009. *What the Buddha Thought*. London: Equinox Publishing.

Gonda, J. 1950. *Notes on Brahman*. Utrecht: J. L. Beyers.

Gonda, J. 1955. "Etymologies in the Ancient Indian Brāhmaṇas." *Lingua* 5: 61–85.

Gonda, J. 1965. "*Bandhu* in the Brāhmaṇas." *Adyar Library Bulletin* 29: 1–29.

Gonda, J. 1967. "A Note on Indra in Purāṇic Literature." *Purāṇam* 9, no. 2 (July): 222–61.

Gonda, J. 1975/1977. *A History of Indian Literature*, vol. 1 Vedic Literature (*Saṃhitās and Brāhmaṇas*); vol. 2 *The Ritual Sūtras*. Wiesbaden: Otto Harrassowitz.

Grinshpon, Y. 2003. *Crisis and Knowledge: The Upanishadic Experience and Storytelling*. New Delhi: Oxford University Press.

Hanefeld, E. 1976. *Philosophische Haupttexte der älteren Upaniṣaden*. Freiburger Beiträge zur Indologie, 9. Wiesbaden: Otto Harrassowitz.

Helfer, J. S. 1989. "Yājñavalkya." In *The Perennial Dictionary of World Religions*, edited by K. Crim, 810–11. San Francisco: Harper & Row.

Hiltebeitel, A. 1976. *The Ritual of Battle: Kṛṣṇa in the Mahābhārata*. Ithaca, NY: Cornell University Press.

Hiltebeitel, A. 2001. *Rethinking the Mahābhārata: A Reader's Guide to the Education of the Dharma-King*. Chicago: University of Chicago Press.

Hock, H. 2002. "The Yājñavalkya Cycle in the Bṛhad-Āraṇyaka-Upaniṣad." *Journal of the American Oriental Society* 122: 278–86.

Horsch, P. 1966. *Die vedische Gātha- und Śloka-Literatur*. Bern: Francke Verlag.

Insler, S. 1989/1990. "The Shattered Head Split and the Epic Tale of Śakuntalā." *Bulletin d'Études Indiennes* 7–8: 97–139.

Jaini, P. S. 2001. *Collected Papers on Buddhist Studies*. Delhi: Motilal Banarsidass.

Jamison, S. 1986. "Brāhmaṇa Syllable Counting, Vedic *tvac* 'Skin,' and the Sanskrit Expression for the Canonical Creature." *Indo-Iranian Journal* 29: 161–81.

Jamison, S. 1991. *The Ravenous Hyenas and the Wounded Sun: Myth and Ritual in Ancient India*. Ithaca, NY: Cornell University Press.

Jamison, S. 1996. *Sacrificed Wife/Sacrificer's Wife: Women, Ritual, and Hospitality in Ancient India*. New York: Oxford University Press.

Jamison, S., and M. Witzel. 2003. "Vedic Hinduism." In *The Study of Hinduism*, edited by Arvind Sharma, 65–113. Columbia: University of South Carolina Press.

Jha, D. N. 2002. *The Myth of the Holy Cow*. New York: Verso.

Jha, S. 1998. *Yājñavalkya*. Makers of Indian Literature series. New Delhi: Sahitya Akademi.

Kane, P. V. 1968. *History of Dharmaśāstra*. vols. I–IV. Reprint, Poona: Bhandarkar Oriental Research Institute.

Keith, A. B. 1925. *Religion and Philosophy of the Veda*. Harvard Oriental Series, vol. 32. Cambridge, MA: Harvard University Press.

Kenghe, C. T. 1971. "Some Further Observations on the Problem of the Original Yogayājñavalkya." *Annals of the Bhandarkar Oriental Research Institute* 52: 49–65.

Knipe, D. 1977. "Sapiṇḍīkaraṇa: The Hindu Rite of Entry in Heaven." In *Religious Encounters with Death: Insights from the History and Anthropology of Religions*, edited by. F. Reynolds and E. Waugh. University Park: Pennsylvania State University Press.

Krishnamurti, E. R. 1984. *Yogeeswara Yajnavalkya*. Madras: Hoe and Co.

Kuvalayananda, S., and R. Kokaje. 1956. "A Reply to Sri P. C. Divanji's Comments on Bṛhadyogiyājñavalkyasmṛti." *Annals of the Bhandarkar Oriental Research Institute* 37: 279–89.

LaCapra, D. 1994. *Rethinking Intellectual History: Texts, Contexts, Language*. Reprint, Ithaca, NY: Cornell University Press.

Lindquist, S. 2003. "Enigmatic Numismatics: Kings, Horses, and the *Aśvamedha* Coin-Type." *South Asian Studies* 19: 105–12.

Lindquist, S. 2004. "Yājñavalkya's Riddle (BĀUK 3.9.28)." In *Problems in Sanskrit and Vedic Literature: Felicitation Volume in Honor of Dr. G. U. Thite*, edited by M. Deshpande, 192–211. Delhi: New Indian Book Center.

Lindquist, S. 2005. "Book Review of J. Grinshpon's *Crisis and Knowledge: The Upanishadic Experience and Storytelling* (New Delhi: Oxford University Press, 2003)." *Journal of the American Oriental Society* 125, no. 1 (2005): 141–43.

Lindquist, S. 2008. "Gender at Janaka's Court: Women in the Bṛhadāraṇyaka Reconsidered." *Journal of Indian Philosophy* 36, no. 3: 405–26.

Lindquist, S. 2009. "Book Review of Black's *The Character of the Self in Ancient India: Kings, Priests, and Women in the Early Upaniṣads*." *Journal of the American Oriental Society* 129 no. 2: 355–57.

Lindquist, S. 2011a. "Literary Lives and a Literal Death: Yājñavalkya, Sākalya, and an Upaniṣadic Death Sentence." *Journal of the American Academy of Religion* 77, no. 1: 33–57.

Lindquist, S. 2011b. "One Yājñavalkya . . . Two? On the (Questionable) Historicity of a Literary Figure." In *Religion and Identity in South Asia and Beyond*, edited by Steven E. Lindquist, 69–82. New York: Anthem Press.

Lindquist, S. 2011c. "Lines of Descent and Dissent: Genealogy, Narrative and the Upaniṣads." *Religions of South Asia* 5, no. 1/2: 29–49.

Lindquist, S. 2016. "Narrating the Upaniṣads." In *Narrating Religion*, edited by Sarah Johnston, 303–16. Macmillan Handbook Series on the Interdisciplinary Study of Religion, general editor Jeffrey Kripal. New York: Macmillan Reference.

Lindquist, S. 2018a. "The Social Background: Caste and Gender in the Upaniṣads." In *The Upanishads: A Complete Guide*, edited by Signe Cohen, 81–92. New York: Routledge.

Lindquist, S. 2018b. "Prominent Characters in the Upaniṣads." In *The Upanishads: A Complete Guide*, edited by Signe Cohen, 95–106. New York: Routledge.

Lindquist, S. 2020. "'Transcending the World' in World Literature: The Upaniṣads." In *The Ethical Turn: Third Millennium BCE to 600 CE*. Vol. 1 of *The Wiley-Blackwell Companion to World Literature*, edited by Ken Seigneurie et al., 55–68. Hoboken, NJ: Wiley Blackwell.

Macdonell, A. A., and A. B. Keith. (1912) 1967. *Vedic Index of Names and Subjects*, 2 vols. Reprint, Delhi: Motilal Banarsidass.

Mayrhofer, M. 1986. *Etymologisches Wörterbuch des Altindoarischen*. Heidelberg: C. Winter.

Mehendale, M. A. 1977. "Aṃsalá." In *Beiträge zur Indienforschung: Ernst Waldschmidt zum 80*, 315–18. Berlin: Museum fur Ind. Kunst.

Monier-Williams, M. 1999. *Sanskrit-English Dictionary* Reprint, New Delhi: Munshiram Manoharlal Publishers.

Murty, S. S. N. 2003. "The Questionable Historicity of the Mahābhārata." *Electronic Journal of Vedic Studies* 10, no. 5. http://users.primushost.com/~india/ejvs.

Mylius, K. 1965. "Geographische Untersuchungen zur Entstehungsgegend des Śatapatha Brāhmaṇa." *Wissenschaftliche Zeitschrift der Karl-Marx-Universität Leipzig* 14, no. 4:759–61.

Mylius, K. 1972. "Das geographische Milieu der mittelvedischen Literatur." *Mitteilungen des Instituts für Orientforschung*, 17, 3: 369–382.

Nadkarni, D. 2001. *Tales from the Upanishads*. Amar Chitra Katha series, issue 649. Reprint, Mumbai: India Book House Ltd.

Nakamura, H. 1967. "Yājñavalkya and Other Upaniṣadic Thinkers in the Jain Tradition." *Adyar Library Bulletin* 31, no. 2: 216–28.

Nye, J. 1985. "Upapurāṇa and Mahapurāṇa: Appendix and Appendee?" Paper Presented at Conference on the Purāṇas, University of Wisconsin, Madison. August.

Oertel, H. 1902. "Contributions from the Jaiminīya Brāhmaṇa to the History of the Brāhmaṇa Literature." *Journal of the American Oriental Society* 23: 325–49.

Oertel, H. 1926. *The Syntax of Cases in the Narrative and Descriptive Prose of the Brāhmaṇas. I. The Disjunct Use of Cases*. Heidelberg: C. Winter.

Oldenberg, H. 1971. *Buddha, His Life, His Doctrine, His Order.* Translated by William Hooey Reprint, Indological Book House: New Delhi.

Olivelle, P. 1993. *The Āśrama System: The History and Hermeneutics of a Religious Institution*. New York: Oxford University Press.

Olivelle, P. 1997. "Amṛtā: Women and Indian Technologies of Immortality." *Journal of Indian Philosophy* 25: 427–49.

Olivelle, P. 1998. "Unfaithful Transmitters: Philological Criticism and Critical Editions of the Upaniṣads." *Journal of Indian Philosophy* 26: 173–87.

Olivelle, P. 1999. "Young Śvetaketu: A Literary Study of an Upaniṣadic Story." *Journal of the American Oriental Society* 119: 46–70.

Olivelle, P. 2005b. "Power of Words: The Ascetic Appropriation and the Semantic Evolution of *Dharma*." In *Asceticism and Power in the Asian Context*, edited by P. Flügel and G. Houtman. London: Curzon.

Pande, G. C. 1990. "The Socio-cultural Milieu of the Mahābhārata: An Age of Change." In *Mahābhārata Revisited*, edited by R. N. Dandekar. New Delhi: Sahitya Akadami.

Patton, L. 1996. "The Fate of the Female Ṛṣi: Portraits of Lopāmudrā." In *Myth and Mythmaking: Continuous Evolution in Indian Tradition*, edited by J. Leslie. Richmond: RoutledgeCourzon.

Rao, S. (text), and P. B. Kavadi (illustrations). 2000. *Nachiketa and Other Tales from the Upanishads*. Amar Chitra Katha series, 702. Reprint, Mumbai: India Book House Ltd.

Rao, V. N. 1993. "Purāṇa as Brahminic Ideology." In *Purāṇa Perennis: Reciprocity and Transformation in Hindu and Jain Texts*, edited by W. Doniger, 85–100. Albany: State University of New York Press.

Rao, V. N. 2004. "Purāṇa." In *The Hindu World*, edited by S. Mittal and G. Thursby, 97–115. New York: Routledge.

Rau, W. 1970. *Weben und Flechten im vedischen Indien*. Akademie der Wissenschaften und Literature. Abhandlungen der Geisten- und Sozialwissenschaftlichen Klasse, 11. Weisbaden: Steiner Verlag.

Reich, T. 1998. *A Battlefield of a Text: Inner Textual Interpretation in the Sanskrit Mahābhārata*. Unpublished dissertation, University of Chicago.

Reinvang, R. 2000. "A Critical Survey of the Dialogue between Yājñavalkya and Maitreyī in Bṛhadāraṇyaka Upaniṣad 2.4 and 4.5." *Acta Orientalia* 61: 145–201.

Renou, L. 1948. "La relation du Śatapathabrāhmaṇa avec la Bṛhadāraṇyakopaniṣad et la personalité de Yājñavalkya." *Indian Culture* 14: 75–89.

Renou, L. 1965. *The Destiny of the Veda in India*. Delhi: Motilal Banarsidass.

Rocher, L. 1986. *The Purāṇas*. In *History of Indian Literature*, vol. 2, fasc. 3, edited by J. Gonda. Wiesbaden: Otto Harrassowitz.

Ruben, W. 1947. *Die Philosophen der Upaniṣaden*. Bern: A. Francke.

Ruben, W. 1954. *Geschichte der indischen Philosophie*. Berlin: Deutscher Verlag der Wissenschaften.

Santucci, J. 1976. *An Outline of Vedic Literature*. Missoula, MT: Scholars Press.

Sathaye, A. 2015. *Crossing the Lines of Caste: Viśvāmitra and the Construction of Brahmin Power in Hindu Mythology*. New York: Oxford University Press.

Schrapel, D. 1970. *Untersuchung der Partikel iva und anderer lexikalisch-syntaktischer Probleme der vedischen Prosa nebst zahlreichen Textemendationen und der kritischen Übersetzung von Jaimīniya-Brāhmaṇa 2, 371–373 (Gavamāyana 1)*. Marburg an der Lahn: Fotodruck E. Mauersberger.

Sullivan, B. M. 1999. *Seer of the Fifth Veda: Kṛṣṇa Dvaipāyana Vyāsa in the Mahābhārata*. Reprint, Delhi: Motilal Banarsidass.

Sutton, N. 2000. *Religious Doctrines in the Mahābhārata.* Delhi: Motilal Banarsidass.

Thapar, R. 2000. "Genealogical Patterns as Perceptions of the Past." In *Cultural Pasts: Essays in Early Indian History,* 709–53. New Delhi: Oxford University Press.

Thite, G. U. 1975. *Sacrifice in the Brāhmaṇa-Texts.* Poona: University of Poona.

Thompson, G. 1997. "The *Brahmodya* and Vedic Discourse." *Journal of the American Oriental Society* 117: 13–37.

Tull, H. 1989. *The Vedic Origins of Karma: Cosmos as Man in Ancient Indian Myth and Ritual.* Albany: State University of New York Press.

Van Buitenen, J. A. B. 1955. "Notes on *Akṣara.*" *Bulletin of the Deccan College Research Institute* 17: 204–15.

Van Buitenen, J. A. B. 1959. "*Akṣara.*" *Journal of the American Oriental Society* 79: 176–87.

Van Buitenen, J. A. B. 1964. "The Large Ātman." *History of Religions* 4: 103–14.

Venkataramiah, D. 1952. "Maitreyī's Choice." In *Prof. M. Hiriyanna Commemoration Volume,* edited by N. Sivarama Sastry and G. Hanumantha Rao. Mysore: Prof. M. Hiriyanna Commemoration Committee.

Vishva Bandhu. 1935. *A Vedic Word Concordance* (10 vols. in 3 parts). Lahore: VVRI.

Weber, A. 1961. *The History of Indian Literature.* Translated from the 2nd German edition by J. Mann and T. Zachariae. Varanasi: Chaukhambhā Sanskrit Series Office.

Wezler, A. 1992. "Sanskrit Prāṇabhr̥t or What Supports What?" In *Ritual, State, and History in South Asia: Essays in Honor of J. C. Heesterman,* edited by A. W. Van Den Hoek, D. H. A. Kolff, and M. S. Oort, 393–413. Leiden: E. J. Brill.

Witzel, M. 1987a. "On the Localization of Vedic Texts and Schools." in *India and the Ancient World: History, Trade, and Culture before A.D. 650,* edited by G. Pollet, 174–213. Orientalia Lovaniensia Analecta, 25. Leuven: Department Oriântalistiek.

Witzel, M. 1987b. "The Case of the Shattered Head." *Festschrift für W. Rau = Studien zur Indologie und Iranistik* 13/14. Reinbek, 363–415.

Witzel, M. 1989. "Tracing the Vedic Dialects." In *Dialectes dans les littératures Indo-aryennes,* edited by C. Caillat, 97–265. Publications de L'Institut de Civilization Indienne 55. Paris: de Boccard.

Witzel, M. 1997. "The Development of the Vedic Canon and Its Schools: The Social and Political Milieu." In *Inside the Texts Beyond the Texts: New Approaches to the Study of the Vedas,* edited by M. Witzel, 257–345. Harvard Oriental Series Opera Minora, 2. Cambridge, MA: Department of Sanskrit and Indian Studies.

Witzel, M. 2003. "Yājñavalkya as Ritualist and Philosopher, and His Personal Language." In *Paitimāna: Essays in Iranian, Indo-European, and Indian*

Studies in Honor of Hanns-Peter Schmidt, edited by Siamak Adhami, 103–143. Costa Mesa, CA: Mazda Publishers.

Wujastyk, D. 2017. "The Yoga Texts Attributed to Yājñavalkya and Their Remarks on Posture." *Asian Literature and Translation* 4, no. 1: 159–86.

Wynne, A. 2011. Review of Johannes Bronkhorst, *Greater Magadha: Studies in the Culture of Early India*. H-Buddhism, H-Net Reviews. July, 2011. http://www.h-net.org/reviews/showrev.php?id=31537.

Zysk, K. G. 1993. "The Science of Respiration and the Doctrine of the Bodily Winds in Ancient India." *Journal of the American Oriental Society* 113: 198–213.

Index

boon, 167; Sun to Yājñavalkya, 145, 151–153; Yājñavalkya to Janaka, 60–62, 103–105, 125, 254, 311n43
Brahma Purāṇa, 197–199, 307n31
brahmahatyā (killing a Brahmin), 192–194, 196
brahmaloka (world/s of *brahman*), 115, 224, 262–263, 271–272, 296n106, 309n19; as zenith, 163
brahman, 1, 7, 77, 81, 83, 121, 122, 129, 170, 225–226, 240, 264, 266–268, 288n79, 311n51; answer (?) to riddle, 86, 92, 96–102 passim, 245; asking beyond, 83, 116–117, 120; clear and not obscure, 221–223; as formulation of truth, 107, 290n21; as free from fear (*abhaya*), 105, 272; highest *brahman*, 139, 144, 154; as immortal (*amṛta*), 105, 269, 272; incomplete claims about, 108, 109, 246–251; lineage, as progenitor of, 75, 113, 278–279, 283n9; teaching narrative, 104; theme of, 103; and *tyad*, 237. See also *ātman, brahmaloka; brahmavādin; brahmavādinī; brahmiṣṭha; brahmodya*
Brahmāṇḍa Purāṇa, 183–186, 187, 191–194, 305n14, 306n17
brahmavādin (talker about *brahman*, m.), 169
brahmavādinī (talker about *brahman*, f.), 124–126, 272. *See also* Maitreyī
brahmavarcasin, (having luster of *brahman*), 32–33, 51
brahmavittama (ultimate knower of *brahman*), 144, 192
Brahmin (class), 211, 231, 283n14, 305n1; Brahmin maleness, 111, 122–123, 298n125, 298n131; Brahmin-by-birth vs Brahmin-by-practice, 121; ideal Brahmin, 8, 39, 119, 223, 270, 271–272, 286n67, 309n16, 309n17; killing of, 192, 193, 196; kings, in relationship with, 7, 15, 59, 60–62, 135, 136, 175, 180, 197–199, 203–206, 287n73, 295n93; lineage, Gārgī's possible Brahminical, 112–114; *varṇa*, transgressing Brahmin, 167–169, 287n71; Yājñavalkya cursed by, 52; Yājñavalkya disputing with other, 4, 42, 43–46, 52, 53, 62–64, 65–69, 77–102 passim, 106, 133, 155; Yājñavalkya, in attendance with, 6, 58, 59–60, 157, 160, 168, 184, 185, 187, 208, 213, 240, 244, 306n16, 306n17; Yājñavalkya reborn in Brahmin family of disrepute, 190; Yājñavalkya sneaking away from, 53–54, 60; wealth, laying claim to by, 185–186. See also *kṣatriya* and *rājanya*
brahmiṣṭha (most learned in *brahman*), in BĀU, 33, 78, 85, 158, 213–214, 308n2; in BP, 184; in JB, 287n76; in MBh, 161, 163, 169, 174, 303n47; in ŚB, 62–63
brahmodya (religious debate), 62, 231, 234, 297n123; Janaka's court, at, 84, 154, 173, 181, 205, 308n8; women in 1, 111, 189, 295n86
Bṛhadāraṇyaka Upaniṣad, 3, 11–12, 17, 71–132 passim, 157–158, 179, 281n4, 283n12, 290n33, 295n86; *Bhāṣya*, 18, 282n4; cow theme, 55; debate in, 78–84, 106–107, 153, 154, 161, 294n72, 306n17; gender in, 110–131, 187–189, 205, 209; genealogy, 112–113, 156, 158, 168, 289n15, 296n99, 303n43, 304n62; Janaka, teaching of, 102–106, 108–109; JB connections, 57, 62, 64;